MARXISM I[N]

THE USSR

MARXISM IN THE USSR

A Critical Survey of Current Soviet Thought

JAMES P. SCANLAN

Cornell University Press

ITHACA AND LONDON

This publication was prepared under a grant from
the Woodrow Wilson International Center for Scholars,
Washington, D.C. The statements and views
expressed herein are those of the author and are
not necessarily those of the Wilson Center.

First published 1985 by Cornell University Press.

International Standard Book Number 0-8014-1649-3
Library of Congress Catalog Card Number 84-45802
Printed in the United States of America
Librarians: Library of Congress cataloging information
appears on the last page of the book.

The paper in this book is acid-free and meets the guidelines for
permanence and durability of the Committee on Production Guidelines
for Book Longevity of the Council on Library Resources.

To Marilyn

Contents

Preface

This book seeks to explore the broad domain of what is called "Marxist-Leninist" philosophy in the USSR—the philosophy that enjoys a protected monopoly in the Soviet intellectual world. Since a dominant philosophy is a revealing indicator of the character and quality of a culture, the examination of contemporary Marxism-Leninism in all its breadth, from metaphysics to morality, should teach us much about the life of the spirit in the Soviet Union in the late twentieth century.

I shall contend that the intellectual culture of the USSR is somewhat richer and more vital today than is often supposed and that, behind its facade of dogmatic unanimity, Soviet Marxism-Leninism is marked by fundamental searching and dispute. The dogmatism and the rigorous political controls under which Soviet philosophy labors are undeniably oppressive, and they tragically confine the spiritual potential of the Russian people and of the other great and creative peoples of the USSR. Yet for all the controls, the direst prophecies of George Orwell concerning thought in a totalitarian order have not been realized in the Soviet Union. The vocabulary of discourse has indeed been constricted, as Orwell foresaw, but the result has not been to make some thoughts altogether unthinkable or to eliminate disagreement or debate. Power over the dictionary, which Soviet authorities have enjoyed for decades, has not given them complete power over minds, for they have not been able to control fully the meanings that people attach to the authorized terms in actual use. In practice people will invest whatever words they have with the meanings they find necessary in order to make sense of their experience. And since neither experience nor requirements for making sense are identical for everyone, ambiguities, misunderstandings, and other impediments to unanimity will arise in any intellectual community. The abundance of such impediments in the USSR may be concealed by the impoverished vocabulary in which Soviet philosophers are compelled to display their findings, but this state of affairs should not prevent us from looking beneath the words to the variety of meanings they bear. To take such a closer look is the task of this book.

Chapter 1 presents an overview of Marxist-Leninist philosophy that focuses on diverse Soviet conceptions of the nature of philosophy itself as an intellectual enterprise. Each subsequent chapter is a relatively self-contained investigation of one broad topic or field within Soviet philosophy. Chapters 2, 3, and 4 deal with subjects treated under the heading 'dialectical materialism' in the USSR: materialism as an ontological theory (Chapter 2), the ontological aspects of dialectics (Chapter 3), and epistemology and logic (Chapter 4). The last four chapters are devoted to the major subfields under the general rubric 'historical materialism': philosophy of history (Chapter 5), social and political philosophy (Chapter 6), ethics, or the philosophy of morality (Chapter 7), and aesthetics, or the philosophy of art (Chapter 8). The conclusion offers some general observations concerning the present condition of Marxist philosophy in the USSR.

In each chapter, the first section is a summary of Marxist-Leninist orthodoxy in the area as it may be distilled from elementary Soviet textbooks but without the usual polemical tone of the latter; in these sections I try to give a straightforward, noncritical account of the elements of Soviet philosophical dogma in a particular field. In most fields, however, a simple primer by no means reflects the actual state of Marxist-Leninist philosophical doctrine on the questions at issue, so that for a fuller picture it is necessary to proceed to the more specialized, professional level of Soviet philosophy—the level at which probing questions are raised and basic disagreements revealed—and also to note the significant changes in dogma that have taken place since the end of the Stalin era. At least one section in each chapter, then, analyzes recent Soviet philosophical scholarship and dispute in the area. Critical evaluation is ordinarily reserved for a separate, concluding section, though this pattern has not been imposed mechanically in fields in which it is difficult to divorce analysis from evaluation. In each chapter, at any rate, the reader may expect to find exposition, analysis, and criticism, in roughly that order.

It is not my intention to judge Soviet philosophy by the special standards of some other philosophical system. Rather, I appeal to broadly accepted criteria of intelligibility, coherence, scope, and supportability. Since Soviet philosophers endorse these same criteria, my work has the character of an immanent critique. I do not mean, however, that it is part of a squabble among feuding disciples of the same master. Neither the views of Marx himself nor those of any non-Soviet champion of his thought are defended in this book. By the same token they are not on trial, though undoubtedly some of the criticisms addressed here to Soviet Marxism-Leninism apply to other varieties of Marxism as well. From time to time inconsistencies are noted between Soviet views and the views expressed by Marx, in order to provide information rather than to praise or blame. My question is not whether Soviet Marxism-Leninism is true to Marx but whether it is true to itself—that is, whether it constitutes a philosophical outlook that is consistent, defensible, and illuminating.

A critical treatment of Soviet philosophy of the kind here proposed should fill a gap in recent Western scholarship. A number of older studies exist, ranging in value from a 1946 exercise in apologetics by John Somerville through Herbert Marcuse's idiosyncratic *Soviet Marxism* in 1958 to the scholarly studies of J. M. Bocheński, Richard T. De George, Gustav Wetter, and other writers in the 1950s and 1960s.[1] But these works are now outdated, and even the better of them have other shortcomings as well. Some take a historical approach and slight Soviet thought after Lenin; others, such as Wetter's *Dialectical Materialism* (1952) and a 1969 study by Bernard Jeu, do focus on post-Lenin Soviet philosophy, but they confine themselves to its more technical aspects, ignoring historical, social, political, ethical, and aesthetic thought. Perhaps the best balance between depth and breadth was achieved by Wetter's *Soviet Ideology Today*, but that work was first published (in German) in 1962, and in it Wetter draws heavily on his earlier examination of Soviet thought during the Stalin era. Since the 1960s there have been no attempts to describe and assess the present state of Soviet Marxism-Leninism as an overall philosophical system.

Yet there have been many changes in the Soviet philosophical world in the past three decades. Stalin himself provided the impetus for some of these changes: his 1950 pronouncements on the subject of linguistics set in motion theoretical shifts in Marxism-Leninism that continued to be felt long after their originator could be credited with them. Stalin's successors, too, have substantially altered the body of dogma they inherited. In recent years, for example, Brezhnev and his ideologists elaborated a new social and political theory, centering on the concepts of 'developed socialism' and 'the all-people's state', successor to 'the dictatorship of the proletariat'. Changes of another sort may be traced to the post-Stalin thaw. Although short-lived as a visible cultural phenomenon, in Soviet philosophy the thaw had among its less evident but more lasting results the emergence and growth of a world of professional scholarship that is insulated at least to a degree from immediate political demands. In this scholarly world, specialized philosophical disciplines such as logic, ethics, aesthetics, and the

---

[1]Full publication data for the works mentioned in this paragraph may be found in the Bibliography.

[11]

philosophy of history have been granted separate existence within what was once considered to be the indivisible monolith of Marxism-Leninism. In many of these areas opposing schools of thought may now be discerned, all claiming the mantle of Marxism-Leninism but in fact contradicting one another on major philosophical issues. Thus in recent years both politicians and philosophers have contributed to innovation in Soviet philosophical thought.

One thing that has not changed, however, is the prominent place occupied by Marxism-Leninism in Soviet life. For two-thirds of a century, Soviet leaders have viewed themselves as struggling in the name of an idea to remake not only human society but humanity itself, and they continue today to accord that idea a social role of overwhelming importance. Though some observers have suggested that Marxist philosophy has lost its force in the USSR, it is difficult to agree with their analysis. For a supposedly exhausted ideology, Marxism-Leninism occupies a remarkably large share of the time and energies of the Soviet state and its citizens. It is true, of course, that those citizens on the whole display no transforming enthusiasm for Marxism-Leninism—none of the revolutionary fervor that fired the Bolsheviks of the early twentieth century. But when has great enthusiasm for any philosophy been exhibited by a population whose social, economic, and political life has been relatively stable for decades? A philosophical teaching need not inspire ardent devotion to be a major factor in shaping the thinking of its audience. When we observe the thorough and exclusive access that Marxist-Leninist philosophy has to the minds of the Soviet citizenry, and the wealth of resources expended on that philosophy, we cannot conclude that it leaves those minds untouched.

The production and dissemination of Marxist-Leninist thought is one of the principal industries of the USSR. A vast army of scholars, teachers, writers, and editors is engaged in these activities, and the magnitude of their product beggars the imagination. Considering books alone, each weekly issue of *Knizhnaia letopis'* (The book chronicle) lists at least twenty and often thirty, forty, or more new Soviet titles on philosophical and ideological topics, many of them textbooks and handbooks printed in editions of tens of thousands of copies. Obviously, none of these publications is critical of Marxism-Leninism; the last book legally printed in the USSR that expressed opposition to Marxist-Leninist principles appeared in 1930.[2] Moreover, no books that might propose alternatives to Marxism-Leninism, such as works published outside the socialist bloc, are

---

[2]The philosopher A. F. Losev, writing not long before all publishing activity was nationalized in the USSR, was able to assert that "dialectical materialism is a crying absurdity" (*Dialektika mifa* [Moscow, 1930], p. 147).

available in the Soviet Union to anyone but an advanced scholar; there is
no public sale of such books, and currency and postal restrictions make
it impossible for the ordinary citizen to obtain them from abroad. Marxist-
Leninist principles set the publication and censorship policies that preserve
the monopoly of Marxism-Leninism, and thus these principles form the
conceptual framework within which every topic is discussed in the philosophical literature available in the USSR.

The Soviet educational system is likewise built on Marxist-Leninist principles, and schools of every sort and at every level provide instruction in
Marxism-Leninism. At Moscow State University alone, well over two
hundred faculty members are engaged in the teaching of philosophy,[3] and
smaller contingents of experts in Marxism-Leninism are found in every
institution of higher learning in the land. Active programs of ideological
training are carried beyond the schools to factories and farms as well, so
that continuing exposure to the outlook is assured not simply for intellectuals but for all Soviet citizens, however humble their calling. And of
course the mass media, too, are charged with furthering the philosophical
education of the citizenry. It is no accident that Viktor Grigorevich Afanasyev, a noted popularizer of Marxism-Leninism whose textbook *Marxist
Philosophy* has gone through four editions since 1960, is the current editor-
in-chief of *Pravda*. It may be hard to gauge the actual effect of all this
ideological activity on the minds of the Soviet people, but a substantial
impact must be assumed even to account for the government's ability to
replenish the legions of scholars, teachers, writers, and editors who engage
in it.

Some Western observers have doubted the solidity of the ideology's hold
on the minds of the Soviet leaders, despite Khrushchev's assurance that
he and his fellow Communists would not abandon the teachings of Marx,
Engels, and Lenin "until a shrimp learns to whistle." It is by no means
clear, however, what evidence could be said to support such doubts. Often
they seem based on nothing more than the conviction that, because Marxist-Leninist philosophy is so inconsistent with reality, no one in his right
mind—and certainly no hard-headed political leader—could sincerely believe in it. But this conviction, even if we accept its premise, greatly under-
estimates the capacity of the human mind for faiths that defy rational
explanation.

Everything Communist party leaders say suggests that they firmly believe
in the Marxist-Leninist faith. They tirelessly invoke its articles in their

[3]The 1977–1978 catalogue of the humanities faculties of the university lists philosophy
courses given by 183 instructors, and the natural science faculties have their own separate
departments of philosophy (see *Moskovskii universitet. 1977–1978 uchebnyi protsess. Katalog-spravochnik. Gumanitarnye fakul'tety* [Moscow, 1977]).

public pronouncements, and if these pronouncements sometimes seem pro forma, the reason may be that they have a ritualistic character appropriate to the solemn occasions that call for them. Less momentous occasions, with no special ceremonial or propagandistic significance, demonstrate the same attachment to Marxist-Leninist ideas. Consider, for example, Brezhnev's remark to a domestic audience of ordinary citizens in 1980: "Of course the capitalists have rockets, just as we do. They have a wealth of natural resources, just as we do. They have their talented scientists, engineers, and cultural figures. But they do not have, and they cannot have, a united society."[4] This statement might be mere posturing, but in the absence of indications to this effect it is far more plausible to interpret it as exhibiting a Marxist-Leninist confidence in the inherent superiority of socialist society. Brezhnev could be confident that a capitalist nation not only lacks but *must* lack unity, because from Marxism-Leninism he "knew" that the capitalist order is torn by irreconcilable class antagonisms; and he could be sure that Soviet society, on the contrary, is unified, because Marxism-Leninism teaches that in the socialist order the economic grounds for these antagonisms have been eliminated. At any rate there is no good evidence to show that Soviet leaders wish by statements such as Brezhnev's to make others believe what they themselves do not.

Of course, if we could read the minds of Soviet leaders we might well be able to discern that different elements of the Marxist-Leninist orthodoxy command different degrees of devotion. It might be, for example, that a negative assessment of capitalist society is more deeply rooted in their thinking than the conviction that Soviet socialist society is fundamentally harmonious; the former judgment, after all, is supported not only by Marxist sources but by Tolstoi, Ostrovskii, Dickens, and many other favorites of the Russian reading public. Or perhaps they are more convinced of the virtues of socialism as it is now established in the USSR than they are of the inexorable march of history toward the victory of full communism. But all such surmises can be no more than speculative, for the only testimony to which we have access—the public statements of the leaders themselves—makes no such distinctions among the various articles of the Marxist creed.

Even apart from their repeated statements, we have every reason to expect Soviet leaders to be personally attached to the substance of the principles they proclaim. As survivors of a long apprenticeship in the ideologically supercharged atmosphere of Communist party training and Soviet government service, they even more than other citizens have been

---

[4]Quoted in G. E. Glezerman, M. N. Rutkevich, and S. S. Vishnevskii, eds., *Sotsialisticheskii obraz zhizni* (Moscow, 1980), p. 313.

powerfully exposed to the Marxist-Leninist teachings. In addition they have a special and more intimate relation to these teachings. Soviet ideology today establishes, among other things, the leadership's right to exist and defines the critical contribution that the Communist party makes to society. If it were nothing else, present-day Marxism-Leninism with its doctrine of "the leading role of the Communist party" would be the self-glorification of a ruling class, the theoretical expression of its own self-image—and Marx never suggested that the dominant class does not *believe* its illusions. Moreover there is the proprietary interest that comes with being the interpreter and defender of the ideology. No one can observe the care that goes into the shaping of certain doctrines in the USSR, and the credit that is claimed for them, without concluding that the purveyors of these doctrines view them as substantive additions to knowledge rather than as propaganda exercises. The awarding of the Karl Marx Medal to Brezhnev for "his outstanding personal contribution to the development of Marxism-Leninism" is not for its participants a charade celebrating the duping of the public with the latest inventions of doctrine.[5]

An outsider may view a particular innovation in doctrine as a cynical contrivance, but that does not mean the Soviet leaders view it as such. Indeed if there is any bad faith in the leaders' relation to Marxist-Leninist doctrine, it consists not in the failure of those leaders to mean what they say, but in their failure to recognize the extent to which their ideological pronouncements simply establish by stipulation what they purport to describe. In the end the leaders' doctrinal allegiance may be given not to a body of objective truth but to the objectified consequences of their own decisions, projected onto the world from their positions of dominance in a privileged hierarchy. If that is so, they would not be the first figures in the history of thought to mistake invention for discovery and to worship intellectual gods of their own making. They are, however, among the few who are in a position to compel millions of others to bow down before the same gods.

Nor can we find bad faith in the relation between ideology and Soviet practice. What is seen as Soviet failure to act according to ideology is sometimes advanced as an argument for its irrelevance. If Marxist theory calls for the postcapitalist state to wither away, why are measures being taken to strengthen the state in the Soviet Union? Such questions, however, proceed from a simplistic conception of the theory that fails to note its alteration as circumstances change. Soviet ideology today calls loudly and

---

[5]"Tvorcheskoe razvitie marksistsko-leninskogo ucheniia," *Voprosy filosofii*, 1981, no. 12, p. 8.

clearly for *increasing* the power of the state, and Soviet practice is quite in keeping with that call.

Soviet modifications in Marxist-Leninist theory, we shall find, often strain and sometimes burst the limits of what may reasonably be called "Marxism." Yet these modifications are undertaken by Soviet theorists and political leaders in the name of making Marxism relevant to present Soviet reality, and they are elaborated and defended with close attention to more abstract elements of Marxist-Leninist philosophy that are by no means abandoned. These elements provide the current ideology with whatever philosophical support it has: they include the metaphysical and epistemological principles to which Marxist-Leninists appeal to justify the entire outlook, as well as the overarching historical model in terms of which present-day Soviet society has meaning and direction and by reference to which achievements can be measured and further efforts inspired. These background elements of theory serve as a continuing reservoir of intellectual possibilities, for they are the concepts and principles to which appeal will be made in constructing the modifications of tomorrow as well. Thus, in examining the fundamentals of contemporary Soviet Marxism-Leninism, we shall be investigating not only the philosophical substance of Soviet culture in the present day but the conceptual inventory on which new theorists and leaders will draw in forging the outlook of the future.

A Note on Translation and Transliteration

Because English translations of Soviet philosophical works (most of them provided by Soviet publishing houses) are now more readily available than in years past, English versions have been cited in this study where possible and where the translations are acceptable. It remains the case, however, that the great bulk of Soviet work in philosophy is available in, and is here cited from, Russian-language editions only. Existing English translations of the works of Lenin are frequently untrustworthy, and for that reason as well as for the sake of simplicity, Lenin is cited only from the latest (fifth) Russian-language edition of his works, which is widely available. All translations from Russian sources not otherwise credited are my own. I have consistently given book titles in English in the text, even when only a Russian-language edition exists or is cited. Full publication data for all literature cited appear in the Bibliography. The transliteration system used is the Library of Congress system without diacritical marks, but writers' names are sometimes given in forms used by the writers themselves in translated works published in the USSR or abroad.

PREFACE

Acknowledgments

It has been my good fortune to be helped in many ways by many generous people. No writer, I am sure, has ever enjoyed more encouraging support, both moral and practical, than I have had at every stage of this work from my wife, Marilyn Morrison Scanlan, to whom this book is gratefully and lovingly dedicated. For professional assistance I am indebted above all to George L. Kline, long-time mentor and friend, whose incomparable knowledge of both Marxism and Russian philosophy saved me from many blunders and directed me to valuable points that I would otherwise have missed. The Soviet philosophers who have shared their thoughts and their scholarly resources with me during the several periods since 1964 when I resided in the USSR are too numerous to mention, and to single out publicly those whose generosity has been greatest could do them a distinct disservice; but my silence does not diminish my sense of appreciation. I am also grateful to Jonathan Schonsheck, Samuel Starr, and Tibbie Kposowa, who, as students at the Ohio State University, contributed their research skills to various parts of this volume. And warm thanks go to Mary Lee Raines, Ann Smith, Patricia Sheridan, and especially Kimberly Ann Holle for the care and efficiency with which they typed the manuscript.

This work has been greatly forwarded by financial support from six different sources. The Inter-University Committee on Travel Grants and the International Research and Exchanges Board sponsored the research visits to the Soviet Union that have contributed immeasurably to my understanding of Soviet philosophy. The Ohio State University provided several grants-in-aid for the early stages of the project and a faculty professional leave for the academic year 1982–1983. A fellowship from the Woodrow Wilson International Center for Scholars made possible six months of research and writing at the Center's Kennan Institute for Advanced Russian Studies in Washington, D.C., during 1982. A Fulbright-Hays faculty research award permitted me to spend most of the academic year 1982–1983 at the Institute of East-European Studies of the University of Fribourg in Switzerland, where the hospitality of Guido Küng, Edward Swiderski, and the institute's staff greatly facilitated my work. Finally, I am indebted to the Rockefeller Foundation for an idyllic month of writing at the foundation's study and research center in Bellagio, Italy.

If after so much help the present work is nonetheless flawed, it is not the fault of the individuals or institutions named above, nor should they be blamed for any of the views expressed herein.

JAMES P. SCANLAN

Columbus, Ohio

MARXISM IN
THE USSR

[1]

The Nature of Philosophy

UNLIKE many of their colleagues in other parts of the twentieth-century world, Soviet philosophers do not balk at espousing a philosophical "system" in the old-fashioned sense—a comprehensive, integrated set of supposed truths concerning the world and its denizens. Rejecting the psychological focus of the existentialists, and the linguistic focus of the positivists and their successors, Soviet Marxists have continued to philosophize in the grand manner, advancing a general theory of reality in all its guises, from subatomic particles to international politics. The standard summary statements of this theory, moreover, are drawn from the nineteenth century and in particular from a few well-mined pages of Frederick Engels's *Anti-Dühring* (1878) and *Ludwig Feuerbach and the Outcome of Classical German Philosophy* (1886). In their uniform and insistent repetition of the concepts and indeed the very words of these classic texts, Soviet philosophers provide ground for the charge that they hold doggedly to a philosophical anachronism.

With regard to the nature of philosophy as to other topics, however, acceptance of a system and deference to the wisdom of the founding fathers by no means deprive Soviet philosophy of either innovation or controversy. There has been considerable change in the manner of conceiving philosophy through the history of the USSR, and this change has accelerated in the post-Stalin era. Furthermore, the consensus among Soviet philosophers on philosophical questions in the present day is not nearly as broad as it may seem at first glance. Behind the accepted formulas lie problem areas, in which issues arise and are openly debated; one of the more hotly disputed issues of the past quarter century has been just this question of the identity of philosophy itself as an intellectual enterprise. The precise balance and the internal dynamics of dogma and dispute may separate the Soviet philosophical scene from those played out under other circumstances, but it would be a mistake to view Soviet philosophy—on this or any other question—as nothing but a tired gospel. Debate and development mark it as much as dogma does, and its unanswered questions are as prominent as its articles of settled conviction.

Let us begin, however, with the more familiar, doctrinaire aspects of the conception of philosophy in the USSR before proceeding to points of uncertainty and disagreement.

Dialectical and Historical Materialism as the Philosophy of Marxism-Leninism

Two cardinal premises of dogmatic Soviet philosophy are that Marxism, in its correct, Leninist interpretation—"Marxism-Leninism"—is the only adequate intellectual orientation for modern man and that the philosophical basis of that orientation is best identified in terms inherited from Lenin and from his predecessor, George Plekhanov—namely, "dialectical and historical materialism."[1]

Marxism-Leninism—the orientation as a whole—is customarily presented as having three parts: first, dialectical and historical materialist philosophy; second, political economy, or in other words Marxian economic theory; and third, what is called "scientific communism," or the social and political theory of Marxism-Leninism. Yet pride of place in the three-part doctrine is invariably given to philosophy, and it is not unusual in Soviet writings for dialectical and historical materialism to be dubbed "the Marxist world view," as if the whole outlook were contained in its distinctive philosophical foundations.

If Soviet Marxist-Leninists regard dialectical and historical materialism

---

[1]"Marxism-Leninism' is, of course, a label selected by Soviet authorities themselves. A more descriptive label, given the greater role in the formation of the Soviet outlook played by Marx's colleague Frederick Engels, would be 'Engelsism-Leninism'. The expression 'dialectical and historical materialism' is a common Soviet conjunction of the two terms 'dialectical materialism' and 'historical materialism', both of which were used freely by Lenin and by Plekhanov before him. Plekhanov coined the former term (G. Plekhanov, *Selected Philosophical Works in Five Volumes* [Moscow, n.d.], vol. 1, pp. 478, 741) and Engels coined the latter (K. Marx and F. Engels, *Selected Works in One Volume* [New York, 1968], p. 386). Neither Marx nor Engels ever used the term 'dialectical materialism', though Engels came close when he wrote, "Modern materialism is essentially dialectic" (Marx and Engels, *Selected Works*, p. 415). The widespread but mistaken notion that Marx and Engels employed the term is attributable to such circumstances as its gratuitous insertion as a chapter heading by devout Leninist editors in posthumous editions of Engels's book on Feuerbach (see the editor's acknowledgment in F. Engels, *Ludwig Feuerbach and the Outcome of Classical German Philosophy* [New York, 1941], pp. 9, 42) and Lenin's completely groundless assertion in the preface to *Materialism and Empirio-Criticism* that "Marx and Engels dozens of times called their philosophical views dialectical materialism" (V. I. Lenin, *Polnoe sobranie sochinenii*, 5th ed., 55 vols. [New York, 1958–1965], vol. 18, p. 9 [cited hereafter as *Soch.*]).

as a uniquely adequate set of answers to certain questions about the real world, they acknowledge the questions themselves to be as old as thought. In a current standard textbook, *The Fundamentals of Marxist-Leninist Philosophy*, the questions of philosophy are said to have been with us from "time immemorial," and they are stated in language that would not be out of place in a Christian seminary: "What is the essence of nature? What is the relation between consciousness and the external world, between the spiritual and the material, between the ideal and the real? What is man and what is his place in the world?"[2] "As of old," writes the Soviet philosopher T. I. Oizerman, "philosophy still seeks to know the infinite, the universal, the intransient."[3]

Dialectical and historical materialism, it is held, not only answers such questions in a defensible and scientific manner that is grounded in the direct and disciplined observation of the world; it also asks the right questions in the right order. Soviet philosophers contend that some of the eternal questions are more important than others and that an adequate philosophy will clearly reflect the relative significance and logical order of the questions in the structure of its doctrines.

According to a major tenet of Soviet philosophy, repeated in every text and reference work, the question of the relation of *mind* and *matter* is so fundamental that every philosopher in history is best characterized by his answer to it. For this conviction Soviet philosophers are indebted to Engels, whose words in *Ludwig Feuerbach* are constantly cited: "The great basic question of all philosophy," Engels wrote, "is that concerning the relation of thinking and being." In the Soviet interpretation of these words, 'thinking' and 'being' are labels for the two and only two fundamentally different types of phenomena that the world presents—on the one hand, mental, spiritual, subjective phenomena and, on the other hand, physical, material, objective phenomena. The question, for Soviet philosophers, concerns not the *existence* of these two types of phenomena (both are real enough) but rather which of the two is primary, in a causal sense. The great split in the history of thought, as Soviet Marxist-Leninists see it, has been that between philosophers who regard "being" (the realm of material phenomena) as causally dependent for its existence on "thinking" (the realm of mental phenomena) and philosophers who view the causal dependence as

[2] F. V. Konstantinov, ed., *The Fundamentals of Marxist-Leninist Philosophy*, trans. R. Daglish, (Moscow, 1982), pp. 13–14. This work is a complete English translation (with minor alterations) of F. V. Konstantinov, ed. *Osnovy marksistsko-leninskoi filosofii*, 4th rev. ed. (Moscow, 1978). Other general works in English are A. P. Sheptulin, *Marxist-Leninist Philosophy*, trans. S. Ponomarenko and A. Timofeyev (Moscow, 1978); and V. G. Afanasyev, *Marxist Philosophy*, trans. David Fidlon, 4th rev. ed. (Moscow, 1980).

[3] *Philosophy in the USSR. Problems of Dialectical Materialism*, trans. R. Daglish (Moscow, 1977), p. 26.

[23]

going the other way. They have made up what Engels called "two great camps": "Those who asserted the primacy of spirit to nature ... comprised the camp of idealism. The others, who regarded nature as primary, belong to the various schools of materialism."[4]

Engels argued that there is no third possibility, and Soviet philosophers continue to consider the division as both exclusive and exhaustive. In the Soviet view, any philosopher who advances some seemingly neutral or intermediate position is actually (unless he is simply confused and self-contradictory) a hidden idealist or materialist, usually the former. Favorite Soviet examples of closet idealists are Descartes and twentieth-century positivists. Descartes's mind-body dualism might appear to be a view according to which mind and body are independent substances, neither reducible to the other and hence neither primary. But in fact, according to Soviet philosophers, Descartes's ontology collapses into idealism. For Descartes argues that both body and mind are created by God, a pure spirit. Consequently Descartes's supposedly independent substances are not independent, and an idealistic entity—God—is primary to bodily matter. Twentieth-century positivism also falls into idealism, in the interpretation of Soviet philosophers, even in pretending to avoid taking sides. The positivists contend that their unit of analysis is neither matter nor mind but the phenomenon, the sense datum, or some other supposedly neutral element. In fact, Soviet philosophers argue, these are mentalistic, idealistic entities; if the world is regarded as a construct out of them, what is actually being asserted is that mind is primary to matter.[5]

Needless to say, the Soviet philosopher sides resolutely with the materialist tradition in philosophy. Along with Hobbes, Holbach, and the entire tradition—which he traces to Democritus—he asserts that everything that is is either matter or the product of matter. There is no self-subsistent spirit or God, no soul independent of the body, no Platonic form separable from matter. This materialist position, for the Soviet philosopher (again following Engels), consists of two related theses: in addition to the obvious thesis of the primacy of matter, it also includes the thesis that reality is fully knowable by the mind—that the world has no alien depths inaccessible to human cognitive investigation. For the materialist regards cognition—a secondary, mental phenomenon—as the direct causal product of an objectively existing material world and denies that any other world exists. The world that impinges on our sensory and cognitive apparatus, and in that way makes itself known to us, is the only world there is to

---

[4]Marx and Engels, *Selected Works*, pp. 603–604.
[5]See, for example, I. Khlyabich, *An Outline History of Philosophy* (Moscow, n.d.), p. 41; Sheptulin, *Marxist-Leninist Philosophy*, pp. 18–21.

know. The materialist credo as understood by Soviet philosophers, then, is the dual doctrine that matter is primary and the world is knowable.

Despite its fundamental kinship with earlier forms of materialism, Soviet Marxism-Leninism is also held to be distinguished from them in various ways, chief among which is its *dialectical* character. In the Soviet view a philosophical world outlook is called upon to provide an answer not only to "the basic question of philosophy" but also to a second question that is scarcely less important. In the words of *Fundamentals*, this is "the question of whether the world is in a changeless state or, on the contrary, is constantly changing and developing." The view that upholds the first answer is called by Soviet philosophers "metaphysics." Following Engels they employ the term 'metaphysics' not in the standard Western sense of the general study of being but rather to signify a particular view of the nature of being—and a false view at that. Metaphysicians, according to *Fundamentals*, "consider objects and phenomena in isolation from one another, as things that are essentially immutable and devoid of internal contradictions." Dialecticians, on the other hand, view the world correctly as interconnected and developmental: they consider the elements of reality to be both organically interrelated and dynamically changing, where change is seen as taking place through the conflicting forces or "contradictions" inherent in things. The impoverished atomistic and static world outlook of the metaphysician is thus countered by the richer holistic and dynamic outlook of the dialectician.[6]

The dialectical outlook, like materialism, is not considered a Marxist novelty in the history of philosophy; dialectics too receives a venerable pedigree, extending as far back as Heraclitus. A pre-Marxist peak in its development is found in the philosophy of Hegel, whose writings were carefully studied by the young Marx, by Lenin, and by many Soviet philosophers, especially before and after Stalin's rule. Hegel, however, is viewed as having poisoned his dialectics with idealism. What is philosophically distinctive about Marxism, then, is that it for the first time combined a mature materialism with a mature dialectics and produced in *dialectical materialism* a world outlook that correctly reflects both the primacy of matter and the dynamic and interconnected character of the world's phenomena.

As a general philosophical outlook, dialectical materialism covers the entire world of nature, man, and society. One area of its application, however, has such crucial importance for Marxism-Leninism that it is

---

[6]Konstantinov, *Fundamentals* (1982), pp. 24–25. Engels misleadingly attributed this sense of 'metaphysics' to Hegel (Marx and Engels, *Selected Works*, p. 620); for a discussion of the relation between Hegel's and Engels's uses of the term, see H. B. Acton, *The Illusion of the Epoch. Marxism-Leninism as a Philosophical Creed* (London, 1955), pp. 74–75.

[25]

given a designation of its own as a component of philosophy. This is *historical materialism,* or the philosophical study of human societies and their history. The nature of society and its change through time are of course subject to analysis by the same general categories and principles as hold throughout the natural world. Social reality, like natural reality, manifests the primacy of being (material phenomena) over thinking (mental phenomena), is fully and thoroughly knowable by the human mind, and exists and develops dialectically. Social reality, however, as a special case of the world's wealth of being, is also characterized by categories and principles that do not apply, say, to astronomical bodies—categories such as 'economic class' and 'ideology' and principles such as those describing the succession of social structures through time. It is the task of historical materialism to expound these sociohistorical concepts and principles. Consequently, Soviet philosophers call the philosophical world outlook of Marxism-Leninism not simply dialectical materialism but *dialectical and historical materialism,* conceived as a unity of dialectical materialism, or the general theory of reality (including social reality), and historical materialism, as the special theory of social reality.

The Debate over the Conception of Philosophy as a Science of General Laws

The foregoing brief exposition of dialectical and historical materialism summarizes the standard content of Soviet textbooks, and in so doing it may give the impression that Soviet philosophers unanimously agree on at least the main features of their outlook. In fact, a number of those features are matters of intense controversy within the USSR.

The central issue concerning the nature of philosophy in the post-Stalin period has been the question of the relationship between philosophy and science. If, as we have seen above, a philosophical system is expected to provide an objectively true description of reality, how is philosophy to be distinguished from the sciences? Or is it itself a science? If philosophy is a science, how is it related to and distinguished from the other sciences? And what is it if *not* a science? In elementary texts such questions are often passed by in silence, or are answered without indication of the controversy that surrounds them. Only in more advanced books and in the professional philosophical journals are such questions explicitly raised and debated.

The continuing discussion of the nature of philosophy in recent years may conveniently be dated to 1962, when two Soviet philosophers responded to a critique of their position by the prominent British philosopher

Alfred J. Ayer. Invited to Moscow to lecture in 1961, Ayer was also asked to contribute an article to the leading Soviet philosophy journal, *Voprosy filosofii* (Problems of philosophy)—the first time a non-Marxist had been accorded that honor. Ayer's article, entitled "Philosophy and Science," was one in which he sought to counter the Soviet tendency to meld the two fields. Philosophy, Ayer argued, is not a science: it does not describe the world, it conducts no experiments, it makes no predictions. Philosophy is concerned rather with certain very general conceptual problems, or what he called "the categorical concepts which dominate all our thinking." And these problems are essentially linguistic ones, Ayer contended, adding that, if philosophy can "change the world," it does so not materially but formally—by altering the structure of the language in which we talk about and come to know the world.[7]

As it happened, Ayer's attack came hard on the heels of a pointed ideological directive addressed to Soviet philosophers at the twenty-second congress of the Communist party in October 1961. The twenty-second congress had as its special task the formulation of the first comprehensive program of the Communist party since 1919—a program that is still in effect today. Included in the completed document, along with the usual exhortations to "come out resolutely against bourgeois ideology," was a specific injunction concerning the nature of Marxist-Leninist philosophy. "It is essential," the program stated, "to firmly defend and develop dialectical and historical materialism as the science of the most general laws of development of nature, society, and human thinking."[8] Ayer's article, which not only denied that philosophy is a science but did so in a Soviet philosophy journal, was an obvious bourgeois target, and Soviet philosophers quickly rose to the challenge.

The article was accompanied in the same issue of *Voprosy filosofii* by a ringing reply entitled "No! Philosophy Is a Science," written by Ivan Vasil'evich Kuznetsov (1911–1970), a prominent figure in the Institute of Philosophy and a specialist in the philosophy of science. In subsequent issues of the same year the journal carried another, two-part response written by Bonifatii Mikhailovich Kedrov (b. 1903), also a respected philosopher of science and a member of the Academy of Sciences of the USSR.[9]

---

[7]A. J. Ayer, "Philosophy and Science," *Soviet Studies in Philosophy* 1, no. 1 (1962–1963), p. 19. This journal contains English translations of articles from Soviet philosophy journals.
[8]*The Road to Communism. Documents of the Twenty-second Congress of the Communist Party of the Soviet Union. October 17–31, 1961* (Moscow, n.d.), p. 575.
[9]I. V. Kuznetsov, "But Philosophy Is a Science," *Soviet Studies in Philosophy* 1 (Summer 1962), pp. 20–36 (the title given in the text is a more accurate translation of Kuznetsov's Russian title); B. M. Kedrov, "Philosophy as a General Science," *Soviet Studies in Philosophy* 1 (Fall 1962), pp. 3–24. An interesting account of Kedrov's life and career may be found in Werner G. Hahn, *Postwar Soviet Politics. The Fall of Zhdanov and the Defeat of Moderation, 1946–53* (Ithaca, 1982), pp. 161–181.

The polemical situation caused the two Soviet philosophers to state the case for philosophy as a science with particular force; their articles were much discussed at the time, and they continue to be cited in Soviet philosophical literature to this day.

Briefly, both articles argue that philosophy is a science, that it does describe the world, that it does make predictions, and that it is grounded in empirical observation and experiment. The subject matter of any science, Kedrov and Kuznetsov contend, is a body of laws linking events in some sphere of reality—laws that enable the scientist both to explain and to predict those events. Biology gives us laws of natural organisms and their behavior; chemistry gives us laws of chemical elements, compounds, and their reactions; and so on for the other specialized sciences. In addition to such laws, however, which are limited in domain (the periodic table of elements has no application to economic transactions, for example), there are also laws of greater generality that apply to all phenomena and events whatever. These laws, according to Kedrov and Kuznetsov, constitute the subject matter of philosophy as a "general science."

Although the two Soviet philosophers refrained from directly citing Frederick Engels as an authority, their conception of philosophy was clearly drawn from Engels's definition of dialectics as "nothing more than the science of the general laws of motion and development of nature, human society and thought."[10] Engels, closely following Hegel, had identified three such "laws" or patterns of development; briefly (they will be examined in detail in Chapter 3), they are the laws that sudden qualitative development is precipitated by gradual quantitative development ("the law of the transformation of quantity into quality"), that all developing things contain dynamic opposites ("the law of the interpenetration of opposites"), and that development is both conservative and progressive ("the law of the negation of the negation"). For Engels these laws are absolutely universal in scope; they apply, in his words, "in the animal and plant kingdoms, in geology, in mathematics, in history and in philosophy."[11] Kedrov and Kuznetsov refer to these laws in their articles, though they do not elaborate upon them. And they follow the lead of the Party program of 1961 in substituting 'philosophy' for 'dialectics' as the definiendum of Engel's definition: "Philosophy," Kuznetsov writes, "is, above all else, a *science*, and, specifically, the science of the most general *laws* of the development of nature, society, and thought."[12]

[10]Frederick Engels, *Anti-Dühring. Herr Eugen Dühring's Revolution in Science* (Moscow, 1947), pp. 168–169.
[11]Ibid., p. 168; see also Frederick Engels, *Dialectics of Nature*, trans. and ed. Clemens Dutt (New York, 1940), pp. 26–34.
[12]Kuznetsov, p. 36 (italics in original).

The articles of Kedrov and Kuznetsov presented in sharp relief a view of philosophy that was shared and continues to be shared by many Soviet thinkers. Textbooks such as *Fundamentals* still use the formula uncritically in distinguishing the science of philosophy from the "specialized sciences."[13] In addition to many defenders, however, and despite the authority of the Party program behind it, the view has also had a great many Soviet critics in the years since 1962. Kedrov and Kuznetsov, by explicitly limiting philosophy to the dialectical laws, made it easier to see what is lost in adopting the Engelsian position. And the loss proved to be no small matter, extending as it does to a number of convictions that had been an integral part of the Marxist heritage in Russia. As a result, other Soviet philosophers came forward to press the claims of what were seen as illegitimately excluded elements of philosophy.

The ensuing discussions in the 1960s revealed a considerable diversity of opinion among Soviet philosophers on the subject of the nature of philosophy. The debate, which in modified form continues to the present day, has centered on three distinguishable issues.

Philosophy and the "Basic Question"

The first and perhaps most obvious shortcoming of the Kedrov-Kuznetsov position was its apparent slighting of the hallowed "basic question of philosophy." To define philosophy as the science of the most general laws of development is, it would seem, to ignore the question of the ontological primacy of mind or matter. The idealist and the materialist alike might assume the same "general laws" (as indeed Hegel and Engels had); it is only in their interpretation of the "events" linked by those laws that they would differ. But is not such interpretation crucial to philosophy? How can philosophy be confined to a subject matter that does not include its basic question?

In their original articles, Kedrov and Kuznetsov had not entirely ignored the question, but their efforts to accommodate it took the form of making it at best an appendage to their definition of philosophy. Kedrov announced near the end of his article that the general laws are actually only the "chief nucleus" of philosophy's concerns, which also include "the specific laws of thought constituting the subject matter of (dialectical) logic." Dialectical logic, he then went on to state, gives attention to "the relationship between

---

[13]Konstantinov, *Fundamentals* (1982), p. 27. It is worth noting that, in the years since Ayer wrote, the positivistic position he represented has largely been replaced in Anglo-American philosophy, through the work of Willard Van Orman Quine and others, by a view much closer to the Soviet conception—a view of philosophy as a very general science.

subject and object," which in turn includes "the basic question of all philosophy."[14] In Kedrov's Soviet readers, this language may have struck a sympathetic chord, for Engels, in addition to calling dialectics the study of the most general laws of all development, had in another place called it (together with formal logic) "the science of thought and its laws."[15] But how exactly the basic question is related to the specific laws of *thought*, and why philosophy as a general science should include the study of any *specific* laws at all, were not adequately explained by Kedrov.

A number of other Soviet philosophers in the 1960s attempted to rectify the situation by giving the basic question a more prominent place in their conceptions of philosophy. A. P. Sheptulin in his textbook *Dialectical Materialism* attributed two distinctive features to philosophy: first, it is a "world view" that deals with reality "as a whole," and second, it addresses itself to the question of the relation of consciousness and being.[16] Only in speaking of *Marxist* philosophy, as opposed to philosophy in general, did Sheptulin bring in the general laws, and even then he subordinated them to the basic question: "Dialectical materialism," he wrote, "is a world view and a general methodology developed on the basis of an acknowledgement of the primacy of matter in relation to consciousness and of the study of the most general laws of the movement and development of nature, society, and human thinking."[17] Similar emphasis was given to the basic question in another textbook widely used in the 1960s—*Marxist-Leninist Philosophy*, edited by V. P. Rozhin and others.[18] Neither work, however, offered any logical ground for juxtaposing the basic question and the general laws in a single definition.

The place of the basic question in the definition of philosophy was one of the central points of debate in a special conference devoted to the Kedrov-Kuznetsov conception of philosophy held at Moscow State University on May 18 and 19, 1970. The position defended by Kedrov at the conference (illness prevented Kuznetsov from taking part) was essentially unchanged from that expressed in his 1962 article. He did, however, elaborate on the puzzling matter of how philosophy, as a general science, can claim to cover also the specific laws of thought. It is not really laws relating *solely* to thought that are dealt with in philosophy, he affirmed: laws limited to thought, such as those of formal logic and psychology, are admittedly the domain of special sciences, not philosophy. The laws of

[14]Kedrov, "Philosophy as a General Science," pp. 22–23.
[15]Marx and Engels, *Selected Works*, p. 415.
[16]A. P. Sheptulin, *Dialekticheskii materializm* (Moscow, 1965), p. 3.
[17]Ibid., p. 15.
[18]V. P. Rozhin et al., eds., *Marksistsko-leninskaia filosofiia. Uchebnoe posobie*, 2d ed. (Moscow, 1966), p. 72.

dialectic, on the other hand, are laws of thought that have "the same degree of generality as the most general laws of all motion and development taking place in nature and society," and hence they are appropriately assigned to philosophy, conceived as the science of general laws. Kedrov's point was that the laws of dialectic have both a subjective and an objective dimension: objectively, they describe actual processes that are common to developments in nature, society, and human thought; subjectively, they are all laws of *thought*, for they represent the consciousness or cognition of these common processes: they "have a general character and reflect [subjectively] the most general laws of all [objective] development." Now, it is precisely in this relationship of the two aspects of the general laws that "the materialist resolution of the basic question of philosophy" may be found, according to Kedrov. The implication is that there is no need to make special mention of the basic question in the definition of philosophy: given that "the subjective dialectic reflects the objective," a proper understanding of the essence of philosophy as the science of general (dialectical) laws already incorporates a materialist answer to the question.[19]

Although Kedrov's position drew support at the conference from such prominent philosophers as E. V. Il'enkov, I. D. Pantskhava, and A. Ia. Il'in, it also drew considerable criticism. By identifying philosophy with the study of *dialectical* laws and stressing the cognitive aspects of dialectics, Kedrov and his supporters appeared to their critics to be fastening attention on epistemological questions to the detriment of the fundamental ontological question of materialism versus idealism. As if to forestall objections on this account, Kedrov in his opening remarks at the 1970 conference had rejected what he called "the epistemological tendency" in Soviet philosophy. Still, the perfunctory manner in which he rejected this tendency and the fact that he refused to acknowledge explicitly the ontological issue in the definition of philosophy suggested epistemological leanings of his own. More important, he directed considerably more forceful and sustained criticism at an opposing trend, which he called "the ontological tendency." It consists, he said, in "undervaluing the specific character of the dialectics of thought in relation to the dialectics of objective reality, which leads to refusal to understand dialectical materialism as a theory of thought." He went on to heap scorn on this "ontologization of dialectics," as he called it, pointing out among other things that Lenin himself had spoken of "the coincidence of dialectics, logic, and the theory of cognition."[20]

The individuals at the conference who promoted the basic question

---

[19]"Diskussiia o predmete filosofii," *Vestnik Moskovskogo universiteta. Seriia 7. Filosofiia*, 1971, no. 2, p. 97.
[20]Ibid., pp. 97–98.

approach to the definition of philosophy, on the other hand, were clearly more disturbed by Kedrov's references to dialectical materialism as a "theory of thought" than they were by the ontologization of Soviet philosophy. "Marxist philosophy includes ontology, too," said I. S. Narskii, and the claims of ontology were also supported by G. M. Shtraks, S. T. Meliukhin, and V. P. Chertkov. M. N. Rutkevich contended that Kedrov's definition of philosophy as it stands is only a definition of dialectical logic, and he called for the explicit inclusion of the basic question in the definition; this view was seconded by Narskii, E. D. Modrzhinskaia, A. P. Sheptulin, and others. It was G. G. Gabrielian, however, who put the disagreement squarely in Kedrov's own terms. The threat to Soviet philosophy is not from an "ontological tendency," he contended: "The danger of distorting Marxist philosophy exists along the lines of epistemologism, and this tendency is rooted for the most part in the incorrect understanding of the subject matter of philosophy." The correct understanding, of course, is that philosophy studies the relation of thinking and being; the general laws formula, according to Gabrielian, should be replaced by the basic question in formulating the definition of philosophy.[21]

For all the official Soviet stress on the "indissoluble unity" of dialectical materialism, then, it appears that the two halves of the theoretical composite are capable of generating competing allegiances. Champions of the general laws formula exhibit a preference for dialectics, at the expense of the ontological commitment represented by the basic question. Proponents of the basic question approach insist that the ontological dimension should preponderate, so that Soviet philosophy is first and foremost *materialism*. And since for Soviet philosophy neglect of the ontological dimension *is* neglect of materialism, it is not difficult to see in the published charge of "epistemologism" a veiled reference to a weightier offense—idealism. Indeed, often such references are less veiled: the late Eval'd Vasil'evich Il'enkov (1924–1979), the staunch Hegelian dialectician and a defender of Kedrov's general laws formula, was criticized for "sometimes almost erasing the border between materialism and objective idealism."[22] Thus although the controversy is not publicly couched in such terms, the opposition between the general laws and the basic question formulas at the 1970 conference and thereafter represented not only a clash between dialecticians and ma-

---

[21]Ibid., pp. 98–99.
[22]S. P. Dudel' and G. M. Shtraks, *Zakon edinstva i bor'by protivopolozhnostei* (Moscow, 1967), p. 170. For a good statement of the opposition between epistemologism and ontologism, see "Materialy soveshchaniia po problemam dialekticheskogo materializma v redaktsii zhurnala 'Voprosy filosofii,' " *Voprosy filosofii*, 1982, no. 4, p. 37. See also the continuation of this article, in which there is a reference to "the well-known traditions of ontologism of the Leningrad school" (no. 6, p. 18).

terialists but something approaching an idealist-materialist split within "materialist" Soviet philosophy.

The Status of Historical Materialism

In the eyes of many Soviet philosophers, a second and no less troublesome failing of the definition of philosophy as the science of the most general laws of nature, society, and thought is that it appears to exclude the entire field of *historical materialism*. For if philosophy is confined to the laws that apply to all three of those areas, then clearly the specific laws of the formation of societies and their historical careers through time must be excluded from philosophy.[23] The categories of historical materialism ('base', 'superstructure', 'class', and the like) have no application to the realms of nature or thought, and hence its laws (such as the law of the determining role of material productive forces with respect to relations of production) are not laws of *all* development. And yet both Engels and Lenin plainly regarded historical materialism as part of a unitary Marxist philosophy—a philosophy that is, in Lenin's famous phrase, "forged from a single piece of steel."[24]

Some Soviet philosophers who use the general laws formula gloss over the problem with a purely verbal solution, inspired by the Party program of 1961. When N. V. Duchenko, for example, speaks of "dialectical *and historical* materialism as the science of the most general laws of the development of nature, society, and human thought," he is in fact using the exact words of the Party pronouncement.[25] But of course the simple addition of 'and historical' explains nothing.

The temptation to make the addition, however, is understandable, given an ambiguity in the formula itself. It is possible to read the formula as referring not—or not only—to a set of laws each of which applies to all three of the realms enumerated but also distributively to three different sets of general laws: laws of nature, laws of society, and laws of thought. In such an interpretation, since historical materialism does deal with the most general laws of *society*, it would fall under the definition of philosophy. There is little likelihood, however, that this was Engels's original meaning, and there is no likelihood at all that Kedrov and Kuznetsov had

---

[23]For an explicit statement of this point, see, for example, A. Spirkin, "Filosofiia," in F. V. Konstantinov et al., eds., *Filosofskaia entsiklopediia*, 5 vols. (Moscow, 1960–1970), vol. 5, p. 344.

[24]Lenin, *Soch.*, vol. 18, p. 346.

[25]V. I. Shinkaruk et al., eds., *Dialekticheskii i istoricheskii materializm—Filosofskaia osnova kommunisticheskogo mirovozzreniia* (Kiev, 1977), p. 34 (italics added).

it in mind in 1962. The general laws in question, Kedrov wrote then, "are operative not only in nature or in any single region of it ... , not only in society or some portion of that area, and not only in the sphere of the human psyche alone. They operate simultaneously in all fields of the external world and of its reflection in our consciousness."[26] In this light, historical materialism could not possibly be included within the subject matter of philosophy, and in fact Kedrov and Kuznetsov made no mention of it.

Their silence was symptomatic of an attitude that has been shared by many Soviet philosophers who, like Kedrov and Kuznetsov, have backgrounds and interests in the natural sciences: they have tended to equate Marxist philosophy with *dialectical* materialism. On the opposite side have been those philosophers whose orientation is more toward the social sciences and who insist on including social and historical questions within the core subject matter of philosophy.

The difficulty for the latter group is that of explaining how both dialectical and historical materialism can be joined in one body of "philosophy." Textbooks such as *Fundamentals* often simply assert that historical materialism is an "inseparable part" of Marxist-Leninist philosophy, perhaps adding that in some unspecified sense it is a necessary condition for dialectical materialism: "Without it the dialectical materialist world outlook could not possibly exist."[27] Oizerman approaches the problem historically and argues that the earlier development of historical materialism by Marx and Engels provided the basis for the elaboration of dialectical materialism.[28] A. G. Spirkin contends that no one can understand the latter without first understanding the former.[29] Even if both Oizerman and Spirkin were right, however, that fact would not explain how to put the two fields together in a single definition of philosophy.

Little progress appears to have been made on this issue at the 1970 conference. E. V. Il'enkov, who supported Kedrov's general position, is quoted as holding that philosophy must deal with "those *and only those* laws and forms of development which remain one and the same for all three spheres—i.e., nature, society, and thought"—the position that clearly excludes the special laws of historical materialism from philosophy. V. Z. Kelle, on the other hand, devoted his entire presentation to historical materialism as a "division" of philosophy, and others are said to have

[26]Kedrov, "Philosophy as a General Science," p. 12.
[27]Konstantinov, *Fundamentals* (1982), p. 28. A more fully developed version of this position is found in E. F. Solopov, *Predmet i logika materialisticheskoi dialektiki* (Leningrad, 1973), pp. 184ff.
[28]T. I. Oizerman, *Problemy istoriko-filosofskoi nauki* (Moscow, 1969), p. 272.
[29]Spirkin, p. 343.

discussed the matter as well. The fact that little is reported concerning this discussion is indicative of its inconclusive nature, as is the pointed observation that many participants believed the question of the relation of dialectical and historical materialism should be examined further in a "special discussion."[30]

Under the circumstances, it is not surprising that writers such as Oizerman and Spirkin had recourse in the late 1960s to a highly pragmatic solution to the problem. Pointing out that the actual institutional organization of philosophical teaching and research in the USSR recognizes dialectical materialism and historical materialism as two separate fields under the general heading of "Philosophy," they argued that the success of this arrangement justifies regarding the fields as "two basic constituents of the philosophy of Marxism."[31] The same might be said, incidentally, of such specific philosophical disciplines as formal logic, ethics, aesthetics, and the history of philosophy, all of which also occupy acknowledged places in the administrative structure of Soviet philosophy despite the fact that they, too, appear to fall outside the general laws conception of the subject matter of philosophy.

The Ideological Role of Philosophy

A third and crucial difficulty with the definition of philosophy as a science of general laws is that it says nothing of the ideological or partisan role attributed to philosophy by Karl Marx himself, which is to many people the distinctive feature of a Marxist understanding of philosophy.

Marx, in a classic summary of his views, wrote in 1859 that the intellectual life of a society is determined by "the mode of production of material life" in that society. Specifically, ideas are expressions of economic class interests. They arise as what Marx calls a "superstructure" thrown up by the economic "foundation" of the society; they are "forms of social consciousness" that serve a partisan function in the struggle of economic classes against each other. And Marx explicitly includes philosophy among such ideological instruments of the class struggle: he speaks of "the legal, political, religious, aesthetic, or philosophic—in short, ideological forms in which men become conscious of this [class] conflict and fight it out."[32]

---

[30]"Diskussiia o predmete filosofii," p. 100 (italics added). The question remains unsettled; see, for example, the many references to it in "Materialy soveshchaniia po problemam istoricheskogo materializma v redaktsii zhurnala 'Voprosy filosofii,'" Voprosy filosofii, 1982, no. 5, pp. 35–51.

[31]Spirkin, p. 344; Oizerman, Problemy, p. 274.

[32]Marx and Engels, Selected Works, pp. 182–183.

How is this social, partisan, militant conception of philosophy consistent with the view that philosophy is the scientific study of the most general laws of development?

For many Soviet philosophers, the debate over the subject matter of philosophy in the 1960s is best described as a dispute concerning whether philosophy should be considered science or ideology—an investigation into general laws or a form of social consciousness that provides an intellectual and practical perspective for an economic class. Certainly a substantial number reacted to the scientific conception championed by Kedrov and Kuznetsov by reasserting—though in somewhat muted tones—the demand for partisanship (*partiinost'*) in philosophy that had been advanced so stridently during the Stalin era. Partisanship is "a constitutive determination" of philosophy, Oizerman wrote in 1968.[33] Kopnin affirmed that philosophy is a system of knowledge that is "transformed into the conviction of people, that has become a principle of action of classes, parties, etc."[34] The evil of "epistemologism" was said by its opponents to be not simply that it overemphasized cognitive problems but that it did so at the expense of ideological concerns. Surveying Soviet philosophy just after the 1970 Moscow conference, A. F. Okulov wrote: "In the fifties and sixties disputes flared up concerning the subject matter of Marxist-Leninist philosophy. Individual philosophers attempted to reduce this subject matter to epistemological problems alone, to the investigation of pure thought, cut off from practice, ... from the sharp, militant questions of the ideological struggle, from the tasks of forming the communist world view of the Soviet people." The 1970 conference itself, Okulov continued, showed that this attempt to limit Marxist philosophy to "logical problems"—apparently a reference to the views of Kedrov and his followers—had not yet been "thoroughly overcome."[35]

To overcome it, of course, a more adequate definition of philosophy was needed, and many Soviet philosophers in the 1960s sought alternative definitions that would clearly acknowledge the ideological or partisan character of the field. Consider, by way of contrast with the general laws definition of Kedrov and Kuznetsov, the following definition, which appeared in 1970 in the fifth volume of the Soviet *Philosophical Encyclopedia*: "Philosophy ... is a form of social consciousness directed at developing an integral view of the world and of man's place in it and

[33]T. I. Oizerman, "O smysle voprosa 'Chto takoe filosofiia?' " *Voprosy filosofii*, 1968, no. 11, p. 140.

[34]P. V. Kopnin, "O prirode i osobennostiakh filosofskogo znaniia," *Voprosy filosofii*, 1969, no. 4, p. 133.

[35]A. F. Okulov, *Sovetskaia filosofskaia nauka i ee problemy. Kratkii ocherk* (Moscow, 1970), pp. 14–15.

investigating the resultant cognitive, evaluative, ethical, and aesthetic relationship of man to the world.... Philosophy is always linked in the closest manner with the interests of social classes, with the political and ideological struggle."[36]

Perhaps the most ambitious and sophisticated attempt by a Soviet philosopher in the 1960s to replace the general laws formula with one more suitable to the ideological role of philosophy was that undertaken by Teodor Il'ich Oizerman (b. 1914) in his book *Problems of the Historico-Philosophical Science* (1969). Oizerman argues that 'science' is not the appropriate genus in terms of which to define philosophy.[37] In order to accommodate not only the broad range of philosophies known to history but also the "multiform content" of Marxism-Leninism, which cannot be restricted to "certain universal laws of development," he contends, another, more comprehensive genus is needed. Oizerman advocates for that purpose the category 'world view'—a term with impeccable Marxist credentials.[38] Every philosophy is a world view, he writes—that is, a general intellectual perspective providing explicit or implicit answers to the eternal questions of mankind. No philosophy can avoid these questions, he believes; even modern Anglo-American analytic philosophy, which overtly refuses to acknowledge the questions, presupposes certain answers to them, and thus has a "world-view character."[39] This is not to say, of course, that a philosophy cannot at the same time be *scientific* in the sense of offering answers that are securely grounded in the facts of the empirical world. Indeed a distinguishing feature of the Marxist-Leninist philosophy is just that, for Oizerman. Every philosophy, then, is a world view; Marxist-Leninist philosophy is a scientific world view.[40]

For all its currency in Marxist literature, however, the term 'world view' itself has no accepted meaning; one exasperated teacher of Marxism-Leninism recently begged for release from "those endless arguments about the structure of the concept 'world view'."[41] Oizerman, attempting to avoid excessively broad definitions such as "the sum total of all views of man

---

[36]Spirkin, pp. 332–333.

[37]Oizerman, *Problemy*, pp. 239–240.

[38]Ibid., pp. 273–274. The Russian original of the term—*mirovozzrenie*—is the literal equivalent of the German *Weltanschauung* (world vision, world perception or view) used by generations of German philosophers, including Marx and Engels. It was firmly entrenched in the Soviet philosophical lexicon long before Oizerman's book, and it is used freely in inspirational Party pronouncements on ideology.

[39]Oizerman, *Problemy*, p. 175.

[40]Ibid., pp. 265–274.

[41]V. I. Dobrynina, "Voprosy formirovaniia kommunisticheskogo mirovozzreniia studenchestva," *Filosofskie nauki*, 1976, no. 2, p. 41.

on the surrounding world,"[42] speaks of a world view as consisting of "basic human convictions concerning nature, personal and social life—convictions which play an *integrating, orienting* role in cognition, conduct, creativity, and the joint practical activity of people."[43] With this definition Oizerman can readily accommodate not only the basic question and other eternal philosophical questions but also the ideological function of philosophy. The "orienting role in ... the joint practical activity of people" is just the guiding, leading function that partisan ideology would be expected to fulfill. Philosophical world views would differ, then, in the ideological orientation they provide, and another distinguishing characteristic of Marxist-Leninist philosophy is that it furnishes such an orientation for the proletariat in its struggle against the bourgeoisie—that is, the "people" for whom it performs an orienting role are first and foremost the members of the propertyless, oppressed working class. Thus Marxist-Leninist philosophy can be called not only a scientific world view but a "scientific ideology," and the latter expression is freely used not only by Oizerman but by many other Soviet philosophers.

Oizerman himself was not a participant in the 1970 Moscow conference on the subject matter of philosophy, but the objections of those participants who found the ideological role of philosophy slighted by Kedrov's views were repeatedly couched in the form of the claim that philosophy has what were called "world-view functions"—functions that make it a broad intellectual perspective and guide to action. Philosophy is a form of social consciousness, affirmed V. I. Shinkaruk, and as such it must be directed toward an explanation of "man's goals and tasks in socio-historical activity." Several of the participants insisted, against much opposition from Kedrov and his supporters, that the way philosophy fulfills such a function is by presenting a view of "the world as a whole"—that is, an overarching perspective that includes but is by no means limited to the formulation of general laws. Although Kedrov himself agreed that philosophy does serve a "world-view function," he gave no indication of what he took it to be.[44]

Perhaps surprisingly, the formal summary of the 1970 conference by P. V. Kopnin gave the palm to the Engels-Kedrov-Kuznetsov view, despite all the ideological and other questions that had been raised about it since 1962. Kopnin concluded his remarks with the observation that whatever their differences, "almost all" of the speakers had acknowledged that "our

[42]M. Rosenthal and P. Yudin, eds., *A Dictionary of Philosophy* (Moscow, 1967), p. 482; T. I. Oizerman, "Filosofiia, nauka, ideologiia," in L. N. Mitrokhin et al., eds., *Filosofiia v sovremennom mire. Filosofiia i nauka. Kriticheskie ocherki burzhuaznoi filosofii* (Moscow, 1972), p. 117.

[43]Oizerman, *Problemy*, p. 176 (italics in original).

[44]"Diskussiia o predmete filosofii," p. 100.

point of departure in understanding the subject of philosophy is the position of F. Engels, and in particular this definition, *which no one has rejected*: philosophy is the science of the most general laws of the development of nature, society, and thought."[45] It is true that the definition was everyone's point of departure, inasmuch as the entire conference was devoted to Kedrov's views. But the fact that Kopnin could claim universal acceptance (or at least nonrejection) for the formula, when many of the participants had quite clearly rejected it as an adequate definition not merely of philosophy in general but of Marxist-Leninist philosophy in particular, serves only to underscore the official respect with which the formula was still treated. Whether the respect was attributable to the authority of the Party program in which that view was endorsed is unclear. But if it was, the irony of the situation is remarkable: for the authority of the Party was in that case supporting a position whose shortcomings included a failure to account for the partisan, ideological character of philosophy.

Agreeing to Disagree: Marxist-Leninist Philosophy as a Polyfunctional System of Sciences

In an earlier day, the purpose of an event such as the 1970 Moscow conference on the subject matter of philosophy would have been to terminate dispute and to establish orthodoxy. In the post-Stalin period, however, philosophical disputes have not always been silenced by fiat. A framework of tolerance has been built in Soviet philosophy within which lack of unanimity on many philosophical questions is acceptable. This framework not only allows intellectual diversity but within certain boundaries permits philosophical discussion to follow its natural course—which is to say that it permits discussion to be genuine rather than a ceremonial accessory to the imposition of dogma.

As a result there is in the present day no single, agreed-upon Soviet definition of philosophy—no formula that constitutes orthodoxy for the Soviet philosophical community. At a special conference on the subject matter of Marxist-Leninist philosophy held at Moscow State University on April 19 and 20, 1979, for example, the general laws formula by no means dominated the proceedings as it had the Moscow conference of

---

[45]Ibid. (italics added).

1970.[46] Only one of the nearly forty participants—Z. M. Orudzhev—spoke strongly in its favor, calling it "fully adequate to define the subject of Marxist-Leninist philosophy." And even Orudzhev qualified his endorsement with the observation that that could be said because "every definition should express only the principal content of a subject."[47] Other participants had more serious reservations. Individuals who still utilized the formula qualified it by reference to one or more of the concerns examined in the previous section, producing in some cases portmanteau definitions seemingly designed to accommodate as many of these concerns as possible, if only additively.[48] Others advocated simpler, schematic definitions that avoided mentioning the general laws at all.[49] Whatever the proposal, there appeared to be general agreement with D. I. Dubrovskii, who asserted that attempts to limit philosophy to the general laws "greatly impoverish the real content of Marxist philosophy."[50]

The "real content," moreover, was not restricted to the old chestnuts. A note heard but by no means stressed earlier in Soviet philosophy was sounded repeatedly at the 1979 conference—the need to include the concept 'man' in the definition of Marxist philosophy. A number of speakers showed the influence of the younger, "humanistic" Karl Marx in their contention that Marxism cannot be conceived apart from a stress on human concerns, on the transformative character of human practical activity, and on ethical, aesthetic, and even religious values.[51] An equal number expressed reservations about these demands, however, arguing against what one of them saw as "the reduction of the subject of Marxist-Leninist philosophy only to the problem of man or to the practical activity of social man."[52] But even these critics did not insist on the adequacy of the general laws definition.

---

[46]"O predmete marksistsko-leninskoi filosofii," *Filosofskie nauki*, 1980, no. 2, pp. 142–151. Kedrov was not among the participants, but he reports that he attempted unsuccessfully to have a statement on the subject included in the conference report; see B. M. Kedrov, "Marksistskaia filosofiia. Ee predmet i rol' v integratsii sovremennykh nauk," *Voprosy filosofii*, 1982, no. 1, p. 61.

[47]"O predmete," p. 145.

[48]Ibid., p. 144.

[49]Ibid., p. 151; see also p. 147.

[50]Ibid., p. 146.

[51]See the comments of D. S. Tsotsonova, V. I. Kuptsov, and V. N. Shevchenko reported in ibid., pp. 146, 148, and 149. Associated with this point of view is the effort by some Soviet philosophers to establish "philosophical anthropology" as a legitimate field of Marxist-Leninist philosophy; see V. Lorentson and B. Yudin, eds., *Marxist Dialectics Today* (Moscow, 1979), p. 105. On the whole question of how to incorporate "the problem of man" in Marxist-Leninist philosophy, see Iu. K. Pletnikov and V. N. Shevchenko, "Issledovaniia v oblasti istoricheskogo materializma," *Voprosy filosofii*, 1981, no. 1, p. 27.

[52]"O predmete," p. 147. See also the comments of Iu. N. Miachin and Z. F. Petrovaia, p. 150.

Another, less obvious weakening of the general laws formula in recent Soviet philosophy consists not in supplementing or replacing it with other formulas but in broadening its interpretation to include formerly excluded content—a kind of development by dilution that we shall see repeated in many different areas of Soviet philosophy in the course of this study. In this way historical materialism is now frequently accommodated within the general laws formula—namely, by extending the notion of a general law to include not only absolutely universal laws but also those that are general within a particular realm, in this case the realm of society and its history. Whereas the 1970 conference on the nature of philosophy was marked by pointed opposition to this interpretation, at the 1979 conference on Marxist-Leninist philosophy two of the most prominent philosophers in attendance—S. T. Meliukhin and I. S. Narskii—both advocated it. Meliukhin, referring to "the well-known difficulties" of the general laws formula, argued that it must include not only those "maximally universal laws" that operate in nature, society, and thought but also what he called "regionally universal" laws that apply only within one of the three fields.[53] Narskii called the latter simply "special laws," but he, too, argued that they should be included in the interpretation of the term 'general law'.[54] Narskii acknowledged that this change from the earlier interpretation is contested by a number of Soviet philosophers; indeed it was contested at the 1979 conference by A. P. Sheptulin.[55] Nonetheless its growing respectability demonstrates a process of the attenuation of a traditional formula that has become a modern feature of Soviet philosophical thought.

Thus the strict general laws definition of philosophy formulated by Kedrov and Kuznetsov in 1962, though still found in Soviet textbooks and still part of the Party program, has not been dogmatically imposed on Soviet philosophers. Indeed it appears that more diversity exists now on the question of the nature of philosophy than was demonstrated at the 1970 conference.

The diversity, of course, has its severe limits. The framework of tolerance on the question still brooks no admittedly non-Marxist, not to say anti-

---

[53]Ibid., pp. 142–143. Another recent writer—Yu. A. Kharin in *Fundamentals of Dialectics*, trans. K. Kostrov (Moscow, 1981)—defines general laws as those that "operate either in nature, or in society, or in thought"; the subset of laws operating in all three realms he calls "universal laws" (p. 114).

[54]"O predmete," p. 144.

[55]Ibid. A recent book-length study by a group of Leningrad philosophers argues that historical materialism is neither a part nor a specialized application of dialectical materialism but is "a constitutive feature of the latter, part of its essence, organically amalgamated with it," and recommends the name 'dialectico-historical materialism' for Marxist-Leninist philosophy. See F. F. Viakkerev et al., eds., *Edinstvo dialekticheskogo i istoricheskogo materializma* (Leningrad, 1978), p. 12.

Marxist, viewpoints. Soviet philosophers continue to evince profound respect for the wisdom of the founding fathers and to pursue the great synthetic dialectical materialist vision of philosophy that they believe the heritage requires. And there are more specific elements of agreement as well. The most distinctive of these, however, are two that serve to promote continuing philosophical discussion, and we shall briefly examine these two common threads in current Soviet philosophy. They are a trend toward identifying philosophy as not a single science but a system of differentiated sciences and the growing acceptance of a polyfunctional conception of philosophy.

Marxist-Leninist Philosophy as a System of Differentiated Sciences

The bulk of the opposition among Soviet philosophers currently to the definition of Marxist-Leninist philosophy as a "science of general laws" is addressed to the latter half of that formula. 'Science' is still on the whole the preferred genus for the classification of the field, however its exact subject matter may be specified. At the same time, Soviet philosophers no longer commonly assume that Marxist-Leninist philosophy must constitute a *single* science, whether its subject is general laws or something else. In the earlier years of the Soviet era, there was great resistance to dividing Lenin's "single piece of steel" into separate philosophical disciplines— metaphysics, epistemology, logic, ethics, and the like—as they are known in the West. Marxist philosophy was viewed as a seamless whole that allowed no subdivision and required no supplementation. A factor contributing significantly to the framework of tolerance in Soviet philosophy in recent years, however, has been a movement toward the view that Marxist-Leninist philosophy is a system of related but distinguishable philosophical sciences, some of which may even be said to exist apart from dialectical and historical materialism. This view was well summarized at the 1979 conference by Serafim Timofeevich Meliukhin, whose comments carried special weight in view of his position as head of the department of dialectical materialism at Moscow State University: "Our philosophy should not be identified only with dialectical and historical materialism. By virtue of development and of processes of differentiation, Marxist-Leninist philosophy represents at the present time a system of philosophical sciences: dialectical and historical materialism, the history of philosophy, ethics, aesthetics, scientific atheism, the theory of scientific communism, sociology, logic, philosophical questions of the natural sciences and of the humanities."[56] This tendency is also evidenced, it may be noted, in the

[56]"O predmete," p. 143.

Soviet academic titles "candidate of philosophical sciences" (*kandidat fi-losofskikh nauk*) and "doctor of philosophical sciences" (*doktor filosof-skikh nauk*), as well as in the name of the journal *Filosofskie nauki* (Philosophical sciences), founded in 1958 and held by many Soviet phi-losophers to be a journal of higher professional caliber than its older rival, *Voprosy filosofii* (Problems of philosophy).

Several other participants in the 1979 conference also spoke approvingly of the process of differentiation, though some saw it as taking place *within* dialectical materialism rather than, as Meliukhin suggested, alongside it.[57] All who addressed the question emphasized the close, "organic" relations among the differentiated areas; but they separated the areas nonetheless, even to the point of identifying them by the standard Western term 'dis-ciplines'. Only one speaker—A. P. Sheptulin—clearly opposed the trend, arguing that Marxist-Leninist philosophy is coextensive with an undiffer-entiated dialectical materialism—an argument that was, however, pow-erfully seconded by Kedrov in a 1982 article.[58]

Although the great majority of Soviet philosophers appear to accept differentiation as both an actual and a desirable feature of their field, there is no real agreement among them as to either the number or the identity of the various philosophical sciences. Meliukhin's list, cited above, is longer than most. N. I. Zhukov named six disciplines as constituting philosophy "in the broad sense of the term"—theory of dialectics, theory of cognition, historical materialism, ethics, aesthetics, and scientific atheism.[59] Virtually everyone but Sheptulin now wishes to include historical materialism, and most include ethics and aesthetics; there is considerable disagreement, however, on epistemology, formal logic, the history of philosophy, and other subjects. All such uncertainties as to what is to be included in the list of philosophical sciences were neatly if inconclusively sidestepped by one of the 1979 conference participants, who simply called Marxist-Len-inist philosophy "an integral science ... including all existing philosoph-ical disciplines."[60]

---

[57]Ibid., p. 150; see also Kedrov, "Marksistskaia filosofiia," p. 52.
[58]"O predmete," p. 144; Kedrov, "Marksistskaia filosofiia," pp. 52–62. For a compre-hensive recent treatment of Marxist-Leninist philosophy as a system of relatively independent philosophical disciplines, see G. V. Platonov, G. M. Shtraks, and V. N. Demin, eds., *Mark-sistsko-leninskaia filosofiia kak sistema (predmet, struktura i funktsii)* (Moscow, 1981).
[59]"O predmete," p. 147.
[60]Ibid., p. 149. In the 1960s Soviet philosophers engaged in a lively debate concerning the existence of an independent "dialectics of nature"—that is, an independent science, com-parable to historical materialism, that would have as its specific subject the operation of dialectical laws in the natural world, as opposed to the worlds of society and thought. Although vigorous discussion of the matter ceased in the mid-1960s, the question has not really been settled. See Bernard Jeu, *La philosophie soviétique et l'Occident. Essai sur les tendances et sur la signification de la philosophie soviétique contemporaine (1959–1969)*(Paris, 1969), pp. 130–140.

In Soviet philosophical practice, the determination of what constitutes an "existing philosophical discipline" may hinge on such extraphilosophical factors as the needs, the expectations, or the ambitions of a particular institution. Not surprisingly, a massive establishment such as Moscow State University, the nation's largest and most prestigious institution of higher learning, has reached advanced stages of differentiation. In the university's School of Philosophy (*Filosofskii fakul'tet*), fourteen separate fields currently have the status of departments (*kafedry*), each with its own head, its own offices, and its own professorial and clerical staffs. Their official titles are: Dialectical Materialism, Historical Materialism, Logic, History of Marxist-Leninist Philosophy, History of Philosophy of the Peoples of the USSR, History of Foreign Philosophy, History and Theory of Atheism, Marxist-Leninist Aesthetics, Marxist-Leninist Ethics, Scientific Communism, History and Theory of the International Workers' and Communist Movement, Theory and Practice of Communist Education, Methodology of Concrete Social Investigations, and History of Socialist Doctrines.[61] Other major universities and research institutions offer comparable though not identical schedules of specializations. In smaller institutions, ethics and aesthetics may be combined in a single department, the history of philosophy may be excluded, and so on. In a veterinary school or engineering institute, there may be only a simple department or section of "dialectical and historical materialism." No institution of higher learning is without a philosophy staff altogether, as some training in philosophy is required of all students in whatever field, even the most practical and technical. There is no consensus, however, as to just what disciplines would be included in an ideally complete philosophical education.

Similarly unsettled is the question of how exactly the different disciplines are joined together to form "Marxist-Leninist philosophy." This should not be surprising, given the absence of agreement on a general definition of that term, for to ask what constitutes the unity of the different areas of Marxist-Leninist philosophy is simply another way of asking for a definition of the entire field. Identification of the "system," over and above its component parts, thus awaits the construction of an adequate definition of Marxist-Leninist philosophy.

Meanwhile, the process of differentiation operates to promote a degree of liberalizing pluralism in Soviet philosophy. It allows specialists in some fields to work with relative independence, insulated to some extent from the general theoretical strictures of dialectical and historical materialism.

---

[61]*Moskovskii universitet. 1977–1978 uchebnyi protsess. Katalog-spravochnik. Gumanitarnye fakul'tety* (Moscow, 1977), pp. 200–201. The establishment of a fifteenth department, Dialectical Logic, is actively being discussed; see "Razrabotka teorii dialektiki v vuzovskikh kollektivakh," *Filosofskie nauki*, 1982, no. 1, p. 160.

It encourages professionalism and discourages provincialism in Soviet philosophy by inviting commitment to an intellectual discipline with a worldwide identity, history, and literature. Whether this should be called a form of philosophical convergence with the West is debatable, but it is a fact that Soviet specialists in such areas as logic, aesthetics, and the history of philosophy today are less tied to the traditional categories of Marxism-Leninism and more conversant with the standard international vocabulary and methodology of their fields than were their undifferentiated predecessors of the Stalin era and before. It must be noted, however, that the virtues of disciplinary specialization in philosophy have been questioned by Communist party authorities as well as by some prominent philosophers. Contending that such specialization does not always produce intellectual advancement, the Party's leading theoretical journal, *Kommunist*, found itself compelled in October 1979 to issue a warning against carrying it too far: "Marxist-Leninist philosophy is a unitary conceptual organism, an integral system of views," the journal proclaimed; "none of the disciplines within it can develop independently of the others."[62]

Marxist-Leninist Philosophy as Polyfunctional

Just as Soviet philosophy in the present day is marked by differentiation, or the development of separate and more or less independent philosophical disciplines, so too it displays a tendency to accommodate a number of separate and more or less independent roles or functions. Soviet philosophers, it is true, have always been inclined to view their field as multifarious, but their definitions of it have not always reflected this view: the general laws definition, for example, provides no clear basis for attributing an ideological role to philosophy. The tendency now in the search for an adequate definition is to stress what Soviet philosophers variously call the "multidimensional," "polysystemic," or "multifaceted" character of philosophy.[63] 'Polyfunctionality' is a convenient single label for this character.

One of the principal functions attributed to philosophy in the current Soviet literature is the *cognitive*, or knowledge-generating, function associated with philosophy's nature as a system of sciences. Like all sciences, philosophy is held to yield truths about the objectively existing world, and

---

[62]"O sostoianii i napravleniiakh filosofskikh issledovanii," *Kommunist*, 1979, no. 15 (October), p. 72.

[63]"O predmete," pp. 147, 149; G. A. Brutian, "K voprosu o prirode filosofskogo znaniia," *Filosofskie nauki*, 1976, no. 5, p. 40. Although Kedrov rejects differentiation within Marxist-Leninist philosophy, even he stresses the "diverse sides, aspects, and functions" of that philosophy ("Marksistskaia filosofiia," p. 57).

consequently to form an integral part of mankind's intellectual assimilation of reality.

Another function much emphasized in Soviet writings is the *ideological* or partisan role of philosophy, now frequently captured under the heading of philosophy's "world-view function." In providing a theoretical basis for a world view (as Marxist-Leninist philosophy is the theoretical foundation of Marxism-Leninism), a philosophy is said to furnish a social group with an ideological orientation for practical life, thus arming it in its struggle against antagonistic groups.

A third role assigned to philosophy by many Soviet theorists is the *methodological* function of providing an orientation and a procedure for intellectual investigation. Since the 1920s Soviet philosophers have argued that philosophy has the special responsibility of guiding the work of the other sciences, and the position continues to be defended warmly today. Some individuals treat this methodological role as one of the world-view functions of philosophy; others, however, attribute to philosophy both world-view and methodological functions, as if the two were independent.[64]

Still other, more limited or derivative functions are also freely cited by Soviet philosophers as harmoniously joined with the major functions already enumerated. In its cognitive capacity, philosophy is held to fulfill ontological, epistemological, and logical functions.[65] In its ideological capacity, it is said to offer among other things a basic value orientation and so to perform what G. A. Brutian calls "evaluative and critical functions."[66] Even functions sometimes identified more with "bourgeois" thought than with Marxist-Leninist philosophy can be included within the latter's commodious scope: Brutian allows "a grain of truth" to the view that philosophy functions as a kind of intellectual therapy.[67]

The understanding of the various roles of philosophy as complementary but also relatively autonomous has beneficial consequences for contemporary philosophical discussion in the USSR. One such consequence is that an author can single out a particular function for more thorough examination without becoming subject to attack—particularly if he at least pays lip service to the functions set aside. It is not necessary, then, for every paper on the subject matter of philosophy to dwell on its ideological or partisan role, as was the case during the Stalin era. Openly to *deny* the

---

[64]Konstantinov et al., *Filosofskaia entsiklopediia*, vol. 3, p. 420; Shinkaruk et al., pp. 23, 49; "O predmete," p. 144.

[65]"O predmete," p. 144; Brutian, p. 36.

[66]Brutian, p. 40.

[67]Ibid. Clearly related to the emphasis on the function of philosophy is the recent suggestion by V. S. Gott, E. P. Semeniuk, and A. D. Ursul that philosophy is best defined as a particular sort of *activity* ("O spetsifike filosofii i ee otnoshenii k drugim naukam," *Filosofskie nauki*, 1982, no. 4, p. 23).

ideological role is of course not advisable, but to pass over that role in order to devote time and attention to cognitive, methodological, or other functions is permissible, and I suspect that this device is employed freely by philosophers for whom passing over is in fact the functional equivalent of denying. Polyfunctionality may thus represent a modus vivendi for still more widely divergent views than appear on the surface. A pro forma acceptance of a view a person rejects (for example, that philosophy has ideological functions) may be thought a small price to pay for the ability to develop a view (concerning, say, the methodology of the natural sciences) in which that person is vitally interested.

Furthermore, the boundaries of philosophy's polyfunctionality are not fixed, which means that new functions can be proposed without fear of heresy, as long as they purport to be complements rather than replacements for others. A good illustration is afforded by a 1969 paper by I. V. Novik. Novik notes that much attention has been given in Soviet philosophy to its partisan, world-view, and general methodological functions, but he argues that the discussion "stands in need of a certain supplementation" by still another function. This new function Novik calls the role of philosophy as a "dialectical metalogic" of science, by which he means (in part) the activity of identifying and analyzing general trends in the current development of all the sciences—trends such as, for example, the growing importance of statistics in both natural and social sciences.[68] In another political and philosophical environment, a paper such as Novik's might argue that philosophy is nothing but, or is *best* understood as, a dialectical metalogic of science, and perhaps Novik's paper is read in that light by at least a part of his Soviet audience. The notion of polyfunctionality is eminently suited to allow people to disagree while retaining a semblance of innocuous unanimity.

A natural extension of the view of philosophy as a complex system and as open-endedly polyfunctional would be the admission that no precise definition could ever be adequate to the field's diversity—that philosophy is strictly speaking indefinable. Surprisingly, even this thesis—so out of keeping with the stereotype of an essentially complete and static Marxist-Leninist outlook—has been enunciated by prominent Soviet philosophers. In the 1979 conference, for example, when Z. M. Orudzhev advocated retention of the traditional brief "science of general laws" definition despite its limitations, he did so on the grounds that no definition, however complex, could embrace "all sides" of Marxist-Leninist philosophy.[69] Still more

[68]I. V. Novik, "Some Aspects of the Interrelation of Philosophy and Natural Science," *Soviet Studies in Philosophy* 8 (Winter 1969–1970), pp. 295–296, 302–303, 307.
[69]"O predmete," p. 145.

explicit is T. I. Oizerman, who rejects the traditional definition for precisely the reason given by Orudzhev for accepting it. Because of Marxist-Leninist philosophy's "multiform content" and its openness to new roles in the future, Oizerman argues, neither it nor philosophy in general can be reduced to "a single definition." As philosophy progresses, he asserts, it becomes "a system of historically developing philosophical disciplines enriched with new content."[70]

The Cognitive and Ideological Functions of Soviet Marxist Philosophy in Theory and Practice

Although the conception of philosophy as a system of sciences that perform a number of disparate intellectual functions has clear virtues, it is not without its difficulties as well. For the functions generally held by Soviet philosophers to be harmoniously combined in Marxist-Leninist philosophy include the cognitive function of presenting scientific truth about the world and the ideological function of promoting the interests of a particular social class. To many critics this conception of Marxist-Leninist philosophy as a "scientific ideology" has seemed not merely dubious but absurd. The search for scientific truth, it is argued, requires disinterested objectivity and hence nonpartisanship; the ideological promotion of interests, on the other hand, requires partisan dedication to a cause.[71] At the same time, no feature of Soviet philosophy is more significant in accounting for the way in which philosophy is practiced and taught in the USSR than its insistence that Marxism-Leninism is both objective *and* partisan. In the concluding section of this chapter, we shall first consider the theoretical question concerning the combination and then examine its impact on the practice of philosophy in the USSR.

Is Proletarian Partisanship a Guarantee of Truth?

Soviet philosophers are, of course, aware of objections to the notion of a "scientific ideology," and they seek to counter such objections. Admit-

---

[70]Oizerman, *Problemy*, pp. 273–274. It should also be noted that some Soviet philosophers hold open the possibility that there may be alternative systems of Marxist-Leninist philosophy. "Marxist philosophy," writes P. V. Alekseev, "places a ban not on the idea of a multiplicity of systems but only on systems of an idealist and metaphysical character" (*Predmet, struktura i funktsii dialekticheskogo materializma* [Moscow, 1978], p. 100).

[71]Gustav A. Wetter, *Dialectical Materialism. A Historical and Systematic Survey of Philosophy in the Soviet Union*, trans. Peter Heath (London, 1958), p. 268.

tedly, the authors of *Fundamentals* write, partisanship *may* conflict with objectivity: "Partisanship certainly does not have a scientific character when philosophy expresses and defends the position and interests of the classes that are passing from the historical arena; in such a case philosophy departs from the truth of life, from its scientific evaluation."[72] The authors' point is that it is not partisanship as such that causes the departure from truth but the *character* of the partisanship—that is, not the fact of defending the interests of classes, but rather the fact that the classes in question are "passing from the historical scene"; these are, of course, the reactionary classes, such as the modern bourgeoisie. Doomed classes, Soviet philosophers maintain, have no interest in understanding the world correctly and indeed are motivated to misconceive it.

The interests and the ideology of such classes, it is said, do not correspond to "the objective course of history."[73] They seek to preserve their own position of dominance, and in so doing they are required to deny the objective evidence of the changing world around them—to falsify the laws and processes of historical development that spell their doom. At one time it was common for Soviet philosophers to attribute the bourgeoisie's flight from objectivity to a simple unwillingness to face unpleasant facts—to "the bourgeois dread of looking into what is, for them, a bleak future."[74] But more sophisticated arguments in the present day adduce a clearer linkage between the bourgeoisie's economic interests and its illusory ideas. Thus V. Z. Kelle argues that the bourgeoisie, in the attempt to maintain its ascendancy, is required to develop and disseminate the fiction that its interests are the interests of society at large.[75]

Implicit in this explanation of the failure of partisanship to achieve objective knowledge is, of course, an indication of its possible cognitive success. For when, by contrast, a class is riding the wave of the future and is destined to be victorious in the historical struggle, then its partisan interest is said by Soviet philosophers to lie precisely in revealing the objective truth, in presenting a correct rather than a falsified picture of reality. Marxism-Leninism, it is held, advances the interests of just such a class—the proletariat.[76] The proletariat has nothing to hide or fear, and given its leading role in remaking the world, it is motivated to achieve a comprehensive, correct, undistorted picture of that world in order to operate successfully within it. The linkage between the partisan interests of

---

[72]Konstantinov, *Osnovy marksistsko-leninskoi filosofii*, p. 24.

[73]I. V. Blauberg, P. V. Kopnin, and I. K. Pantin, eds., *Kratkii slovar' po filosofii*, 2d ed. (Moscow, 1970), p. 102.

[74]Wetter, *Dialectical Materialism*, p. 269.

[75]*Philosophy in the USSR. Problems of Dialectical Materialism*, p. 261.

[76]Konstantinov, *Fundamentals* (1982), p. 34.

the proletariat and the attainment of objective knowlege is expounded as follows by N. V. Duchenko:

> Partisanship guides the communist world view to science, to the attainment of maximally adequate knowledge. Such knowledge is essential for making correct appraisals of the surrounding reality from the standpoint of its significance for man. In the communist world view, man's orientation toward the attainment of maximally reliable knowledge is determined by the class interests of the working class, which is vitally interested in the most successful alteration of natural and particularly of social reality.[77]

Thus by a neat conceptual twist it turns out that proletarian partisanship not only is compatible with scientific objectivity but *promotes* it: the more genuinely partisan the proletariat is, the more interested it is in discovering the truth about the world.[78]

This argument will surely be unacceptable to anyone who is not already persuaded of the truth of the Marxist theory of history, since it assumes a number of the theses of that theory, among them that the interests of the bourgeoisie are *not* the interests of society at large and that the proletariat *is* riding the wave of the future. Supposing that the theory can be defended without circularity, however, and granting its truth for the sake of argument, are we then required to accept the above defense of the congeniality of proletarian partisanship and scientific objectivity? Gustav Wetter, despite his severe criticism of the Soviet conception of partisanship, believes that we are: assuming historical materialism, he asserts, "it will readily be seen that one has to adopt the standpoint of the proletariat in order to know reality aright."[79] But is that really the case?

To say of the proletariat that its interests "coincide" with the objective laws of development is not to affirm the automatic identity of what the proletariat believes and the truth; it is presumably to say that the proletariat *wishes* to know the truth about those laws and to disseminate this knowledge. It is, in other words, to affirm a causal connection between the *motives* of the proletariat and what it believes and proclaims. To move from these motives to the identity in question would be to assume that the proletariat never errs—a very big assumption. Who is to say that the proletariat has adequately discovered the truth it seeks to know? It may be wrong as to which facts of the world correspond to its interests. Even more fundamentally, it may be wrong about its interests; for that knowledge, too, must be present if its real interests are to function effectively to

[77]Shinkaruk et al., p. 38.
[78]Wetter, *Dialectical Materialism*, p. 269.
[79]Ibid., pp. 269–270.

yield the truth—unless we assume some magical linkage, operating independently of its consciousness, between its real interests and its beliefs. Hence we must accept the possibility that at any time what the proletariat *thinks* is its interest may not really *be* its interest, so that the motivation provided by the *interest* in seeking the truth does not guarantee its possession.

But why should we assume even that the proletariat would have an interest in seeking the truth? If it is *destined* to be the victorious class, and will become so by processes "independent of the human will," as Soviet Marxists are fond of saying,[80] what does it gain from *knowing* about these processes? It will benefit from them whether it knows about them or not. We may object, however, as Soviet philosophers regularly do, that Marxism is not fatalism, that the talk about independence of the human will is not to be taken literally and that knowledge of the laws and processes of development is in fact a necessary condition for the proletariat's victory. In that case it would be in the interest of the proletariat to understand correctly the workings of the world because, as the above quotation from Duchenko suggests, it would aid the class in bringing about the desired outcome. But if that were true, there would have to be an indeterminacy about the outcome itself such that *it* could not be part of the "objective facts" that the progressive class is motivated to "know": the outcome would be rather a projected ideal to be *brought about*—not known—in accordance with a person's interests. And this possibility has at least two awkward consequences for the Marxist-Leninist philosopher.

First, it is at least arguable that deception and even self-deception would serve the interests of the proletariat more effectively than truth. Convictions as to the rightness of its cause, the superiority of socialism to capitalism, and the inevitability of victory would no doubt serve as powerful incentives to the proletariat in its struggle to prevail, even if those convictions were groundless. If its interest lies in advancing its revolutionary ambitions, that interest would be served by believing whatever armed it best for the fight—from encouraging, even if inaccurate, convictions of tactical strength to the most elaborate myth of the world and a person's rightful place in it. Or even if not deceived itself, the proletariat might well find it advantageous to advance deceiving views. It would be useful if a person's *opponents* believed, for example, that their cause was unworthy, or lost, or both. And when it comes to an urge to disseminate "maximally adequate" knowledge, it might be noted incidentally that one particular proletariat—that of the USSR—has never been known for its eagerness to spread factual information about the world to its own members or about its own members to the world.

[80]Ibid., p. 269.

Second, if there is an indeterminacy about the outcome of the class struggle, so that the victory of one class or another is not an objective datum but a future contingency, it is not clear that the bourgeoisie would be motivated to distort or mask reality or would be intimidated by a bleak future. Indeed it would have exactly the same motivations to accept truth or deception that the proletariat would have. It would be no more and no less susceptible to the power of myth and invigorating illusion. To whatever extent it would be in the interest of the proletariat to understand the workings of the world correctly (in order to operate effectively in the world), to that extent it would similarly be in the interest of the bourgeoisie, and for precisely the same reason. If the progressive class's motive to know the truth is that it needs to know the true mechanisms of history and social life so that it can bring about the desired result, how is its situation any different from that of the bourgeoisie?

The foregoing argument is not intended to show that partisanship and objectivity are incompatible. Logically speaking, there is no reason to deny that what is objectively true might also be useful in promoting the partisan interests of some social group; there is no inherent antagonism between the true and the useful, which have separate and independent grounds. The Soviet philosopher, however, is not content with compatibility; he asserts a stronger connection between proletarian partisanship and objectivity. He persists in assuming that the two exist in "dialectical unity," which signifies an organic connection in which there is mutual support and encouragement. It is the questionable character of this stronger claim that I have tried to show.

Partisanship and Objectivity in Soviet Philosophical Practice

Questionable or not, the claim that there is a special affinity between proletarian partisanship and objectivity continues to be advanced by Soviet philosophers, and it accounts for some noteworthy features of the practice of philosophy in the USSR. By making proletarian partisanship and objectivity dialectically interdependent, Soviet doctrine encourages the conviction that both of them can be achieved by beginning with either one. But since in practice even a dialectician must begin somewhere, this conviction when acted upon produces diametrically opposed approaches to philosophy.

The first approach is to begin with partisanship and to assume that, *because* a view is partisan, it is true. Thus the philosopher's obligation to the truth is adequately discharged by determining what expresses the interests of the working class. This approach is relatively easy and eminently

safe, What is "partisan" can often be determined by consulting pronouncements of the Communist party itself, in whose hands the individual
philosopher's professional fate in any event largely resides. The tendency,
then, is to assume not only that what is good for the Party is good for
philosophy but that what the Party wants to hear is good for it. Matters
are facilitated by the fact that the great majority of the Soviet philosophical
community are members of the Communist party and as such are committed to the cause of advancing the interests of the proletariat as understood by the Party. The presence of a Party office within the academic
precincts of the School of Philosophy of Moscow State University, for
example, serves as a constant reminder of the mission of Soviet philosophy
as the ideological vanguard of a social movement the direction of which
is assumed to be written in the stars.

From this partisan perspective the truth about the world that is philosophy's cognitive objective is often considered to be in the main already
discovered, so that the task of the philosopher today is less to discover
more of it than to persuade the young and the dubious of its existence
and its importance. The chief work of the departments of philosophy in
institutions of higher learning, according to one major Party pronouncement, is "the formation of a Marxist-Leninist world view, a communist
consciousness, and lofty moral qualities in young specialists, educating
them to be active builders of communism, innovators in production, pa-
triots and internationalists."[81] If this activity is what is partisan, and what
is partisan is true, the philosopher can easily come to see his service to the
truth as consisting in communicating Marxism-Leninism effectively and
combatting its enemies.

In this light it is not surprising that the training received by budding
Soviet philosophers is typically one-sided. They find no open advocacy of
non-Marxist positions in their courses, and although they read Plato and
Aristotle, Kant and Hegel, they do so within a critical framework provided
by Marxism-Leninsm. The Soviet books and journal articles they encounter
are predictable in their positive dogmas and in their attacks on the errors
of "bourgeois" philosophy. And not only the content but the form of their
instruction may be heavily partisan. Their instructors are enjoined to display strong conviction, as in the following excerpt from a manual on the
teaching of Marxist-Leninist philosophy: "Conviction has considerable
power, especially moral power, in everything, and particularly in the teaching of philosophy. Hence those instructors act incorrectly who present
their topic without firm conviction, and even with frequent reservations

---

[81]G. M. Shtraks et al., eds., *Osnovnye napravleniia raboty kafedr filosofii* (Moscow, 1969),
pp. 13–14.

such as 'it seems to me,' 'I think,' 'if I am not mistaken,' and the like. Clearly the lecturer has not considered what kind of impression—a negative one, of course—is left in his audience by language so larded with reservations."[82]

The philosopher's research as well as teaching is called to promote the great social purpose. "All our investigations and all our books," wrote one dedicated Soviet philosopher recently, "must serve the most important cause—the cause of building a new world."[83] Militaristic images for intellectual work on behalf of the cause are no longer as common in Soviet writing as they once were, but it is still possible to encounter references to the activities of philosophers at their "stations on the philosophical front."[84] One of these stations is the international philosophical congress, at which Soviet participation is still all too frequently marked by the militant and unyielding advocacy of Marxist-Leninist positions by doctrinaire Soviet philosophers especially selected for ideological reliability and vigor.

But the dialectical unity of proletarian partisanship and objectivity cuts two ways. If it allows a Soviet philosopher to assume that what is partisan is true, it also legitimizes the converse thesis: what is true is partisan. In practice, then, a second approach to philosophical work is possible in the USSR: a person may begin with an inquiry into what is objectively true and may argue in good conscience that, whatever the truth turns out to be, it will serve the real interests of the proletariat and the building of the new world. The emphasis is on rational argumentation and on going where the evidence leads even if doing so requires reinterpretation of cherished dogmas. Although this approach clearly demands greater courage on the part of the Soviet philosopher, it is a justifiable one in terms of orthodox doctrine. In following it the Soviet philosopher can develop views in relative disregard of specific Party demands—at least for a time—and can identify with a form of professionalism in the service of truth that has been honored since the time of Plato.

An enthusiastic endorsement of this second approach can be found in an unlikely place in recent Soviet philosophy—in the article on partisanship in the authoritative *Philosophical Encyclopedia*. The author of the article, Genrikh Stepanovich Batishchev, presents a stinging rebuke to individuals whose first concern is for Party loyalty—who believe, in his words, that "militancy provides a *guarantee* of objectivity in science, that the subjective conviction that one is serving the interests of communism and even the verbal declaration of devotion to communism in themselves assure one's

[82]Ibid., p. 14.
[83]Okulov, p. 190.
[84]Ibid., p. 5.

correctness in a dispute and a true position in the resolution of every problem." This, he argues, is a perverted conception that, following Hegel, he calls "subjective partisanship." It reduces philosophy, he contends, "to the role of a handmaiden of religious, political, legal, and other ideological forces and institutions." True Marxism, on the other hand, stands for "objective partisanship," which he lauds in a remarkable litany:

> The former [subjective partisanship] is the partisanship of the biased, prejudiced distortion of the objective logic of a subject; the latter [objective partisanship] is the partisanship of the unbiased, unprejudiced pursuit of logic all the way to its ultimate conclusions. The former means foisting onto a theory conclusions and evaluations demanded in advance; the latter means accepting and defending only those conclusions and evaluations to which we are bound by the investigation itself.... The former transforms philosophy into an obsequious tool of external ends; the latter signifies the discovery of ends through sovereign philosophical investigation. The former looks at the whole world solely from the point of view of its usefulness or harmfulness to dogma; the latter always places the objective dialectic of the creative quest for truth above subjective considerations of expediency based on previously elaborated principles.

Subjective partisanship, Batishchev argues, appeals to "canonized texts" and leads to "the militarization of the methods and the language of polemic." Objective partisanship, on the other hand, opposes all dogmatism and is "the partisanship of science itself."[85]

It would be difficult to imagine a more ardent defense of objectivity *against* partisanship than is found in Batishchev's defense of "objective partisanship." In fact there is nothing "partisan" at all, in the usual sense, in his conception: the word 'objectivity' could be substituted *simpliciter* for every occurrence of his expression 'objective partisanship'. The presentation of his paean to "sovereign philosophical investigation" as an analysis of *partisanship* is another example of development by dilution in Soviet philosophy: an accepted term—'partisanship'—is stretched to accommodate previously unacceptable content, up to and here including its own opposite. A debate that to plainer minds is simply a clash between the claims of partisanship and those of objectivity is cast in the form of a conflict between two varieties of partisanship. Thus partisanship in the usual sense can be rejected in fact without being rejected in words, and the whole procedure is theoretically justified by the "dialectical unity" that permits Batishchev to assume the *identity* of proletarian partisanship (properly understood) and objectivity.

[85]Konstantinov et al., *Filosofskaia entsiklopediia*, vol. 4, pp. 219, 217.

Batishchev's defense of objectivity is an unusually forceful and straight-forward one, but the attitude it represents is not uncommon among Soviet philosophers.[86] For all the partisan strictures that I have detailed, many Soviet philosophers do regard philosophy as a quest for objective truth. They write books and journal articles in which they strive not only and not principally to build a new world but to use rational argumentation to defend or attack particular philosophical positions. They seek out the philosophical writings of thinkers of other lands and persuasions, both in the original languages and in the increasingly available Russian translations of philosophical classics, from Plato to Ludwig Wittgenstein. They include distinguished scholars who are revered by both their colleagues and their students for the subtlety and sophistication of their thought. And the best of them pass on to their students not only a wealth of information about philosophy beyond the ideological boundaries of Marxism-Leninism but a dedication to the pursuit of truth for its own sake. Just as the presence in the Party program of a particular definition of philosophy does not lead to the universal or even the general acceptance of that definition by Soviet philosophers, as we have seen, so too the pedagogical injunction to teach Marxism-Leninism with firm conviction does not automatically cause all philosophers to operate with mindless dogmatism. Indeed, if there is any causal connection here, it is probably the other way around: the injunction is included in the teaching manual because so many lecturers betray reservations.

The objective approach to philosophy has coexisted uneasily with the partisan approach throughout the Soviet era, and at any given time the character of Soviet philosophy has been determined by the pole that exerts the stronger attraction. It is a thesis of the present study that the years since Stalin's death have seen a swing—uneven and vacillating, but none-theless pronounced—toward the objective pole. Even independently of that development, however, there is justification for undertaking in the present study a philosophical rather than an ideological or political investigation of Soviet philosophy. For however partisan its doctrines may be, as ele-ments of a purportedly "scientific" ideology they must be offered as con-tributions to the truth and hence as subject to the standard philosophical demands of clarity, scope, logical coherence, and defensibility.

[86]See, for example, the editorial "S pozitsii partiinosti" in the January 1974 issue of *Voprosy filosofii* (pp. 47–56).

[2]

Materialism

ALTHOUGH Soviet philosophers lay great stress on the "organic un-ity" of dialectics and materialism, they nevertheless disengage the two principal components of their outlook for purposes of exposition. We shall follow Soviet practice not only in making the separation but in beginning with materialism. The present chapter opens with a primer of orthodox Soviet materialist doctrine, proceeds to the examination of changes that have taken place in the doctrine in recent years, and concludes with a critical assessment of Soviet materialism as a philosophical theory.

Principles of Soviet Materialism

In Soviet philosophy, the doctrine of the primacy of matter means not that minds and other things we call "mental" or "spiritual"—mathematics and love, for example—have no claim to real existence but that, for the claim to hold, these seemingly immaterial things must be causally depen-dent on straightforwardly material entities such as brains and bodies, dependent not merely for their genesis but for their continuing existence as well. Thus although the reality of mental or spiritual *phenomena* is admitted by Soviet materialists, they do not admit the reality of mental or spiritual *things*: such phenomena always require a material foundation. Mathematical reasoning takes place in a physical, spatio-temporal brain (natural or artificial), and nowhere else. Love is unthinkable without a flesh-and-blood lover whose affection it is. Hence materialism is for the Soviet philosopher a sweeping ontological commitment, expressed as fol-lows in *The Fundamentals of Marxist-Leninist Philosophy*: "There is noth-ing in the world that is not a certain state of matter, one of its properties, a form of motion, a product of its historical development, that is not ultimately conditioned by material causes and interactions."[1]

What does such a world exclude? Philosophically, the Soviet materialist rejects every intellectual entity that lacks a material foundation, from Plato's Forms to Hegel's Absolute Idea; they are one and all "idealistic." Closer to the lives of most people, the principal exclusions are the familiar divine natures of the great world religions—gods, lesser spirits, and the human soul. For the Marxist-Leninist such entities are purely imaginary, simply products of the human brains that spawn and harbor them and of the human societies in which they flourish. There are no supernatural, self-subsistent divine spirits, any more than there are ghosts or elves. There are no detachable, spiritual souls capable of surviving bodily human death and enduring in some other, unseen realm. Religion—Marx's "opiate of the people"—is for the Soviet philosopher not merely socially pernicious but descriptively false. Soviet communism is godless as a matter of philosophical principle.

For the positive content of their materialist doctrine, Soviet "Marxist-Leninists" cannot draw on Marx, since he did not develop or defend a materialist ontology.[2] Instead they rely on Engels, who advanced such an ontology in Marx's name, and above all on Lenin, whose *Materialism and Empirio-Criticism* (1909) endorsed and updated Engels's position. Popular Soviet expositions of materialism often limit themselves to formulas drawn from Lenin's book, and even the more specialized and technical treatments invariably take their departure from it and in particular from two contributions to materialist doctrine that it contained.

First, Lenin provided a definition of matter. In the physics of his day, the breakdown of the atom into electrical charges had cast serious doubt on the materialist interpretation of nature. "The atom dematerializes, matter disappears"—such was the antimaterialist attitude that Lenin encountered in the "empirio-criticism" of Ernst Mach, Richard Avenarius, and their Russian followers.[3] In opposition to this view, Lenin argued that it was not matter that was disappearing but an outmoded conception of it—a conception that bound matter to properties (such as impenetrability, inertia, and mass) that actually characterize certain states of matter only. The discovery by physicists of new states lacking those properties, ac-

---

[1] F. V. Konstantinov, ed., *The Fundamentals of Marxist-Leninist Philosophy*, trans. Robert Daglish (Moscow, 1982), p. 75.

[2] For analyses of Marx's views, see George L. Kline, "The Myth of Marx's Materialism," *Annals of Scholarship* 3, no. 2 (October 1984), pp. 1–38; and Frederic L. Bender, "Marx, Materialism and the Limits of Philosophy," *Studies in Soviet Thought* 25 (1983), pp. 79–100.

[3] V. I. Lenin, *Polnoe sobranie sochinenii*, 5th ed., 55 vols. (Moscow, 1958–1965), vol. 18, p. 273 (cited hereafter as *Soch.*).

cording to Lenin, requires philosophers not to abandon the category of matter but to seek a broader understanding of it.

The understanding proposed by Lenin was indeed a broad one, for he argued that matter has only a single defining characteristic: "The *only* 'property' of matter with the recognition of which philosophical materialism is bound up," he wrote, "is the property of *being an objective reality*, of existing outside our mind."[4] So long as we acknowledge that the human mind does not constitute or generate its own objects—that the objects it cognizes ("reflects," to use Lenin's term) have an independent existence—we are, according to this view, philosophical materialists. Lenin frequently stressed the sensory character of the mind's reflection of its objects, as in the following much-quoted statement: "Matter is a philosophical category designating the objective reality that is given to man in his sensations and that is copied, photographed, and reflected by our sensations, while existing independently of them."[5] But he left no doubt that not sensory perceptibility but existence independent of the mind is the only essential token of materiality: "The concept of matter," he wrote, "epistemologically implies *nothing other* than objective reality existing independently of human consciousness and reflected by it."[6] This definition continues to enjoy wide currency in Soviet philosophy, and it should be evident that the two principal theses of Soviet materialism introduced in the previous chapter—the primacy and the knowability of matter—are directly linked to it. The primacy of matter is guaranteed by its existence independent of the mind, and knowability is guaranteed by its availability to be "reflected" by the mind.

Lenin's capacious definition of matter is highly valued by Soviet philosophers for its ability to accommodate scientific change. Since, in the words of *Fundamentals*, the definition does not "reduce matter merely to certain of its forms," it is held to embrace everything now known to science and everything that will be known in the future. Such exotic modern entities as "antiworlds" and "antimatter" thus offer no theoretical difficulties, so long as they are recognized as existing independently of the mind that discovers them. And it is not only "things" that make up the Marxist-Leninist material world. In addition to material *substances*, Soviet philosophers note, there are material *fields*; electromagnetic and gravitational fields, for example, are no less objectively real than rocks or trees.[7]

For many years it was customary in Soviet philosophy to distinguish

---

[4]Ibid., p. 275 (italics in original).
[5]Ibid., p. 131.
[6]Ibid., p. 276 (italics in original).
[7]Konstantinov, *Fundamentals* (1982), pp. 63 (italics omitted), 66; see also V. Afanasyev, *Marxist Philosophy* (Moscow, 1980), p. 44.

between Lenin's *philosophical* conception of matter, regarded as stating the "essence" of matter and as unaffected by scientific progress, and the *scientific* conception of matter, which represented the state of scientific knowledge and hence changed over time. Lenin himself had called it "absolutely impermissible" to confound "any particular doctrine of the structure of matter with the epistemological category" of matter.[8] Beginning about 1951, however, perhaps moved by fears of the irrelevance of philosophy to our advancing knowledge of the world, Soviet philosophers began to avoid the notion that there are two separate conceptions of matter.[9] Only one conception—the philosophical—is now recognized; the sciences are viewed as using this conception to present more and more adequate descriptions of the material world so conceived.

Lenin's second contribution to Marxist materialism is neither as original as the first nor clearly consistent with it. For having announced that objective reality is the only property that a materialist must ascribe to matter, Lenin went on in *Materialism and Empirio-Criticism* to identify several other properties, most of them borrowed from the writings of Engels, as seemingly essential to matter as well. Although the exact status of these additional "properties" remains a subject of controversy, most Soviet philosophers regard Lenin's treatment of them as a major source of Marxist materialist doctrine. They include motion, space, time, infinity, and what is called "the inexhaustibility of matter in depth."

It is the nature of the material world to be in *motion*, in the Engels-Lenin interpretation. Engels's words describing motion as "the mode of existence, the inherent attribute, of matter" are repeated tirelessly by Soviet philosophers, as is Lenin's echoing statement that motion is "an inseparable property of matter."[10] This doctrine plays an important ideological role in Soviet philosophy, for it means that the material world does not need to have motion imparted to it from without by something extramaterial. Religious thinkers who accept the "First Mover" argument for the existence of God, it is held, misconceive the world as essentially static—as a collection of inert bodies requiring an initial impetus. No such external principle is required, according to Soviet philosophers, for the material world and motion are inseparable. Rest and equilibrium, where they exist, are regarded as always relative, as functions of a limited perspective. The boulder may be at rest relative to the surface of the earth, but both boulder and earth are hurtling through space, and the boulder's subatomic con-

---

[8]Lenin, *Soch.*, vol. 18, p. 131.

[9]Gustav A. Wetter, *Dialectical Materialism. A Historical and Systematic Survey of Philosophy in the Soviet Union*, trans. Peter Heath (London, 1958), pp. 288–291.

[10]Frederick Engels, *Dialectics of Nature*, trans. and ed. Clemens Dutt (New York, 1940), p. 35; Lenin, *Soch.*, vol. 18, p. 285.

stituents are likewise vigorously active. Furthermore, even in the absence of spatial displacement matter is characterized by motion, for the term is used so broadly by Soviet philosophers as to be synonymous with 'change'. This aspect of the doctrine, too, goes back to Engels, who argued that "motion in the most general sense...comprehends all changes and processes occurring in the universe, from mere change of place right to thinking."[11]

After motion, the most important properties attributed to matter by Soviet philosophers are *space* and *time*. Lenin cited with approval Engels's statement that "the basic forms of all being are space and time,"[12] and later Soviet philosophers have consistently followed this lead, regarding space and time as inherent, indispensable features of the material world. In *Materialism and Empirio-Criticism*, Lenin's chief concern with respect to space and time was to establish their objectivity, and this remains a major interest of Soviet philosophers. In this respect Marxist-Leninist materialism is traditionally counterposed to the "idealist" views of Immanuel Kant, who regarded space and time as subjective features of the perceiver that could not be attributed to the "thing in itself." Soviet philosophers, however, are as interested in defending the thesis of the inseparability of space, time, and matter as they are in defending the objectivity of space and time. A passage from Engels's *Dialectics of Nature* is regularly cited: "The two forms of existence of matter," Engels wrote of space and time, "are naturally nothing without matter, empty concepts, abstractions which exist only in our minds."[13] In this context the customary opponent is Isaac Newton. Newton did not deny that space and time exist independently of mind, but he wrongly (in the Soviet view) regarded them as existing independently of matter.[14] For the Soviet philosopher the objective reality is *spatio-temporal matter*: there is no matter that does not exist in space and time, and there is no space or time without matter.

Another feature of matter identified by Lenin and much dwelt upon in Soviet philosophy is spatio-temporal *infinity*. A typical presentation of the infinity thesis is the following in a recent textbook:

No matter how enormous any given cosmic system [may be]...it forms part of an even larger system....No matter how far away from us any given stellar system may be, there must be yet other gigantic groups of celestial bodies and cosmic systems of inconceivable extent further away still....No matter how

[11] Engels, *Dialectics of Nature*, p. 35.
[12] Frederick Engels, *Anti-Dühring. Herr Eugen Dühring's Revolution in Science* (Moscow, 1947), p. 67; Lenin, *Soch.*, vol. 18, p. 183.
[13] Engels, *Dialectics of Nature*, p. 327.
[14] Konstantinov, *Fundamentals* (1982), pp. 71–72.

much time may pass up to a certain moment, time will always go on and on....No matter how long ago a certain event occurred it must have been preceded by a countless number of other events.[15]

Soviet philosophers see the infinity thesis as another blow to religion, for in their understanding, creationism thrives on finitist views: to assert that the material universe is finite in time would be to say that it had a beginning, which could have been produced by an act of creation; and to assert that it is finite in space is to suggest that "outside" it there is something immaterial, such as a spiritual creator. In an infinite material universe, it is held, there is neither need nor room for God.[16]

Lenin's observations on the subject of infinity extended not only to space and time but to endlessness of another sort, which Soviet philosophers now generally call matter's property of being *inexhaustible in depth*. In 1909, commenting on the breakdown of the atom, Lenin had suggested that there is no end to this process of analysis and dissolution: "If yesterday the deepening [of our knowledge of objects] did not go beyond the atom, and today does not go beyond the electron and ether, dialectical materialism insists on the temporary, relative, approximate character of all these *milestones* in the cognition of nature by the progressing science of man. The electron is as *inexhaustible* as the atom, nature is infinite." Several years later, reading Hegel's discussion of the unity of the finite and the infinite, Lenin was again reminded of the notion of inexhaustibility, and he included in his *Philosophical Notebooks* a reference to "the overall infinity of matter in depth."[17] Soviet philosophers subsequently developed these passing remarks into a full-fledged materialist thesis, which, since it is not found in Engels or other Marxist theoreticians but is said to be confirmed by the subsequent history of physics, is offered as major evidence of Lenin's originality and acumen.

Although the features of matter thus far considered were endorsed in the writings of Engels or Lenin, another property now accepted by many Soviet philosophers is put forward even at the risk of contradicting the masters. This is the property of *substantiality*. The term 'substance', as we have seen, is sometimes used by Soviet philosophers to identify material bodies such as rocks and trees as opposed to material fields. There is a more general, philosophical sense of the term, however, that Soviet philosophers long avoided—the idea of matter as a common underlying reality

---

[15][F. V. Konstantinov, ed.,] *The Fundamentals of Marxist-Leninist Philosophy*, trans. Robert Daglish (Moscow, 1974), p. 87.

[16]A. P. Sheptulin, *Marxist-Leninist Philosophy*, trans. S. Ponomarenko and A. Timofeyev (Moscow, 1978), pp. 115–117.

[17]Lenin, *Soch.*, vol. 18, p. 277 (italics in original); vol. 29, p. 100.

in which all qualities and properties inhere, or as "substance" in the etymological sense of that which "stands under" the attributes of things. Engels rejected the notion of a "matter as such" that is the uniform basis of all being; he called it "a pure creation of thought."[18] Lenin, too, dismissed the idea of an "absolute substance," finding it incompatible with his conception of the inexhaustibility of matter.[19] As early as 1956, however, a Soviet philosopher, V. P. Tugarinov, strongly defended a substantialist conception of matter as essential to a realist position and a bulwark against idealism, and since that time the substantiality thesis has won wide although not universal acceptance among Soviet philosophers. "Matter is substance," Tugarinov wrote; "it is the *substratum* of movement and of change; it is not only what is general in beings but also the foundation of all things."[20] This substratum, it is held, is not an abstract "matter as such" but is simply the totality of material entities (substances, fields, and whatever other such entities may be identified by science) in which all the features of the world inhere. In this sense substantiality is not only granted to matter but is insisted upon as the ground of the "material unity of the world."[21]

Other properties, too, are actively discussed by Soviet materialists, but beyond those properties already enumerated it is no longer possible to speak of a consensus among Soviet philosophers. Indeed even concerning those properties, the consensus that has been presented is in certain respects more apparent than real. For in order to give a succinct account of Soviet materialism I have been obliged to adopt the techniques employed by Soviet textbook writers and to mask by vagueness and silence a number of troublesome questions. These questions are raised and debated by Soviet philosophers at a more technical level, to which we must now proceed if we wish to understand and assess the Soviet claim that the only reality is knowable, objectively existing matter.

The Debate on Lenin's Definition of Matter

It is characteristic of the changes in Soviet philosophy in the years since Stalin's death that dialectical materialist doctrines that formerly provoked

[18]Engels, *Dialectics of Nature*, pp. 322–323.
[19]Lenin, *Soch.*, vol. 18, p. 277; Wetter, *Dialectical Materialism*, p. 291.
[20]V. P. Tugarinov, *Sootnoshenie kategorii dialekticheskogo materializma* (Leningrad, 1956), p. 49. For a criticism of this view in a recent work, see F. F. Viakkerev et al., eds., *Materialisticheskaia dialektika v piati tomakh. Tom 1. Ob"ektivnaia dialektika* (Moscow, 1981), pp. 93–95.
[21]*Philosophy in the USSR. Problems of Dialectical Materialism*, trans. Robert Daglish (Moscow, 1977), p. 51. See also Sheptulin, *Marxist-Leninist Philosophy*, pp. 100–102.

questions and criticisms only from abroad are now frequently the focus of lively debate among Soviet philosophers themselves. An important recent example is the Soviet discussion of Lenin's definition of matter as objective reality.

A stock Western criticism of the definition is that it fails to distinguish between *materialism*, an ontological position holding that matter is primary in the realm of being, and *realism*, an epistemological position holding that being exists independently of consciousness. Engels, it is argued, began the confusion with the initial formulation of his "basic question of philosophy," by presenting the question first in an epistemological version—What is the relation of being and thinking?—and then tacitly identifying this epistemological question with the ontological question of whether "Spirit" or "Nature" is primary.[22] Lenin compounded and institutionalized the confusion in *Materialism and Empirio-Criticism*, it is held, when he proclaimed that being an objective reality is "the *only* 'property' of matter with the recognition of which philosophical materialism is bound up" but then went on to add to this purely epistemological consideration an ontological characterization of matter as well.[23]

To assert that being is independent of anyone's thinking about it is different from asserting that matter is the primary reality, the critics contend. They support their point by observing that philosophers as far apart as Thomas Aquinas and Hegel would accept the former thesis but reject the latter: both Aquinas's God and Hegel's Absolute Idea satisfy Lenin's conceptual requirement of "being an objective reality, of existing outside our mind," but these entities were certainly not regarded by their proponents as material things. No doubt all materialists are obliged to accept realism, it is admitted by the critics, but the reverse does not hold: Aquinas and Hegel were realists but not materialists. The conscious or unconscious identification of the two positions is seen not only as saddling Soviet philosophy with what Gustav Wetter calls a "fatal misunderstanding" but also as giving the materialist ontology of Marxism-Leninism illicit support: in the writings of Soviet philosophers, considerations that lend force to realism, an intrinsically more plausible and very widely held view, are enlisted in favor of materialism. The result, Wetter complains, is that "the philosophically untutored reader is often left with the impression that materialism is nothing other than the philosophy of ordinary common-sense, directed merely against 'cranky' idealist beliefs."[24]

---

[22]Wetter, *Dialectical Materialism*, pp. 281–284; Gustav A. Wetter, *Soviet Ideology Today*, trans. Peter Heath (New York, 1966), pp. 30–31.

[23]Lenin, *Soch.* vol. 18, p. 275 (italics in original); Wetter, *Dialectical Materialism*, pp. 287–288.

[24]Wetter, *Dialectical Materialism*, pp. 281, 284.

Criticisms such as these, tending as they do to call into question either the philosophical ability or the intellectual honesty of both Engels and Lenin, were long rejected out of hand by Soviet philosophers. In the post-Stalin period, on the contrary, Lenin's definition of matter has become an open topic, and the resulting debate has demonstrated the existence of a range of Soviet views on the subject, extending to views that some Soviet critics have found to be scandalous idealist "revisions" of the Leninist position.

Although "revisionist" endeavors in Soviet materialism were evident as early as the 1950s in the work of V. P. Tugarinov and others,[25] the focus of recent controversy has been a book entitled *Matter in Its Unity, Infinity, and Development*, published in 1966 by the prominent Moscow philosopher S. T. Meliukhin. In that work Meliukhin openly acknowledged the distinction between materialism and realism in a passage that contains a rare example in Soviet philosophy of a direct, verbatim rejection of a statement of Lenin's:

> Upon an initial general approach to matter, that among all its properties which reveals itself first of all is objective reality, independence of human consciousness. But this by no means signifies that objective reality is *the sole property of matter with the recognition of which dialectical materialism is bound up.* . . . In itself the recognition of the objectivity of matter in relation to human consciousness is possible not only within the framework of materialism but in theories of objective idealism as well, such as in the doctrine of Hegel and in contemporary neo-Thomism.[26]

Meliukhin's positive characterization of matter consists in a lengthy list of properties, which not surprisingly includes those mentioned by Engels and Lenin. But it also includes features of matter not specified by the masters, and Meliukhin leaves no doubt of his opinion that a number of them are more important to materialism than is objective reality in relation to consciousness. Indeed he regards the latter feature as derivative from two more basic properties of matter, which he calls "interaction" and "coexistence": objective reality, he contends, is dependent on a relation, which appears only at an advanced level of material evolution, between

---

[25]For a discussion of these developments, see two articles by Helmut Fleischer: "The Materiality of Matter," *Studies in Soviet Thought* 2 (1962), pp. 12–20; and "Open Questions in Contemporary Soviet Ontology," *Studies in Soviet Thought* 6 (1966), pp. 168–184. An excellent summary and critique of Soviet discussions of matter up to the early 1960s may be found in N. Lobkowicz, "Materialism and Matter in Marxism-Leninism," in E. McMullin, ed., *The Concept of Matter in Modern Philosophy* (Notre Dame, 1978), pp. 154–188.

[26]S. T. Meliukhin, *Materiia v ee edinstve, beskonechnosti i razvitii* (Moscow, 1966), p. 48 (italics added).

a co-present object and subject: "Interaction and coexistence are more fundamental attributes of matter than objectivity in relation to consciousness. Objectivity itself arises as a concrete form of their manifestation, but only at higher stages of the evolution of matter, when there appears a cognizing subject which distinguishes itself from all of nature and counterposes nature to itself as something objective in relation to itself."[27]

More basic still is the property that Meliukhin calls the "absoluteness" of matter, which he defines as "its uniqueness as the substantial basis of all phenomena."[28] This is Meliukhin's version of the "substantiality" feature accepted by many Soviet philosophers today, and he attributes great importance to it. The universality, the uncreatability, and the indestructibility of matter are all functions of this basic property, he contends. Indeed the property of absoluteness, he affirms, "is primary in regard to all the other attributes of matter, including [he adds, in yet another reference to the inadequacy of the traditional Leninist formula] objectivity and independence of our mind."[29] Other properties Meliukhin identifies are structure (*strukturnost'*), the capacity for self-development, and the properties described by the three laws of dialectics.[30]

Meliukhin's and other "ontological" expansions of materialist theory have dominated the Soviet philosophical discussion of this question in recent years, but the ontologists by no means have a monopoly on Soviet materialist doctrine. They are opposed from both less doctrinaire and more doctrinaire positions—each of which, ironically, claims to represent the true spirit of Lenin against the ontologists' revisionism.

The less doctrinaire position is that of those Soviet writers, especially natural scientists, who openly embrace the negative or purely epistemological conception of matter implicit in Lenin's minimum formula and deny any need for philosophy to supplement that characterization by elaborating positive, "ontological" features of matter. The eminent Soviet astrophysicist Viktor Ambartsumian, for example, writing with his colleague Vadim Kaziutinskii, speaks with favor of the fact that Lenin "gave a definition of the philosophical concept of matter freed from the constraint of a link with any concrete physical properties of material objects."[31] Meliukhin accurately characterizes this view as the position of those who believe that Marxist materialism requires the acknowledgment of only two propositions: that matter is an objective reality independent of our consciousness and that the world is knowable. In such a view, he notes, the

[27]Ibid., p. 54.
[28]*Philosophy in the USSR. Problems of Dialectical Materialism*, p. 52.
[29]Meliukhin, *Materiia*, p. 75.
[30]Ibid., p. 48; *Philosophy in the USSR. Problems of Dialectical Materialism*, p. 56.
[31]*Philosophical Concepts in Natural Science* (Moscow, 1977), p. 59.

question of the actual properties and laws of the material world is given over to the natural sciences: philosophy has nothing to say to the issues of whether the world is created or uncreated, finite or infinite, and the like. Such an approach, Meliukhin contends, "in fact emasculates the world-view content of dialectical materialism," and he expresses satisfaction that "the majority of Marxist philosophers" reject it.[32]

Although Meliukhin may be correct in saying that most (Soviet) Marxist *philosophers* reject the epistemological view, among scientists it is no doubt more widespread. Only by assuming its continuing vitality can we account for the persistent attacks upon it in Soviet philosophical literature—attacks that sometimes extend to the same ultimate charge that surfaced in another context in the previous chapter: that the epistemological view is a form of idealism. Meliukhin himself does not explicitly make the charge, but it is clearly implied not only by his comment about the "world-view content" of dialectical materialism but also by his further assertion that the view reduces dialectical materialism to "the theory of thought or to a certain generalized theory of activity"—to a theory, in other words, that excludes the material world.[33] No doubt many proponents of the epistemological view, however, care little whether their view is called "materialism," "realism," or even "idealism," so long as it permits them to proceed with scientific work unimpeded by excess conceptual freight.

But if the epistemological view is suspected of idealism when it is compared with Meliukhin's moderate "ontological" view of matter, the latter is in turn branded "idealism" by a more doctrinaire view that has been prominent in Soviet philosophical literature in recent years. Its most vigorous champion has been Vladimir Viacheslavovich Orlov, a professor of philosophy at Perm' State University and a warm defender of Marxist-Leninist orthodoxy. In a number of writings in the late 1960s and early 1970s, Orlov complained of what he called "negative elements" in the writings of Tugarinov, Meliukhin, and others, including what he saw as deviations from the "conceptual unity" and the partisanship of Soviet materialism.[34] In 1973 Orlov was answered publicly by a supporter of Meliukhin, M. N. Matveev,[35] and a year later the two sides confronted each other in an acrimonious interchange in the journal *Filosofskie nauki*. Orlov opened the 1974 debate with the following observations:

[32]S. T. Meliukhin, "Problemy filosofskoi teorii materii," *Filosofskie nauki*, 1974, no. 5, pp. 60–61.
[33]Ibid.
[34]V. V. Orlov, "K voprosu o filosofskom poniatii materii," *Filosofskie nauki*, 1970, no. 4, pp. 123, 131–132.
[35]M. N. Matveev, "Analiz razvitiia. Deistvitel'nye trudnosti i mnimye paradoksy," *Filosofskie nauki*, 1973, no. 5, pp. 61–69.

As is well known, in the past ten to fifteen years the opinion has been advanced in a number of publications that the Leninist definition of matter as objective reality is inadequate, and certain authors have come to regard the definition as a purely epistemological one. In this connection a tendency has arisen to "supplement" the Leninist definition of matter with supposedly broader, ontological definitions, which in effect signifies a *revision* of the only possible conception of matter in scientific philosophy. This cannot fail to arouse a certain alarm.[36]

The substance of Orlov's complaint is that Meliukhin rejects Lenin's pronouncement that objective reality is "the *only* 'property' of matter" and instead views it as one property among many—and a subsidiary one at that. A dangerous consequence of this approach, according to Orlov, is that it removes the supposedly more primary properties "beyond the bounds of the feature of objectively real (material) existence" and hence directs a double blow at the notion of objective reality: it deprives that notion of all content and represents the other properties as "not existing objectively, materially."[37] But what Orlov finds "truly incredible" is Meliukhin's contention that objectively real existence "arises" only at the stage of evolution at which consciousness appears. This is plainly an idealist view, in Orlov's opinion—one that he finds indistinguishable from Avenarius's doctrine of the "coordination in principle" (*printsipial'naia koordinatsiia*) of self and environment that Lenin had condemned in *Materialism and Empirio-Criticism*: "Thus [Orlov writes] S. T. Meliukhin arrives at...the assertion that an object (the objective) does not exist without a subject, or in other words, if we are to call things by their proper names, at the theory of the 'coordination in principle' of object and subject, at subjective idealism. With such an approach the concept of objective reality is deprived of all profound materialist content, is emasculated and devalued."[38] And Orlov makes it clear that ideologically as well as philosophically there is no more critical notion than that of objective reality independent of consciousness: "The partisanship of Marxist-Leninist philosophy, understood as its most profound and fundamental materialist

[36]V. V. Orlov, "O nekotorykh voprosakh teorii materii, razvitiia, soznaniia," *Filosofskie nauki*, 1974, no. 5, p. 47.
[37]Ibid., p. 49. This quotation includes what George L. Kline has called "the Leninist comma" in one of its principal uses—to insinuate that there is no difference between realism (the view that things exist objectively) and materialism. The comma suggests that the words it separates are synonymous; but its user, if pressed, can argue that it is meant simply as a conjunction.
[38]Ibid., p. 48. English translations of Lenin's works prepared in the USSR have consistently misrendered *printsipial'naia koordinatsiia* as "principal coordination"; see, for example, V. I. Lenin, *Materialism and Empirio-Criticism. Critical Comments on a Reactionary Philosophy* (New York, 1927), pp. 59–69.

determination, which excludes every other philosophy, is organically bound up with the truly scientific objectivity of the philosophy of Marxism."[39]

Orlov's insistence on the literal acceptance of the Leninist definition of matter as objective reality might appear to throw him in league with the less doctrinaire epistemologists. But such is not the case, for Orlov argues that Lenin saw "being an objective reality" as a characteristic of a very special sort—not as one property among all those that might be attributed to matter, but rather as "*the integral substantial feature*, which expresses the *entire content* of the concept of matter and includes within itself a series of 'derivative' features." These "derivative" features—motion, space, time, and the other attributes mentioned by Lenin—Orlov refers to variously as "elements," "sides," "aspects," and "manifestations" of objective reality. What they are *not* is features that, in Orlov's words, " 'supplement' the concept of objective reality as equal and coordinate with it." Indeed, all the ordinary features of matter, both universal and particular, he asserts, are "properties and manifestations of objective reality."[40]

The issue between Meliukhin and Orlov should not be seen as simply a scholastic dispute concerning the relative primacy of various features of matter. Far more significant is the difference in the two philosophers' approaches to the identification and establishment of those features, or in other words, the difference in what might be called their ontological methods. Orlov, the old-liner, in his attempt to remain faithful to the letter of "the only possible conception of matter in scientific philosophy," to retain the purity of the Leninist teaching and thereby to buttress materialist partisanship, is led not only to absolutize Lenin's formula but to regard as built into the notion of objective reality all the other features of the material world that Lenin identified. Because, for Orlov, "the category of matter includes within itself the whole series of general features" of matter, it is sufficient in ontology to explore and develop Lenin's conception; certainly it is unnecessary to replace that conception with another.[41] The result in practice is to make the particular properties of matter identified by Lenin a fixed dogma in Marxism-Leninism.

Meliukhin, on the other hand, opposing the traditionalism so common in Soviet philosophy during the Stalin era, speaks for the less doctrinaire majority of Soviet philosophers who view the theory of matter as a general scientific theory—a theoretical construct in which the attributes ascribed to matter hinge on the findings of the sciences, not on an a priori relation to some sacrosanct formula. These attributes, Meliukhin writes, "cannot

[39]Orlov, "K voprosu," p. 132.
[40]Ibid., pp. 124 (italics in original), 129, 132.
[41]Orlov, "O nekotorykh voprosakh," p. 49; Orlov, "K voprosu," p. 123.

be deductively elucidated from the concept of objective reality; they are not contained in it implicitly, as V. V. Orlov thinks." They can be discovered, he adds, only by "experimental and theoretical investigation of real actuality." One implication is that new properties of matter might be found in the future: "At the present time we know only a very small part of the universal properties and laws of the being of matter which together express the objective dialectic of nature. The world is infinite in structure, space, and time, and we may assume that an infinite multitude of universal properties and laws of matter exists objectively."[42] Another implication, though Meliukhin does not mention it, is that revisions in science could lead to the abandonment of some previously accepted "property" of matter—even one so blessed as to be named in the pages of *Materialism and Empirio-Criticism.*

The Meliukhinite position is clearly closer in spirit to the less doctrinaire, epistemological conception of materialism than it is to Orlov's conception. The Meliukhinites share a basic antidogmatic assumption with the epistemologists: neither group is willing to accept an ontological doctrine on faith. The principal difference between them is that the epistemologists would prefer to have the theory of matter developed by scientists rather than philosophers. The Meliukhinites, in requiring a *philosophical* theory of matter, contend that philosophy itself, and not simply natural science, is committed to providing a descriptive account of the nature of matter. Not surprisingly, this account typically proceeds in broadly Leninist terms— in terms, that is, of "properties" in some way related to objectivity, infinity, and the like. At the same time the sciences, not Lenin's words, are asked to provide substantiation: the properties in question may have been seen by a prescient Lenin, but they must be validated by modern science.[43]

According to both of the less dogmatic versions of Soviet materialism, then, the actual development of materialist doctrines cannot go counter to the direction of scientific progress. That Soviet materialism has in fact developed in step with scientific progress and that these less doctrinaire positions have increasingly prevailed in the handling of scientific issues in Soviet philosophy are the theses of the following section.

Soviet Materialism and Modern Physics

To say that Soviet materialism has evolved along with advances in the sciences is not to say that the evolution has been spontaneous or smooth.

[42]Meliukhin, "Problemy filosofskoi teorii materii," pp. 62–63.
[43]*Philosophy in the USSR. Problems of Dialectical Materialism*, p. 50.

It has come, rather, in often reluctant and belated response to inconsistencies between the philosophical doctrine and new theories in various branches of physics. Just as Lenin was obliged to refine Marxist materialism to make it consistent with the physics of his day, so his Soviet successors have been required to modify their materialist theories to accommodate subsequent scientific developments. We shall examine here some of the more significant accommodations, having to do with the doctrines of objectivity, infinity, and inexhaustibility.

Problems of Objectivity in Relativity and Quantum Theories

Although Einsteinian relativity physics and the principle of complementarity in quantum mechanics are now fully acceptable to Soviet philosophers, such was not always the case. Both theories were victims of the anti-Western hysteria in Soviet philosophy and science fanned by the pronouncements of the powerful A. A. Zhdanov and others in the years immediately following World War II.[44] Opposition to them reached a high point in 1952 with the publication of the notorious "Green Book," a collective diatribe against "bourgeois physics" prepared by the Soviet Academy of Sciences.[45] Only in the mid-1950s and later did the two theories begin to win legitimate status in the eyes of dedicated Marxist-Leninists.

With regard to relativity theory, the theoretical problem that occasioned the opposition was a straightforward one. The Leninist thesis of the objectivity of the material world, accepted in one form or another by all Soviet philosophers, asserts that matter is independent of human consciousness. The objective world is as it is regardless of the standpoint, attitude, or wishes of the observer; the subject does not, by means of perception or cognition, either bring the object into existence or create or modify its properties. Einstein's Special Theory of Relativity, on the other hand, rejects the notion that material things possess absolute or entirely objective spatio-temporal characteristics. According to Einstein, physical determinations such as that of the simultaneity of two events, the interval between two points in time, the position of a body, and the length and mass of a body cannot be made in abstraction from the observer. The length of a speeding train, for example, is different, depending on whether

---

[44]For a detailed discussion see Loren R. Graham, *Science and Philosophy in the Soviet Union* (New York, 1972), pp. 69–138. For a recent reassessment of Zhdanov's role in these developments, see Werner G. Hahn, *Postwar Soviet Politics. The Fall of Zhdanov and the Defeat of Moderation, 1946–53* (Ithaca, 1982).

[45]A. A. Maksimov et al., eds., *Filosofskie voprosy sovremennoi fiziki* (Moscow, 1952).

it is measured by someone on the train or by a stationary observer off the train.[46] And neither of these lengths—nor any other that might be determined from still a third standpoint—is the "true" length of the train. In this case as in those of simultaneity, time interval, and other spatio-temporal determinations, a definite value can be assigned only for a given reference system—in other words, only for a given standpoint of the observer.

To many Soviet philosophers in the late 1940s and early 1950s, such "subjectivist," "relativist" views were simply unacceptable. A vigorous campaign against Einstein was mounted, led by philosophers whose ignorance of physics was so profound, as Loren Graham has observed, that they rejected even Galilean relativity in their anti-Einsteinian zeal: A. A. Maksimov, attributing to Einstein the view that "a body has no objectively given trajectory existing independently of the choice of a system of coordinates," pronounced the notion "completely antiscientific."[47] In the Green Book, I. V. Kuznetsov called for new, "materialist" theories to replace the theory of relativity: "Only the complete rejection of Einstein's conception, and not compromises and half-measures regarding it," he claimed, "will permit us...to move science ahead."[48]

This unrestrained opposition to relativity did not long outlive Stalin, however. As early as 1955 an authoritative endorsement of Einstein's views appeared in Voprosy filosofii, and in subsequent years the earlier, negative appraisal was reversed so thoroughly that greater homage may now be paid to Einstein in the USSR than in any other country.[49] Pronouncements in support of realism are now found in Einstein's writings, and his views in general are held to be very close to Marxist-Leninist materialism. Indeed he is identified as a "spontaneous materialist and dialectician"—that is, as someone who arrived at an essentially dialectical materialist position without calling it that.[50] In the opinion of one recent Soviet admirer, only a Western intellectual atmosphere poisoned by the anti-Marxist hostility of bourgeois ideologists prevented Einstein from espousing dialectical materialism openly.[51]

[46]Bertrand Russell, The ABC of Relativity (New York, 1925), p. 78.

[47]Graham, Science and Philosophy, pp. 116–117; A. A. Maksimov, "Marksistskii filosofskii materializm i sovremennaia fizika," Voprosy filosofii, 1948, no. 3, p. 114.

[48]Maksimov, Filosofskie voprosy, p. 72.

[49]See, for example, the great attention paid to the Einstein centennial year (1979) in the journal Voprosy filosofii, beginning with no. 2 and continuing in subsequent issues; and E. M. Chudinov, ed., Einshtein i filosofskie problemy fiziki XX veka (Moscow, 1979).

[50]D. P. Gribanov, "The Philosophical Views of Albert Einstein," Soviet Studies in Philosophy 18 (Fall 1979), pp. 76–77.

[51]Ibid., p. 74.

Whatever the reasons for the change in the Soviet appraisal of Einstein,[52] what is important for our purposes is that it could not have come about without a philosophical revision, however subtle and unpublicized, in Marxist-Leninist materialist doctrine. Einstein's expressed support for realism notwithstanding, the Special Theory does make certain characteristics of the "external world" depend upon the standpoint of the observer. If the Marxist requirement of independence of human consciousness is taken to mean that the object with all its commonly recognized characteristics must exist apart from the observer—as there is every reason to think that it did mean both for Lenin and for Soviet philosophers before 1955—it seems clear that relativity *did* conflict with Soviet materialism. On the basis of that earlier understanding of materialism, Soviet philosophers were simply being consistent in rejecting not only Einsteinian relativity but even the pre-Einsteinian notion that a moving body describes no "objective" trajectory.

Hence for Soviet philosophers to accept relativity, a weakening of the earlier standard of objectivity was required. The concept of objective reality had to be extended to cover the world described by modern physics, and it was so extended in Soviet philosophy after 1955. The weakening consisted in abandoning the requirement that all the "characteristics" of a material object as it is known to common sense belong to that object independently of its relation to the observer. In place of this strong objectivity requirement, Soviet philosophers now insist on only two minimum conditions: first, the *existence* of the object apart from the observer, and second, the availability of at least *some* objective truth about the object's characteristics. The inherent vagueness of the second condition is useful and perhaps crucial to the Soviet interpretation: it allows Soviet philosophers to deny that all the scientifically relevant features of the physical world are inherent objectively in that world without being committed to any particular set of features that *are* inherent. This helpful indefiniteness is evident, for example, in D. P. Gribanov's version of the two conditions in his recent warm defense of Einstein: "The conclusion that physical knowledge was relative," Gribanov writes, "did not lead Einstein to deny the existence of the external world or the objectivity of truth."[53] The extent of the objective truth in question is not specified—though clearly it need not extend so far as to deny that *some* "physical knowledge" is "relative." A similarly useful nebulousness concerning the extent of reality's objective characteristics is seen in the writings of Aleksandr Danilovich Aleksandrov

[52]Siegfried Müller-Markus, "Soviet Philosophy in Crisis: The Unity of Science and Ideology," *Cross Currents* 14 (Winter 1964), pp. 43–44. For a more detailed discussion, see the same author's *Einstein und die Sowjetphilosophie*, 2 vols. (Dordrecht, 1960, 1966).
[53]Gribanov, "The Philosophical Views of Albert Einstein," p. 90.

(b. 1912), a mathematician who is one of the Soviet Union's foremost interpreters of relativity theory. The structure of space-time, Aleksandrov writes, "exists as a fact," and for that reason "everything associated with it" takes place independently of our desires and aims.[54] Given this formulation, everything that *does* prove to be dependent on the observer—simultaneity and other spatio-temporal values, for example—may simply be said to be not "associated" with the *objectively* existing space-time structure as long as some minimum of "fact" can still be specified for that structure.

With respect to relativity, then, the result is that, although there is not nearly so much "in" the independently existing object as was previously assumed, it is still possible to claim for it two features—independent existence and susceptibility to objective description in at least some respect. Thus independence of consciousness and knowability are both preserved, despite the clear implication that there is less that *is* independent and knowable than was formerly thought. Essentially the same course of conceptual adjustment has been taken by Soviet materialists in dealing with problems in quantum mechanics, but in this field the adjustment was somewhat slower in coming.[55]

Quantum theory takes its start from what are now well-established and thoroughly described relations of events in the microworld of subatomic particles.[56] However paradoxical it may be, experiments show that microobjects such as electrons and photons are characterized by incompatible sets of properties. In some respects, these objects behave like corpuscles or like particles that can be located at points in space. In one type of experiment, a precise value for the position of an electron can be determined: it makes a spot on a photographic plate. In other experiments, however, the same "objects" act not in a corpuscular but in an undulatory fashion; the momentum or velocity of an electron can be determined only through measurements that treat it as a wave extending indefinitely in space. Furthermore, there are no measurements in which position and momentum can be determined simultaneously. As the Heisenberg uncertainty relation demonstrates mathematically, the more exactly one of these magnitudes is measured, the less exact must be the measurement of the other. Already, then, we have an apparent limitation on the knowability

[54]A. D. Aleksandrov, "Space and Time in Contemporary Physics in the Light of Lenin's Philosophical Ideas," *Soviet Studies in Philosophy* 10 (Winter 1971–1972), p. 257.
[55]For a candid account of the Soviet treatment of quantum mechanics beginning in the 1930s, see I. S. Alekseev, *Kontseptsiia dopolnitel'nosti. Istoriko-metodologicheskii analiz* (Moscow, 1978), pp. 194–209.
[56]Excellent expositions of the elements of quantum mechanics and of Soviet reactions to them may be found in Graham, *Science and Philosophy*, pp. 69–110, and in the same author's "Quantum Mechanics and Dialectical Materialism," *Slavic Review* 25 (1966), pp. 381–410.

of the microworld. We can at best know *some* of the properties of micro-objects at any given time.

Still, this limitation on knowledge does not in itself call into question the objectivity of the external world. A possibility of deeper conflict with Marxist materialism arises when we go further and seek an interpretation of the uncertainty relation—when we attempt, in other words, to explain how it is that microbodies can possess seemingly incompatible properties. Among the interpretations that have been advanced by physicists, perhaps the best known and the most controversial is the "Copenhagen interpretation" developed by Niels Bohr and Werner Heisenberg utilizing Bohr's "principle of complementarity." This principle, in its simplest terms, resolves the "contradiction" by rejecting the assumption that an object has the conflicting properties independently of the measurement in which they make their appearance. The principle states that each property exists only at the moment of measurement and that it is therefore meaningless to speak of either position or momentum in itself, apart from the constitutive influence of the measuring apparatus. Thus to the limits on knowability implicit in the uncertainty relation itself, the principle of complementarity adds a still more unsteadying departure from the bedrock of Marxist materialism: the suggestion that significant features of the microworld do not exist independently but are brought into being by acts of the observer.

Zhdanov alluded only briefly to the problems of quantum mechanics in his 1947 speech attacking Western science.[57] The full power of the opponents of complementarity soon became apparent, however, when in the same year the new philosophy journal *Voprosy filosofii* made the mistake of publishing a defense of the Copenhagen interpretation by the prominent Soviet theoretical physicist Moisei Aleksandrovich Markov (b. 1908).[58] Markov's article provoked a storm of criticism that silenced Markov himself for years to come, cost the chief editor of *Voprosy filosofii* (at that time B. M. Kedrov) his job, and ushered in what Loren Graham has called "the age of the banishment of complementarity."[59] Apparently the banishment was more effective in philosophy than in physics, however. The 1955 edition of the *Philosophical Dictionary* still complained of "subjective idealist distortions" on the part of "certain Soviet physicists," and Soviet physicists in general were accused of having failed to fulfill their charge to create a "consistent materialist interpretation" of quantum me-

---

[57]A. A. Zhdanov, *Vystuplenie na diskussii po knige G. F. Aleksandrova "Istoriia zapadnoevropeiskoi filosofii." 24 iiunia 1947 g.* ([Moscow,] 1951), p. 43.

[58]M. A. Markov, "O prirode fizicheskogo znaniia," *Voprosy filosofii*, 1947, no. 2, pp. 140–176.

[59]Graham, *Science and Philosophy*, p. 80.

chanics.[60] A leading Soviet philosopher of science at that time, the late Mykhailo Erazmovych Omel'ianovskii (1904–1979), attempted in 1956 to show recalcitrant physicists the way to an acceptable interpretation based on the premise that only "the enemies of materialism" could accept the Copenhagen interpretation.[61]

In the end, however, it was the physicists who showed the philosophers the way, and beginning about 1960 the tide turned increasingly in favor of complementarity. In the 1963 edition of the *Philosophical Dictionary*, the principle of complementarity is dignified with an entry of its own, in which the writer complains about not the principle itself but "idealist and metaphysical" views of it.[62] Soviet physicists are no longer charged with subjective idealist distortions, and indeed the "distortions" themselves are now treated less as enduring threats to materialism than as temporary, "neopositivist" aberrations that were transcended even by the better bourgeois scientists.[63] In short, Soviet philosophers in the 1960s came to the position that the principle of complementarity, properly understood, is not incompatible with Marxism-Leninism, and this position has prevailed to the present day.

The standard Soviet account of the shift avers that it is due not to any changes in Marxism-Leninism but to corrections in the understanding of complementarity by its champions, above all by Bohr himself. Great stress falls on Bohr's supposed movement away from positivism and idealism in his later years: he worked his way, in the words of Omel'ianovskii, "not directly, but by a zigzag path, to a materialist and dialectical interpretation of quantum mechanics."[64] Similar comments by the distinguished physicist Vladimir Aleksandrovich Fock (1898–1974) are generally credited with beginning the reversal in the Soviet attitude toward complementarity; in the talks he had with Bohr in Copenhagen in 1957, Fock reported, it became clear that Bohr "fully acknowledges the objectivity of atoms and their properties."[65] Accordingly, Soviet philosophers now state the principle of complementarity in a version that is considered to be more appropriate to the Danish scientist's mature "materialist" views. That is, they do not express it in the extreme form originally identified as the "Copenhagen interpretation," in which it asserts that the properties of the micro-

[60]M. Rozental' and P. Iudin, eds., *Kratkii filosofskii slovar'*, 4th rev. ed. (Moscow, 1955), p. 193.

[61]M. E. Omel'ianovskii, *Filosofskie voprosy kvantovoi mekhaniki* (Moscow, 1956), p. 47.

[62]M. Rosenthal and P. Yudin, *A Dictionary of Philosophy* (Moscow, 1967), p. 87. The Russian edition of this work appeared in 1963.

[63]Ibid., p. 56; M. E. Omelyanovsky, *Dialectics in Modern Physics*, trans. H. C. Creighton (Moscow, 1979), p. 311.

[64]Omelyanovsky, *Dialectics*, p. 311.

[65]V. A. Fock, "Nil's Bor v moei zhizni," *Nauka i chelovechestvo* 2 (1963), p. 519.

world do not exist independently of the act of measurement. Rather, they have followed many Western scientists and philosophers of science in adopting a minimum interpretation of the principle, as simply asserting the necessity of employing complementary sets of concepts to characterize the microworld.[66] The 1980 *Philosophical Dictionary* phrases the principle as follows: "To show the wholeness of a phenomenon at a given, 'intermediate' stage of its cognition, it is necessary to apply mutually exclusive and mutually limiting 'complementary' classes of concepts, which may be utilized separately, depending on special (experimental and other) conditions, but only taken together exhaust all of the information that lends itself to determination."[67]

The Soviet view that Bohr, like Einstein, became a convert to dialectical materialism is of course debatable, and even an occasional Soviet commentator rejects it as an explanation of the new acceptability of complementarity in the USSR.[68] But even if we grant it and adopt the minimum interpretation of complementarity, there are still problems to be faced by the Soviet materialist who wishes to affirm the principle. Does not the need to acknowledge, as the 1980 minimum formulation does, a dependence on experimental conditions still signify a subjective and consequently "idealist" interference by the observer? And does not the impossibility of determining certain values simultaneously signify an unacceptable limit to the knowability of the world? Within the framework of the older Soviet conception of materialism, answers to these questions could only be affirmative. For the answers to change, revisions in materialist doctrine were necessary.

Perhaps the clearest indication of the nature of the revisions that have come to be accepted may be found in the philosophical views of the physicist V. A. Fock—views that now receive strong support from philosophers in the USSR. In Fock's interpretation, an understanding of quantum mechanics must begin with the recognition of the fundamental difference between the macroworld to which classical mechanics applies and the microworld of subatomic processes. Human beings with their sense organs and the measuring instruments that they construct to supplement those organs belong to the former world, whereas the microobjects under study are part of a radically different realm, to which what Fock calls "the idealizations and abstractions" associated with the classical description of physical phenomena cannot be extended.[69]

---

[66]Graham, *Science and Philosophy*, pp. 71, 94.
[67]I. T. Frolov, ed., *Filosofskii slovar'*, 4th ed. (Moscow, 1980), p. 103.
[68]Alekseev, *Kontseptsiia dopolnitel'nosti*, p. 208. Cf. Paul K. Feyerabend, "Dialectical Materialism and the Quantum Theory," *Slavic Review* 25 (1966), p. 416.
[69]V. A. Fock, "Quantum Physics and Philosophical Problems," in M. E. Omelyanovsky, ed., *Lenin and Modern Natural Science* (Moscow, 1978), p. 209.

One such "abstraction," Fock affirms, is "the assumption that all physical processes are completely independent of the conditions of observation," that processes occur "by themselves," undisturbed by the act of observation.[70] This "absolutization" of physical processes is the basis of classical physics, he holds, and it is perfectly justified within that domain. It is not justified, however, in the microworld, where it is necessary to admit what he calls "the principle of relativity to the means of observation"—a principle regarded by some Soviet philosophers as a generalization of the Einsteinian notion of relativity to a reference frame.[71] Armed with this principle, Fock finds nothing puzzling about the fact that different "properties" of microobjects manifest themselves fully only under mutually exclusive conditions.

A second "abstraction" that Fock singles out for criticism is the assumption that it is possible to give an exhaustively complete description of the operation of a given measuring instrument or a given physical system.[72] In classical mechanics, again, this assumption creates no difficulties. By determining the coordinates and momentums of the masses in a given system, we can describe the system fully, and we can simultaneously judge various aspects of a phenomenon, approximately at least. But in quantum mechanics we cannot simultaneously determine the coordinates and the momentum of a particle. Hence in that area this abstraction, too, must be abandoned. In the microworld, some things simply cannot be known because they cannot be determined in observation.

What Fock does not note is that the two views he is rejecting as "abstractions" would surely have been identified by both Engels and Lenin as simple statements of the requirements of Marxist materialism. For it was precisely the macroworld assumptions appropriate to classical mechanics that formed the content of the Leninist notion of matter derived from Engels and amply displayed in the pages of *Materialism and Empirio-Criticism*. What is "independence of the conditions of observation" if not the status of matter as an objective reality according to the founders? And what is the assumption of an exhaustive description of physical events if not the requirement of knowability that served as the ground of the traditional "cognitive optimism" of the Marxist materialist?[73] By applying the label 'abstractions' to these formulations of the classical demands of

---

[70]Ibid.; V. A. Fock, "Quantum Physics and Philosophical Problems," *Soviet Studies in Philosophy* 10 (Winter 1971–1972), p. 253. Although the last two essays cited have the same title, their contents are not the same.

[71]Fock, "Quantum Physics," *Soviet Studies in Philosophy*, p. 252; Fock, "Quantum Physics," in Omelyanovsky, *Lenin and Modern Natural Science*, p. 216.

[72]Fock, "Quantum Physics," *Soviet Studies in Philosophy*, p. 252; cf. Fock, "Quantum Physics," in Omelyanovsky, *Lenin and Modern Natural Science*, p. 216.

[73]Müller-Markus, "Soviet Philosophy in Crisis," p. 36.

Marxist materialism, Fock is in effect stating that they are inadequate to capture the real state of affairs. In other words, "objective reality" and "knowability" cannot be interpreted as strictly as hitherto if we are to accept the empirical findings of quantum mechanics.[74]

How, then, can the two requirements be interpreted? As in the case of relativity theory, a minimum conception of each notion is retained by Soviet philosophers. The very need for applying complementary concepts to the microworld, according to Fock, is "a reflection of objective properties of nature"; that is, given the character of the microworld, it is objectively true about it that an object displays precise spatial localization only when approached with one type of measuring device and a precisely determinable momentum only when approached with another.[75] For this analysis to hold, the conditions of objectivity and knowability appear to require simply that microobjects *exist* independently of human consciousness and be the bearers of at least *some* properties that can be objectively known.

The properties in question, it must be noted, need not include such commonsense features as spatial locatability or any other of the actual measured states of microobjects, for these *are* inseparable from "human consciousness" in the form of the cooperation of the observer in a measurement process. Rather, the objective properties of the microworld that Fock identifies are the *capacities* that microobjects possess to be actualized in those ways—capacities that Fock calls "potentialities."[76] Antecedent to measurement, according to Fock, the state of the object described by the mathematical formulas of quantum theory is objective in that

> it is an objective (independent of the observer) description of the potentialities of various results of the interaction of the atomic object with the instrument. It is in this sense that it relates to the given, individual object. But this objective state is not yet actual, in the sense that for the object in the given state the indicated potentialities have not yet been realized. The transition from the potential to the realized, to the actual, takes place in the final stage of the experiment.[77]

The objectively real, then, is not what is actual: it is a state of openness to alternative actualizations. Supporting this conception, Omel'ianovskii

[74]A similar point is made with respect to findings in astronomy in Omelyanovsky, *Lenin and Modern Natural Science*, p. 259.

[75]Fock, "Quantum Physics," *Soviet Studies in Philosophy*, p. 254; Frolov, p. 103.

[76]The actual Russian expression used by Fock—*potentsial'nye vozmozhnosti*—is an unfortunate pleonasm, meaning literally "potential possibilities."

[77]V. A. Fock, "Ob interpretatsii kvantovoi mekhaniki," in P. N. Fedoseev et al., eds., *Filosofskie problemy sovremennogo estestvoznaniia. Trudy Vsesoiuznogo soveshchaniia po filosofskim voprosam estestvoznaniia* (Moscow, 1959), p. 223.

warns that we must not mistakenly equate objective reality with "the actual" or "the real": "The category of possibility," he writes, has "an objective character from the standpoint of dialectical materialism."[78]

The philosophical acceptability of Fock's doctrine of "potentialities" demonstrates, even more clearly than the parallel developments in the treatment of relativity theory, how far Soviet materialists have departed from the traditional Marxist conception of matter as an "objective reality." For the Leninist conception was precisely an actualist one, or in other words one that identified matter with the actual spatio-temporal properties it displays on the macro level. To move from that conception to one that identifies matter with possibilities is to make a radical departure from the earlier orthodoxy. At the very least it moves Marxist-Leninist materialism notably closer to John Stuart Mill's celebrated definition of matter as "a permanent possibility of sensation"—a definition roundly condemned as "idealist" by Soviet philosophers from Lenin to the present day.[79]

Similarly evident is the revision with respect to knowability. For Fock the formulas of quantum mechanics provide an adequate description of the microworld, despite the impossibility of determining simultaneously such values as the position and the momentum of a microobject. "Inasmuch as all potentialities are covered in such a description," he writes, "it is doubtless complete. What else is there to demand besides reflection of all existing potentialities?"[80] His point, supported by other Soviet writers as well, is that it is senseless to speak of limitations to knowability when a person has all the knowledge of which a given situation is susceptible.[81] Though undoubtedly reasonable, such a consideration does nonetheless represent a deviation from the earlier orthodoxy. Thus when the 1980 *Philosophical Dictionary* in defining complementarity refers to "all of the information *that lends itself to determination*," it is acknowledging a limit to knowability that was vigorously rejected in 1956.[82] Seeking to know what is knowable about a subject is a far less ambitious program than seeking to know everything about the subject. Indeed in this light it is no longer clear what content the knowability thesis can retain in Soviet philosophy, since any further limitation to knowledge encountered in the future can likewise be dismissed as a case in which there is nothing in the situation to know. In sum, the thesis that the world is knowable is now

---

[78]Omelyanovsky, *Dialectics*, p. 59; see also pp. 171–179.

[79]Lenin, *Soch.*, vol. 18, p. 108; Rosenthal and Yudin, *Dictionary of Philosophy*, pp. 291–292.

[80]Fock, "Quantum Physics," *Soviet Studies in Philosophy*, p. 256.

[81]Müller-Markus, "Soviet Philosophy in Crisis," p. 56.

[82]Frolov, p. 103 (italics added).

compatible in Soviet philosophy with an indefinitely large area of unknowability.

Modern Cosmology and the Infinity of the Material World

Soviet views concerning the infinity of the material world, like those concerning its objectivity, have brought dialectical materialism into conflict with modern science, and for that reason much controversy has surrounded the discussion of infinity in Soviet philosophy in recent years.

In scientific cosmology, a prime consequence of the application of relativity theory to questions of the origin and structure of the universe has been the development of alternative cosmological models. And since the characteristics of space and time, according to relativity theory, depend on the distribution of matter in the universe, in different models space and time have different characteristics. In some, the universe is infinite in space and time; in others it is finite in one or both of those respects. Finitist models, moreover, are more than mere theoretical possibilities, for they have received special support from a discovery in astrophysics—the discovery that light from distant nebulae, when analyzed spectrographically, presents a pattern in which there is a distinct displacement toward the red end of the spectrum. Although other interpretations of this "red shift" could be devised, among cosmologists it is now universally regarded as a Doppler effect, or in other words as signifying the movement of the light's source away from the observer. This interpretation in turn has served as the basis for the so-called "expanding universe" theory, according to which the material world may be assumed to have begun its expansion at a particular time from a small, dense mass. In this theory the origin of the expansion is generally thought to have been a primal explosion—an initial "big bang" that set the world's matter hurtling outward; and in recent years this view has received powerful support with the discovery of what is assumed to be the remnant radiation from such an explosion.[83]

The reaction of Soviet ideologists to these hypotheses during the dark years of the *Zhdanovshchina* was dominated by the fear that they could be used (as indeed they were used by some Western scientists and philosophers) to make room for a religious philosophy—to see the big bang as God's act of creating the universe. Zhdanov himself, in his 1947 address, lamented that "many followers of Einstein" were "talking about the finiteness of the world, about its limitedness in time and space."[84] In 1948,

---

[83]Nigel Calder, *Einstein's Universe* (New York, 1979), pp. 127–131; Graham, *Science and Philosophy*, pp. 139–146.
[84]Zhdanov, p. 43.

the expanding universe theory was condemned at a Soviet conference on ideological problems in astronomy, and vigorous opposition to the theory continued for many years thereafter.[85] In the 1960s, however, Soviet cosmology began to reap the benefits of liberalization that we have already seen at work in relativity and quantum physics. Champions of the expanding universe theory emerged and made their mark, with the result that there is now, in stark contrast to the *Zhdanovshchina*, virtually universal acceptance of the theory, in some form at least, among Soviet philosophers as well as scientists.[86] But this is not to say that Soviet philosophers, particularly those writing at the popular level, have ceased to be disturbed by the possible creationist implications of the expansion hypothesis.

The typical approach in the more ideologically oriented literature today is to accept the expanding universe theory with respect to observable portions of the universe but to question or deny its applicability to the universe as a whole. The Soviet writers who adopt this tack are following a suggestion of Zhdanov, who in 1947 condemned the practice of arriving at cosmological theories by "transferring the results of research into the laws of the movement of a finite, bounded region of the universe to the whole infinite universe."[87] A. P. Sheptulin's textbook, *Marxist-Leninist Philosophy* (1978), elaborates: "So the expansion of the observed part of the Universe in no way means that its other parts are also expanding at this moment. They may expand, or they may contract. *It is more likely* that processes of expansion and contraction are taking place in the Universe in equal measure, that one tendency is predominant in one part for a certain period of time and another tendency in another part."[88] The same assumption of the greater likelihood of contraction in other parts of the universe is made in the most recent (1982) edition of *Fundamentals*, which assures readers that "there are grounds for believing that this expansion is a local process and that in the Universe apart from our Galaxy there are countless other cosmic systems."[89] What the textbook does not say is that the "reasons" in question are primarily ideological in nature, having

---

[85] Müller-Markus, "Soviet Philosophy in Crisis," p. 37; Wetter, *Dialectical Materialism*, p. 436.

[86] Ia. B. Zeldovich and I. D. Novikov, "Contemporary Trends in Cosmology," *Soviet Studies in Philosophy* 14 (Spring 1976), pp. 28, 40, 47.

[87] Zhdanov, p. 43. Zhdanov was in turn using a distinction drawn earlier by Engels for another purpose; see Engels, *Dialectics of Nature*, p. 164.

[88] Sheptulin, *Marxist-Leninist Philosophy*, p. 117 (italics added). It might be noted that the word 'Universe' (*Vselennaia*) is always capitalized in Soviet philosophical writings, unlike the word 'God' (*bog*), which is almost never capitalized. If, as George L. Kline has suggested, the latter practice is appropriately dubbed "orthographic atheism" (*Religious and Anti-Religious Thought in Russia* [Chicago, 1968], p. 112, n. 14), perhaps the former should be called "orthographic pantheism."

[89] Konstantinov, *Fundamentals* (1982), p. 75.

to do with the role of the infinity thesis in "the struggle against the religious-idealist world view."[90]

This grudging, qualified acceptance of the expanding universe theory in Soviet textbooks by no means exhausts the recent development in this area of Soviet thought, however. Popular works on the whole operate with an unanalyzed, commonsense conception of infinity that is assumed dogmatically for purposes of discussing cosmological theories. Far more important from a philosophical point of view is the discussion of the nature and status of the infinity thesis in the more specialized, professional literature of Soviet philosophy. For this discussion has produced radical departures from the earlier dogmatic approach to the subject.[91]

The dogmatic approach is now widely mentioned in the advanced literature as the "traditional" conception of infinity. L. B. Bazhenov and N. N. Nutsubidze dubbed it the "naive traditional view" in an influential study of 1969, in which they described this approach as proceeding from two basic assumptions: "(1) It is considered that we possess a sufficiently definite, intuitively clear and complete concept of infinity. This concept is essentially negative and expresses the absence of any sort of boundary or limit. Infinity signifies simply the absence of an end in any direction. (2) This concept of infinity is established by philosophy and presented to natural science." Proponents of this conception, the authors continue, are convinced that "the world is infinite in space and time and [that] any discussion of this question is simply inappropriate, for it contradicts dialectical materialism." To such thinkers, the only thing needed, Bazhenov and Nutsubidze contend, is "to 'confirm' this view over and over again by the findings of the natural sciences."[92]

Bazhenov and Nutsubidze do not openly identify the "naive traditional view" as that advanced by Frederick Engels, but in fact their first assumption quoted above comes in part directly from the definition of infinity that Engels provided in 1878 in his *Anti-Dühring*: "Eternity in time, infinity in space, signify from the start, and in the simple meaning of the words, that there is *no end in any direction*, neither forwards nor backwards, upwards or downwards, to the right or to the left."[93] The Estonian philosopher Gustav Ioganovich Naan (b. 1919) credits Engels with having

[90]A. S. Karmin, "Kosmologicheskie predstavleniia o konechnosti i beskonechnosti Vselennoi i ikh otnoshenie k real'nosti," *Filosofskie nauki*, 1978, no. 3, p. 22.

[91]For a treatment of these developments during the period 1959-1969, see Bernard Jeu, *La philosophie soviétique et l'Occident. Essai sur les tendances et sur la signification de la philosophie soviétique contemporaine (1959–1969)* (Paris, 1969), pp. 88–114.

[92]L. B. Bazhenov and N. N. Nutsubidze, "K diskussiiam o probleme beskonechnosti Vselennoi," in V. V. Kaziutinskii et al., eds., *Beskonechnost' i Vselennaia* (Moscow, 1969), p. 129.

[93]Engels, *Anti-Dühring*, p. 65 (italics added).

established the notion of *real infinity* as "the objective source of our ideas of infinity"—a contribution that Naan regards as the basis of the materialist approach to the problem. But he also finds in Engels the typical pre-Riemannian confusion of infinity with boundlessness, or in other words a failure to see that an unbounded space, such as would be traversed by one moving freely over the surface of a sphere, can at the same time be finite. And he admits that Engels's conception dominated Soviet published work in philosophy until the beginning of the 1960s.[94] By the traditional view, then, these present-day Soviet philosophers have in mind Engels's conception of infinity as endlessness, taken as a complete and intuitively clear philosophical category that identifies a real, objective feature of the world.

Although many Soviet scientists and philosophers are agreed that the traditional conception of infinity is inadequate, there is no consensus on a single conception to replace it. Rather, a number of different positions have evolved in the professional literature of Soviet philosophy, representing a range of outlooks from more doctrinaire to less so. All of these outlooks share, however, an opposition to unthinking dogmatism and a willingness not only to accommodate the expanding universe theory but more generally to yield a large place in the study of infinity to the natural sciences.

The most unorthodox position is one adopted by a number of scientists and best represented in recent Soviet philosophical literature by the late Ernst Kol'man (Arnosht Kolman, 1892–1979), a Czech philosopher-scientist who, although he spent much of his professional life in the USSR, fled the country in 1976 and died in Sweden.[95] Not only was Kol'man one of the earliest critics of the traditional view of infinity, he steadfastly refused to adopt in any form the thesis of the real infinity of the material world.[96] Nothing in Marxist philosophy, he argued, rules out a finitist cosmology. Dialectical materialism, Kol'man wrote, "is not bound to the recognition of any particular ideas of time and space for all eternity, just as it is not bound, for example, to the recognition of any particular ideas about the structure of matter, or the character of causality, and so on.... Dialectical materialism is equally compatible with the assumption both of the spatial infinity and of the spatial finiteness of the Universe."[97] Kol'man stopped

[94]G. I. Naan, "Poniatie beskonechnosti v matematike i kosmologii," in Kaziutinskii et al., p. 71.
[95]For further information on Kol'man's life, see Kurt Marko, "No Juvenal of Bolshevism," *Studies in Soviet Thought* 22 (1981), pp. 147–149, and the notes that Kol'man appended to his article "The Philosophical Interpretation of Contemporary Physics," *Studies in Soviet Thought* 21 (1980), pp. 13–14.
[96]Bazhenov and Nutsubidze, p. 129.
[97]E. Kol'man, "O konechnosti i beskonechnosti Vselennoi," in Kaziutinskii et al., pp. 147–148.

short of affirming finitism as a proven principle, or even as a conclusion confirmed by physical evidence; both the infinity and the finiteness of the material world are "indemonstrable and irrefutable," he contended. But he argued that finitism is the hypothesis or postulate that should be adopted on methodological grounds: it is, he believed, heuristically the most productive in stimulating the advancement of physics.[98] Kol'man denied, furthermore, that there is any special "philosophical" conception of infinity not connected with the work of the sciences.[99]

The other nontraditional views of infinity in current Soviet philosophy are not so iconoclastic as to share what Kol'man called his "finitist 'heresy.' "[100] All of them in some sense accept the "real infinity" of the objective material world. This does not mean, however, that they are diametrically opposed to Kol'man's position, with which in fact they have much in common.

Closest to Kol'man is a group of writers headed by G. I. Naan and including L. B. Bazhenov, N. N. Nutsubidze, and others. Like Kol'man, these writers have great respect for the natural sciences, and they scorn the dogmatism and the obsequious deference to authority that mark the traditional view. To treat the sciences as if they were "summoned to illustrate and concretize" a philosophical conception of infinity, Naan writes, runs the risk of turning Marxist-Leninist philosophy into "something resembling a materialist theology."[101] They also agree with Kol'man that infinity cannot be conclusively proved, but at the same time they contend that we are compelled to postulate it in order to understand the world. For Naan there appears to be an intuitive perception of the unlimited without which human beings cannot make sense of their surroundings. Amid the transient and relative phenomena of existence we nonetheless assert that, in Naan's words, "there is in the world something intransient, enduring, absolute (God, matter)."[102] But this statement does not mean that we have a clear conception of the infinity that idealists ascribe to God and materialists to matter: "We know that the material world is infinite," Naan writes, "but we never know in precisely what sense."[103] It remains for the various sciences, viewing this "real infinity" from different sides, to identify and clarify its features, according to Naan and his associates.

[98]Bazhenov and Nutsubidze, p. 131; Orlov, "O nekotorykh voprosakh," p. 53; Kol'man, "O konechnosti," p. 150; Kol'man, "Philosophical Interpretation," p. 11. The latter work, as Kol'man explains in a note on pp. 13–14, was refused publication in the USSR for political reasons.
[99]Kol'man, "O konechnosti," p. 148.
[100]Kol'man, "Philosophical Interpretation," p. 11.
[101]Naan, "Poniatie beskonechnosti," p. 75.
[102]Ibid., p. 68; see also pp. 76–77.
[103]Ibid., p. 77.

No special, separate "philosophical" conception of infinity reveals aspects of infinity unknown to the natural sciences. Rather, philosophy performs the functions of analyzing and synthesizing the conceptions of infinity attained by the separate sciences.[104]

A third nontraditional approach to the problem of infinity in current Soviet philosophy is that of a group of philosophers who, although they reject the naive, "endlessness" conception of Engels, persist in arguing for a specifically philosophical conception of infinity, distinguished from the conceptions of the sciences. For this reason the group is dubbed "quasi-nontraditionalist" by Bazhenov and Nutsubidze;[105] it includes the Leningrad philosophers Vladimir Iosifovich Sviderskii (b. 1910) and Anatolii Solomonovich Karmin, the Moscow philosopher S. T. Meliukhin, and others. There is no clear consensus within this group as to the content of the philosophical conception of infinity. An increasingly common tendency among them, however, is to link philosophical infinity not with the spatio-temporal characteristics of the material world but with the Leninist category of inexhaustibility. The cosmological question of the spatio-temporal finiteness or infinity of the universe as it is known to science, according to Karmin, concerns not a philosophical issue but rather the question of whether the astronomical universe is finite or infinite in a mathematical or "metrical" sense—in the sense applicable to four-dimensional space-time. The philosophical question of infinity, he argues, is the question of the inexhaustibility of the material world: "The infinity of space and time in this conception appears as the inexhaustible diversity of the spatio-temporal forms of matter."[106] Thus Karmin and others, in distinguishing between the astronomical universe on the one hand and the material world on the other, are not doing so in order to suggest, as traditionalists have done for years, that a metrically infinite world might surround our seemingly finite one. Rather they are pointing to a different kind of consideration in dealing *philosophically* with the nature of matter—a consideration of the infinite variety rather than the infinite extent of the world.[107]

Not all of the "quasi-nontraditionalists" who look to the concept of inexhaustibility as the key to infinity agree that the notion is *purely* nonmetrical, however. S. T. Meliukhin has worked for a number of years to develop a philosophical conception of infinity that, although based on

---

[104]Ibid., p. 76; cf. pp. 63–66 and Bazhenov and Nutsubidze, p. 136.
[105]Bazhenov and Nutsubidze, p. 132.
[106]Karmin, "Kosmologicheskie predstavleniia," p. 22; see also A. S. Karmin, *Poznanie beskonechnosti* (Moscow, 1981).
[107]I. Z. Tsekhmistro, review of V. P. Lebedev, *Beskonechna li Vselennaia?* (Minsk, 1978), in *Filosofskie nauki*, 1979, no. 5, pp. 157–158.

nonmetrical inexhaustibility, seeks to link that feature with other characterizations of infinity as well, including the metrical.[108] In his willingness
to incorporate spatio-temporal infinity in the philosophical conception,
Meliukhin is closer to the traditional view than are other nontraditionalists.
Yet even Meliukhin's position is set apart from the traditionalists' both
by its comprehensiveness and by its avoidance of dogmatism. There can
be, Meliukhin writes, "no complete and final proof" of the real infinity
of the material world.[109] Similar disclaimers of dogmatism are made by
other "quasi-nontraditionalists" as well. Karmin, for example, writes that
metrical infinity can never be proved, because of the impossibility in principle that human experience could ever extend to a spatio-temporally
endless universe, and he holds that the philosophical conception of infinity
as asserting an inexhaustible diversity of material structures is really no
more than a methodological principle, on a par with the principles of
simplicity and causality.[110]

Some part is still taken in the higher-level Soviet discussions of infinity
by admitted "traditionalists," though it is a diminishing and an increasingly
ineffective part. V. V. Orlov in his 1974 critique of Meliukhin and others
gave special attention to their views of infinity. He found these views
"alarming," particularly for their appeal to what he called "alien concepts"
such as that of the postulational character of infinity. Marxist philosophy
proves the infinity of the world, Orlov insists, and that infinity is grounded
in spatio-temporal endlessness. To accept the view that the world has a
finite radius, he warns, would inevitably lead to the denial of its infinite
diversity as well and then perhaps to the ultimately unacceptable conclusion—that the world has a beginning and end.[111] Orlov's article, however,
was accompanied in the same issue of *Filosofskie nauki* by three sharply
critical replies. The first, written by Meliukhin, defended Naan, Sviderskii,
and others (but not Kol'man) and charged that Orlov in no way advances
the investigation by assuming that truth is "in his pocket." Progress is
possible, Meliukhin concludes, only when "the norms of scientific discussion are observed and principles of genuine scientific creative work sup-
plant the spirit, still sometimes encountered, of clamorous and scholastic
pretentiousness."[112] The other critics, V. S. Tiukhtin and L. B. Bazhenov,

---

[108]Meliukhin, *Materiia*, p. 48. See also Meliukhin, "Filosofskie osnovaniia idei beskonechnosti Vselennoi," *Filosofskie nauki*, 1978, no. 1, pp. 101–105.
[109]*Philosophy in the USSR. Problems of Dialectical Materialism*, p. 66.
[110]Karmin, "Kosmologicheskie predstavleniia," p. 22.
[111]Orlov, "O nekotorykh voprosakh," pp. 52–53.
[112]Meliukhin, "Problemy filosofskoi teorii materii," pp. 64, 67.

also showed Orlov no quarter.[113] And the nontraditionalists had the last word in the debate, as no rebuttal by Orlov was published.

In current Soviet philosophy, then, the classic dialectical materialist thesis of the infinity of the material world has an aspect far different from the one it bears in antireligious tracts or other ideologically oriented works. In literature of the latter sorts, the thesis is presented as a substantive and provable philosophical truth, to which the findings of the sciences must be accommodated and which asserts the metrical, spatio-temporal endlessness of the physical universe. In the philosophical literature, on the other hand, the status and content of the infinity thesis are open questions; metrical endlessness is widely rejected, and the thesis is generally seen as an unprovable postulate that is adopted for its utility in scientific investigation.

The Concept of Inexhaustibility in Soviet Materialism

The attempt on the part of some Soviet philosophers to interpret infinity as inexhaustibility lends still greater significance to what is in any event regarded by Marxist-Leninists as an important characteristic of matter. Whether or not inexhaustibility is the key to infinity in general, there is no doubt that it is what Lenin had in mind when he spoke of "the overall infinity of matter in depth," and a recent Soviet work calls the notion "one of the most important in materialist dialectics."[114]

Just what "infinity in depth" amounted to was long considered unproblematic in dialectical materialist philosophy. Lenin had advanced the notion in attempting to deal with the supposed "disappearance" of matter as the atom was broken into constituent parts. When in the face of these developments he not only reaffirmed materialism but added that "the electron is as *inexhaustible* as the atom, nature is infinite," the most direct interpretation of these lines was that Lenin believed that every material unit reached by scientific analysis would in turn prove divisible into still other material units.[115] As Kedrov expounded Lenin's view in 1948: "However simple and elementary a given particle of matter may appear to us, in fact it can never be absolutely simple or elementary; there can never be anything like an ultimate building-block."[116] Western scholars, too, took

---

[113]V. S. Tiukhtin, "K sootnosheniiu obraza, znaka i struktury," *Filosofskie nauki*, 1974, no. 5, pp. 71, 73; L. B. Bazhenov, "Nekotorye zamechaniia po povodu publikatsii V. V. Orlova," *Filosofskie nauki*, 1974, no. 5, p. 75.

[114]Viakkerev et al., *Materialisticheskaia dialektika*, p. 100; Lenin, *Soch.*, vol. 29, p. 100.

[115]Lenin, *Soch.*, vol. 18, p. 277 (italics in original).

[116]B. M. Kedrov, "Leninskii vzgliad na elektron i sovremennaia fizika," *Bol'shevik*, 1948, no. 2, p. 45.

this straightforward approach to Lenin's statements. J. M. Bocheński, noting that Lenin had also endorsed Dietzgen's thesis that "nature in its sum as well as in its parts has no beginning and no end," concluded Lenin meant that matter is "infinitely divisible."[117]

As with other properties attributed to matter by Soviet materialists, however, the property of inexhaustibility has encountered theoretical difficulties, stemming in this case from findings in elementary particle physics. Recent years have seen an astounding proliferation of microobjects in the subatomic world, until at present there is evidence to support the existence of hundreds of different particles, from the old familiar electrons, protons, and neutrons to the newer and more exotic monopoles, vector bosons, and quarks. At the same time, despite ritual Soviet pronouncements to the effect that the "profound insight" of Lenin's thesis concerning the infinity of matter in depth has been "completely confirmed" by modern developments in particle physics,[118] it is far from clear, as most Soviet philosophers and scientists now realize, that the "elementary" particles found in the microworld are accurately described by the vocabulary of "divisibility" and levels of "depth." As the Soviet Ukrainian physicist and philosopher Volodymyr Svyrydovych Gott (Hott) writes:

When, let us say, high-energy protons collide with other protons and new particles arise as a result, the notion "division" no longer works, for the number and the types of new particles depend on the energy of the colliding particles. The new particles are not constituents of the particles through the collision of which they arose. A proton, for example, may be obtained as the result of a collision between a neutron and a pi-meson, or between a lambda-hyperon and a K-meson; but this does not mean that the proton is part of their structure, that they "consist of" protons.... The question of what a given elementary particle "consists of" is devoid of meaning.[119]

We engage in an unjustifiable extrapolation, the late Ernst Kol'man contended, when we reason that because bodies consist of molecules, molecules of atoms, and atoms of nucleons and electrons, then the latter must also be divisible, and so on to infinity. "Not a single elementary particle," Kol'man wrote in 1975, "has yet been divided into smaller parts."[120]

At this point we might expect Soviet scientists and philosophers to argue that the mere failure, thus far, to find the "smaller parts" of so-called

[117]Bocheński, *Soviet Russian Dialectical Materialism*, p. 78; see also Graham, *Science and Philosophy*, p. 48.
[118][Konstantinov,] *Fundamentals* (1974), p. 79.
[119]V. S. Gott, "Material'noe edinstvo mira i edinstvo nauchnogo znaniia," *Voprosy filosofii*, 1977, no. 12, p. 32. See also *Philosophical Concepts*, p. 127.
[120]Kol'man, "Philosophical Interpretation," p. 11.

elementary particles does not prove the nonexistence of such parts or preclude a future scientific breakthrough in which they will be found. Certainly Western scientists continue to entertain the possibility that presently known particles may be shown to be various combinations of more fundamental elements such as quarks. On the contrary, Soviet scholars have instead increasingly moved away from the notion of the divisibility of subatomic particles into simpler elements. S. T. Meliukhin puts the retreat from infinite divisibility in terms familiar to Russian readers by using the image of the *matroshka*, a set of nested dolls: "Structural infinity cannot be understood in the sense of an unlimited hierarchical sequence of systems in the structure of every microparticle, like a series of Russian dolls fitting inside one another.... [The] structures of elementary particles... turn out to be different from the structures of all other systems."[121] Earlier Meliukhin had criticized the much-abused traditionalist V. V. Orlov for advancing such a model of a *matroshka* universe composed of an infinite hierarchy of levels of matter "stretching downward."[122] And even a *Pravda* article speaks of "the old naive conceptions about matter's being divisible into parts."[123]

But if we can no longer assert that matter is infinitely divisible, it would appear that we have no ground for calling it "infinite in depth." Are we not obliged then to abandon the Leninist thesis of the inexhaustibility of matter? Understandably, given Lenin's status as a philosophical authority in the USSR, there is no rush to abandon the letter of the thesis. At the same time the difficulty is clearly seen by Soviet scholars, and their response is to seek a new spirit in which to understand Lenin's pronouncement. As the physicist V. A. Barashenkov remarks, the inexhaustibility of the material world "does not necessarily have to be realized through unlimited division."[124] Consequently, new interpretations of the inexhaustibility thesis are proposed, in an attempt to give it a reasonable content that is consistent with the findings of elementary particle physics.

[121]*Philosophy in the USSR. Problems of Dialectical Materialism*, p. 68. See also V. L. Ginzburg, *Key Problems of Physics and Astrophysics*, trans. Oleg Glebov (Moscow, 1976), pp. 61, 81. For technical discussions of the concept of divisibility in Soviet philosophy of physics, see L. Ia. Stanis et al., eds., *Novye filosofskie voprosy fiziki (Materialy konferentsii 1973–1975 gg.)* (Moscow, 1977), pp. 58–78.

[122]Meliukhin, "Problemy filosofskoi teorii materii," p. 65.

[123]Quoted with approval in Omelyanovsky, *Dialectics*, p. 221. Only the most doctrinaire and superficial works, such as Yu. A. Kharin's *Fundamentals of Dialectics*, trans. Konstantin Kostrov (Moscow, 1981), continue to speak of microparticles as divisible (see p. 59). Critics of Marxist-Leninist philosophy, however, still commonly assume that the Marxist-Leninist is committed to the doctrine of infinite divisibility; see, for example, Jiři Marek and L. E. Musberg, "Matter in Its 'Infinity,' " *Studies in Soviet Thought* 27 (1984), pp. 25–30.

[124]*Philosophical Concepts*, p. 140. Cf. *Philosophy in the USSR. Problems of Dialectical Materialism*, p. 69.

Kol'man, true to his finitist approach, argued that it is not necessary to assume any sort of actual infinity, much less infinite divisibility, in order to accept the inexhaustibility thesis. "Lenin's thesis that the universe is inexhaustible," he wrote in 1969, "remains in force even in the case where it is a true proposition that the universe is in all respects finite but is inconceivably enormous in comparison with the scale of the human species."[125] This sense of 'inexhaustible', however, in which the term means "inexhaustible for practical purposes" or "greater than human powers of comprehension," has little appeal to most Soviet scholars, who remember that Lenin included in his famous sentence on inexhaustibility the further clause "nature is infinite." Hence the majority seek an interpretation that will link inexhaustibility with a "real infinity" of some sort though not with an infinite divisibility.

Three such interpretations, not always clearly distinguished in the Soviet literature, have been suggested. The first is stated succinctly by Sheptulin: "The world is infinite in its diversity and therefore inexhaustible."[126] The shift from divisibility to diversity is of course a significant one: no longer is it being said that however small an entity may be, it must be a whole composed of still smaller parts. All that is required by Sheptulin's formulation is that the world be characterized by an endless variety of material states or structures—what Meliukhin calls, in speaking of matter, "the infinity of its forms."[127]

A second interpretation stresses not so much the infinity of *forms* of matter as the infinity of the *succession* from one form to another. V. P. Lebedev phrases it as follows: "The dialectical principle of inexhaustibility assumes...that every object of nature, however small or great it may be, must develop, must pass over into other states of matter, while the succession of stages of development itself must be an infinite process."[128] Such a succession, of course, is compatible with there being a *finite* number of different material states and structures that recur in the process of change; the second conception requires that change from one state to another never stop, not that the variety of different states be endless.

Still a third interpretation of inexhaustibility in recent Soviet philosophy requires neither an endless diversity of material forms nor an endless succession of changes in the material world but simply the endless advance of our knowledge of that world. Epistemological inexhaustibility is stressed

---

[125]Kol'man, "O konechnosti," p. 150.

[126]Sheptulin, *Marxist-Leninist Philosophy*, pp. 155–156.

[127]*Philosophy in the USSR. Problems of Dialectical Materialism*, p. 70. See also *Philosophical Concepts*, p. 18.

[128]Lebedev, *Beskonechna li Vselennaia?* p. 127; see also Sheptulin, *Marxist-Leninist Philosophy*, p. 97.

by a wide range of Soviet philosophers, though usually without explicitly excluding the ontological dimension. Some writers move easily from one to the other as the occasion demands, noting no difference between asserting that objects have an inexhaustible number of properties and asserting that "the world *as an object of cognition* is inexhaustible."[129] The attractiveness of the latter, weaker thesis is no doubt responsible for the warnings in more dogmatic works that it is not sufficient: "The recognition of the epistemological inexhaustibility of the world," a recent book insists, "necessarily presupposes the inexhaustibility of matter in the ontological sense."[130]

Although they arose as substitutes for the notion of infinite divisibility, none of these three contemporary Soviet interpretations of the inexhaustibility of matter is incompatible with that notion. They are clearly far broader than the traditional interpretation, in such a way that they are consistent both with it and with the physical findings that called the traditional interpretation into question. The thesis that matter is inexhaustible—like so many other theses of Marxism-Leninism—has been greatly loosened in recent Soviet philosophy. Once thought to require the endless breaking down of every bit of matter into smaller elements—a matroshka universe with no smallest doll—the thesis now commits its proponents to nothing more than the view that the material world is endlessly varied, or that it is an arena of constant change, or (least demanding of all) that our knowledge of it can never be considered final or complete. Significantly, all these views are widely accepted outside as well as within dialectical materialist philosophy, and none of them seems likely to run afoul of further developments in physics or any other science.

In its weakened state, the inexhaustibility thesis—especially in its epistemological version—is frequently invoked by nontraditionalist Soviet philosophers as an antidote to the very dogmatism that once accompanied it. For its message is now above all that existing knowledge of the world is always partial and approximate—that there is always more knowledge to be gained. Since no particular direction—such as further divisibility—in which to seek that knowledge is any longer mandated, the thesis has changed its character from a substantive dogma to the broadest of heuristic principles: never assume that all truth is known. In this sense Soviet philosophers can readily and with a clear conscience accept the pronouncement of the Central Committee of the Communist party when, on the centenary of Lenin's birth, it declared that Lenin's "idea of the inexhaus-

---

[129]V. Gott, *This Amazing, Amazing, Amazing But Knowable Universe*, trans. John Bushnell and Kristine Bushnell (Moscow, 1977), p. 98 (italics added). See also Kol'man, "Philosophical Interpretation," p. 11.

[130]Viakkerev et al., *Materialisticheskaia dialektika*, p. 101.

tibility of matter has become the general principle of natural science."[131]
In this same sense, however, there is no basis other than ritual piety for
crediting *Lenin* with the establishment of so broad a principle, particularly
one that has been a mainstay of Western scholarship for some twenty-five
centuries.

A Critical Assessment of Soviet Materialism

It should be evident from the foregoing discussion that Marxist-Leninist
materialism, although popularly represented both inside and outside the
USSR as a straightforward, monolithic creed, is in fact not a precisely
defined doctrine or one on which there is close agreement among Soviet
writers. Given the broad differences among them in the interpretation of
key materialist concepts, including the concept of matter itself, it is no
longer accurate to speak of Marxist-Leninist materialism as a single philosophical position. And for this reason, the blanket condemnations that
have been the typical Western response to simplistic Soviet expositions are
no longer helpful. I do not mean that no general critical conclusions can
be offered but only that such conclusions must be responsive to the actual,
sometimes elusive content of the various positions that are Soviet
materialism.

With respect to what we identified as the purely epistemological conception of materialism that appeals strongly to many Soviet scientists, there
is very little content to criticize. This "scientists' materialism," as it may
be called, amounts to nothing more than the familiar doctrine of realism,
or the view that there is a world of reality apart from the subject who
perceives and studies it. Soviet scientists are perfectly willing to subscribe
to this view, particularly now that it has been given a minimum interpretation within which it is consistent, as we have seen, with both relativity
and complementarity. And on the whole they have no objection to calling
it "materialism." "The truly materialist position," writes the physicist V. L.
Ginzburg, "consists in the acknowledgement of the existence of the Universe apart from dependence on human consciousness and prior to the
appearance of that consciousness."[132] To say, as Ginzburg does, that materialism does not simply *include* but *consists in* that acknowledgment is
to require very little of materialism. The same minimum demand is evident
when Omel'ianovskii writes that science, since it must seek to understand
nature just as it is, without "arbitrary additions" by the subject, "cannot

[131]Quoted by Sheptulin, *Marxist-Leninist Philosophy*, p. 87.
[132]V. Ginzburg, "Astrofizika. Dostizheniia i perspektivy," *Kommunist*, 1965, no. 4, p. 62.

help being materialist."[133] Clearly, in Omel'ianovskii's mind the acceptance of an independent reality is a sufficient condition for the materialist position.

At the minimum level, there is really nothing controversial about Marxist-Leninist materialism aside from the propriety of labeling so undemanding a view "materialism." It is consistent with all of the world's great religions and with most of the world's philosophies, so that it can be affirmed in all sincerity by those with the most diverse personal convictions. It is the well-nigh universal assumption in terms of which scientists around the world proceed and against the background of which even controversies such as those in relativity physics and in quantum mechanics take place. Einstein insisted upon it, and Bohr accepted it, as we have seen. In this sense Soviet philosophers are entirely justified in contending that not only Einstein and Bohr but all "true scientists" are "unconscious" or "spontaneous" followers of Marxist-Leninist materialism—meaning simply that they accept realism but do not call it "materialism." Along with Soviet scientists and philosophers they accept, in other words, what Bernard d'Espagnat describes as the tenaciously held notion that "the world outside the self is real and has at least some properties that exist independently of human consciousness."[134]

Despite frequent Soviet claims of the provability of materialism, the realist doctrine is typically either simply taken for granted or advanced with merely a nod in the direction of support. Many Soviet works content themselves with citing the authority of Engels and Lenin or with assurances that materialism is a "natural, rational explanation of phenomena" that is confirmed by "practice."[135] Occasionally a work will reproduce a supporting point used by Lenin, such as the evolutionary argument to the effect that since minds developed out of mindless matter, it must be possible for the latter to exist without the former.[136] These points, however, are not elaborated or dwelt upon, much less defended as logical support for realism.

But even if in Soviet philosophy the objective status of the material world is simply a postulate, devoid of logical proof, dialectical materialism is not necessarily at a disadvantage with respect to the rest of the scientific world. D'Espagnat describes the postulate's status in science generally as that of an "intuitive notion" to which we cling not because we can prove it but because of dissatisfaction with the implications of rejecting it: to assert that observable regularities have no underlying objective causes, he

---

[133]Omelyanovsky, *Dialectics*, p. 27.

[134]Bernard D'Espagnat, "The Quantum Theory and Reality," *Scientific American* 241 (November 1979), p. 177.

[135][Konstantinov,] *Fundamentals* (1974), pp. 72, 200–201.

[136]Ibid., p. 86.

believes, would be to trivialize the scientist's quest.[137] Soviet scholars may have an ideological predisposition toward the realist postulate, but it is clearly not dependent on that circumstance for its broader scientific appeal. To the extent, then, that the assertion of the primacy of matter in Soviet philosophy means only that there is an objective world independent of the knower, absence of proof is no compelling charge against it. For it consists in a minimum assertion that is shared by virtually the entire world of science and that commits the thinker—as Soviet scientists are fond of stressing—to no specific features of that objective world.

For many Soviet philosophers, however, as we have seen, materialism does mean more than realism. The positive or "ontological" conception of matter that is developed in the writings of S. T. Meliukhin and others ascribes to matter not only an existence independent of mind but also a catalogue of properties such as motion, infinity, and inexhaustibility. This view provides an identifiable subject matter for philosophy as distinguished from the "special" sciences, and it would appear to commit one to a far more demanding outlook than the scientists' materialism. Let us call this seemingly stronger position "the philosophers' materialism."

On the basis of our analysis in the previous section, however, we can now see that the appearance of being a more demanding outlook is in large part illusory. For the philosophers' materialism receives at the hands of its proponents so broad an interpretation that once again there is very little in it to which a person might object. The property of motion, for example, embraces every imaginable form of change, including those far removed from spatial displacement; hence to say that matter and motion are inseparable comes to mean, for the Soviet philosopher, simply that everything in the material world is subject to change of some sort and that there is no change without something that changes. The traditional Soviet claim that the material world is infinite is not any longer typically regarded as committing the Marxist-Leninist philosopher to the rejection of finitist models of the universe; the assertion can mean no more than that the material world presents to limited human cognition a picture of endless diversity. To say that matter is inexhaustible, similarly, is not to be bound to the view that no material particles are truly elementary and that all are further divisible; for many Soviet philosophers it means only that we should continue the quest for fuller and more adequate knowledge of the world, whatever particular results may have been obtained at a given point in the development of science.

There is nothing that could be called argumentation for these theses in contemporary Soviet philosophy, but at the same time it is difficult to see

---

[137]D'Espagnat, p. 177.

what facts could possibly contradict them. The trouble with them is not that they are narrow, implausible, and unyielding—as Marxist philosophical theses are often presumed to be—but that they are so loose and permissive that every imaginable factual finding is consistent with them. Of course this immunity to empirical contradiction has its price: the price is vacuousness, or the failure to make any genuine commitment concerning what will and what will not be found in the real world. As Soviet philosophers have come to use the terms, there is no conceivable evidence that could be offered to show that the material world is *not* "moving," "infinite," and "inexhaustible"—simply because to affirm that it is all those things is not to commit oneself to any particular features of the world. It is at most to commit oneself to certain ways of talking about and studying the world.

Conceivably, of course, these ways of talking and studying could be useful: it might be argued that they can stimulate further insights and guide the course of scientific investigation in profitable ways. Hence to call the theses in question "vacuous" is not necessarily to dismiss them as worthless. Some Soviet philosophers, indeed, appear to be content with claiming only heuristic value for dialectical materialism.[138] For the majority, however, who present the philosophers' materialism as a positive and substantive ontological doctrine, the charge of vacuousness cannot be ignored.

The two forms of Soviet materialism distinguished thus far share a basic orientation toward the sciences. Both are characterizations of the material world studied by the sciences—one a minimum, realist account that leaves all the details to the sciences, the other a substantive philosophical description of the world that seeks to be consistent with the findings of the special sciences. For still a third group of Soviet writers, however—including those who write the popular textbooks—materialism means more than any particular characterization of the material world: it means that the material world is all there is, or in other words that there is nothing in reality *but* spatio-temporal matter. In this third sense, Marxist-Leninist materialism can no longer be called vacuous: it commits its adherents to the rejection of the reality of all purely ideal or spiritual entities.

This strengthened conception of materialism has little attraction for Soviet scientists or philosophers of science, whose concerns are with the empirical world. It is of paramount importance, however, to those Soviet philosophers with strong ideological concerns, and for that reason it seems appropriate to call it "the ideologists' materialism." The world-view sig-

[138]Loren Graham argues in *Science and Philosophy* that Soviet scientists have been guided fruitfully in their work by dialectical materialism (see pp. 5–6, 52, 63–64). For a critique of Graham's position, see James P. Scanlan, "Dialectical Materialism in Soviet Science and Philosophy," *Slavic Review* 32 (1973), pp. 788–796.

nificance of Marxist materialism is closely bound up with the rejection of supernatural religion. If materialism did not clear the world of gods and spirits, it would not serve the partisan interests of the masses wakening from opiation; it would have less claim to being a "progressive" philosophy; perhaps it would not even need to be directed by the Communist party. Such considerations are not, of course, openly scorned even by the nontraditionalists among Soviet philosophers. Meliukhin's acceptance of "absoluteness" as a property of matter is, among other things, a way of acknowledging the materialist's claim to a monopoly on reality, and when Soviet philosophers speak of "the material unity of the world," they have in mind not simply that the matter of the world is unified but that there is in the world nothing apart from matter. But if there is something of the ideologist in most Soviet philosophers, it is the more ideologically inclined traditionalists such as Orlov whose conception of materialism is rooted in the denial of a nonmaterial realm.

Since the ideologists' materialism makes a clear substantive claim concerning the nature of being, we would expect to find positive arguments offered on its behalf. Yet there is in Soviet philosophy nothing more in the way of support for this strengthened version of materialism than airy assurances to the effect that it is "proved by the whole history of the development of science."[139] The ideological importance of establishing atheism, we might think, would dictate the need for special attention to the philosophical bases of this position, but such attention is not to be found. Soviet philosophers do not even address themselves critically to opposing arguments, such as the well-known "proofs" of the existence of God. Rather, the theses of the idealist or theist are typically treated by Soviet philosophers as symptomatic of some defect or deprivation—particularly a socio-economic deprivation resulting from a class position—which leads the thinker to advance an absurd and consequently indefensible view. The postulation of nonmaterial entities is viewed as an aberration to be handled by removing its causes rather than by presenting arguments against it.

To say that arguments are lacking is not to say, however, that the ideologists' materialism is groundless. Lenin, it will be remembered, required anything knowable to be not only objective but also "given to man in his sensations," and this empiricist proclivity has been a feature of Marxist materialism ever since.[140] On this basis, for the Soviet philosopher the reason there is something wrong with the assertion that God exists is simply that there is no sensory evidence of such a being. Gustav Wetter

---

[139]Z. M. Orudzhev, *Dialektika kak sistema* (Moscow, 1973), p. 135.
[140]Lenin, *Soch.*, vol. 18, p. 131.

has argued in rebuttal that such a consideration might be sufficient to support an agnostic position, but that since the Soviet materialist wishes to espouse atheism it is incumbent upon him to supply "positive arguments in support of his claim."[141] Wetter's objection, however, overlooks the fact that, *on an empiricist basis*, the absence of factual evidence is sufficient for the rejection of an existence claim. For the empirically minded Soviet philosopher, then, the burden of proof clearly rests on the other side, and to ask for arguments establishing that God does *not* exist is viewed as tantamount to asking for a refutation of the presence before one of an unseen and unseeable ghost.

Beyond this single issue of the existence of a nonmaterial realm, the doctrines of the ideological traditionalist no longer play much part in discussions of materialism in the USSR. The dogmatic defense of the Leninist conception of matter found in the writings of Orlov, for example, is largely ignored by serious philosophers. With its jurisdiction essentially reduced to the doctrine of atheism, however, the ideologists' materialism has at the same time been strengthened, in that it is just in the area left to it that it can be absolutely safe from scientific shocks: precisely this area cannot be questioned by science, for anything discovered by the latter must belong to the material world, not to the extramaterial.

Generally speaking, then, the substantive claims of the ideologists' materialism hang simply on the truth of the empiricist theory of knowledge— a feature of Soviet philosophy that we shall examine more fully in a separate chapter to follow. When in popular outlines and textbooks we find Soviet writers asserting that space exploration has disclosed no trace of God in the heavens, we must realize that this primitive "argument" is merely symbolic of a broader empiricist approach.[142] The philosopher may blush, but he will not be able to counter the point on a factual basis. It is this aspect of Soviet philosophy that led H. B. Acton, in his pioneering study *The Illusion of the Epoch*, to conclude that Marxist materialism is essentially positivistic and that it owes much of its appeal to that circumstance: "Marxist atheism is a consequence of Marxist positivism," Acton writes, and he argues that in a technological age this feature of Marxism is enough to recommend it to a broad public.[143]

Acton's observation is surely apt with respect to the third or ideological variety of Soviet materialism as we have examined it. But a more comprehensive reason for the acceptability of Marxist materialism in the USSR

---

[141]Wetter, *Soviet Ideology Today*, p. 30.

[142]Clemens Dutt, ed., *Fundamentals of Marxism-Leninism. Manual*, 2d rev. ed. (Moscow, 1963), p. 35.

[143]H. B. Acton, *The Illusion of the Epoch. Marxism-Leninism as a Philosophical Creed* (London, 1955), p. 65.

may be that it is at least three significantly different views, each of which has a distinctive appeal to a different constituency. How can so large a number of persons, many of them highly educated, in a society as immense as the Soviet Union, so uniformly assert allegiance to a single philosophical creed? Part of the answer, with respect to materialism at least, is that they are subscribing to a number of different creeds with the same name.

The distinction between the scientists', the philosophers', and the ideologists' materialisms is not drawn openly by Soviet writers, but we should not think they do not perceive it. In the ideologically dominated society of the USSR, the confusion of these three views has clear advantages. The scientist and the philosopher can justify their activities by appeal to the mandatory concept of materialism and in so doing can satisfy ideological authorities at the same time that they proceed largely unimpeded by dogmatism in their work. The ideologist, on the other hand, can point to the support of scientists and philosophers in his preaching of materialism and can draw on the plausibility and popularity of the other forms of materialism as recommendations for his own. Thus the illicit confusion of materialism and realism, the "cheap confidence trick" designed to fool the philosophical tyro that so angers Gustav Wetter and other critics of Soviet Marxism,[144] is actually something more than that. It is an integral and mutually beneficial aspect of a perverse intellectual community in which science is freed to progress and even philosophy has a certain independence while nonetheless ideology is enthroned. Without the confusion this aim could not be achieved, and consequently there is no interest on any side in eliminating the confusion. It would be the death of the Soviet scientific and philosophical intelligentsia if, in endorsing materialism, all sides were compelled to talk about the same thing. And they must therefore insist that they *are* talking about the same thing and must vigorously reject the analysis presented in this chapter.

[144]Wetter, *Soviet Ideology Today*, p. 31.

[3]

Objective Dialectics: Dialectics
in the Nature of Things

IF, with respect to materialism, a systematically ambiguous Marxist-Leninist "orthodoxy" has been created that both satisfies Soviet philosophers and does no violence to modern science or to secular common sense, the same cannot be said for dialectics. Called the "living soul" of the Marxist doctrine by Lenin,[1] dialectics is also its most troubled element, a center of fundamental disagreements not simply between philosophers, scientists, and ideologists but among the philosophers themselves. To many Western observers, moreover, dialectics renders Marxist philosophy both puzzling and suspect, as if a familiar outlook—materialism—that most people find intelligible even if they regard it as false has suddenly been transformed into an alien and quite possibly nonsensical set of views. In short, the dialectics component of dialectical materialism is a controversial subject both inside and outside the USSR, and for this reason I shall consider it in some detail in Chapters 3 and 4.

The complexities of the subject include the fact that Soviet philosophers identify within it both an ontological theory concerning the character of the material world (named "objective dialectics" by Engels) and an epistemological theory concerning the character of our knowledge of the material world ("subjective dialectics").[2] Since, in good "materialist"—that is, realist—fashion, our knowledge is held to be derivative from and to reflect the world itself, I shall begin with objective dialectics, and I shall reserve Chapter 4 for an examination of the corresponding epistemological theories of subjective dialectics.

[1]V. I. Lenin, *Polnoe sobranie sochinenii*, 5th ed., 55 vols. (Moscow, 1958–1965), vol. 20, p. 84 (cited hereafter as *Soch.*).
[2]Frederick Engels, *Dialectics of Nature*, trans. and ed. Clemens Dutt (New York, 1940), p. 206.

Basic Elements of Dialectics as an Ontology

For all their disagreements, Soviet dialecticians unanimously endorse a number of broad characterizations of reality that were originally adapted from the philosophy of Hegel by Engels and Lenin. Most Soviet textbook expositions of dialectics limit themselves to these characterizations, which are typically summarized under the three headings of *principles, categories,* and *laws* of dialectics.

The *principles* of dialectics are identified variously by different writers, but a prominent place is always given to two that a recent work calls "the principles of universal connection and development."[3] The superiority of dialectics to "metaphysics," as we saw in Chapter 1, is that the former acknowledges just these two features of the world. To approach something dialectically, it is held, is to consider it, first, as interacting with its environment; to approach it metaphysically, by contrast, is to view it as a separate entity unrelated to other things. For the dialectician, furthermore, reality is changeable and develops over time; the metaphysician, on the other hand, sees reality as static and ahistorical. Hence whatever else a dialectical world may be for Soviet philosophers, it is an interconnected and dynamic world.

Even at this level of generality, it is easy to see that a dialectical outlook inclines the Soviet philosopher toward certain modes of thought. A leaning toward historical analysis, an expectation of evolution and revolution, a tendency to raise questions of genesis and direction, to expand an inquiry to include additional sides of a question, to link an item of investigation with other things or events—all these attitudes are to be expected of a dialectician. Similarly, it is easy to understand the dialectician's readiness to dismiss as "metaphysical" such beliefs as that there is a fixed, timeless "human nature" or that a spiritual phenomenon like religion can fruitfully be examined in isolation from its socioeconomic setting.

A second broad way in which Soviet dialecticians characterize the world is by the use of *categories*—philosophical concepts of the greatest generality that are held to identify the most essential, universal properties and relations of everything that is. Every science has its basic concepts, which capture the fundamental features and connections of its distinctive subject matter, the Marxist-Leninist argues; dialectics, ontologically exhaustive in scope, deals with concepts of maximum abstraction, applying equally to the realms of nature, society, and thought. In elementary Soviet treatments

[3]Yu. A. Kharin, *Fundamentals of Dialectics*, trans. Konstantin Kostrov (Moscow, 1981), pp. 110–111, 164. For a much more elaborate treatment, see F. F. Viakkerev et al., eds., *Materialisticheskaia dialektika v piati tomakh. Tom 1. Ob"ektivnaia dialektika* (Moscow, 1981), pp. 13–81.

of dialectics, there is some variation in the lists of categories presented, for reasons we shall examine later in this chapter. Virtually every list, however, includes 'matter', 'motion', 'space', 'time', 'infinity', and such correlative pairs as 'particular' and 'universal', 'quantity' and 'quality', 'cause' and 'effect', 'necessity' and 'chance', 'possibility' and 'actuality', 'content' and 'form', 'essence' and 'appearance'.[4]

The significance of the categories is of course that they specify universal features of the real world. For the Soviet philosopher, to identify 'cause' and 'effect' as categories is equivalent to asserting the principle of universal causal determinism. "All phenomena in the world, all changes and processes must be induced by certain causes," we read in *Fundamentals*.[5] Similarly, the categorial status of 'essence' and 'appearance' signifies the universality of a real distinction much appealed to in Soviet philosophy—the distinction between the underlying, inner nature of a thing or process (the deep currents of a river, in Lenin's example) and some changeable, superficial phenomenon that is consequent upon that essence (the foam on the river's surface);[6] this distinction gives the Soviet philosopher a doctrine of natural kinds and moreover one that, because of its categorial universality, applies to social and intellectual entities as well as natural. A related Soviet doctrine of broad significance is linked with the categories of 'necessity' and 'chance'. 'Chance', for the Soviet philosopher, means neither that a phenomenon is uncaused nor that we are ignorant of its cause; it signifies, rather, the absence of *necessary* causal determination or determination that proceeds from the essence of the phenomenon in question. Given the physical, cubical nature of a die, when cast on a flat surface it comes to rest of necessity on some one of its sides; *which* side is a matter of chance, being dependent on causes inessential to the die. Capitalists hire workers of necessity; workers sometimes become capitalists by chance.[7]

A third traditional way of characterizing the dialectical real world, and the way on which most textbooks dwell, is by specifying general *laws* that it purportedly obeys. Many such laws are identified by Soviet philosophers in one or another context, but chief among them are the three "basic laws" named by Engels and often regarded as constituting the principal subject matter of philosophy. They are the law of the transformation of quantity into quality and vice versa, the law of the interpenetration of opposites,

[4]F. V. Konstantinov, ed., *The Fundamentals of Marxist-Leninist Philosophy*, trans. R. Daglish (Moscow, 1982), pp. 123–146.

[5]Ibid., p. 129.

[6]Lenin, *Soch.*, vol. 29, p. 116.

[7]A. P. Sheptulin, *Marxist-Leninist Philosophy*, trans. S. Ponomarenko and A. Timofeyev (Moscow, 1978), p. 209.

and the law of the negation of the negation.[8] Even Soviet philosophers who reject the general laws definition of philosophy pay homage to these three laws, which are held to capture critical features of a dialectical reality.

The universal respect accorded the laws is not matched, however, by consensus concerning their exact statement or sphere of application. Neither Engels nor Lenin formulated them in so many words, and there is much debate about their content in Soviet philosophy; for these reasons the laws are far more often named than stated, even in specialized studies. Popular texts are almost invariably vague, often to the point of incoherence, in their efforts to suggest the substance of the laws while at the same time avoiding troublesome questions of interpretation. One of the virtues of the textbook *Fundamentals of Marxist-Leninist Philosophy* is that it hazards actual formulations, which we shall follow here.

The law of the transformation of quantity into quality and vice versa, according to the authors of *Fundamentals*, states:

> There is an interconnection and interaction between the quantitative and qualitative aspects of an object thanks to which small, at first imperceptible, quantitative changes, accumulating gradually, sooner or later upset the measure of that object and evoke fundamental qualitative changes which take place in the form of leaps and whose occurrence depends on the nature of the objects in question and the conditions of their development in diverse forms.[9]

Central to this formulation, as to most other statements of the law by Soviet philosophers, are the notions that quantitative aspects of things or events can be distinguished from qualitative aspects and that the two are related in such a fashion that relatively gradual quantitative changes precipitate relatively sudden qualitative changes.

According to this law, all processes of development are punctuated by what Engels (following Hegel) called "nodes," at which change is both accelerated and deepened. Hegel and Engels used the illustration of the boiling and freezing points of water. The temperature of water changes gradually as quantities of heat are added; at 100 degrees centigrade (the "node"), however, a more sudden and radical alteration takes place: the water changes in character ("quality") from liquid to vapor. The range of temperatures between zero and 100 degrees is a "measure"—that is, a range over which quantitative change proceeds without producing quali-

---

[8]Engels, *Dialectics of Nature*, p. 26.
[9]Konstantinov, *Fundamentals* (1982), p. 109 (italics omitted). The term 'measure' has been substituted here for the term 'proportion', which the translator uses to render the Russian *mera*. 'Measure' is the accepted English equivalent of 'mera' in this context.

tative change. The transition from one quality to another that takes place at the node is called a "leap"—a term that appropriately suggests both relative suddenness and movement to another level.[10] Other favorite illustrations in Soviet philosophical literature are the change effected when the division of some quantity of a chemical compound reaches the level of a single molecule, beyond which the substance is no longer (say) H_2O but separate atoms of H and O; the emergence, after long processes of evolution, of organic life from nonliving matter; and, of course, social revolutions—sudden qualitative leaps such as the transition from capitalism to socialism, precipitated by gradual quantitative changes in society. The point of the "and vice versa" addition (which is often, as in the *Fundamentals* formulation that I gave above, tacitly understood rather than stated) is simply to acknowledge that quantitative changes are preceded as well as followed by qualitative changes. In real development, for the Soviet dialectician, periods of evolution alternate with revolutionary leaps to ever different qualitative levels.

The second basic law of dialectics—Engels's "law of the interpenetration of opposites"—is now usually called by Soviet philosophers "the law of the unity and struggle of opposites." In *Fundamentals* it is formulated as follows:

> According to this law all things, phenomena and processes possess internal contradictions, opposing aspects and tendencies that are in a state of interconnection and mutual negation; the struggle of opposites gives an internal impulse to development, leads to the building up of contradictions, which are resolved at a certain stage in the disappearance of the old and the appearance of the new.[11]

Thus the dialectical world is a scene of dynamic contention. There are, of course, apparent stabilities and unities, but these are without exception analyzable into deeper oppositions that are the seeds of change. From the positive and negative electrical charges within an atomic nucleus to the conflict of economic classes in a social system, the presence of what the Soviet philosopher calls "objective contradictions" is a universal feature of reality.

Whereas the first law characterizes the *manner* in which development occurs, the law of the unity and struggle of opposites is often said by Soviet

---

[10]Frederick Engels, *Anti-Dühring. Herr Evgen Dühring's Revolution in Science* (Moscow, 1947), pp. 59, 151. For Hegel's discussion of these points, see the section entitled "Nodal Line of Measure Relations" in *Hegel's Science of Logic*, trans. W. H. Johnson and L. G. Struthers, 2 vols. (London, 1929), vol. 1, pp. 386–390.

[11]Konstantinov, *Fundamentals* (1982), p. 117 (italics omitted).

philosophers to indicate the *source* of development: development results from the dynamism of conflicting elements within matter itself.[12] Here we encounter once again the notion of the *self-movement* of matter, so important to Soviet ideologists as obviating the need for an external "First Mover" of the material world. No less important is the ideological application of the law in the social sphere. Affirmation of the reality of "objective contradictions" in society is often seen as the first line of defense against "opportunists" and "revisionists" who argue that the relations of bourgeoisie and proletariat under capitalism can be cooperative rather than antagonistic.[13]

The third basic law of dialectics—the "law of the negation of the negation"—is the least fixed in its formulation. In some statements it appears to add little to the first two laws; the Soviet *Philosophical Encyclopedia*, for example, presents it as the law according to which "development unfolds in definite cycles, within the framework of which the contradictions characteristic of each are resolved."[14] Considerably richer is the formulation in *Fundamentals*:

> The law of the negation of the negation is a law whose operation conditions the connection and continuity between that which is negated and that which negates. For this reason dialectical negation is not naked, "needless" negation, rejecting all previous development, but the condition of development that retains and preserves in itself all the progressive content of previous stages, repeats at a higher level certain features of the initial stages and has in general a progressive, ascending character.[15]

This formulation captures Engels's Hegelian notion that dialectical development is both progressive and conservative—that successive qualitative leaps beyond ("negations of") a previous state do not simply annihilate it but eventually return on a higher level, spiral-fashion, to what was positive in the old state. In Engels's example, the barley plant "negates" the seed from which it grows, in the sense of replacing the seed in the natural cycle; but the plant is in turn replaced ("negated") not by one seed but by the dozens it produces; and if we bring in "the gardener's art," Engels adds, the result of the double negation could be not simply more but better seeds.[16] More commonly cited by Soviet philosophers is a sociohistorical

[12]M. F. Vorob'ev, "O soderzhanii i formakh zakona otritsaniia otritsaniia," *Vestnik Leningradskogo universiteta*, 1956, no. 23, p. 57.
[13]A. P. Sheptulin, *Osnovnye zakony dialektiki* (Moscow, 1966), p. 101.
[14]F.V. Konstantinov et al., eds., *Filosofskaia entsiklopediia*, 5 vols. (Moscow, 1960–1970), vol. 4, p. 188.
[15]Konstantinov, *Fundamentals* (1982), p. 122.
[16]Engels, *Anti-Dühring*, pp. 162–163.

example used by both Marx and Engels: the institution of private property
negated the communal form of land ownership found in primitive societies,
according to the Marxist reading of history; but the proletarian revolution,
in negating the institution of private property, returns to common ownership not in its original form but in "a far higher and more developed
form" in which it is no longer an obstacle to high economic productivity.[17]
Because of this emphasis on what is called in *Fundamentals* the "positive,
ascending character" of development, the third law is sometimes said to
indicate the *direction* of development, as the first two indicate its manner
and source.[18]

The Fortunes of Dialectics under Stalin and After

Popular Soviet treatments of dialectics typically do not openly indicate
that there are theoretical difficulties with the subject. In fact, however, in
dialectics the intellectual problems of Soviet philosophy are at their most
acute, as discussions on the more specialized, technical level of philosophy
amply testify.

The problems go back to the very beginnings of systematic dialectical
materialism and specifically to the tensions created by grafting an essentially idealist conceptual apparatus—dialectics—onto a materialist ontology. These tensions first surfaced in Soviet philosophy in the 1920s in the
form of bitter disputes between a group of scientifically inclined materialists
called "mechanists" (among them were Aleksandr Aleksandrovich Bogdanov [1873–1928] and Nikolai Ivanovich Bukharin [1888–1937]) and a
group of dialecticians with a strong admiration for Hegel, called "Deborinists" after their leader, Abram Moiseevich Deborin (1881–1964).[19] When
in 1929–1930 the dispute between the two sides was terminated, it was
not by any philosophical resolution but by the imposition of a Stalinist
philosophical orthodoxy that required the denaturing of both positions
and the acceptance of a purely external combination of "dialectics" and
"materialism." Under the banner of "the unity of theory and practice," a
new Soviet philosophical establishment, led by Mark Borisovich Mitin (b.

[17]Ibid., p. 165.
[18]Vorob'ev, p. 57.
[19]A good brief summary of the controversy may be found in Richard T. De George, *Patterns
of Soviet Thought. The Origins and Development of Dialectical and Historical Materialism*
(Ann Arbor, 1966), pp. 179–184. The tensions between dialectics and materialism have been
noted by many critics of Marxist philosophy; see, for example, V. P. Vysheslavtsev, *Filosofskaia nishcheta marksizma*, 2d ed. (Frankfurt am Main, 1957), pp. 45–48; and Gustav
A. Wetter, *Dialectical Materialism. A Historical and Systematic Survey of Philosophy in the
Soviet Union*, trans. Peter Heath (London, 1958), pp. 364–365.

1901) and Pavel Fedorovich Iudin (1899–1968), stressed ardent Communist partisanship and the practical application of dogmas at the expense of serious philosophical investigation.

Although in principle dedicated to a dialectical outlook, the Marxist-Leninist orthodoxy of the 1930s and 1940s permitted little attention to the finer points of dialectics as presented in Engels's *Dialectics of Nature* or Lenin's *Philosophical Notebooks*, not to mention Hegel's *Science of Logic*. The intellectual level of the treatment of dialectics in the Stalin era was set by the essay entitled "Dialectical and Historical Materialism," which appeared in 1938 as part of chapter 4 of *A History of the Communist Party of the Soviet Union (Bolsheviks). Short Course.* Later attributed to Stalin himself but almost surely ghostwritten, this superficial exposition of Marxist doctrine quickly became the gospel for Soviet philosophers. In it all talk of "categories" and "laws" was abandoned in favor of a simplified version of dialectics that identified four "features" of the dialectical world—interconnectedness, dynamic development, the transition from quantity to quality, and the presence of internal contradictions.[20] Although the last two of these features preserved in germ the first two of Engels's laws, no trace remained of the law of the negation of the negation—an omission that cynics have attributed to Stalin's fear of being "negated" himself. Hailed by sycophants, on the other hand, as the liberation of dialectics from Hegelian mystification, the *Short Course* presentation fixed the limits of the philosophical treatment of dialectics in Stalin's time.

Release of Soviet philosophers from the Stalinist straitjacket after 1953 has meant a return to the texts of Lenin, Engels, and Hegel and the reopening of the many questions raised by the attempt to develop dialectics on a materialist foundation and in a modern scientific world. Very soon after Stalin's death, a multidimensional dialogue on dialectics began, the results of which have been the production of an enormous body of literature and the reemergence of the mechanist-Deborinist controversy without the old labels.

To characterize the post-Stalin debate briefly, let us take only one of the standard Soviet approaches to dialectics—namely, category theory. A problem confronting Soviet dialecticians was the lack of any model to follow in developing a *materialist* theory of dialectical categories. Neither Marx nor Engels attempted to construct such a theory. Lenin gave considerable attention to categories in his *Philosophical Notebooks* (1914–1915), but he did so in the form of a running commentary on Hegel's

[20]*History of the Communist Party of the Soviet Union (Bolsheviks). Short Course*, edited by a Commission of the Central Committee of the C.P.S.U. (B.) (New York, 1939), pp. 106–109.

Science of Logic, without offering an explicit system of his own.[21] Indeed Lenin seemed to suggest that the Hegelian categorial system would be perfectly adequate once freed from its idealist trappings. Further reflection, however, suggests that freeing it would be no easy task, for the very identification and ordering of the categories in the Hegelian system was grounded in the equation of being with thought. Surely a materialist dialectician could endorse neither Hegel's relegation of the category 'matter' to a subordinate position nor his giving so prominent a role to the category 'nothing'—a notion that can have no ontological significance for the materialist. And many other Hegelian categories as well—'contradiction' and 'the absolute' prominently among them—seem appropriate for the world of thought but not for a world of matter. What, then, are the categories of a *materialist* dialectics, and how are they related?

Serious attempts to answer these questions began early in the post-Stalin period. Vasilii Petrovich Tugarinov in *The Correlation of the Categories of Dialectical Materialism* (1956) drew selectively on Hegel to present a system of more than fifty categories, beginning with the fundamental categories of substance ('nature', 'being', 'matter', 'phenomenon'), proceeding to attributive categories ('motion', 'space', 'time', and others), and concluding with relational categories ('quantity-quality-leap', 'content-form', and many more).[22] In the same year, M. M. Rozental' and G. M. Shtraks in *Categories of Materialist Dialectics* suggested that, since all knowledge of reality begins with the perception of phenomena, the initial categories might be the pair 'phenomenon-essence', followed by a succession of categories each with some conceptual link to its predecessor—'cause', 'effect', 'necessity', 'chance', 'law', and so on, through a total of eighteen categories.[23] Both efforts met with some favor, but they also stimulated other Soviet philosophers to try their hands; and in the ensuing years a wide variety of categorial systems have been suggested by a large number of writers, including V. S. Bibler, B. M. Kedrov, V. S. Lutai, V. I. Mal'tsev, A. P. Sheptulin, and D. I. Shirokanov. The diversity of these schemes with respect to both the number and the order of the categories is seen by one recent Soviet observer as proceeding from differences in "images of dialectics, in ideas of what the essence of the theory of dialectics is and of what are the ways of constructing it and the methods of expounding it."[24]

[21]Lenin, *Soch.*, vol. 29, pp. 79–218.

[22]V. P. Tugarinov, *Sootnoshenie kategorii dialekticheskogo materializma (Leningrad, 1956).*

[23]M. M. Rozental' and G. M. Shtraks, eds., *Kategorii materialisticheskoi dialektiki* (Moscow, 1956), pp. 50, 62ff.

[24]A. P. Kapustin, "Spory o putiakh izlozheniia dialektiki (Obzor)," *Voprosy filosofii,* 1979, no. 6, p. 169. Concerning the range of Soviet positions, see Z. M. Orudzhev, *Dialektika kak sistema* (Moscow, 1973), pp. 13–23; Guy Planty-Bonjour,*The Categories of Dialectical Materialism. Contemporary Soviet Ontology,* trans. T. J. Blakeley (New York, 1967), pp. 39–59; and T. V. Bogomolova and V. I. Kirillov, "Problema vzaimosviazi kategorii dialektiki (obzor literatury)," *Filosofskie nauki,* 1981, no. 2, pp. 43–55.

The diversity, in fact, extends beyond those philosophers who seek to construct finished systems of traditional philosophical categories. For they are the modern-day Deborinists, neo-Hegelians who see the world as fitting a web of interdependent philosophical concepts essentially discerned by Hegel, for all his idealistic errors. Ranged against them are the neomechanists—the more positivistically minded, less traditionalistic Soviet philosophers who reject what one of them, I. S. Narskii, has called "a kind of 'cult' of the idealistic dialectics of Hegel." Fundamentally opposed to the notion of a system of timeworn categories ringing a few materialist changes on the *Science of Logic*, these philosophers argue that dialectics must be responsive to conceptual developments in the sciences. "It would be a great mistake," writes Narskii, "to limit epistemological investigations to categories of dialectical materialism developed earlier," and he argues for the recognition and study of new categories such as 'sign', 'structure', 'fact', 'information', and 'model'.[25] V. I. Sviderskii, contending that Hegel's concepts have been superseded, urges "the development of ever newer and newer categories of dialectics."[26]

Some antitraditionalists in Soviet philosophy, finally, reject the very idea of a categorial "system," whether composed of old, "philosophical" (that is, Hegelian) concepts or newer, scientific ones. One argument, advanced by A. S. Arsen'ev and others, is that systematization is contrary to the true spirit of dialectics as a science of pervasive change and genuine qualitative novelty.[27] A quite different, thoroughly anti-Hegelian argument was presented by the distinguished Georgian philosopher and historian of philosophy Konstantin Spiridonovich Bakradze (1898–1970) and his followers. For there to be a "system" of categories, Bakradze contended, the categories must be, as Hegel thought they were, immanently and necessarily related; each must be conceptually "contained" in the others, must "pass into" the others. But all such talk is purely figurative, Bakradze believed, and he held that, to avoid intellectual confusion and the idealistic imposition of the characteristics of the world of thought on the world of being, we must keep categories separate and distinct, each doing its own job.[28]

Thus on a broad range of questions concerning the most general concepts available to philosophy to describe the real world, contemporary Marxism-Leninism is marked by fundamental and persistent disputes. The number and identity of the categories, their relations to each other, the need for

---

[25] F. V. Konstantinov et al., eds, *Dialektika i logika nauchnogo poznaniia. Materialy Soveshchaniia po sovremennym problemam materialisticheskoi dialektiki, 7–9 aprelia 1965 g.* (Moscow, 1966), p. 366. For earlier comments on the continuation of the Deborinist-mechanist debate in the post-Stalin period, see J. M. Bocheński, "Philosophy Studies," *Soviet Survey*, 1960, no. 31 (January-March), pp. 73–74.

[26] Konstantinov et al., *Dialektika*, p. 250.

[27] Orudzhev, *Dialektika kak sistema*, pp. 16–18.

[28] K. S. Bakradze, *Sistema i metod filosofii Gegelia* (Tbilisi, 1958). pp. 433ff.

and the possibility of new categories, the possibility and the character of a categorial system—on all these questions Soviet philosophers continue to disagree.[29]

The existence of such basic disagreement is met with ambivalence in the Soviet philosophical community. On the one hand the disputes are welcomed—especially by the more independently minded philosophers—as a sign of intellectual vitality and a precondition for philosophical progress. The path to truth, G. S. Batishchev reminded his colleagues in 1979, lies through "disputatious interactions among different conceptual tendencies."[30] On the other hand the persistence of disputes at the very heart of dialectical materialism is something of an embarrassment to many Soviet philosophers, and the embarrassment is the more acute the closer the philosopher is to the seats of power and orthodoxy in Soviet life. How can the "world-view" functions of philosophy be performed, how can dialectical materialism play its crucial role of orienting progressive forces in the struggle to build communism, if it is not clear what concepts, in what relations, constitute a materialist dialectics, or even whether the model for constructing one is to be Hegel or modern science?

Concern over such matters has lent urgency to the troublesome questions of dialectics and has led to the lavishing of bureaucratic and academic attention on the field. Scholarly conferences on dialectics have abounded in the post-Stalin period.[31] Research and publication in dialectics has been given special impetus by the establishment of "task forces" (*problemnye gruppy* or *problemnye sovety*), the aim of which is said to be "the creation of fundamental works in the theory of materialist dialectics."[32] One such group, headed by B. M. Kedrov, has worked in Moscow since the late 1950s;[33] others operate in Leningrad, Rostov-on-Don, Kiev, and Alma Ata. For all this activity, however, Soviet philosophers have not yet, in the three decades since Stalin's death, raised dialectics to a state of perfection acceptable to the Communist party. The Party newspaper, *Pravda*, ad-

---

[29]For a summary of these disputes, see Bogomolova and Kirillov. In the light of these disagreements it is not surprising that in the past few years Soviet philosophers have increasingly turned from proposing still further "systems" of categories to examining more fundamental, methodological questions concerning the nature and role of a philosophical category; see, for example, M. I. Konkin, *Problema formirovaniia i razvitiia filosofskikh kategorii* (Moscow, 1980).

[30]*Dialekticheskoe protivorechie* (Moscow, 1979), p. 40.

[31]The largest such conference met in Moscow in April 1965; some six hundred philosophers took part (see Konstantinov et al., *Dialektika*, p. 2).

[32]"O sostoianii i napravleniiakh filosofskikh issledovanii," *Kommunist*, 1979, no. 15, p. 71.

[33]Kedrov describes the work of his group in "Lenin's Plans for Elaborating the Theory of Materialist Dialectics," in V. Lorentson and B. Yudin, eds., *Marxist Dialectics Today*, 2d ed. (Moscow, 1979), pp. 48–82.

dressing itself in 1975 to what it called "The Lofty Duty of Soviet Philosophers," wrote that "among the tasks confronting philosophical science at the present time, development of the theory of dialectics is central."[34] *Kommunist*, the Party's chief theoretical journal, declared in a 1979 editorial that "the chief shortcoming of philosophical investigations continues to be the slow resolution of the task, bequeathed us by Lenin, of developing the theory of dialectics as an integral system of doctrines."[35] One consequence of this heightened recent concern has been the establishment of still larger task forces with still more ambitious programs.[36]

What has been accomplished by this massive attack on the problems of materialist dialectics? It is impossible in a chapter to assess the entire sweep of current Soviet work in dialectics as an ontological theory. By focusing on the traditional three basic laws of dialectics, however, we can judge the accomplishments of Soviet philosophers on some matters of critical importance for dialectical theory.

An Appraisal of Soviet Work on the Three Basic Laws of Dialectics

Not long after the death of Stalin the law of the negation of the negation made its reappearance in Soviet philosophy books, and Engels's three laws replaced Stalin's four features as the favored format for presenting dialectics. Subsequently, despite attempts on the part of individual philosophers to reduce one or another of the laws to a lesser status or to add new laws, Engels's three laws have retained their hold on the minds of Soviet dialecticians, all of whom affirm their importance. More than that, they affirm the *truth* of the laws: they all accept the thesis that each of the laws is a correct description of the objective world. Perhaps surpris-

---

[34]"Vysokii dolg sovetskikh filosofov," *Pravda*, September 19, 1975, p. 3.

[35]"O sostoianii," p. 71. See also *Pravda*, August 11, 1983, pp. 2–3.

[36]Three of the most prominent figures in Soviet philosophical officialdom—the Academicians L. F. Il'ichev, F. V. Konstantinov, and M. B. Mitin—are now directing such groups at the Institute of Philosophy, Leningrad State University, and Moscow State University, respectively. Il'ichev's group has published the first three volumes of a proposed four-volume work entitled *Materialisticheskaia dialektika kak obshchaia teoriia razvitiia* (Moscow, 1982–1983). The group headed by Konstantinov plans a five-volume study (*Materialisticheskaia dialektika v piati tomakh*), of which the first three volumes—including that edited by F. F. Viakkerev et al., cited above—have been published (Moscow, 1981–1983). Of the eight volumes proposed by Mitin's group under the general title *Marksistsko-leninskaia dialektika v vos'mi knigakh*, only the first—*Materialisticheskaia dialektika kak nauchnaia sistema*, ed. A. P. Sheptulin—has yet appeared (Moscow, 1983). Each of the last two groups consists of over a hundred scholars (see "Razrabotka teorii dialektiki v vuzovskikh kollektivakh," *Filosofskie nauki*, 1982, no. 1, p. 159).

ingly, however, this element of ideologically inspired dogmatism does not forestall disputes concerning the laws in the USSR; it simply affects the form that those disputes take.

For the problem, as the Soviet philosopher sees it, is to find the *sense* in which the laws can be said to describe the objective world correctly. Instead of asking, as another philosopher might, whether or not these laws are true, and what facts of the world tell for or against them, the Soviet philosopher asks, rather, to what facts of the world these laws must be addressed, and what must they say about these facts, given that the laws are true. The Soviet philosopher confronted with the laws of dialectics is in a position comparable to that cited by Naan with respect to infinity in the previous chapter: he "knows" that the laws are true, but he does not know what they mean. Nonetheless his search for meaning, provided it is honest and informed (as it often is), can be as solicitous of the facts of the world as the other philosopher's search for truth. Let us see what progress has been made in interpreting each of the three laws in recent years.

The Law of the Transformation of
Quantity into Quality and Vice Versa

In itself the notion that relatively abrupt qualitative changes are produced by relatively gradual quantitative changes is a suggestive one, and even a modern thinker as distant from Marxism as Teilhard de Chardin has made use of it.[37] It stands as a useful warning against simplistic reductionism in the sciences. Certainly many processes in nature and in social life conform to it: cooling water to zero degrees centigrade does create a sudden change in its condition, and a worker must accumulate free capital, as Marx observed, in order to make a qualitative leap into the bourgeoisie. Soviet philosophers, however, are not content to regard the formula as merely cautionary or as describing large numbers of events. They view it, rather, as a universal law of change. And in that regard it must be said that Soviet philosophers have experienced great difficulty in finding an interpretation of the law that would allow it to be true of every process in the realms of nature, society, and thought.

I do not say that no faulty versions of the law have been put to rest since Stalin's day. It is no longer generally believed by Soviet philosophers that every qualitative leap is a progressive or "ascending" development. Stalin, in presenting the feature of dialectics that corresponds to the first

[37]Pierre Teilhard de Chardin, *The Phenomenon of Man*, trans. Bernard Wall, 2d ed. (New York, 1965), p. 152.

law, had spoken of qualitative transition as "an onward and upward movement ... , a development from the simple to the complex, from the lower to the higher."[38] Obviously, however, the movement from water to ice is not a movement from lower to higher, or if it were, the equally common reverse movement from ice to water would then disprove the law. The standard Soviet position now is that the law does not assert that all change is progressive, but simply that all change can be characterized by the quantity-quality interrelation.[39]

Other problems have not been so easy to handle. A number of them are associated with the Hegelian concept of a "measure" within which quantity and quality are linked. According to the law, a given measure persists until a node is reached at which further quantitative change cannot be accommodated without an alteration in quality. This point is reached, to recall the formulation of the law in *Fundamentals*, through "small, at first imperceptible, quantitative changes, accumulating gradually." Hence a measure has often been interpreted as a range of values over which, in the words of *Fundamentals*, "one can change certain quantitative properties of an object without its undergoing any significant [that is, qualitative] changes."[40] The difficulty with this interpretation is that it precludes many of Engels's favorite examples of quantity-quality transition from having measures. Engels was fascinated by the atomic relationships found in the periodic table of elements and in regular compound series such as that of the oxides of nitrogen; indeed it was in chemistry, he thought, that the law scored its greatest triumphs.[41] Prominent among his own examples are cases such as the difference between an oxygen molecule (O_2) and a molecule of ozone (O_3) and the difference between the nitrogen oxides NO and N_2O. But in these cases the qualitative difference in the substances is produced by the addition of a single atomic unit. In such instances, far from there being "small, at first imperceptible, quantitative changes," there is altogether absent any range within which quantitative changes do *not* produce qualitative changes.[42]

To avoid the problem, Soviet philosophers now often define 'measure' in a weaker manner that is no doubt closer to what Engels and Hegel had in mind—namely, as expressing a correlation between quantitative and qualitative changes without any commitment as to the range of the former.

[38] *History of the Communist Party*, p. 107.
[39] See, for example, E. K. Voishvillo, D. P. Gorskii, and I. S. Narskii, eds., *Dialektika nauchnogo poznaniia. Ocherk dialekticheskoi logiki* (Moscow, 1978), p. 16.
[40] Konstantinov, *Fundamentals* (1982), p. 105.
[41] Engels, *Dialectics of Nature*, pp. 30–33. Hegel also stressed chemistry, and indeed the oxides of nitrogen, in his discussion of the quantity-quality connection (*Hegel's Science of Logic*, pp. 388ff).
[42] Gustav A. Wetter, *Soviet Ideology Today*, trans. Peter Heath (New York, 1966), p. 115.

One of the most careful formulations of this correlation in recent Soviet philosophical literature reads as follows, where X_1 is a particular state of a system X:

> For every X there must exist some definite [quantitative] value A, such that as soon as X_1 acquires a value less than A, the corresponding quality is immediately destroyed, inasmuch as the measure is broken. Likewise for every variable there must exist a [quantitative] value B, such that as soon as the corresponding variable acquires a value greater than B there is a departure from the limits of the measure and the given qualitative determination is destroyed. The corresponding values of the variables form the upper and lower limits of the space of the measure.[43]

This formulation does not, of course, rule out a range of quantitative changes on a given qualitative level: values intermediate between A and B would form such a range. But Engels's single-unit alterations can also be accommodated, for the difference between A and B could be small to the point of nonexistence; nothing in the formulation prevents A from equaling B.[44]

We have solved the immediate problem, but at the same time we have found another difficulty with the category of 'measure' in Soviet discussions of the first law. For if at the one extreme the difference between A and B could be nonexistent, at the other extreme it could be indefinitely great. Quantitative changes might continue over an indefinitely large range without "breaking" the measure—that is, without getting from A to B. What is the measure of a fossil, which endures now as it has for eons? Quantitative microchanges are no doubt going on within it; but when will they produce a qualitative change in the nature of the fossil? To take a process of another sort, in subdividing a small heap of sand we shall soon reach a node at which further quantitative diminution can take place only by breaking down a grain of sand into molecules of silica and other substances. But could we not *add* grains of sand to the heap forever without breaking a measure?

Soviet philosophers have thus far answered such questions only with the faith that all processes eventually, if continued long enough, reach a node: in the language of *Fundamentals*, quantitative changes "sooner or later" upset a given measure.[45] On the face of it, the indeterminateness of

---

[43]Viakkerev et al, *Materialisticheskaia dialektika*, p. 278.

[44]Even when they provide an interpretation of 'measure' that does accord with Engels's examples, however, Soviet philosophers sometimes lapse into the old formulations. Thus we read that "in every fixed relationship there exists an interval of quantitative changes within the bounds of which they do not lead to qualitative changes"(ibid., p. 296).

[45]Konstantinov, *Fundamentals* (1982), p. 109.

this answer is helpful to Soviet philosophers. They need never accept the persistence of a given measure, however lengthy, as evidence against the law; they can always maintain that the measure in question—whether that of a fossil or that of the capitalist socioeconomic system—is simply a very long one. In fact, however, this openness with respect to the duration of a measure renders the law vacuous by robbing it of all predictive value. For any given process with which we are not already familiar independently of the law, the law provides us with no clues to future change; at no point in the process does the law give us grounds for expecting either that quantitative change *will* take place without qualitative (for the node may be at hand) or that quantitative change *will not* take place without qualitative (for the node may be yet to come).

If the category of measure creates problems for the first law, the same is true of the notion of a qualitative leap. In traditional formulations of the law, as we have seen, a qualitative change is said to be distinguished from the quantitative change that precedes it by its relative suddenness. Certainly such a distinction may plausibly be applied to many processes in nature and society, from the freezing of water to the Bolshevik revolution. On the other hand there are also many processes that do not so happily show qualitative change to be leaplike. Molten glass (as Harry Acton observed) hardens gradually—a circumstance that permits it to be worked.[46] The emergence of new biological species, which Soviet philosophers themselves frequently cite as examples of qualitative change, cannot be said to take place suddenly.[47] But by far the most serious case for Soviet philosophers is a process that, paradoxically, has never actually been carried to completion but is said to be going on now in the USSR—namely, the qualitative but gradual transition from socialism to communism. According to Marxist-Leninist social theory, no revolutionary leap is required to move from the present socialist order, in which some class differences and a state still exist, to the eventual paradise of stateless, classless communism. The need to accommodate in dialectical theory a protracted evolution to communism has been one of the principal spurs to discussion of the first law in the post-Stalin period.

The accommodation, it might seem, could best be made by dropping the requirement that a qualitative change must be a "leap." In fact, the term was not used by Stalin when he made his influential proclamation in 1950 to the effect that qualitative changes need not be "explosions" but could take place gradually.[48] Subsequent Soviet philosophers, however,

[46]H. B. Acton, *The Illusion of the Epoch. Marxism-Leninism as a Philosophical Creed* (London, 1955), p. 86.
[47]Sheptulin, *Marxist-Leninist Philosophy*, p. 256.
[48]I. Stalin, *Marksizm i voprosy iazykoznaniia* ([Moscow], 1950), pp. 55–59.

adopted the confusing policy of retaining the word 'leap' but expanding its meaning, to the point of including what its plain sense rules out—namely, gradual, progressive changes. In making this choice, Soviet philosophers were perhaps moved by revolutionary devotion to the word, perhaps by the fact that no less an authority than Engels allowed leaps to be gradual.[49] In any event, the expression 'gradual leap' is now coin of the realm in Soviet philosophical transactions, and it turns out that gradual leaps are not even exceptional but are one of the two "typical and most general forms" of leaps.[50]

The least that might be expected of Soviet philosophers is that, having adopted this novel usage, they accept its implications as well and recognize that they can no longer employ relative gradualness as a distinguishing feature of quantitative alterations. But many philosophers refuse to do so; and either victimized by their own semantic shift or seeking to exploit it for pedagogical or ideological purposes, they end up contradicting themselves, sometimes on adjoining pages. Thus Sheptulin in his textbook *Marxist-Leninist Philosophy*, after distinguishing quantitative changes, which take place "gradually, continuously," from qualitative changes, which occur "abruptly,...as a break in continuity," immediately goes on to speak of qualitative changes that occur "by way of gradually accumulating the elements of a new quality and discarding those of the old."[51]

For the more careful Soviet philosopher, the only acceptable course is to give up gradualness and seek to distinguish between quantitative and qualitative changes by reference to more essential characteristics. This task might seem to be easy, but quite the reverse has proved to be the case in Soviet philosophical discussions. Traditionally, Soviet philosophers have adhered fairly closely to a Hegelian notion of 'quality' as meaning not any property of a thing but its inner nature, the "determinateness" of the object that makes it the object it is.[52] Around this vague core of meaning, however, Soviet philosophers have developed a wide range of conflicting views of quality, none of which seems capable of handling all the counterexamples that are now raised almost as freely by Soviet philosophers in criticizing each other as by Western critics of Soviet philosophy. Among the issues that divide Soviet thinkers are such substantive questions as how to distinguish between the categories of 'quality' and 'essence', whether a thing has one quality or many, and whether things have properties that are neither quantitative nor qualitative.[53]

[49]Engels, *Anti-Dühring*, p. 83.
[50]Konstantinov, *Fundamentals* (1982), p. 107.
[51]Sheptulin, *Marxist-Leninist Philosophy*, pp. 254–255.
[52]Konstantinov, *Fundamentals* (1982), p. 103.
[53]Sheptulin, *Osnovnye zakony dialektiki*, pp. 38–48, 60–74.

In the welter of opposing views, two may be singled out as representative of major tendencies—a more traditional view and a more innovative one. The former is that of Aleksandr Petrovich Sheptulin (b. 1929), who follows the Hegelian usage of identifying quality with "what a thing is"; quantity, on the other hand, Sheptulin defines as "the totality of properties indicating a thing's dimensions or magnitude."[54] Chlorine, in his view, is a gas, poisonous, yellowish-green in color, and so on; such properties he calls its "qualities." Properties that make up its quantity, on the other hand, are that it is 2.5 times heavier than air, that its nucleus contains seventeen protons, and the like. Sheptulin does not restrict quality to essential properties; any property that characterizes "what a thing is" during any part of its existence or in any set of circumstances, he argues, is a quality of that object. Thus liquidity is a quality of H_2O despite the fact that it is displayed only between zero and 100 degrees centigrade. Such temporary or conditional properties Sheptulin calls "nonbasic qualities"; "basic" qualities are those that a thing "has always, in any relation and under any conditions," such as, in the case of H_2O, having one oxygen atom in its molecule.[55]

Sheptulin's view addresses a number of the key questions in the debate, but clearly its ultimate value depends on the soundness of his initial distinction between "what a thing is" and its dimensions or magnitude. Not only does Sheptulin fail to defend this distinction adequately, it breaks down repeatedly in his own illustrations of the law. Thus after stating that the presence of seventeen protons in its nucleus is a *quantitative* characteristic of chlorine, Sheptulin writes on the next page that having one oxygen atom in its molecule is part of the basic *quality* of water.[56] In another example, he asserts that it is a qualitative characteristic of an angle in plane geometry that it has two sides and a quantitative characteristic that it subtends a particular number of degress; but why is the possession of *two* sides any less quantitative than the subtending of *n* degrees?[57] The problem becomes still more acute when we consider the latitude that can be given the term 'nonbasic quality' in Sheptulin's conception. Being 47 degrees centigrade characterizes "what water is" at a certain point in the transition from ice to steam; why is it not, then, a nonbasic *qualitative* property of water? But in that case the change of water from 46 to 47 degrees is just as much a qualitative as a quantitative change. It is perhaps in response to anticipated objections of this sort that Sheptulin advances the dark doctrine that in fact every property of an object "possesses" *both*

[54]Ibid., p. 45; Sheptulin, *Marxist-Leninist Philosophy*, p. 248.
[55]Sheptulin, *Marxist-Leninist Philosophy*, p. 249.
[56]Ibid., pp. 248–249.
[57]Sheptulin, *Osnovnye zakony dialektiki*, p. 45.

quantity and quality.[58] This muddies the waters hopelessly, for to say of any property that it has quantity and quality is presumably to say that *it* is characterized by both quantitative and qualitative properties, each of which must in turn have properties of both sorts, and so on without end.

The second, innovative conception represents a tendency that has won extensive support in Soviet philosophy in recent years, to the point where it might be considered the new orthodoxy in discussions of the first law of dialectics. This is what is called the "systems" or "systems-structural" approach to the quantity-quality relation, and it has been associated with the advocacy, by V. I. Sviderskii and others, of the idea that the categories of 'element' and 'structure' are central to dialectics. Sviderskii's 1962 book on those categories applied them to the quantity-quality distinction, among others; and despite criticism by traditionalists, many Soviet philosophers more inclined to respect post-Newtonian science than Hegel have been impressed with the analysis.[59] It figures prominently in much Soviet work in the philosophy of biology, in the Soviet *Philosophical Encyclopedia* article on the first law, and in other authoritative works.[60]

Central to the systems approach is the view of an object or phenomenon as a system of more or less numerous elements in more or less numerous and complex relations with each other. The number of elements and relations is clearly a quantitative dimension. More than that, the elements of a system are said to have varying "magnitudes." Hence quantity, in this approach, is a combination of the two values of number and magnitude.[61] The term 'quality', on the other hand, is held to refer to the structure of the system as a whole—that is, to the particular, more or less stable organization of elements that characterizes it overall. A qualitative transition, then, according to V. Tiukhtin, is "a transition from a system of one sort of stability and organizational character to another," a transition that may consist in a restructuring of the relations among components of the system, a change in the "composition" (*sostav*) of the elements of the system, or both.[62]

Over and above its possible virtues in providing a way of distinguishing between quantitative and qualitative change, the systems approach has a particular merit that may be responsible for some of its appeal to Soviet

[58]Ibid.

[59]V. I. Sviderskii, *O dialektike elementov i struktury v ob"ektivnom mire i v poznanii* (Moscow, 1962), pp. 59–66. See also O. S. Zel'kina, *Sistemno-strukturnyi analiz osnovnykh kategorii dialektiki* (Saratov, 1970).

[60]V. Tiukhtin, "Perekhod kolichestvennykh izmenenii v kachestvennye," in Konstantinov, *Filosofskaia entsiklopediia*, vol. 4, pp. 239–240; Naftali Prat, "Diamat and Contemporary Biology," *Studies in Soviet Thought* 21 (1980), pp. 189–202.

[61]Viakkerev et al., *Materialisticheskaia dialektika*, p. 163.

[62]Tiukhtin, "Perekhod," p. 239.

philosophers. It provides a convenient conceptual apparatus for distinguishing between sudden and gradual qualitative "leaps" in a complex structure such as a society. For according to this analysis, systems may have subsystems, the qualitative change of which creates in turn a qualitative modification in the overall system. When all or many subsystems are altered simultaneously or in quick succession, the corresponding qualitative change in the overall system is explosive or fast-paced; but when subsystems change one by one at a slower rate, the overall system is altered gradually. Even Soviet philosophers who do not generally espouse a systems approach resort to this conception to explain the difference between the sudden socialist revolution on the one hand and the subsequent gradual "leap" from socialism to communism on the other.

In other respects, however, it is not clear what contribution is made by the systems approach to the understanding of the first law. To equate quality with structure and quantity with number and magnitude is a start, but much more remains to be done by Soviet philosophers. The authors of one recent work admit that there is yet no satisfactory understanding of what constitutes the "magnitude" of an element or subsystem.[63] Even in as simple a case as the transition from water to steam, it is by no means obvious how to apply the concepts; is the increased distance between molecules a case of changed magnitude (quantity) or structure (quality)? The problem of indefiniteness with respect to the duration of a measure has not been addressed by proponents of the systems approach; they have largely ignored the cases of apparently "measureless" transitions, and they still allow a measure to be indefinitely extended. Even the resolution of a "contradiction" within a system need not terminate a measure, we read: "Frequently what takes place is the prolonged dynamic preservation of the system."[64]

Furthermore, how does the systems approach deal with the *alternation* of quantitative and qualitative processes that appears to lie at the heart of "the transformation of quantity into quality and vice versa"? The question of exactly how changes in number and magnitude can be said both to produce and to be produced by changes in structure requires attention. The Israeli scholar Naftali Prat has argued in effect that such questions cannot be answered adequately by Soviet systems theorists because of a fundamental incompatibility between their approach and the first law. In a genuine structural change such as a gene's loss of a nucleotide, Prat

---

[63]Viakkerev et al., *Materialisticheskaia dialektika*, p. 161.
[64]Ibid., p. 282.

contends, there is no "transition" from quantity to quality or vice versa, since the two are at best different aspects of the same process.[65]

Vigorously opposed to the systems-structural interpretation of the first law are its traditionalist critics within the USSR, who see it as simply a disguised departure from the truly dialectical understanding of quantity and quality. Something of the flavor of the argument can be gained from the following remarks at the 1965 dialectics conference by E. V. Il'enkov, the late neo-Hegelian, who had one of the sharpest minds and tongues in recent Soviet philosophy:

> Comrade Sviderskii spoke here, and he said that today we must not understand 'quality' in the old way, we must understand it "in a new fashion." How it was understood in the old way—that is, in classical dialectics, including Marx and Lenin—he did not deem it necessary to elucidate. Instead, striving to clarify the "new" understanding, he made an expressive gesture with his arms, trying to take in as much air with them as possible, and he explained: it is, he said, both "structure," and "the relation of structure to its elements," "and so forth."
> This is "development" of the categories of dialectics?[66]

Il'enkov proceeds with charges that make clear the broader significance of this dispute: it is a renewed battle of the dialecticians against the mechanistic materialists:

> The category of 'quality' . . . simply disappears, replaced by other categories having nothing in common with it and instead resembling purely quantitative definitions, conceptions of contemporary mathematics.
> What remains of 'quality' is only the word, the name. And a completely opposite meaning is given to it. Just try to combat mechanism using this "new" definition of 'quality'. I am sure that such "development" of the category of 'quality' would bring great joy not only to Stepanov-Skvortsov and Sarab'-ianov [mechanists of the 1920s] but to all intemperate worshippers of cybernetics who see nothing anywhere but "structures," "relations of elements," and other things expressed without remainder in numbers and equations.[67]

The dispute between the original mechanists and the Deborinist dialecticians in the 1920s was resolved by the imposition of a philosophically impoverished orthodoxy. It remains to be seen what will become of the current disagreement between neomechanists such as Sviderskii and neo-

---

[65]Prat, p. 201.

[66]Konstantinov et al., *Dialektika*, p. 143.

[67]Ibid. For a broad Soviet critique of the systems-structural approach to category theory, see Orudzhev, *Dialektika kak sistema*, pp. 6–7, 20–21, 53–83.

Deborinists such as Il'enkov, who represent the same centrifugal tendencies of a philosophy seeking to be both materialist and dialectical. The neo-mechanists bear the burden of being associated in Soviet thinking not simply with mechanism in general but with the long condemned "tectology" or "organization science" of the renegade Bolshevik Bogdanov, which was the first and is still the fullest development of a systems-structural theory in the Russian philosophical literature.[68] On the other hand Sviderskii and his colleagues have the authority and achievements of the sciences and the powerful aura of modernity behind them, not to mention the ability to explain gradual leaps. Furthermore, the untimely death in 1979 of Il'enkov, the dialecticians' most erudite and effective spokesman, cannot but weaken the neo-Deborinist cause. At the moment, the balance in an inherently unstable situation is tilting toward those who put contemporary science before Hegel; and in the absence of another night of darkness, the "transformation of quantity into quality" may be expected to make its own gradual leap away from traditional dialectics to a systems-structural or other interpretation more in keeping with the conceptual needs of the sciences.

The Law of the Unity and Struggle of Opposites

In the jottings on dialectics contained in Lenin's *Philosophical Notebooks*, the second of Engels's three dialectical laws occupies the central place. Dialectics, Lenin writes, may be defined briefly as "the doctrine of the unity of opposites."[69] Because of this Leninist emphasis, and because the "opposites" in question are the "internal contradictions" that account for dialectical development, as we have seen, many Soviet philosophers regard Engels's second law as the fundamental law of dialectics and place it first in the order of exposition.[70] Also recommending the law is its worldview significance: by rooting opposition in the nature of things, we impart ontological justification to the class struggle.[71]

Indeed the very aptness of the law to describe social conflict has led many commentators, Soviet as well as non-Soviet, to question its supposed status as a universal law of nature. Only by an anthropomorphization, it is held, can the term 'struggle' (in Russian, *bor'ba*, the same word used

[68]For a recent study of Bogdanov's thought, see Kenneth M. Jensen, *Beyond Marx and Mach. Aleksandr Bogdanov's Philosophy of Living Experience* (Dordrecht, 1978).
[69]Lenin, *Soch.*, vol. 29, p. 203.
[70]Vorob'ev, p. 57; Konstantinov et al., *Dialektika*, pp. 47, 223, 244.
[71]This point is made by Z. A. Jordan in "The Dialectical Materialism of Lenin," *Slavic Review* 25 (1966), p. 283, and by Gustav Wetter in *Dialectical Materialism*, pp. 341–342.

for wrestling) be applied even to living nonhuman nature; and when it comes to describing relations in the inorganic world such as that of the positive and negative poles of a magnet (one of Engels's favorite examples), 'struggle' seems completely out of place. For such reasons, and noting that Lenin himself in places set the word off with quotation marks, some Soviet philosophers as early as 1956 suggested rephrasing or at least renaming the law, perhaps by going back to Engels's original designation, "the law of the interpenetration of opposites."[72] At a conference in 1980, S. T. Meliukhin proposed 'interaction' and 'counteraction' as appropriate replacements for 'struggle'.[73]

In this case as in so many others in Soviet philosophy, however, lexical conservatism has generally prevailed—aided, no doubt, by the revolutionary ring of the term in question. Instead of reserving the term 'struggle' for special, chiefly social cases of interpenetrating opposites, the term has been diluted to allow it to apply to all cases in nature, society, and thought, even those most free of conflict. In its most general form the concept of a struggle of opposites must cover, the authors of *Fundamentals* write, "all kinds of mutual negation and exclusion of opposites," including action and counteraction, attraction and repulsion of every kind, the movement of a living thing toward its death or end, the fact that an organism loses old components and acquires new ones, and more.[74] 'Struggle', in other words, must be interpreted broadly enough to include both the mortal combat of wild animals and the blooming of a rose. In view of the extreme breadth allowed the concept, we must of course resist the temptation to attribute anything resembling a Manichaean ontology to Soviet Marxism-Leninism, despite the images of conflict that the second law's title may conjure up.

Even in the social field, a weak interpretation of 'struggle' is required to accommodate Marxist-Leninist doctrines. A difficult question faced by Soviet theorists has been that of how socialist society develops. Capitalism, of course, is an arena of dynamic conflict between opposed economic forces. After the revolution, however, when those oppositions have been overcome, we seem to face a dilemma: either society will stagnate in the absence of social "contradictions," or new antagonisms, new struggle and conflict, will develop, leading to another revolutionary leap. The first alternative is ontologically unacceptable, for a dialectical world knows no rest; the second is politically unacceptable, for socialism must be a realm

---

[72]Lenin, *Soch.*, vol. 29, p. 317; S. P. Dudel' and G. M. Shtraks, *Zakon edinstva i bor'by protivopolozhnostei* (Moscow, 1967), p. 65.

[73]N. I. Gribanov and S. A. Lebedev, "Aktual'nye voprosy teorii materialisticheskoi dialektiki," *Vestnik Moskovskogo universiteta. Seriia 7. Filosofiia*, 1981, no. 4, p. 75.

[74]Konstantinov, *Fundamentals* (1982), pp. 110–111.

of harmony, not strife, and must require no revolutionary negation. The way out of this dilemma was provided by the introduction in the late 1940s of a distinction between *antagonistic* and *nonantagonistic* contradictions.[75] The former are those holding between hostile social forces, whose interests are irreconcilably opposed; polarization and disruptive struggle ensue, ending with the destruction of one of the forces. Socialism, on the other hand, is said to be characterized by the existence of nonantagonistic contradictions, such as that between the workers and the peasantry, whose "struggle" takes place on a foundation of broad common interests; the contradictions between them can thus be overcome peacefully, without a revolution. Through the resolution of nonantagonistic contradictions, socialism can move forward dynamically along an unbroken path to full communism.[76]

Whatever we may think of this conceptual maneuver, it seems clear that, if the second law is to retain any substantive meaning, it must do so in virtue of its claim that oppositions open to being called "contradictions"— whether the "contradictory" elements are antagonistic or not, whether they may appropriately be said to "struggle" or not—nonetheless inhere in all things and account for their development. For that reason most philosophical discussion of the second law has centered on the interpretation of the term 'contradiction'. In this discussion sharp and fundamental disagreement among Soviet philosophers has been disclosed; and given the key position of dialectics in the Marxist-Leninist outlook, this dispute has been regarded by many Soviet philosophers as the central controversy of contemporary dialectical materialism.

The concern that fuels the dispute within Soviet philosophy is the same one that has led non-Marxists from Dühring on to question dialectical materialism at its foundations—namely the puzzle of what it can mean to say that there are contradictions in the real world. For the Soviet dialectical materialist, the second law is ontologically descriptive; it characterizes reality as containing what are called "objective contradictions" as essential constituents of all things. And these contradictions are held to be not only real but functional: they are the source of change. For the philosopher trained in traditional, Aristotelian logic, on the other hand, there are no such things as contradictory objects. Contradiction is not something that "exists" in the real world but rather a relation that holds between two

[75]Wetter, *Dialectical Materialism*, p. 342.

[76]Konstantinov, *Fundamentals* (1982), p. 114. Although most Soviet philosophers restrict the distinction between antagonistic and nonantagonistic contradictions to the social sphere, the view that it may also be found in the natural world is defended by some. See G. V. Platonov, "Protivorechiia i ikh rol' v razvitii zhivoi prirody," *Vestnik Moskovskogo universiteta. Seriia 7. Filosofiia*, 1981, no. 5, pp. 11–13.

thoughts—or better, two assertions (hence the term 'contra*diction*')—such that, if one of them is true, the other is necessarily false: for example, 'today is Monday' and 'today is not Monday'. The original phrasing of the principle of noncontradiction rules out a contradictory *thing* as an object of meaningful speech: the same attribute, Aristotle wrote, cannot both belong and not belong to the same subject at the same time and in the same respect. Grass can be both green and not green, but only if it is, say, green today and not green tomorrow, or green with respect to its leaves and not green with respect to its roots.[77] For traditional logic, a contradiction arises from some confusion, error, or incompleteness in thought or speech; it is not "real," and certainly is no source of development in the real world.

The question of what to do about this apparent clash between dialectics and logic was at one time "settled" in Soviet philosophy by the facile assumption that the latter in its Aristotelian form is simply "metaphysical" and hence incapable of dealing with a dynamic, dialectical world.[78] With the rehabilitation of formal logic as a field of study in the late 1940s, however (see the following chapter), a search began for ways of harmonizing its principles—including the principle of noncontradiction—with dialectics. But here again the tensions between the scientifically oriented neomechanists and the Hegelian dialecticians came into play, and by 1958, when a conference on the subject of contradiction was held in Moscow, the split between them on this question was sharp and open.

On one side were such independently minded anti-Hegelians as Ernst Kol'man, the philosopher M. K. Mamardashvili, and the mathematical logician Alexander Zinoviev (Aleksandr Aleksandrovich Zinov'ev, b. 1922), who contended that dialectics does not require us to give up or to weaken the logical law of noncontradiction. *Logical* contradictions, they argued, are the result of error (or of the use of an inadequate conceptual framework) and must be avoided in any context, however "dialectical." They are not a sign of a contradictory state of the world; "there are no such things," Mamardashvili stated, as "logical contradictions that reflect real contradictions."[79] *Real* contradictions, nonetheless, can be said to exist, but they are not analogous to the logical variety. What they are, according to these thinkers—whose position was subsequently labeled "polarism"— is empirically manifested oppositions between antithetical forces, tendencies, or aspects of things in the real world. Hence Kol'man defined

---

[77]*The Works of Aristotle*, vol. 8: *Metaphysics*, trans. W. D. Ross (Oxford, 1954), p. 1005b, lines 19–20.

[78]Wetter, *Dialectical Materialism*, p. 524.

[79]G. A. Volkov, "Konferentsiia po voprosam protivorechii," *Voprosy filosofii*, 1958, no. 12, pp. 170–171.

(objective) contradiction at the 1958 conference as follows: "Contradiction is a material difference, a lack of correspondence between two different, polar aspects of one and the same real object which leads them to clash with each other. Such polar aspects are the different internal and external forces and tendencies which act on a given body (phenomenon) within the limits of a given motion or in the course of the development of society."[80]

To the polarists, then, the second law of dialectics asserts the universality of oppositions such as those between forces of attraction and repulsion in physics and conflicting economic classes in history—oppositions the existence and the causal role of which are matters of straightforward scientific investigation. The acknowledgment of such real or objective "contradictions" requires no logical concessions; "the presence of opposing tendencies," Zinoviev wrote in 1971, "is not a logical contradiction."[81] Nor is a logical contradiction even required to *state* a real contradiction; the latter is in effect a "contradiction" *in different respects*, and therefore can be expressed in logically noncontradictory form. This interpretation of dialectical "contradictions" as signifying opposing forces or conflicting sides or aspects of a situation continues to be advocated vigorously by many Soviet philosophers. Among its more prominent defenders in the present day are I. S. Narskii, V. I. Sviderskii, V. I. Metlov, and V. N. Porus.

Yet polarism is far from enjoying a monopoly on the subject of objective contradiction in Soviet dialectical materialism. It is rejected by many Soviet philosophers who see its "opposing forces" approach to ontology as a mechanistic retreat from a truly dialectical view of the world. These philosophers, whose position may be called "antinomism," argue on the contrary that there are genuine, "same respect" logical contradictions that reflect real features of the world. In particular they point to the antinomies that arise in the course of our attempts to understand the world—the wave-corpuscle "contradiction" in quantum mechanics, for example—and above all to two classic antinomies formulated by Marx and Engels. One occurs in the chapter of Marx's *Capital* entitled "Contradictions in the General Formula [for Capital]." Seeking to explain the origin of capital, Marx argues that it can arise only in processes of economic exchange ("circulation") but also that it appears impossible for it to arise in that way; capital, he writes, "must have its origin both in circulation and not in circulation."[82] The second antinomy derives from Engels's Hegelian

---

[80]Ibid., p. 165. The position is called "polarism" by G. S. Batishchev in *Dialekticheskoe protivorechie*, pp. 42–58.

[81]A. A. Zinov'ev, *Logika nauki* (Moscow, 1971), p. 206.

[82]Karl Marx, *Capital. A Critical Analysis of Capitalist Production*, vol. 1, trans. Ben Fowkes (New York, 1977), p. 268.

interpretation of Zeno's paradoxes of motion, such as the Greek philosopher's contention that a flying arrow is really at rest. Instead of concluding from the paradoxes, as Zeno did, that motion is illusory, Engels argues that it is real but inherently contradictory: "Even simple mechanical change of position," he writes, "can only come about through a body being at one and the same moment of time both in one place and in another place, being in one and the same place and also not in it." Here we have, in Engels's view, a contradiction that is "objectively present in things and processes themselves," and since the argument is generalizable for all changes of state of whatever sort, such fundamental contradictions must pervade the universe.[83]

In its extreme form Marxist-Leninist antinomism is more an attitude than a developed philosophical position—an attitude that V. A. Lektorskii sarcastically ascribed to those who believe that "truly dialectical thinking consists in the formulation of a multitude of unresolved antinomies."[84] At the 1958 conference V. M. Boguslavskii complained of "those comrades who contend that every object possesses one or another feature and at the same time and in the same sense and respect doesn't possess it."[85] Many seem to think, G. S. Batishchev wrote in 1979, that to be accepted as a dialectician one need only swear that one admits "contradiction in the same respect." We must get beyond these "antinomian prophets of contradiction," he urged.[86]

The developed position that is closest to extreme antinomism is that of Il'enkov, who, although he did not regard antinomies as unresolvable, saw their contradictory form as directly and truthfully expressing a contradictory reality. Resisting the very distinction between "logical" and "objective" contradictions, Il'enkov distinguished instead between those trivial "contradictions" that result from careless thinking, on the one hand, and real contradictions, which are both logical and objective, on the other. In the latter cases, he argued in 1958, the violation of the traditional law of noncontradiction is not a product of error but "flows of necessity from the most correct movement of thought in accordance with the logic of the subject." Such, he contended, are the paradoxes of motion, which point to genuine problems in the nature of motion that cannot be dismissed verbally but will be resolved only by advancing to deeper levels in our understanding of space and time. Thus for dialectics a contradiction is not

---

[83]Engels, *Anti-Dühring*, pp. 144–145. On the lively discussion of this paradox in Soviet journals in the 1960s, see Orudzhev, *Dialektika kak sistema*, pp. 251–252.

[84]*Dialekticheskoe protivorechie*, p. 336. Batishchev uses the term 'antinomism' to refer to this extreme position only (p. 43).

[85]Volkov, p. 172.

[86]*Dialekticheskoe protivorechie*, pp. 246, 249.

an impassable obstacle but "a springboard from which thought should effect a leap forward in the concrete theoretical and experimental investigation of the object."[87]

One of the most forceful presentations of Il'enkov's influential antinomist position came just before his death in 1979. In it, Il'enkov states that contradiction, like all the dialectical categories, is "a universal form of the development of 'being.'" Marx's paradox of capital, he holds, is "the theoretically correct expression of a real antinomy," for it is in the "unfolding" of this real contradiction that capital in fact arises. Hence what we need in order to understand the world is "the art of thinking objective contradictions dialectically." Formal logic, long since superseded by Hegel's more adequate dialectical logic, should be relegated to the instruction of young people, as Lenin suggested; nothing should prevent an adult from confronting the contradictions in things "without fearing these contradictions and without trying to evade them through verbal dexterity." The correct approach to the study of reality, Il'enkov affirms, is first to "fix the real contradictions in the makeup of the object under investigation precisely and with maximum sharpness" and then to proceed to investigate "that process—the real process—through which these opposites *are transformed into* each other."[88]

The polarists today do not dismiss antinomies as abruptly as they once did. They acknowledge that antinomies may signal the need for further investigation of a subject, and they grant that some antinomies have an objective basis of a sort. But they continue to deny that antinomies are a kind of knowledge of the world, as Il'enkov's supporters insist. Marx's paradox of capital, though treated with respect, is not interpreted by polarists as directly mirroring a "contradictory" reality. As early as the 1958 conference Zinoviev argued that Marx's meaning was that exchange is a necessary but not a sufficient condition for the origination of capital, which requires processes of production as well as exchange.[89] A fuller recent analysis by V. N. Porus adds to Zinoviev's treatment the concession that Marx's antinomy may be seen as a way of formulating a genuine scientific problem and to that extent is "an element of the reflection of a specific reality." But in Porus's view the "reality" in question is not the contradictory nature of the origin of capital but rather the inner contradictoriness of the conceptual apparatus of classical economics that led to the paradoxical expression and in its turn is grounded in "the root contradictions of bourgeois reality itself." Thus for Porus the "objective basis"

[87]Volkov, pp. 168–169.
[88]*Dialekticheskoe protivorechie*, pp. 131, 256, 265, 133, 260.
[89]Volkov, p. 169.

of Marx's contradictory statement is a highly indirect and distant one—
and one that, it will be noted, is thoroughly analyzable in the polar terms
of social antagonisms. There is no "contradictory situation," Porus states,
called "capital arises and does not arise in circulation." Rather, through
that paradoxical assertion Marx was able to advance to the more adequate
conceptual structure of Marxian economics that truly (and nonantinom-
ially) reflects the origin of capital.[90]

As for Engels's paradoxes of motion, they are accorded still less attention
by the polarist philosophers. Zinoviev at the 1958 conference rejected
them for the reason most often adduced by mathematicians and scientists
everywhere—namely, that the appearance of contradiction depends on
confusing an *interval* of time (over which, of course, a thing *can* be in
more than one place "at the same time") with a durationless *moment* of
time (in terms of which we can speak of *neither* motion *nor* rest, both of
which make sense only with respect to duration).[91] A few courageous Soviet
philosophers have criticized Engels publicly on this score. Kol'man did so
at the 1958 conference, offering in excuse for Engels that, in speaking of
a moving object's being simultaneously "in one and the same place and
also not in it," he was employing almost verbatim an unfortunate locution
of Hegel's and moreover that he was limited by the state of scientific
knowledge in the 1870s.[92] Bakradze and other Soviet philosophers are also
reported to have openly rejected Engels's conception.[93] The majority of
polarists today, however, simply do not refer to the subject, apparently
finding the case adequately made by their predecessors.

Meanwhile, Soviet antinomists continue to affirm that "motion itself is
a contradiction."[94] Their position would of course be strengthened if they
could present a coherent account of a "contradictory" object or state of
affairs that does not resolve upon analysis into a case of opposed forces
or aspects. They are still faced with the problem made explicit by B.A.
Lastochkin in 1979: "how to understand and how to express in the logic
of concepts the *contradictoriness of a single thing* 'in the same place,' 'at
the same time,' and 'in the same respect.' "[95] Efforts to resolve the problem
continue but without notable success.

Some efforts, indeed, border on the ludicrous. F. F. Viakkerev offers, as
an example of the working of "internal contradictions," the case of the

[90]*Dialekticheskoe protivorechie*, pp. 167–168, 280.
[91]Volkov, p. 169.
[92]Ibid., p. 165.
[93]John Somerville and Howard L. Parsons, eds., *Dialogues on the Philosophy of Marxism. From the Proceedings of the Society for the Philosophical Study of Dialectical Materialism* (Westport, 1974), p. 65.
[94]Dudel' and Shtraks, p. 167.
[95]*Dialekticheskoe protivorechie*, p. 181 (italics in original).

struggle for survival among individuals of the same biological species. The clue to such contradictions, Viakkerev believes, is provided by Darwin when he observes that members of the same species inhabit a common locality, require the same food, and are exposed to the same dangers. Viakkerev's presentation of the "contradiction," then, is as follows: "From what has been said it is clear that the coincidence, the identity of opposites (opposite tendencies among individuals of the same species) in the same respect (with respect to food, to place of habitation, etc.) and at the same time are the necessary condition of the intraspecies struggle (of the internal contradiction)." "Real contradictions" are best understood, then, according to Viakkerev, as "coinciding opposites."[96] But surely this explanation will not do. The "coinciding opposites" that the classical conception of contradiction excludes are the simultaneous ascription and denial of the same attribute to the same subject in the same respect; the "coincidence" of opposite (that is, different and struggling) *individuals* with respect to food and place of residence, on the other hand, involves no logical contradiction whatever and is easily understandable in polarist terms.

Lastochkin, for his part, attributes the lack of progress by his fellow Soviet dialecticians in this area to their failure to develop an adequate modal ontology. The way to conceive of an object as essentially contradictory, Lastochkin believes, is to see it as containing real possibilities over and above its actual states at any moment. The essence of an object, in this view, is not simply what it is but the "opposite" thing it may become by inner necessity.[97] Once again, however, this explanation will not do. There is no actual contradiction in the same respect in saying, for example, that "the acorn both is and is not an oak tree," for this is simply an abbreviated way of stating that the acorn is potentially but not actually an oak, and being-in-actuality and being-in-potentiality are manifestly distinguishable respects.

One of the more ambitious attempts in current Soviet philosophy to defend at least a modified form of antinomism against polarism has been undertaken by Zaid Melikovich Orudzhev (b. 1932) of Moscow State University. Conceding the polarists' contention that there is a fundamental distinction between logical contradictions and dialectical or "real" contradictions, Orudzhev argues that a cardinal aspect of that distinction has been overlooked. Logical contradictions, he writes, are bare, immediate oppositions of incompatibles; in dialectical contradictions, on the other hand, mutually exclusive opposites are mediated by intervening stages or steps—"intermediate links" that make possible the coexistence, coinci-

[96]Viakkerev et al., *Materialisticheskaia dialektika*, p. 305.
[97]*Dialekticheskoe protivorechie*, pp. 180–190.

dence, and intertransformation of the extreme elements.[98] By way of example Orudzhev presents such "dialectical contradictions" as that between the input and the output of a computer system, which are, he says, mediated by the system's organization; and that between production and consumption in an economic system, where the intermediate links are the activities of exchange and the other economic processes that characterize the system in question. Quantum mechanics, Orudzhev believes, stands today at the threshold of resolving its basic contradiction—that between the undulatory and the corpuscular characteristics of microobjects; and the contradiction will be resolved, in his view, by the disclosure of the intermediate links in the internal structure of matter that allow the otherwise incompatible poles to be joined. But these poles, Orudzhev insists, are not simply contraries; for he argues that *in themselves* (that is, considered *apart* from their intermediate links) such opposites as the positive and negative electrical charges on an atom are contradictories *in the same respect* ("in respect of charge").[99] A dialectical contradiction, then, is defined by Orudzhev as "a unity of opposites, mediated by intermediate links, which opposites are taken at one and the same time, in one and the same respect (and sense)."[100]

It should be evident from Orudzhev's examples, however, that he fails to acknowledge still another difference between logical and "dialectical" contradictions. For in Orudzhev's analysis the extreme members that are "mediated" in a dialectical contradiction are not affirmations and denials, like the relata of a logical contradiction, but features, aspects, or characteristics of the real world such as production and consumption. Logically, it is only in regard to pairs of affirmations and denials that the condition "in the same respect" makes sense. To speak, as Orudzhev does, of "opposites . . . taken in the same respect" is without meaning when the "opposites" in question are objects or features of objects. What does it mean to "take" undulatory and corpuscular characteristics in the same respect? To *ascribe* undulatory features to a given microobject and simultaneously *and in the same respect* to deny such ascription would of course be contradictory. But none of that is going on in the microobject itself; in it the "opposite" characteristics simply coexist, and it is up to our theoretical analysis of the situation (as Orudzhev rightly observes) to show us how the two are compatibly related. "Respects" come into play when we wish

---

[98]Z. M. Orudzhev, "Some Problems of Dialectical Logic," in *Philosophy in the USSR. Problems of Dialectical Materialism*, trans. R. Daglish (Moscow, 1977), p. 240. For Orudzhev's position see also *Dialekticheskoe protivorechie*, pp. 78–95, 223–232; and A. V. Aver'ianov and Z. M. Orudzhev, "Dialectical Contradiction in the Evolution of Knowledge," *Soviet Studies in Philosophy* 18 (Winter 1979–1980), pp. 63–82.

[99]F. Kumpf and Z. Orudzhev, *Dialekticheskaia logika. Osnovnye printsipy i problemy* (Moscow, 1979), p. 103; see also *Dialekticheskoe protivorechie*, pp. 89–90.

[100]*Dialekticheskoe protivorechie*, p. 94.

to *talk* about them meaningfully, but then we are operating in a domain of conceptions, not objects. Orudzhev attempts to use the "same respect" condition in order to get the appearance of a genuine contradiction, but he transports it to a realm in which it has no application.

Confusion of the two realms is an unfortunate product of the Hegelian heritage in Soviet Marxism, by which even moderate antinomists such as Orudzhev are greatly affected. They seek to describe a world of material objects, but the conceptual apparatus they use confounds it with a world of thoughts. To say such things as that "an object relates negatively to itself" or that opposites "mutually presuppose" each other is possible in a Hegelian universe, in which conceptual relations such as negation and presupposition *are* relations of real things.[101] The Hegelian wing of Soviet philosophy, although supposedly rejecting Hegel's ontology, nonetheless assumes that the same relations Hegel ascribed to the realities of his world must exist in the material world considered apart from thought. And with that assumption comes conceptual trouble. In seeking a direct analogue for contradiction in the material world, the antinomists are engaged in a quest for a conceptual impossibility—a real thing that has the same structure as a logical contradiction. Logical contradiction joins one relatum with its *denial*, and that is something no material entity can do. And when we add that for the antinomist the contradiction not only must be "real" but must *account for development*, the enormousness of the problem becomes still more obvious.

Narskii, Sviderskii, and the other neomechanists are surely right in believing that polarism, with its appeal to opposing "forces" or "aspects" of real things, comes as close as is possible to a defensible analogue to Hegel's antinomism in the material world. But that is not very close, as the antinomists are quick to note. To present opposition "in different respects" as an adequate analysis of dialectical contradiction is, for the antinomists, to commit a kind of philosophical treason. "The whole grandiose history of dialectics," Orudzhev complains, "is thus reduced to the allegation that a non-contradictory form of relation, long since regarded in formal logic as non-contradictory, is declared to be a dialectical contradiction."[102] The power of intellectual traditions remains strong in Soviet philosophy, and the departure of polarism from a truly dialectical spirit is keenly felt by many Soviet philosophers. The facts, moreover, that polarism is associated with the more independently minded, positivist segment of the Soviet philosophical community and that leading polarists such as Kol'man and Zinoviev became (for other reasons) politically undesirable to the Soviet state, have not helped the polarist cause.

---

[101]Ibid., p. 61; Viakkerev et al., *Materialisticheskaia dialektika*, pp. 300–301.
[102]Orudzhev, "Some Problems," p. 240.

The polarists, however, have the distinct advantage of defending a co-herent position: they can explain what a "real contradiction" is, give plausible examples such as the struggle of one economic class against another, and claim by this approach to provide a genuine explanation of development as the product of the interaction of opposing forces. I do not mean that the polarist interpretation establishes the law of the unity and struggle of opposites as a universal truth. But at least it makes the law scientifically assessable. *Is* the interaction of opposing forces at the root of every change in nature, society, and thought? Probably not, but only concrete investigation by the special sciences can answer the question.

The polarists' sense of 'contradiction', moreover, is all that is needed for normal political and ideological purposes in the USSR. The Party can no longer do without the term 'contradiction', that much is clear; the word is omnipresent in the Soviet ideological vocabulary. But the uses to which it is put plumb no antinomian depths. Sometimes it is simply synonymous with a (usually regrettable) difference of some sort, such as the "contra-diction" between the living standards of different regions of the USSR or the "contradiction" between the wealth of resources available for economic production and the limited utilization of those resources.[103] In most cases something more than a mere inequality or disproportion is intended, but in all of those instances the polarists' language of opposing forces or tendencies is entirely adequate, for they consist invariably in the counter-posing of elements that, though they work against each other in fact, are perfectly compatible logically—bourgeoisie and proletariat, the world sys-tems of capitalism and socialism, nationalistic and internationalistic tend-encies within a given state, and so on.[104] By providing a simple, readily intelligible conceptual framework for such oppositions, polarism makes its contribution to the world-view role of philosophy. Thus the interests of ideological effectiveness reinforce those of philosophical coherence in promoting the anti-Hegelian, neomechanist cause of the polarists.

In 1875, Marxist philosophy's early critic, Eugen Dühring, remarked on "the uselessness of the incense which has occasionally been lavished on the dialectics of contradiction."[105] If Dühring had known what clouds of incense would be lavished on the subject in a Marxist state, he might have redoubled his critical efforts. Still, some progress has been made. Not even the antinomist philosophers are any longer guilty of what Karl Pop-per once charged all dialecticians with doing—namely, discarding the law

---

[103]V. E. Kozlovskii, "XXVI s"ezd KPSS i problemy materialistichskoi dialektiki," *Filo-sofskie nauki*, 1981, no. 5, pp. 10–11.

[104]Ibid., pp. 3–4, 7.

[105]E. Dühring, *Cursus der Philosophie als streng wissenschaftlicher Weltanschauung und Lebensgestaltung* (Leipzig, 1875), p. 32.

of noncontradiction altogether.[106] The polarist majority fully accepts the law in its traditional, Aristotelian sense, and the antinomists accept it at certain levels of discourse. Most Soviet philosophers agree that contradictions must be "resolved" in some manner—though the polarists see the resolution as a matter of intellectual clarification, whereas the antinomists view it as taking place through the development of "being." But such issues are now openly joined. The antinomists know what the law of noncontradiction requires, and they recognize that the "oppositions" with which the polarists and the Communist party are content are not really contradictions. Perhaps eventually they too will stop trying to square the circle and will cease their attempts to write a materialist sequel to "the grandiose history of dialectics."

The Law of the Negation of the Negation

By comparison with the attention given Engels's first two laws of dialectics, the third law has consistently been slighted in the Marxist-Leninist literature. Engels himself, though he devotes a chapter to the law in *Anti-Dühring*, barely mentions it in *The Dialectics of Nature*. Lenin, in his list of sixteen "elements of dialectics," refers to the law only in points 13 ("the repetition at a higher stage of certain features, properties, etc., of the lower") and 14 ("the apparent return to the old [negation of the negation]").[107] In Lenin's brief essay, "On the Question of Dialectics," there is no clear reference to the law at all.[108] In this light, the absence of the law from the *Short Course* essay of 1938 is simply an extreme case of a general tendency. Even today, the third law never receives as much attention as the first two in Soviet texts and reference works.

We might be tempted to conclude that the law is relatively uncontroversial. On the contrary, the law of the negation of the negation remains the least settled of the three, and if less is written about it, that may reflect not philosophical satisfaction but puzzlement concerning its interpretation. For there are difficulties with the third law that are now perceived not only by its non-Marxist critics but by its Soviet supporters, and some prominent Marxist-Leninists are convinced that we can find an adequate interpretation of the law only by ceasing to regard it as universal.

Standard interpretations of the law, consistently with Lenin's fragmentary comments, envisage dialectical change as a succession of qualitative

---

[106]Karl R. Popper, "What Is Dialectic?" in *Conjectures and Refutations. The Growth of Scientific Knowledge*, 3d ed. (London, 1969), p. 316.

[107]Lenin, *Soch.*, vol. 29, p. 203.

[108]Ibid., pp. 316–322.

transformations ("negations") in which there is a kind of cyclical return to what has gone before (that is, something is preserved or reappears in the process), but where the return takes place on a "higher level," in the fashion not of a simple cycle but an ascending spiral (that is, progress is made). Concerning both of these supposed dimensions of dialectical change—the conservative and the progressive—serious questions arise when they are ascribed to all processes in the real world.

As for the conservative dimension, it has long been noted by Marxists and non-Marxists alike that in a great many processes the negation of a negation does not effect a return to a positive content. A case in point is the succession of socioeconomic formations postulated by Marxist historical materialism. The institution of communal property in primitive societies, in the Marxist conception, is "negated" by slaveholding societies, which introduce the institution of private property. But when the slave system is in its turn negated by the feudal order, there is no return to communal property; feudalism retains the institution of private property.

Soviet philosophers are aware of this problem, and they deal with it by weakening the law—specifically, by interpreting the law as requiring not that the *second* negation in a series effect a return to the starting point but only that *somewhere* in the series there be such a return. Lenin prompted this approach by quoting favorably, in his *Philosophical Notebooks*, Hegel's animadversions against the mechanical application of the three-stage schema introduced into philosophy by Johann Gottlieb Fichte—the triad consisting of an initial, positive *thesis*, its negation by an *antithesis*, and finally a *synthesis* that, in negating the antithesis, overcomes the one-sidedness of the latter and incorporates or "sublates" the positive content of the thesis as well. Lenin does not deny that in a dialectical process there is a return to the positive content of an earlier stage, but he appears to follow Hegel in holding that triplicity as such is a superficial, merely formal aspect of the process and that it is a matter of little concern whether the actual return takes place at the third, the fourth, or some other step.[109] In post-Stalin Soviet philosophy these suggestions became theses: "It would be incorrect ... to regard 'triplicity' as an *a priori* scheme which must be imposed on all processes," wrote the authors of an authoritative textbook in 1959; "the development of an object need not and often does not take

---

[109]Ibid., pp. 210–211. The Russian verb translated as "to sublate"—*snimat'* (perfective aspect: *sniat'*)—is the equivalent of Hegel's *aufheben*, and it contains much of the latter term's semantic richness, combining elements of "canceling," "preserving," and "raising to a higher level." It should be noted that Hegel never applied the terms 'thesis', 'antithesis', and 'synthesis' to his own philosophy, though they are now often associated with it. He used the terms sparingly and only in criticizing the views of others.

three stages but takes more or fewer."[110] The favorite example of a return taking more stages is just the case of the evolution of socioeconomic formations mentioned above; for with the defeat of capitalism, it is said, the socialist order does finally reintroduce (on a higher level) the institution of communal property found in primitive society.

The difficulty with this proposed solution is that by giving up the definiteness of three stages in favor of "more or fewer," we have lost the ability to pin down the law to a definite commitment. The resulting vagueness is amply demonstrated in Sheptulin's *Marxist-Leninist Philosophy*, where it is asserted that in different subject matters the repetition of a stage may require not two but "a greater number of negations, e.g., four, eight, and so on"; achievement of the opposite of a given negation, it is said, is "only the ultimate result."[111] Thus, going along with the indefinitely prolonged measure of the first law, we now have the indefinitely prolonged *series* of measures of the third law; at no point in the series need we admit that the law has finally been proved wrong. Vacuousness is again the price of weakening a principle to avoid awkward facts.

In the post-Stalin age, however, many Soviet philosophers are no longer content with facile but in the end philosophically self-defeating stratagems, and other, more adventurous treatments of the law are offered. One possibility is simply to give up cyclicality; negation of the negation, in this interpretation, is a process of stepwise progression without return to a former state.[112] More actively discussed in the post-Stalin period, however, has been an approach found in the writings of Mikhail Nikolaevich Rutkevich (b. 1917) and other Soviet philosophers: that is, to retain the cyclical interpretation but to argue that the law is not universal in scope.[113]

Rutkevich, in a concise presentation of his position in 1965, divides Marxist-Leninist philosophers into three groups as concerns the scope of the third law: some see it as describing qualitative change in general, others as describing progressive qualitative change, and still others as describing only progressive qualitative change that has a spiral form. Identifying himself with the last group, Rutkevich contends that Lenin, in espousing the law, meant simply to acknowledge the existence of spiral change among other forms. Not even all *progressive* change has a spiral form, Rutkevich argues. In the grand evolutionary advance from inorganic matter to living nature to human society, he asks, what features of inorganic matter are "lost" in living nature and then reappear (on a higher level) in society?

[110]F. V. Konstantinov, ed., *Osnovy marksistskoi filosofii* (Moscow, 1959), p. 287.
[111]Sheptulin, *Marxist-Leninist Philosophy*, p. 280.
[112]Voishvillo, Gorskii, and Narskii, p. 91.
[113]For the first fully developed presentation of the view, see M. N. Rutkevich, *Dialekticheskii materializm. Kurs lektsii dlia estestvennykh fakul'tetov* (Moscow, 1959), pp. 373ff.

Again, what characteristics of man's remote progenitors disappeared among his more immediate ancestors only to appear once more in *Homo sapiens*? Finally, what will be the cyclical elements in the development of communism, once it is established? Communist party pronouncements, Rutkevich argues somewhat archly, make many predictions about communism, but in none of them is there any reference to the repetition at higher levels of earlier communist stages. Communism might better be understood, he suggests, as a realm of *"straightening the spirals* of social development," not continuing them. Rutkevich does not deny that the law has broad application, and he does not oppose its return to the dialectical fold from Stalinist exile. "But in correcting the mistakes of Stalin," he writes, "we must return to Lenin, not Hegel . . . , and must conform to a real picture of the world." That picture, as Rutkevich sees it, includes the law of the negation of the negation as a "highly general" but not a universal law.[114]

If cyclicality cannot be considered universal in real processes of change, according to some Soviet philosophers, neither can advancement to a higher state. The progressive dimension of the law has in fact been one of the thorniest issues in Soviet dialectics, generating still more concern than the conservative or cyclical dimension. In Soviet philosophical literature, it was long more or less assumed that progressiveness is an inherent feature of dialectical development. Engels, after all, consistently discussed the third law in terms of the evolution of "higher" and "more developed" forms, and of course he regarded the dialectical laws as laws of all motion or change.[115] Much Soviet philosophical literature, especially at the popular level, continues to make the same suggestions today.[116] If nothing else, there are good ideological reasons for stressing progressiveness: Marxist-Leninists have always regarded their world view as an optimistic, forward-looking one suitable for the builder of communism. Showing philosophically that a better future is dialectically rooted in the very nature of things could be an important way of keeping that "revolutionary optimism" alive—or at least of indicating that it is still firmly planted in one's own outlook.

The trouble with the assumption of universal progress is that it hardly corresponds to "a real picture of the world"—that is, to the facts of change as we see it. Surely not all processes, even in the social sphere, can be seen as passages to "higher levels" of being or organization: world wars, the cult of personality, and the nuclear arms race may be cited as counter-examples, to take only cases that might appeal to a contemporary Marxist-

[114]Konstantinov et al., *Dialektika*, pp. 217–223 (italics in original).
[115]Engels, *Anti-Dühring*, p. 165.
[116]Sheptulin, *Marxist-Leninist Philosophy*, p. 273.

Leninist. And when we move to the natural world, questionable cases are everywhere. The evolution from unicellular organisms to man might be considered, with appropriate definitions and qualifications, a case of progress; but is there any reasonable sense in which an earthquake, the boiling of water, or the evolution of one more species of beetle is a transition from "lower" to "higher" forms?

Different Soviet attitudes toward the third law may be seen in the ways in which Soviet philosophers have responded to such counterexamples. The first impulse of the extreme doctrinaire when faced with awkward facts is to reject them. Blind dogmatism of this sort has become increasingly rare in Soviet philosophy, and to find a clear instance of it in connection with the third law it is necessary to go back to a 1961 book by G. M. Domrachev, S. F. Efimov, and A. V. Timofeeva. Responding to alleged cases of nonprogressive change adduced by Rutkevich, the authors claim to see in his procedure the weaknesses of what they call "trivial empiricism." The dialectical laws, they contend, describe the *essence* of things, which does not correspond with "what is immediately observed." The "facts" before us must be understood in their inner nature. What is their inner nature? That described by the dialectical laws, of course. "What we immediately observe," the authors state, "can be understood only when we grasp it by proceeding from the universal laws." In effect, then, we are urged to beg the question by assuming the truth of the laws even though, as the authors admit, "certain features and aspects of the laws of dialectics are insufficiently clearly manifested or are not manifested at all in particular processes."[117]

The more sophisticated present-day defense of the universality of progressiveness acknowledges that the counterexamples adduced are real and not simply apparent but urges that they can be accommodated nonetheless by a slight weakening of the law. The weakening consists in asserting that the law describes not every phenomenon and process individually but rather the underlying tendency of systems of phenomena and processes. Instances of regressive change, the authors of *Materialist Dialectics* hold, appear incompatible with the third law only if, "metaphysically," we regard progressive, regressive, and neutral change as independent of each other and equal in status. Actually these types of change exist in a hierarchical interrelationship: progressive development, the authors write, "dominates the other two types of change, which are only a condition and a consequence of development." Approaching the material world as a whole, they go on, "motion from the lower to the higher expresses inte-

---

[117]G. M. Domrachev, S. F. Efimov, and A. V. Timofeeva, *Zakon otritsaniia otritsaniia* (Moscow, 1961), pp. 6–8.

grally the unity of all processes occurring in it." Thus, for example, the nonprogressive intertransformation of microparticles in physics is only a component or aspect of the more global, progressive processes of the evolution of cosmic matter in the metagalaxy. Because, then, progress is "the chief form and the main direction" of change overall, the universality of the law is held to be preserved.[118]

This approach clearly depends upon a shift in the conception of the law from one describing every process of change distributively to one describing a changing world as a system. But however questionable it may be to call a principle of the latter sort a "universal law," still more doubtful is the gratuitous assumption that, within the overarching system, progressive development is dominant and the source of all other change. No evidence is presented that could approach being adequate to establish a proposition of such cosmic sweep, and it is here that Soviet critics of the universality thesis such as Rutkevich decisively part company with those who support the approaches to the law just examined.

To begin with, these critics contend, it cannot be argued that there is progress or indeed directedness of any kind in the material world as a whole. There are, they grant, processes of synthesis, movements from the simple to the more complex, that could be called "progress." But there are also disintegrative, regressive processes: stars dim, complex atoms break down. Overall, Rutkevich wrote with heavy emphasis in 1966, "the Cosmos *has no set direction in its development*."[119] This conclusion is sometimes supported by an argument calculated to appeal to the ideological interests of Soviet philosophers—namely, that to acknowledge a given direction of cosmic development would be to ascribe to the material universe a beginning and an end.[120] And that, E. F. Molevich writes, "would lead straight into the arms of religion."[121]

At best, then, according to this view, progress is found in particular regions of the objective world, the identity of which is an empirical question. Inorganic nature is the realm least susceptible to analysis in terms of progressive development, and many though not all Soviet philosophers regard the law of the negation of the negation as virtually inapplicable to it. In his 1958 book *The Problem of the Finite and the Infinite* and later in *On the Dialectics of the Development of Inorganic Nature* (1960), S. T. Meliukhin argued convincingly that the concepts of 'higher' and 'lower' have no place in the analysis of most physical and chemical processes. The

---

[118]Viakkerev et al., *Materialisticheskaia dialektika*, pp. 234–235, 352.

[119]Konstantinov et al., *Dialektika*, p. 201 (italics in original). See also Rutkevich, *Dialekticheskii materializm*, p. 385.

[120]Rutkevich, *Dialekticheskii materializm*, pp. 385–386.

[121]Konstantinov et al., *Dialektika*, p. 190.

sole exception Meliukhin allows is inorganic processes that enter into the evolution of living matter.[122] Another exception is sometimes made for geological processes, no doubt because Engels specifically mentioned geology as a science within which the basic laws of dialectics apply.[123] Meliukhin, however, pointedly includes geological changes among those in which no distinction can be made between more or less "progressive" events.[124]

In living nature, by contrast, Soviet philosophers generally see an ascending line of development in the evolutionary process from the "lowest" organisms to man.[125] Even in this area, resistance to identifying "higher" and "lower" forms is not unknown in the USSR; as early as 1952, the prominent Soviet botanist L. M. Krechetovich wrote that 'progress' and 'regress' are subjective concepts.[126] On the whole, however, both scientists and philosophers in the USSR think of the evolutionary process as a progression, and in this they are not distinguishable from most of their colleagues in the West, who also typically speak of evolutionary progress to "higher" forms, even if they sometimes place the word in quotation marks.[127] Western biologists and philosophers of biology, moreover, might well endorse the definition of progress that is presented in *Materialist Dialectics*—"an increase in the strategic possibilities of a system."[128] Such a definition is a systems-structural version of the view, frequently encountered in Western literature, that evolutionary advance consists in the opening up of new and greater opportunities for adaptive response on the part of the organism.[129]

The area, finally, in which there is both the greatest apparent consensus among Soviet philosophers and the greatest difference from the West with regard to progressiveness is the area of social change. In this sphere the law of the negation of the negation clearly has world-view significance, and not a single Soviet philosopher today is on record as denying either that human social history is a domain marked by a consistent progressive movement or that communism is its end. Not every social process is accounted progressive, of course; counterrevolutions and other temporary

[122]S. T. Meliukhin, *Problema konechnogo i beskonechnogo* (Moscow, 1958), p. 202; S. T. Meliukhin, *O dialektike razvitiia neorganicheskoi prirody* (Moscow, 1960), pp. 8–9.
[123]Voishvillo, Gorskii, and Narskii, p. 16; Engels, *Anti-Dühring*, p. 168.
[124]Meliukhin, *O dialektike*, p. 8.
[125]Ibid., pp. 8–9.
[126]L. M. Krechetovich, *Voprosy evoliutsii rastitel'nogo mira. Sbornik statei* (Moscow, 1952), pp. 158–159.
[127]Ernst Mayr, "Evolution," *Scientific American* 239 (September 1978), p. 51.
[128]Viakkerev, *Materialisticheskaia dialektika*, p. 344.
[129]Mayr, p. 51.

setbacks are acknowledged.[130] But as to the primary law-governed line of development from primitive communalism through the various forms of social order based on the institution of private property to the eventual triumph of socialism and subsequently communism throughout the world, there is no expressed doubt in the literature of Soviet philosophy. In this area we are essentially dealing with a doctrine of historical materialism, to which we shall return in Chapter 5.

Rutkevich, who fully accepts the applicability of the law to the social domain, suggests that an ideological impulse may be responsible for its unwarranted extension to other regions: because "bourgeois" philosophers tend to deny progress in *both* (inorganic) nature and society, he writes, "some comrades" may have thought that the ideological struggle demands identification of progress with the very concept of change in general. The truth, as Rutkevich sees it, is that the third law is not universal, and that progress arises only where conditions favorable for it exist. Seeking to defend himself against ideologically inspired objections, he poses a rhetorical question: "How will Marxism suffer," he asks, "if we see a constant *possibility* of progress at the foundation of matter?"[131] Actually there is no simple answer to Rutkevich's question. It seems clear that Marxism as an objective theory of the world would not suffer but benefit, for it could then accept a point that critics have legitimately pressed for a century and more—namely, that the "law" of the negation of the negation describes some but far from all real processes. Marxism as an instrument of partisan ideology, however, might well suffer, for if progress is only a cosmic *possibility*, the ontological ground is cut out from under the faith in an inevitable "bright future" that has sustained many Marxists.

Marxist-Leninist dialectics is sometimes regarded by casual critics as a set of dogmas on which there is total if blind agreement among Soviet philosophers. Soviet philosophers themselves, on the other hand, typically view dialectics as an area in which there is unanimity among them on basic questions but disagreement on a number of subsidiary issues.

The foregoing analysis suggests that neither of these assessments is accurate. In fact there are very few significant points of agreement among Soviet philosophers on the subject of dialectics—points, that is, that go beyond the trivial ("the world changes," "things are interconnected"), the ultrasensitive ("communism is the goal of history"), or the purely verbal ("there are real contradictions"). In case after case, expressed agreements prove not to be grounded in substantive agreements. Dialectics, the heart

[130]Sheptulin, *Marxist-Leninist Philosophy*, p. 258.
[131]Konstantinov et al., *Dialektika*, pp. 203–205 (italics in original).

of Marxist-Leninist philosophy, is an accepted vocabulary but not an accepted body of claims about the world.

In good part the reason is that no claims are being made. When a person's only assertion is that change will come "sooner or later," that person is committed to nothing. When "measures" may be indefinitely short or long, when "negations" may succeed each other endlessly without a return to the starting point, when "struggle" may be without conflict and "leaps" without speed, *anything* can happen—and it cannot be the function of a description of the world to say no more than that. Regrettably, refusal to make commitments has become a familiar phenomenon in Soviet philosophical life. Kedrov links it directly with the rubbery use of terms: "The imprecision of the concepts with which some [Soviet] authors operate," he writes, "reaches at times the point that they adopt deliberately undefined and even clearly equivocal definitions of very important philosophical concepts, so that the reader himself, at his own discretion, may invest them with whatever meaning he wishes."[132]

Such obliging but fatal vagueness, however, does not tell the whole story of current Soviet dialectics. Through the work of serious philosophers such as Kedrov, Il'enkov, Meliukhin, Rutkevich, Sviderskii, and Tugarinov, the weaknesses of traditional doctrines and familiar modes of argumentation are being recognized and addressed. Meaningful claims are being made and real issues are being joined. These issues, however, are proving to be not secondary or derivative but fundamental. There are no more basic questions in dialectics than those concerning the number, the definitions, and the relations of the categories; but Soviet philosophers take a range of positions on all these questions. There is no more important dialectical category than contradiction; but Soviet philosophers advance conflicting views of it. The "basic" laws of dialectics were thought to be basic because they applied in every domain of reality; but it is debated whether this is true of all the laws. Clearly, much of the consensus that exists is merely verbal; it masks profound substantive disagreements.[133]

[132]*Dialekticheskoe protivorechie*, p. 320.
[133]At a Moscow conference in 1981, V. N. Shevchenko acknowledged the presence in Soviet philosophical literature of a point of view that "directly and unequivocally denies the very possibility of a single, in the sense of universal, mechanism of development" ("Materialy soveshchaniia po problemam istoricheskogo materializma v redaktsii zhurnala 'Voprosy filosofii,'" *Voprosy filosofii*, 1982, no. 6, p. 27). B. M. Kedrov is the only Soviet philosopher who has publicly admitted a wide range of *radical* disagreement among Soviet philosophers on questions of dialectics, and he recently condemned it vigorously: "On such fundamental questions of principle," he wrote in 1982, "it is intolerable for there to be such profound disagreements among philosophers who consider themselves to be in equal measure adherents to the same philosophical school.... No such pluralism of views can be justified here" ("Materialy soveshchaniia po problemam dialekticheskogo materializma v redaktsii zhurnala 'Voprosy filosofii,'" *Voprosy filosofii*, 1982, no. 7, p. 85).

It has been a thesis of this chapter that many of the disagreements are products of a conflict, inherent in dialectical materialism, between the Hegelian dialectical heritage elaborated by the Deborinists in the 1920s and the positivist, empiricist proclivities associated with materialism, developed by the mechanists in the same period. The fact that this dispute has emerged once more in the present day shows that there is increased opportunity for philosophical debate in the post-Stalin period, but it also testifies to the depth of the antagonism between dialectics and materialism. Soviet philosophers acknowledge that an ontology harmonizing the two has yet to be constructed, despite Herculean efforts since the 1950s. We may wonder what it will take to convince them that the task is not simply difficult but impossible.

[4]

Subjective Dialectics: Logic and Epistemology

SUBJECTIVE dialectics, or the Soviet theory of the dialectical character of our knowledge of the world, is no more free of controversy than its ontological counterpart, objective dialectics. Indeed the very identification of a branch of dialectics devoted to processes of cognition, despite its endorsement by Engels himself, is not a settled point of Marxist-Leninist doctrine, as we shall see. At the same time, Soviet philosophers did inherit a fund of views concerning logic and epistemology from their Marxist forebears, and in the post-Stalin age they have increasingly sought to develop this heritage into a dialectical theory of knowledge distinguishable from ontology. Their efforts have produced to date both a rough consensus on a general theory, which we shall summarize in the first section, and a large literature of specialized but controversial studies, which we shall examine in subsequent sections of this chapter.[1]

Principles of the Marxist-Leninist Theory of Knowledge

In epistemology, as in many other areas, "Marxist-Leninist" philosophy took its start not from Marx but from Engels. The "basic question of philosophy," as Engels identified it, contains a clearly epistemological di-

---

[1]For other studies of Soviet epistemology, see Thomas J. Blakeley, *Soviet Theory of Knowledge* (Dordrecht, 1964), and Bernard Jeu, *La philosophie soviétique et l'Occident. Essai sur les tendances et sur la signification de la philosophie soviétique contemporaine (1959–1969)* (Paris, 1969), pp. 281–371.

mension—"the relation of thinking to being."[2] It cannot be said that Engels explored the philosophical ramifications of that relation, however; rather, from his confident realist position he simply made certain assumptions about it. Being exists independently of thinking; thinking is derivative from it; ontologically, matter produces mind; epistemologically, the word that occurred to Engels to describe the relation of dependence was 'reflection': properly structured, Engels argued, our ideas of the real world produce "a correct reflection of reality."[3] Lenin in his turn adopted Engels's idiom, speaking of the cognitive process as "the *reflection* [*otrazhenie*] of nature in man's thought;" Lenin's famous realist characterization of matter, it will be remembered, identified it as an objective reality that is "copied, photographed, and reflected [*otobrazhaetsia*] by our sensations."[4] Given this authoritative support, it is no surprise that Engels's notion of *reflection* has come to occupy a central place in Marxist-Leninist epistemology.

For Soviet philosophers, reflection is not a phenomenon that exists in cognitive processes alone. Lenin suggested in *Materialism and Empirio-Criticism* that something analogous to sensory reflection is found throughout the material world, and his Soviet followers now argue that reflection is in fact a universal property of matter, consisting in the capacity of any one bit of matter to be affected by other bits.[5] According to the Soviet *Philosophical Encyclopedia*, reflection is "the reaction . . . of any thing (phenomenon) in interaction with another thing"—a notion broad enough to cover not only the knowing of reality by the mind but the reflective action of a mirror, the bouncing of a ball off a hard surface, and indeed every other instance of the response of one material object to another.[6] Rather than reducing cognition to physics, however, the Soviet philosopher

---

[2] Karl Marx and Frederick Engels, *Selected Works in One Volume* (New York, 1968), p. 604.

[3] Ibid., p. 605. The impression that Marx used the same terminology in *Capital* was created by Engels's tendentious editing of the English translation prepared after Marx's death and published in 1887. Where Marx wrote that the ideal is "nothing other than the material transposed [*umgesetzte*] and translated [*übersetzte*] in the human mind" (Karl Marx and Friedrich Engels, *Werke*, vol. 23 [Berlin, 1968], p. 27), the translators working under Engels's direction rendered the passage as "nothing else than the material world reflected by the human mind, and translated into forms of thought" (Karl Marx, *Capital. A Critique of Political Economy*, vol. 1, trans. S. Moore and E. Aveling, ed. F. Engels [New York, 1967], p. 19). And unfortunately an almost identical rendition is found in a modern translation that, although in some respects superior to the Moore-Aveling translation edited by Engels, still relies heavily on the latter (Karl Marx, *Capital. A Critique of Political Economy*, vol. 1, trans. Ben Fowkes [New York, 1977], p. 102).

[4] V. I. Lenin, *Polnoe sobranie sochinenii*, 5th ed, 55 vols. (Moscow, 1958–1965), vol. 29, p. 177 (italics in original); vol. 18, p. 131 (cited hereafter as *Soch.*).

[5] Lenin, *Soch.*, vol. 19, p. 91. See, for example, Z. M. Orudzhev, *Dialektika kak sistema* (Moscow, 1973), p. 289.

[6] F. V. Konstantinov et al., eds., *Filosofskaia entsiklopediia*, 5 vols. (Moscow, 1960–1970), vol. 4, p. 184.

postulates a hierarchy of levels of reflection, beginning with purely physical and chemical reactions and proceeding through the simpler animate levels (irritability, sensation) to the highly complex and distinctively human forms of reflection we call "understanding," "generalizing," "theorizing," and the like.[7]

These higher cognitive forms utilize data generated initially by sensory reflection, so that Marxist-Leninist epistemology is fundamentally a species of empiricism. Sensations, we read in a recent textbook, are "ultimately the source of all our knowledge of objects and phenomena."[8] Soviet philosophers themselves, however, reject the label 'empiricism' for their position; they regard the higher forms of cognition as theoretical rather than empirical, inasmuch as they require the active transformation and supplementation of sensory material by intellectual operations. Thus Marxist-Leninists do not see themselves as subscribing to a "copy theory" of knowledge, despite Lenin's statement that our sensations are "copies" of material reality. What at the level of sensation is appropriately called "copying" is superseded at more advanced levels of abstract cognition by concept formation, the invention of hypotheses, the making of predictions, and so on.

Although these advanced forms of reflection depart from sensory immediacy, they are for the Soviet philosopher by no means departures from the objective world. However indirectly, they still show us an independently existing reality, about which truth is attainable at all levels of cognition. That Leo Tolstoy was born in 1828, that birds have beaks, and that chemical elements have atomic weights (to cite examples given in *The Fundamentals of Marxist-Leninist Philosophy*) are all cases of correct reflection providing us with objective and even "eternal" truths. The concept of reflection thus goes along in Soviet philosophy with a correspondence theory of truth: our ideas are true to the extent that they conform to the actual state of reality. Soviet philosophers, like Lenin himself in *Materialism and Empirio-Criticism*, go so far as to entertain the notion of *absolute truth*, meaning by that expression the full and totally correct reflection of reality in human cognition. This notion of the ideal totality of objective truths is usually (though not always) regarded as a limit unattainable in practice: "In principle man is capable of knowing everything in the world,"

[7]F. V. Konstantinov, ed., *The Fundamentals of Marxist-Leninist Philosophy*, trans. R. Daglish (Moscow, 1982), pp. 89–91; Yu. A. Kharin, *Fundamentals of Dialectics*, trans. K. Kostrov (Moscow, 1981), pp. 81–88.

[8][F. V. Konstantinov, ed.,] *Fundamentals of Marxist-Leninist Philosophy*, trans. R. Daglish (Moscow, 1974), p. 108.

the authors of *Fundamentals* write, "but in reality this ability is realized in the process of the practically infinite historical development of society."[9]

Lenin introduced the term 'relative truth' for the imperfect state of our knowledge at a given time, incomplete and in need of correction. Relative truth, in the words of *Fundamentals*, "reflects reality truly in the main, but *not completely*, and only within certain limits, and with the further movement of knowledge it becomes more accurate and more profound"; Lenin in the same spirit writes that absolute truth is "composed of the sum of relative truths."[10] The recognition of relative truth, in this view, is by no means an espousal of epistemological relativism, for there must be an objective truth at the heart of every relative truth. In the Soviet view the "relativity" of Euclidean geometry and Newtonian mechanics, for example, consists not in dependence on the situation of the knower, and certainly not in inapplicability to the real world, but in their lack of perfect application to all phenomena.

But how do we determine which of our statements and beliefs qualify even as relative truths? How can we judge the adequacy of a supposed "reflection"—especially in theoretical cognition, where we cannot simply compare a mental copy with the perceived original? To these fundamental questions of epistemology Soviet philosophers provide a brief, unanimous answer—*practice*. Marx himself found practical activity, it is held, to be not only the source and the purpose but the test of knowledge, as is shown by a much-cited passage from the *Theses on Feuerbach*: "The question whether objective [*gegenständliche*] truth can be attributed to human thinking is not a question of theory but is a *practical* question. In practice man must prove the truth, that is, the reality and power . . . of his thinking."[11] Engels, always attracted to the natural sciences, defined practice as "experiment and industry," and he included within it both the testing of our understanding of a natural object by synthesizing it in the laboratory and such refined scientific "practice" as the discovery of the planet Neptune on the basis of Leverrier's calculations.[12] Lenin, though he went no further in fleshing out the practice criterion, left no doubt that he believed in it: "The supremacy over nature which manifests itself in the practice of mankind," he wrote in *Materialism and Empirio-Criticism*, "is the result of the objectively true reflection in the head of man of the phenomena and processes of nature, is the proof that this reflection (within the bounds of what practice has shown us) is the objective, absolute, eternal

[9]Konstantinov, *Fundamentals* (1982), p. 163.
[10]Ibid., p. 164 (italics in original); Lenin, *Soch.*, vol. 18, p. 137.
[11]Marx and Engels, *Selected Works*, p. 28 (italics in original).
[12]Ibid., pp. 605–606.

truth."[13] Soviet philosophers have subsequently devoted considerable attention to elaborating the notion of practice as the criterion of truth and seeking to distinguish the Marxist-Leninist view of these matters from other views in modern epistemology.

One of the more difficult distinctions to make is that between Marxism-Leninism and pragmatism. In many popular Soviet expositions of the practice criterion, it has a decidedly pragmatic ring: "In order to establish the truth of an idea [A. P. Sheptulin writes] it is necessary to perform certain practical actions based on this idea. If the results are as expected, the idea is true; otherwise it is false. To establish, for instance, the truth of the statement that heat may be converted into mechanical motion, we build a steam engine which operates on the principle of conversion of thermal into mechanical energy."[14] Yet ever since Lenin included an uncomplimentary footnote on pragmatism in *Materialism and Empirio-Criticism*,[15] relations between the two movements have been strained, and for many years pragmatism was condemned in Soviet philosophical works as a vicious tool of Wall Street imperialism. Even in the less strident rhetoric of the present day it is still rejected as a subjective idealist outlook that "reflects the narrow practicism of the American bourgeois." Pragmatism, it is said, judges the success of action on the basis of the personal satisfaction of the agent or the interests of the exploiting class, whereas for Marxism-Leninism practice is aimed at establishing objective truth and serves the interests of all mankind.[16]

Both the reflective and the practical character of the cognitive process, in the Soviet conception, are closely linked with a third major feature of knowledge stressed by the Marxist-Leninist—namely, its *dialectical* character. Objective dialectics teaches that the world itself is dialectical—that it harbors inner contradictions that work themselves out in dynamic development. To reflect that world faithfully, the Marxist-Leninist argues, cognition, too, must be dialectical in its content and methods. Lenin's fascination with the Hegelian dialectic clearly stemmed from a conviction that the conceptual relations discussed by Hegel could be read "materialistically"—that is, as characterizing the material world; Lenin was convinced that, in Kedrov's words, "the dialectics of concepts . . . reflects the dialectics of things."[17] From there it was an easy step to the view that the

[13]Lenin, *Soch.*, vol. 18, p. 198.
[14]A. P. Sheptulin, *Marxist-Leninist Philosophy*, trans. S. Ponomarenko and A. Timofeyev (Moscow, 1978), p. 150.
[15]Lenin, *Soch.*, vol. 18, p. 363.
[16]I. T. Frolov, ed., *Filosofskii slovar'*, 4th ed. (Moscow, 1980), p. 291; M. B. Mitin et al., eds., *Sovremennye problemy teorii poznaniia dialekticheskogo materializma*, vol. 2 (Moscow, 1970), p. 20.
[17]*Dialekticheskoe protivorechie* (Moscow, 1979), p. 321.

activity of acquiring and testing knowledge is a dialectical process—a conclusion Lenin stated in a passage that has become a byword of Marxist-Leninist epistemology: "From living contemplation [that is, sensation] to abstract thought *and from there to practice*—such is the dialectical route of the cognition of *truth*, the cognition of objective reality."[18] Following this lead, Soviet philosophers have applied dialectical terminology to most of the features of the cognitive process that we have identified above, seeing in the progressively increasing adequacy of our knowledge of the world a "dialectic of absolute and relative" in which the positive (that is, absolute) content of relative truth is sublated in more absolute, less relative truth.

The dialecticization of a reflection theory of knowledge, however, raises questions as to the status of both epistemology and logic. If *dialectics* cognitively reflects the movement of the real and describes the knowledge process from initiation to application, of what use are epistemology and logic in the traditional senses? Lenin, in the Hegelian enthusiasm of his *Philosophical Notebooks*, saw no reason to retain them as separate philosophical disciplines. "Dialectics *is* the theory of knowledge of (Hegel and) Marxism," he wrote. As for logic, Hegel gave its name to his dialectics of concepts and dismissed Aristotelian or formal logic as an outmoded, limited field, to be subsumed in the true logic of dialectics. Lenin agreed, and although he accepted traditional logic as a useful school subject he identified true logic as well as theory of knowledge with dialectics: "In *Capital*," he wrote, "the logic, dialectics, and theory of knowledge (three words are not needed: it is one and the same thing) of materialism are applied to a single science."[19]

The full meaning of Lenin's statement has yet to be agreed upon by Soviet philosophers, and a systematic body of doctrine corresponding to his dialectical trinity has yet to be constructed. Just as objective dialectics awaits definitive statement, so, too, subjective dialectics is an unformed, nascent discipline in Soviet philosophy. But Lenin's statement is viewed as a call to action: the principal task of the philosopher working in these fields, it is held, is to construct both a dialectical theory of knowledge and a dialectical logic. Traditional logic is tolerated, but in general works on dialectical materialism it is usually relegated to a subordinate and sometimes a distinctly nonphilosophical status, with warnings against the dangers of "absolutizing" its principles and methods—that is, regarding them as fully and exclusively adequate for the study of reasoning. In the popular

---

[18]Lenin, *Soch.*, vol. 29, pp. 152–153 (italics in original).
[19]Ibid., pp. 321 (italics in original), 301.

philosophical literature, dialectics reigns supreme, and all aspects of the acquisition and proof of knowledge are held to be connected with it.

Formal Logic in the Post-Stalin Period

It is a paradoxical feature of the current philosophical scene in the USSR that, for all the official emphasis on dialectics, formal logic is nonetheless cultivated fruitfully by many scholars without the slightest attention to dialectics. Despite Lenin's assurance that the words are synonymous, in Soviet usage the unqualified term 'logic' means, not only to the man in the street but to most philosophers, very much what it means in Western discourse—that is, the science of correct reasoning based on the classical laws of thought originally identified by Aristotle: the law of identity (A equals A), the law of noncontradiction (not both A and not-A), and the law of excluded middle (either A or not-A). Furthermore, the subject taught and investigated in departments of logic in universities and in sectors of logic in research institutes is the same familiar subject called "logic" in Western institutions; Soviet specialists in "dialectical logic" are found not in those divisions of such institutions but in the divisions of dialectical materialism. Nondialectical logic, moreover, is a surprisingly vital part of the training of Soviet philosophers. In the philosophy curriculum of Moscow State University, the required program in formal logic occupies a demanding 200 hours of student class time—the same number of hours devoted to dialectical materialism. And when we add the extensive work in formal logic carried on in departments of mathematics and specialized institutes, we see that the Marxist-Leninist commonplaces summarized in the previous section are far from telling the whole story of the Soviet approach to questions of knowledge and reasoning.

Soviet work in formal logic is largely a product of the postwar period, though its development was powerfully abetted by the survival of a group of older scholars—Valentin Ferdinandovich Asmus (1894–1975), Sof'ia Aleksandrovna Ianovskaia (1896–1966), Petr Sergeevich Novikov (b. 1901), and others—who provided a link to an earlier tradition of Russian work in logic reaching back into the nineteenth century.[20] Through the first fifteen years of the Stalin period, the little attention paid to logic in the Soviet Union favored "dialectical logic" at the expense of formal, which

---

[20]Guido Küng, "Bibliography of Soviet Work in the Field of Mathematical Logic and the Foundations of Mathematics, from 1917–1957," *Notre Dame Journal of Formal Logic* 3 (1962), p. 2; Alexander Philipov, *Logic and Dialectic in the Soviet Union* (New York, 1952), pp. 51–54.

was viewed as a kind of class enemy.[21] The essay attributed to Stalin in the *Short Course*, however, with its heavily "ontological" approach to dialectical materialism, signaled a lessening of interest in dialectics generally, and there is some evidence that the rehabilitation of formal logic was planned as early as the late 1930s, before the onset of World War II. In any event, in the fall of 1946, instruction in formal logic was introduced in Soviet high schools and universities by decree of the Central Committee of the Communist party, and extensive work in the field began.[22]

In the absence of Soviet textbooks in logic, a prerevolutionary work by G. I. Chelpanov was hastily reissued, but the void was soon filled more adequately by translations and original Russian works. Through the efforts of Ianovskaia and others, important books by major Western logicians were made available in the Russian language, beginning with *Principles of Theoretical Logic*, by Hilbert and Ackermann, in 1947 and Alfred Tarski's *Introduction to Logic and to the Methodology of Deductive Sciences* in 1948. The new Soviet works, all of which had a classical, Aristotelian orientation and avoided the more modern developments in mathematical logic, included texts by M. S. Strogovich, V. F. Asmus, S. N. Vinogradov, and others.[23]

Despite their conservative character the Soviet works provoked a storm of criticism for their "formalism" and lack of political commitment, and a heated discussion of them erupted on the pages of *Voprosy filosofii*.[24] But at that point another favorable development gave the fortunes of formal logic a needed theoretical boost. Stalin's "Letters on Linguistics," published in 1950, were directed against the theories of Academician Nikolai Iakovlevich Marr (1864–1934), whose "dialectical" and thoroughly class-conscious analysis of language led to the view, among others, that formal logic is incompatible with Marxism-Leninism. Stalin in reply said nothing about logic, but his pronouncement that the vocabularies and the grammatical structures of languages are class-neutral and serve society as a whole was easily extendable to the rules of formal logic as well.[25] The extension was made authoritatively by an editorial in *Voprosy filosofii* in

[21]Philipov, pp. 34–35.

[22]Ibid., pp. 40–41; Gustav A. Wetter, *Dialectical Materialism. A Historical and Systematic Survey of Philosophy in the Soviet Union*, trans. Peter Heath (London, 1958), p. 525.

[23]Philipov, pp. 40ff.; Wetter, *Dialectical Materialism*, p. 525.

[24]Philipov, pp. 55–56; J. M. Bocheński, "Soviet Logic," in J. M. Bocheński and T. J. Blakeley, eds., *Studies in Soviet Thought*, I (Dordrecht, 1961), p. 30.

[25]I. Stalin, *Marksizm i voprosy iazykoznaniia* ([Moscow], 1950), pp. 10–23. Roy A. Medvedev has noted that the ideas on linguistics expressed by Stalin had been advanced repeatedly by Marr's scholarly opponents, and Medvedev contends that one of them, the Academician V. V. Vinogradov, "gave Stalin much help" in preparing the letters (*Let History Judge* [New York, 1972], p. 51). See also Philipov, pp. 60ff.

1951, in which the critics of formal logic were assured that the forms and laws of thought studied by the discipline are the property of all mankind, inasmuch as they are a reflection of an objective reality, and that the historical changes to which they are subject are not the explosive alterations produced by class antagonisms but are the same gradual, continual changes we find in the evolutionary transition from socialism to communism.[26] Formal logic, then, was granted the right to exist.

Dialectics was far from vanquished by this development, however, for even at that time it was said by many to provide a conceptual framework within which formal logic could occupy a delimited and a philosophically inferior place. Furthermore, the death of Stalin and the end of the authority of the *Short Course* brought strong efforts to redialecticize Soviet Marxism-Leninism, and calls for the development of a truly dialectical logic increased. Yet the Stalinist acceptance of formal logic was not rescinded, and since that time a more or less official "two logics" policy has been pursued by the Soviet philosophical establishment. Despite the clear precedence given dialectics in official pronouncements and in the philosophical literature, both fields have been essentially free to develop, on different but often intersecting tracks, with periodic collisions and a continuing state of tension between them.

Different tactics have been employed by defenders of formal logic in coping with its status as the lesser of two equals. Some—most prominently the Georgian philosopher K. S. Bakradze—have been outspoken opponents of the idea of a "dialectical logic." There can be only one science of correct reasoning, Bakradze argued, and that is formal logic; dialectics, in his view, is a broad philosophical discipline, combining epistemology with ontology and at best providing a general methodology for the sciences.[27] Another early opponent of dialectical logic was N. I. Kondakov, who along with Bakradze was one of the principal targets of a 1955 editorial in *Voprosy filosofii* warning ominously that Bakradze's views were no longer "the individual mistakes of an aberrant logician" but represented "a profoundly erroneous and pernicious tendency, obstinately defended by one segment of our logicians."[28]

A more common approach, especially in recent years, is that of the champions of formal logic who proclaim themselves to be champions of dialectical logic. A good example is a recent work by D. P. Gorskii, E. K. Voishvillo, and I. S. Narskii. Though all three are well known for

---

[26]"K itogam obsuzhdeniia voprosov logiki," *Voprosy filosofii*, 1951, no. 6, pp. 143–149.

[27]K. S. Bakradze, "K voprosu o sootnoshenii logiki i dialektiki," *Voprosy filosofii*, 1950, no. 2, pp. 198–209.

[28]"Protiv putanitsy i vul'garizatsii v voprosakh logiki," *Voprosy filosofii*, 1955, no. 3, p. 158.

their interest in formal logic, they describe their book as devoted to "a systematic exposition of the basic principles, laws, and concepts of the dialectics of scientific cognition, which is viewed in the present work as coinciding with dialectical logic."[29] Not surprisingly, such protestations of fealty to dialectical logic are often regarded with considerable skepticism by the dialectical opposition. Voishvillo, for example, has been described privately by a prominent dialectician as someone who now "pretends" to accept dialectics but is actually "worse than Bakradze." So deep do the suspicions run that Narskii has been criticized openly for calling dialectical contradiction a "problem" in the title of one of his books (*The Problem of Dialectical Contradiction*).[30]

But more common still, and considerably more important with respect to the actual development of formal logic in the USSR, is the attitude of those mathematicians, logicians, and philosophers who, protected by their academic specializations outside dialectical materialism, simply ignore dialectics and avoid the potential controversy inherent in either opposing or defending it.

The most talented and for many years the most successful representative of this approach was Alexander Zinoviev, several of whose logical works were published in the West even before he fled the country in 1978 and became better known as a writer of fiction and social criticism. Although he could not avoid at times coming into open conflict with antiformalist views, as at the 1958 Moscow conference on contradiction discussed in the previous chapter, Zinoviev's scholarly writings were consistently devoted to the serious discussion of substantive, often technical and specialized questions of modern nonclassical logic and its applications in the analysis of the language of science, without any reference to the question of one logic or two. This avoidance of troubled issues in Marxist philosophy, along with the high professional quality of his work, accounts for Zinoviev's success in publishing in the USSR what he has called his "six non-Marxist books" in logic over the years 1960 to 1972.[31] The same designation "non-Marxist" might be applied to the continuing work of such Soviet logicians as A. V. Kuznetsov, L. L. Maksimova, A. G. Dragalin, V. N. Sadovskii, and V. M. Popov, whose work is similarly technical and ideologically noncommittal.

[29]E. K. Voishvillo, D. P. Gorskii, and I. S. Narskii, eds., *Dialektika nauchnogo poznaniia. Ocherk dialekticheskoi logiki* (Moscow, 1978), p. 3.
[30]A. M. Minasian, ed., *Dialektika sotsializma* (Rostov-on-Don, 1971), p. 111.
[31]Zinoviev's books on logic published in the West include *Philosophical Problems of Many-Valued Logic*, trans. G. Küng and D. D. Comey (Dordrecht, 1963), and *Foundations of the Logical Theory of Scientific Knowledge (Complex Logic)*, trans. T. J. Blakeley (Dordrecht, 1973). Zinoviev's best-known work of social criticism is the satirical novel *The Yawning Heights*, trans. Gordon Clough (New York, 1979).

Substantively, what has been accomplished in formal logic by Soviet scholars? In broad terms, they have brought the Soviet Union into the mainstream of international activity in the field and have raised Soviet work to advanced levels of sophistication in a wide variety of logical specialties. The progressive achievement of this status may be observed in a series of Soviet studies surveying the logic scene in the USSR. The first, written by S. A. Ianovskaia in 1948, used the bulk of its space to defend Soviet logicians and their subject against Marxist-Leninist misgivings and to describe the achievements of prewar Russian logicians.[32] In a comparable survey by Ianovskaia eleven years later, however, ideological defense is no longer necessary; mathematical logic is presented as an acknowledged branch of science and not (as in 1948) a philosophical appendage to mathematics, and far more Soviet works are cited, including numerous advanced monographs on such topics as constructivist ("intuitionist") mathematics and the theory of algorithms—two areas in which much work has been done by Soviet logicians.[33]

A survey by A. F. Okulov in 1970 reported extensive new work in many areas, including that of Zinoviev on logical inference, Gorskii on abstraction and the definition of concepts, Voishvillo on the theory of concepts, A. L. Subbotin on syllogistics and the application of algebraic methods in logic, and P. V. Tavenets, V. K. Finn, and E. D. Smirnova on logical semantics.[34] The most recent stock-taking, by V. A. Bocharov, E. K. Voishvillo, A. G. Dragalin, and V. A. Smirnov, was prepared for an international congress in 1979, and so it is not surprising that the authors present a favorable picture of Soviet logic.[35] What is remarkable is that, apart from the names of the logicians cited and the blatant fiction that "in Marxist philosophy, logic, in all its aspects, has always been accorded great importance,"[36] the report might be a survey of logic in any scientifically advanced country today. Work is described in all the chief areas of con-

[32]S. A. Ianovskaia, "Osnovaniia matematiki i matematicheskaia logika," in *Matematika v SSSR za tridtsat' let 1917–1947* (Moscow-Leningrad, 1948), pp. 11–45.
[33]S. A. Ianovskaia, "Matematicheskaia logika i osnovaniia matematiki," in *Matematika v SSSR za sorok let 1917–1957*, vol. 1 (Moscow, 1959), pp. 13–120; Küng, "Bibliography," p. 3; G. Küng, "Mathematical Logic in the Soviet Union (1917–1947 and 1947–1957)," in Bocheński and Blakeley, p. 41.
[34]A. F. Okulov, *Sovetskaia filosofskaia nauka i ee problemy. Kratkii ocherk* (Moscow, 1970), p. 87. For a more detailed appraisal by a Western scholar at about the same time, see Jürg Hänggi, *Formale und dialektische Logik in der Sowjetphilosophie. Dissertation zur Erlangung der Doktorwürde von der philosophischen Fakultät der Universität Freiburg in der Schweiz*, 2 vols. (Zurich, 1971).
[35]V. A. Bocharov et al., "Nekotorye problemy razvitiia logiki," *Voprosy filosofii*, 1979, no. 6, pp. 102–114. This paper has been published in English translation as "On Problems of the Evolution of Logic," *Soviet Studies in Philosophy* 18 (Spring 1980), pp. 31–52.
[36]Bocharov, "On Problems," p. 45.

temporary logic—the theory of deduction, modal logic, relevant logics, the philosophical foundations of mathematics, the application of logic to particular problems of mathematics and problems in the methodology and philosophy of science, and the history of logic. The work outlined is not cranky or ideologically tainted, and although only a specialist could make a final judgment of its merit, in both range and depth it appears comparable to work produced in other countries.[37]

The integration of logic with general philosophy through the analysis of language, in the manner of modern, postpositivist analytic philosophy, is not well developed in the USSR but it is far from unknown. Its principal center is the remote, ideologically neutralized science preserve known as the "Academy town" (*Akademgorodok*) at Novosibirsk. There, in the Institute of History, Philology, and Philosophy that is part of the Siberian division of the Academy of Sciences of the USSR, a select group of philosophers and linguists follows the latest writings of Saul Kripke and Jaako Hintikka and discusses developments in "possible world semantics" as eagerly and knowledgeably as any readers of *Synthese* in Princeton or Helsinki. An example of their work is a recent volume entitled *Logic and Ontology* (1978), published by the prestigious *Nauka* (Science) publishing house in Moscow. This book follows a pattern now very familiar in Soviet scholarly publishing. An initial quotation from the works of Marx or Engels establishes the importance of the subject to be investigated (here, language); this appeal to scripture is then supported by a brief indication that a properly "materialist" (that is, realist) approach will be followed (in this case, that the book will be devoted to aspects of "the reflection of reality by language").[38] Thereupon the authors leave behind all national and ideological distinguishing marks and proceed to discuss their subject in another vein entirely. The idiom of modern analytic philosophy is used to examine technical questions in the philosophy of language, in essays bearing titles such as "The Game-Theory Approach to the Semantics of Natural Language" and "Two Approaches to the Problem of the Foundations of Logical Modalities." Work of this sort has only a limited impact on the broader philosophical community in the USSR, but it is available in published books and articles.

The application of logic to the "special sciences" has always been important to Soviet philosophers, given their stress on the methodological significance of Marxism-Leninism. Understandably, however, the extension of *formal* logical analysis to science has met with resistance from

---

[37]For this provisional judgment I am indebted to my Ohio State University colleague George Schumm.

[38]V. V. Tselishchev et al., eds., *Logika i ontologiia* (Moscow, 1978), p. 3.

dialecticians. The very expression 'the logic of science' is suspect in some quarters in the USSR, as it is used principally to describe the application of formal concepts and techniques in the philosophy of science, by those Soviet philosophers presumed to be tainted by the positivist mentality.[39] Thus when Zinoviev entitled his 1971 book *The Logic of Science* (rather than, say, *The Dialectics of Scientific Cognition*), it was an aesopic declaration that the book examined the logical structure of science from a formal, not a dialectical, standpoint.

Despite dialectical resistance, however, formal methods are being actively extended to scientific work in the USSR. To date their most fruitful applications have come in two related fields in which there has been great interest among Soviet scholars in the post-Stalin period, doubly fostered by the practical significance of the fields and by the fact that both can derive some support from the principles of dialectical materialism. They are *cybernetics* and *systems theory*.

Loren Graham has well described the Soviet enthusiasm for cybernetics that peaked in the 1960s, nourished by the hope that the fledgling science of control processes would facilitate the rational direction of the centralized socioeconomic system of the USSR.[40] Beginning in the 1950s a number of prominent Soviet scientists and philosophers, led by Ernst Kol'man, S. L. Sobolev, and A. I. Berg, championed the new discipline and provoked lively and far-ranging discussion of it. The works of Western pioneers in the field were translated into Russian, and a Soviet literature developed that swelled to vast proportions—including literature concerning the use of formal logic in cybernetic analysis. In recent years the interest in cybernetics as a socioeconomic panacea has waned considerably in the USSR, but paradoxically the cybernetic significance of formal logic has increased. For as cybernetics has lost authority as an overarching science of control and communication, the term in Soviet usage has come to be used as a generic label for a group of more specialized and technical disciplines— computer science, information theory, game theory, decision theory, and the like—in all of which modern mathematical logic has powerful applications. Work in these areas is pursued at well-supported centers such as the Institute of Applied Mathematics, the All-Union Institute of Scientific and Technical Information, and the Institute of Cybernetics of the Ukrainian Academy of Sciences.[41]

---

[39]See, for example, G. Sadovskii, "Logika revoliutsionnogo myshleniia i klassovyi podkhod v logike," *Kommunist*, 1979, no. 11, p. 69; and Okulov, p. 90.

[40]Loren R. Graham, *Science and Philosophy in the Soviet Union* (New York, 1972), pp. 324–354.

[41]Küng, "Bibliography," pp. 3–4; N. I. Zhukov, *Informatsiia (filosofskii analiz tsentral'- nogo poniatiia kibernetiki*, 2d ed. (Minsk, 1971), p. 159; Bocharov, "On Problems," p. 44.

Over and above the application of formal methods in cybernetic disciplines, Soviet philosophers also continue to devote attention to various concepts associated with cybernetics and to the relations of these concepts to the categories of dialectical materialism. To the extent that cybernetics deals with the organization of dynamic sets of elements, a natural affinity to dialectics has generated much discussion. But the greatest Soviet attention is given to the concept 'information', which is seen to parallel the category 'reflection' in Marxist-Leninist epistemology. Many Soviet philosophers, indeed, contend that the two concepts are coextensive. K. E. Morozov, defining information as the content of a signal, argues that every process of reflection, whether in inorganic or living nature, has information as its content, inasmuch as reflection is simply "a change taking place in one system ... under the influence of signals coming from another system."[42] Other writers, however, argue that although reflection is a universal property of matter, information is not, usually on the ground that information requires interpretation by a receiver—a feature of material interaction not found in the inorganic world.[43] But even the latter writers see the concepts as closely related. In his interesting book *Information* (1971), N. I. Zhukov elaborates the concept of reflection at some length in order to locate 'information' on the Marxist-Leninist philosophical landscape, but he also looks to the latter notion to "deepen" our understanding of the former—a benefit that Soviet cybernetics enthusiasts believe could be extended to many categories of dialectics if cybernetic notions were systematically applied to them.[44]

Systems theory is a more recent and now a more widely discussed direction in which the apparatus of modern logic is being applied in the USSR. Regarded by many Soviet philosophers and scientists as a comprehensive theory that incorporates cybernetics as a special case, "the systems approach" has in the past fifteen years become the most significant and influential trend in Soviet philosophy of science. It is the subject of a flood of literature, and is cited in virtually every discussion of scientific methodology.[45]

Soviet work in systems theory, like most work in the area worldwide,

[42]K. E. Morozov, "Model' sviazi informatsii s dvizheniem," in L. Ia. Stanis et al., eds., *Novye filosofskie voprosy fiziki (Materialy konferentsii 1973-1975 gg.)* (Moscow, 1977), p. 40.
[43]Ibid., pp. 39–40; Zhukov, pp. 42–55.
[44]Zhukov, pp. 256–257.
[45]A statistical study of the literature may be found in *Sistemnye issledovaniia. Ezhegodnik. 1978* (Moscow, 1978), pp. 127–135. A bibliography of over four hundred items is included in I. V. Blauberg, V. N. Sadovsky, and E. G. Yudin, eds., *Systems Theory. Philosophical and Methodological Problems*, trans. S. Syrovatkin and O. Germogenova (Moscow, 1977), pp. 294–318.

is heavily indebted to the writings of Ludwig von Bertalanffy (1901–1972), the Austrian theoretical biologist who is credited with laying the foundations for a general systems theory in the postwar period.[46] Soviet systems theorists do not ignore the tectology of Alexander Bogdanov, and in systems circles in the USSR Bogdanov's pioneering efforts in constructing a general science of organization are more and more widely and sympathetically discussed. Nonetheless the texts of von Bertalanffy and other Western innovators in the field such as Russell L. Ackoff, W. Ross Ashby, and Kenneth Boulding are widely available to Soviet scholars through translations, whereas Bogdanov's writings have not been printed in the USSR since the 1920s. Original Soviet literature in the field began to appear in the mid-1950s, but only within the past decade has it grown to its present large proportions. The first Soviet research group specifically devoted to systems theory was established in Odessa in 1966. Another active center for systems research is the Sector for Systems Studies in Science, established in 1967 as a division of the Institute of the History of Science and Technology in Moscow; headed by Igor Viktorovich Blauberg, this group sponsors many publications in the field, including (since 1969) the annual *Systems Research*.[47] In the 1970s still another center was formed, the All-Union Scientific Research Institute for Systems Investigations in Moscow.[48]

Although Soviet philosophers disagree on many points concerning the nature and scope of systems theory, among the discipline's supporters there is a consensus that it provides a general scientific methodology for the study of complex objects, whatever their type or origin (natural, social, or artificial), considering such objects as "sets of interconnected elements functioning as single wholes."[49] Although most Soviet systems theorists question von Bertalanffy's contention that the laws of different spheres of reality are isomorphic, they agree nonetheless that common principles of structure and function can be found in systems as different as biological organisms and economic systems and consequently that it is fruitful to take a common "systems approach" toward complexes of all sorts.[50] The affinity of systems theory to another much discussed contemporary method—structuralism—is acknowledged by Soviet writers, but they take pains to point up differences between the two approaches, one of which is the stress placed by the systems approach on formal aspects of meth-

[46]For an account of von Bertalanffy's career and ideas, see Blauberg, Sadovsky, and Yudin, pp. 42–68.
[47]Ibid., pp. 26–27, 80–81.
[48]*Sistemnye issledovaniia*, p. 5.
[49]Blauberg, Sadovsky, and Yudin, p. 33.
[50]Ibid., pp. 13–14, 35, 59–61.

odology. "Unlike structuralism and functionalism," E. G. Iudin writes, "systems theory not only borrows logical and mathematical apparatus from other fields of knowledge but makes ever more persistent attempts at constructing its own formalized calculi." These attempts, undertaken by Sadovskii, Smirnov, and others, include not only work in the direction of axiomatizing general systems theory but what Iudin calls the "development of particular specialized instruments for the formalization of systems research."[51]

Clearly, however, it is not its penchant for formalization that makes systems theory tolerable to the dialectical materialist. It is, rather, the fact that elements of the systems approach can, without much strain, be seen as applications of a more general "dialectical" methodology. Systems research, according to Iudin, starting from the idea of the wholeness of the system under investigation, studies the connections among elements that constitute the system's structure and organization, deals with the "self-organizing" features of systems, and considers the problems of goal-oriented activity and development within systems.[52] It is small wonder, then, that systems research should be considered by some as "realizing" (to use I. G. Glazunov's word) the principles of dialectics, which portray the entire material world as complex, interconnected, self-moving, and subject to progressive development.[53] Soviet champions of systems theory make no secret of this tie. "It is exactly this connection with dialectics," Blauberg, Iudin, and Sadovskii write, "that gives an added significance to systems methods both in science and practice in Soviet society."[54]

The precise nature of the connection between the systems approach and dialectics is a much debated question in Soviet philosophy, however. Advocates of the approach tend to see systems theory as not simply a "realization" of dialectics but a philosophical propaedeutic to it, a way of interpreting dialectics that gives new content to traditional categories and allows us "to interpret the conceptual apparatus of dialectical materialism in a new light."[55] Furthermore, application of the method in the scientific study of objects in the world is held to be not simply consistent with dialectics but uniquely or peculiarly appropriate to it as well as peculiarly effective: "The systems approach to the study of complex, evolving objects

[51]Ibid., p. 37; see also pp. 73, 87–88, 204, and *Metodicheskoe posobie po dialekticheskomu materializmu. Dlia slushatelei ZVPSh pri TsK KPSS* (Moscow, 1977), pp. 120–122.
[52]Blauberg, Sadovsky, and Yudin, pp. 37–41.
[53]I. G. Glazunov, "O razvitii dvukhstupenchatykh gnoseologicheskikh struktur vo mnogostupenchatye," *Vestnik Moskovskogo universiteta. Seriia 7. Filosofiia*, 1981, no. 5, p. 14.
[54]Blauberg, Sadovsky, and Yudin, p. 9.
[55]Ibid., p. 93.

is *inherent in* Marxism-Leninism," Blauberg writes, "and represents one of the greatest victories in the history of knowledge."[56] In this view, Marx himself is held to be the real inventor of the method: his analysis of modern industrial capitalism in *Capital* is said to be the first true application of what could just as well be called the "systems method" as the "dialectical method"—a method used, of course, by Lenin also, in his analysis of imperialism.[57] Blauberg does assert that the dialectical method is broader, inasmuch as the systems approach is applicable only to the study of "real objects characterized by complex organization." But it is difficult to see what object of study in a dialectical universe would *not* be real and complex. Moreover, there seems little use for a broader method (at least in the social sphere) when we are assured by Blauberg that in socialist society the systems approach "is being applied with ever greater success to solve all major economic and social problems."[58]

Soviet critics of systems theory, granting its dialectical features but concerned that, as Glazunov phrases it, "the general theory of systems is elaborated primarily on a mathematical basis as a formal logical theory," seek to show that dialectics is both theoretically more basic and practically of wider use than systems theory.[59] The correct approach to understanding the relation between them, according to Zaid Orudzhev, "consists in the application of the universal categories of the materialist dialectic to the theory of systems, and not in the reverse." Systems theory is a more "concrete" method that adds nothing to our understanding of dialectics, Orudzhev argues, and he faults it for being indifferent to the *direction* of changes within systems: it views both progress and regress as "equally necessary and legitimate alterations." Like cybernetics, systems theory is not really a *philosophical* study at all for Orudzhev, and consequently it does not provide a universally applicable method. What it does provide is a useful *general* method, on a par with induction, deduction, modeling, and the like, which is still in its formative stages and cannot be perfected without "the skillful utilization of materialist dialectics."[60]

Whatever the exact connection between systems theory and dialectical materialism, advocates of the former must avoid Bogdanov's fate of having

---

[56]Ibid., p. 106 (italics added).

[57]Ibid., pp. 104–106; Iu. V. Gritskov, "Problema utochneniia statusa obshchei teorii sistem," *Vestnik Moskovskogo universiteta. Seriia 7. Filosofiia*, 1981, no. 5, p. 50. The fullest analysis of Marxism as a systems theory is found in V. P. Kuz'min, *Printsip sistemnosti v teorii i metodologii K. Marksa*, 2d ed. (Moscow, 1980).

[58]Blauberg, Sadovsky, and Yudin, p. 111.

[59]Glazunov, p. 14.

[60]Orudzhev, *Dialektika kak sistema*, pp. 77, 63, 7, 83.

their views interpreted as an *alternative* to Marxism.[61] Since there are no alternatives to the truth, the believer in systems theory must find an interpretation of that truth that will permit his views to share in it.

The Search for Dialectical Logic

The development of formal logic and of methodologies exploiting it, however vigorously pursued by many Soviet philosophers, is either ignored or opposed by most. The majority, whether for intellectual or political reasons, take seriously Lenin's remark about the identity of dialectics, logic, and the theory of knowledge and seek approaches to the scientific understanding of the world that are *essentially* dialectical and not simply, in the words of one dialectician, limited to "formal logic with an occasional admixture of dialectics."[62] On the current Soviet scene this attitude is ideologically reinforced by the frequent repetition of Lenin's catchphrase and by authoritative warnings against the dangers of "absolutizing" formal logic. A 1979 article in *Kommunist* by G. Sadovskii, perhaps occasioned by the flight of Alexander Zinoviev from the USSR several months earlier, characterized excessive devotion to formal logic as a pernicious attempt to replace the proletarian and revolutionary doctrine of Marxism with "the abstract truths of bourgeois objectivism." Logic, the article goes on, cannot be politically neutral and "indifferent generally to truth and falsehood." "The only weapon capable of dealing with every fideistic diversion of bourgeois ideology and of manifesting consistently, in every ideological encounter, the class position of the proletariat," according to Sadovskii, is "dialectics as the logic and theory of knowledge of contemporary materialism."[63]

The notion of dialectics as logic was not always so warmly recommended. In the later Stalin era, as we have seen, subjective dialectics fell into relative disfavor as a consequence of what Kedrov has called the "absurd 'ontologization' " of Soviet philosophy in the essay attributed to Stalin in the *Short Course*. In that work, Kedrov argues, *thought* was in effect excluded from the subject-matter of Marxist-Leninist philosophy: the field was reduced to the study of the general laws of nature and society,

---

[61]Blauberg, Sadovsky, and Yudin, p. 27. However lively the interest in systems theory in some quarters in the USSR, there is no basis for the extravagant claim that it has replaced Marxism-Leninism as the theoretical basis of Soviet ideology (cf. Criton Zoakos, "The Surfacing of Holy Mother Rus: A Documentary Report," *Executive Intelligence Review*, July 26, 1983, pp. 16–31).

[62]Orudzhev, *Dialektika kak sistema*, p. 348.

[63]Sadovskii, pp. 65, 69, 72.

and no mention was made of dialectical logic or epistemology. And Stalin's authority was so great, Kedrov points out, that anything not mentioned in a work supposedly authored by him became suspect. At some philosophy conferences in the early 1950s, Kedrov reports, acknowledging a dialectical logic was likened to stabbing dialectical materialism in the back.[64] Such ontologization was also evident in the long-awaited textbook *Dialectical Materialism* (1953), where again no reference was made to "dialectical logic."[65]

Kedrov and G. Gurgenidze wrote a detailed critique of the textbook, and although publication of the critique was blocked for a year and a half, it did finally appear in the Party journal *Kommunist* in 1955.[66] With that signal of authoritative support, other writers joined in, and the advocacy of dialectical logic came to be both a symbol of rejection of the Stalinist past and an indication of genuine interest in the creation of a dialectical Marxist philosophy. Kedrov sees the recognition of dialectical logic in the next approved textbook, *Fundamentals of Marxist Philosophy* (1958), as a turning point, and monographs by Rozental', A. M. Kasymzhanov, M. N. Alekseev, and others pursued the growing interest.[67]

But what is dialectical logic? What did Lenin mean by his famous remark that "three words are not needed," since dialectics, logic, and the theory of knowledge are "one and the same thing?"[68] In this as in most areas of post-Stalin Soviet philosophy, a diversity of viewpoints has developed, and in the present case the diversity is so great that Soviet writers do not even agree on how to classify the conflicting positions.[69] Even if we exclude positions like Bakradze's that reject the very notion of a dialectical logic, the range of disagreement is wide. By way of characterizing it in reasonable compass, we shall focus on two divergent approaches to the question and a few of the more important subpositions that fall under the second, more common approach.

The first and simpler approach is that of the literalists who believe that

---

[64]B. M. Kedrov, *Edinstvo dialektiki, logiki, i teorii poznaniia* (Moscow, 1963), pp. 12, 117, 119.

[65]G. F. Aleksandrov, ed., *Dialekticheskii materializm* (Moscow, 1953).

[66]B. Kedrov and G. Gurgenidze, "Za glubokuiu razrabotku leninskogo filosofskogo nasledstva," *Kommunist*, 1955, no. 14, pp. 45–56. The review is reprinted in Kedrov, *Edinstvo*, pp. 278–291.

[67]Kedrov, *Edinstvo*, p. 18. For a description of Soviet work in the field, see Okulov, pp. 66–71.

[68]Lenin, *Soch.*, vol. 29, p. 301.

[69]See, for example, Okulov, pp. 67–70; Konstantinov et al., *Filosofskaia entsiklopediia*, vol. 3, p. 216. When it comes to systems of dialectical logic, wrote D. I. Dubrovskii in 1982, "almost every author has his own" ("Materialy soveshchaniia po problemam dialekticheskogo materializma v redaktsii zhurnala 'Voprosy filosofii,'" *Voprosy filosofii*, 1982, no. 4, p. 37.

Lenin meant exactly what he said—that dialectics, logic, and the theory of knowledge are "one and the same thing." Since Lenin's statement was made in the heat of his enthusiasm for Hegel, and in fact suggests statements made by Hegel himself,[70] it is not surprising that one of the more prominent defenders of the literalist position should have been the doyen of the Soviet Hegelians, E. V. Il'enkov. Pointing to Lenin's related statement that "dialectics is the theory of knowledge of (Hegel and) Marxism," Il'enkov strongly defended the thesis of the identity of the three fields. "Dialectical logic," in this view, is simply logic, which is simply dialectics—the same (Hegelian) dialectics explored with favor in Lenin's *Philosophical Notebooks* and discussed in the previous chapter under the heading "objective dialectics."[71] And just as there is no distinction between dialectics and logic for Il'enkov, so there is no distinction between objective and subjective dialectics: the same laws govern thinking as well as nature and society. "Logic, being dialectical," Il'enkov writes, "is not only the science of 'thinking' but also the science of the development of all things, both material and 'spiritual.' "[72] This identification of (dialectical) logic with (dialectical) philosophy in general may also be seen in the Soviet *Philosophical Encyclopedia*, where dialectical logic is defined simply as, in that most familiar of Soviet characterizations of *philosophy*, "the science of the most general laws of the development of nature, society, and human thought."[73] For one group of Soviet philosophers, then, dialectical logic is not a special science with a special subject matter: it *is* the Marxist-Leninist materialist dialectic.

The second approach has increasingly gained adherents in recent years, to the point that it has become clearly dominant in Soviet philosophy.[74] As early as 1955 a report prepared by the Institute of Philosophy in Moscow spoke not of the "identity" but simply of the "unity" of dialectics, logic, and the theory of knowledge, and the latter expression was taken by Kedrov as the title of his influential book of 1963, in which he developed the general position on the question that is now accepted by the majority of Soviet philosophers. Lenin's statement that "three words are not needed" should not be taken literally, Kedrov argued, for Lenin himself on occasion made such distinctions as that between the logical and the epistemological

---

[70]See, for example, G. W. F. Hegel, *Enzyklopädie der philosophischen Wissenschaften im Grundrisse (1830)* (Hamburg, 1969), p. 58.
  [71]E. V. Ilyenkov, *Dialectical Logic. Essays on Its History and Theory*, trans. H. G. Creighton (Moscow, 1977), p. 312.
  [72]Ibid., p. 8.
  [73]Konstantinov et al., *Filosofskaia entsiklopediia*, vol. 3, p. 209. See also E. F. Solopov, *Predmet i logika materialisticheskoi dialektiki* (Leningrad, 1973), pp. 42, 123; and E. F. Solopov, *Vvedenie v dialekticheskuiu logiku* (Leningrad, 1979), p. 135.
  [74]Okulov, p. 69.

aspects of a particular issue.[75] According to Kedrov the "identity" of the three fields must be regarded not as abstract or absolute but as a dialectical unity, an "identity in difference" that not only does not rule out but presupposes that the things unified have distinct identities. Thus there is nothing to prevent the unified fields from having different (albeit related) subject matters.

Dialectics, Kedrov held, is the broadest of the three, studying the most general laws of all development, both in the external world (nature and society) and in human cognition. The two domains have distinctive features, however, whence the need to distinguish between objective dialectics, which studies the relations of external things to each other, and subjective dialectics, which studies the relations of events in the world of cognition. *Dialectical logic*, concerned like all logic with "thought and its laws" (Engels's definition), is for Kedrov equivalent not to dialectics in general but to subjective dialectics: it studies the dialectics of human cognition. *Theory of knowledge*, finally, is not reducible to either of the above, for it has to do with the connections between the two dialectics; by the "materialist" (that is, realist) principle, the subjective processes reflect objective processes, and for Kedrov this relationship between the two provides epistemology with its distinctive subject matter.[76]

Creation of a niche for dialectical logic, however, does not yet answer the question of how it differs from logic in general. As Il'enkov never tired of observing, Lenin in enumerating his trinity said simply "logic," not "dialectical logic." Kedrov, a consistent defender of the "two logics" policy, made room for formal logic in his 1963 work with the curt statement that dialectical logic "is the only one intended when we speak of the unity of logic with dialectics and the theory of knowledge."[77] Still, he did not provide an account of its distinguishing features as opposed to formal logic, and the relation between the two remains an open and much debated question in Soviet philosophy.

Among the more widely and uncritically held views is that dialectical logic is distinguished by the *type* of thought it studies. There is a temptation to identify that type as *dialectical* thought and to think of formal logic, by contrast, as concerned with "metaphysical" thought only; often Soviet philosophers do at least tacitly suggest such a distinction.[78] Explicitly,

[75]Kedrov, *Edinstvo*, pp. 21, 24. For a recent development of this view, see I. S. Narskii, "Eshche raz o probleme tozhdestva logiki, dialektiki, i teorii poznaniia," *Filosofskie nauki*, 1981, no. 5, pp. 44–55.

[76]Kedrov, *Edinstvo*, pp. 22–23, 275–276. For a more recent use of the same scheme, see Z. M. Orudzhev, S. Rodriges, and B. Rote, "O strukture dialekticheskoi logiki kak nauchnoi distsipliny," *Filosofskie nauki*, 1980, no. 5, p. 39.

[77]Kedrov, *Edinstvo*, p. 22.

[78]Sadovskii, p. 69.

however, the comparison—less invidious but still ordinarily implying a clear difference in value—is between a broader, synthetic, and innovative type of thinking and a more limited, analytic, and unproductive type. N. K. Bakhtomin speaks for many Soviet philosophers when, without rejecting formal logic, he links dialectical logic with genuine advances in knowledge: "Dialectical logic studies creative thinking, the categorial synthesis that produces knowledge that is new in principle. Formal logic studies formal logical deduction, which analyzes existing knowledge."[79] Many Soviet philosophers thus proceed on the assumption that dialectical logic is a synthetic logic of discovery rather than an analytic logic of proof.

Another common view is that the two logics deal not with different types but with different aspects of thought. Thus it is often held that since formal logic deals only with the form or structure of thinking, dialectical logic must deal with its content.[80] This view is particularly attractive to those who believe that a "true" logic cannot be indifferent to the question of the truth or falsity of thought, as that question can readily be identified with "content." It can be held, for example, that in thinking, dialectics supplies the truthful content and formal logic the correctness of structure.[81] There is also, however, considerable opposition to this simplistic division of functions between the two logics, if only because many philosophers wish to maintain that human cognition is marked by dialectical forms as well as dialectical content.[82]

If dialectical logic as a separate discipline went no further than the foregoing suggestions, neither of which is well elaborated in the Soviet literature, we could dismiss it as devoid of philosophical interest or value. Within the past fifteen years, however, more serious attempts have been made by some Soviet philosophers to develop and codify dialectical logic as a science distinct from general dialectics, the theory of knowledge, and formal logic—attempts which, despite their shortcomings, do raise the subject to a respectable level of philosophical discourse. We can see this development in S. B. Tsereteli's book *Dialectical Logic* (1971), published in Tbilisi in an edition of only a thousand copies,[83] but it may be examined

---

[79]N. K. Bakhtomin, *Praktika-Myshlenie-Znanie. K probleme tvorcheskogo myshleniia* (Moscow, 1978), p. 98. See also Konstantinov, *Fundamentals* (1982), p. 183.

[80]For a recent example, see *Dialekticheskoe protivorechie*, p. 72.

[81]For an extreme example, see S. P. Dudel' and G. M. Shtraks, *Zakon edinstva i bor'by protivopolozhnostei* (Moscow, 1967), pp. 150–151.

[82]Z. M. Orudzhev, "Some Problems of Dialectical Logic," in *Philosophy in the USSR. Problems of Dialectical Materialism*, trans. R. Daglish (Moscow, 1977), p. 247. It is significant, however, that there have been no attempts by Soviet philosophers to formalize dialectical logic.

[83]S. B. Tsereteli, *Dialekticheskaia logika* (Tbilisi, 1971). The movement to develop dialectical logic as a distinct science is also evident in the proposal mentioned above (Chapter 1, n. 61) to establish a separate department of dialectical logic at Moscow State University.

more productively in the recent, widely disseminated writings of Z. M. Orudzhev, whose moderate antinomist views on the nature of objective contradiction were analyzed in the previous chapter.

Orudzhev rejects the notion that formal logic is limited in its application to a certain type or aspect of thinking. All human thought, on every level, he believes, is subject to the traditional "laws of thought" (identity, non-contradiction, and excluded middle); he argues that the "formality" of the logic of Aristotle and his followers consists not in having no application to the content of thinking but in being equally applicable to every sort of content. Even thought about processes of development—often excluded from the range of competence of formal logic by Soviet philosophers—must accord with the demands of formal logic, Orudzhev contends. "The assertions 'everything develops' and 'nothing develops' are by their form classical judgments (assertions) of formal logic," he writes.[84] Thus for Orudzhev adherence to the rules of formal logic is a necessary condition for thinking of every sort, and so it cannot be counterposed to dialectical logic.

Nonetheless there is, according to Orudzhev, a common kind of thinking for which formal logic is not only a necessary but a sufficient condition of adequacy—that is, for which dialectical logic is not needed. There is nothing "dialectical," he asserts, in judgments such as 'I have a toothache' or 'If you put your finger into boiling water, you will feel pain'.[85] In general, he holds, dialectical logic has no application at what he calls the "everyday and empirical level of cognition"—the level at which "things and phenomena are given us in direct space-time connections and relations."[86] By contrast, formal logic is not sufficient to deal with another kind of thought, which Orudzhev calls "theoretical thinking." At that level, both formal and dialectical logics are required, and it is here that the latter subject finds its distinct identity. "Dialectical logic," he writes, "is the scientific doctrine of the laws and forms of the movement and development of theoretical thinking (cognition)."[87]

By "theoretical thinking," Orudzhev has in mind not some exotic or specifically philosophical thought process but the thinking engaged in by any scientist when he goes beyond what is directly given in experience. Addressed as it is, then, to "the laws and forms of the movement and development" of this kind of thinking, dialectical logic becomes for Orudzhev essentially a study of theory formation and change in the sciences—

[84]Orudzhev, Rodriges, and Rote, p. 44.
[85]Ibid.
[86]F. Kumpf and Z. Orudzhev, *Dialekticheskaia logika. Osnovnye printsipy i problemy* (Moscow, 1979), p. 7; Orudzhev, "Some Problems," p. 247.
[87]Orudzhev, Rodriges, and Rote, p. 40.

a study of how theories arise, are developed, refined, tested, and discarded. His thesis, of course, is that these processes are dialectical in nature, following patterns outlined in the writings of Hegel, Marx, and Marx's followers.

Theoretical thinking as described by Orudzhev is subject to the operation of what he calls "basic principles of dialectical logic," three of which are discussed at some length (and others less fully) in the book *Dialectical Logic* (1979), which Orudzhev coauthored with the East German philosopher Friedrich Kumpf. One is the principle of comprehensiveness, according to which all aspects of an object or situation must be examined in their interconnections. In all of Orudzhev's writings it is assumed—usually with reference to the methodology of *Capital*, where Marx worked his way to the concept 'surplus value' as the key feature of modern industrial capitalism—that a comprehensive analysis of any subject will lead to the identification of some core element or nucleus that reveals the "essence" of the matter at hand, enabling us to understand it as an integrated whole. Thus Orudzhev speaks of locating in a given situation the "substantial property" that determines the other properties. The objective is to produce a *theory*, which Orudzhev defines as "a system of categories and laws reflecting in its structure the essence of the subject of investigation as a whole—that is, its integral structure."[88]

Another basic principle of dialectical logic discussed at length by Orudzhev is a direct corollary of the general dialectical law of the unity and struggle of opposites. Calling it (using Lenin's words) the principle of "the splitting of a whole and the cognition of its contradictory parts," Orudzhev regards the procedure as a necessary step in the comprehensive understanding of any object or situation and a universal feature of scientific theorizing.[89] Since he is not an extreme antinomist in ontology, Orudzhev does not see the opposed elements of a real situation as contradictory in the formal sense. Rather, he argues that, although "in themselves" contradictory, in reality opposing elements are rendered compatible by intermediate links, as the positive and negative electrical charges of an atom are mediated by its structure. According to this second principle, then, theoretical knowledge, in dealing with any subject, must "join its poles into a single whole with the aid of a system of mediating links."[90]

A third basic principle expounded in Orudzhev's and Kumpf's *Dialectical Logic* is the principle of the "ascent from the abstract to the con-

---

[88]Kumpf and Orudzhev, pp. 115–119, 194. The portions of the book written by Orudzhev are identified on p. 2.

[89]Lenin,, *Soch.*, vol. 29, p. 316; Kumpf and Orudzhev, p. 100.

[90]A. N. Aver'ianov and Z. M. Orudzhev, "Dialectical Contradiction in the Evolution of Knowledge," *Soviet Studies in Philosophy* 18 (Winter 1979–1980), p. 79.

crete."[91] That expression, used by Marx in his *Grundrisse* to describe his own method in the analysis of capitalism, has received much attention in recent Soviet philosophy, particularly since the appearance in 1960 of Il'enkov's book *The Dialectics of the Abstract and the Concrete in Marx's Capital.*[92] Essentially the expression refers to the procedure, thoroughly exploited before Marx by Hegel in his *Science of Logic*, of moving in a conceptually necessary progression from simpler, one-sided notions (Hegel's 'being', Marx's 'commodity') to more complex and richer ones (Hegel's 'spirit', Marx's 'surplus value') in which the positive content of the simpler notions is sublated; the more complex notions offer a fuller picture of the subject under investigation.[93] This procedure, in the minds of many Soviet philosophers, is by no means restricted to Hegelian ontology and Marxian economics but represents an important feature of all productive theoretical thinking; in the words of the current Soviet *Philosophical Dictionary*, the method of ascent from the abstract to the concrete is "a universal form of the unfolding of scientific knowledge, of the systematic representation of an object in concepts."[94] All other methods (induction, deduction, analogy, modeling, and the like) are held by Orudzhev to be sublated in the method of ascent, which "embraces the whole process of theoretical thought."[95]

Suggestive as Orudzhev's "basic principles" may be, clearly they are not precise or specific enough to function as rules of inference or patterns for the conduct of theoretical reasoning in particular cases. Orudzhev assures us that they have a "fully determinate logical function in the system of dialectical logic,"[96] but when we examine critically what is offered as their application in actual instances of scientific reasoning, the weaknesses of Orudzhev's conception become all too apparent. As one such instance, let us consider briefly a favorite illustration of his—the work of Nils Bohr and Georg von Hevesy on the relation between atomic weight and the

[91]Kumpf and Orudzhev, p. 135.

[92]E. V. Il'enkov, *Dialektika abstraktnogo i konkretnogo v "Kapitale" Marksa* (Moscow, 1960). An English translation by Sergei Syrovatkin was published by Progress Publishers in Moscow in 1982.

[93]Sheptulin, *Marxist-Leninist Philosophy*, pp. 167–168. It should be noted that in the Hegelian senses of the terms 'abstract' and 'concrete' that Marx employed in the *Grundrisse* passage, the distinction is one between different types of *concepts*—in Hegelian terminology, between one-sided, unrelated, inadequately mediated concepts and many-sided, fully related, adequately mediated ones—and does not coincide with the more familiar distinction between "abstract" concepts and "concrete" matters of empirical fact. In other places, however, Marx does use the terms in the latter senses, and Soviet writers frequently do so as well.

[94]Frolov, p. 4.

[95]Orudzhev, "Some Problems," p. 256.

[96]Kumpf and Orudzhev, p. 99.

chemical properties of isotopes.[97] Although repeatedly advanced as an example of the insufficiency of formal logic and the successful application of dialectical logic, the case actually presents a catalogue of the typical shortcomings displayed by Soviet dialectical logicians in their attempts to establish their discipline.

One shortcoming is an ignorance of, or a willingness to flout, even the most elementary rules of formal logic. Despite his insistence on the universal validity and the importance of formal logic, Orudzhev sees Bohr and von Hevesy as initially blocked by having validly derived a false conclusion from true premises—a situation that is simply not possible in formal logic. The scientists began, Orudzhev says, with two true premises (not apparently true, but *true*)—the first being Mendeleev's periodic law (expressed by Orudzhev as "the chemical properties of chemical elements depend on their atomic weight") and the second being "isotopes are chemical elements." From these premises it follows that "the chemical properties of isotopes depend on their atomic weight"—but this conclusion was shown experimentally to be false. Formal logic, it seems, has brought us to a contradiction, and we must therefore go beyond it.[98]

In the above considerations, however, a second shortcoming in Orudzhev's procedure is already evident—a lack of precision in formulating the problem. We could, by giving more precise meaning to the vague expression 'depends on', just as well read Orudzhev's first premise as false, and using another interpretation we could read both that premise and the conclusion as true—in either case eliminating the problem. The interpretation given 'depends on' is actually beside the point, however, for the second premise of Orudzhev's syllogism is certainly false: isotopes, as the very research in question resulted in showing, are not "chemical elements" but *species* of a given chemical element, which differ from each other precisely in having different atomic weights (because of having different numbers of neutrons in their nuclei) but the same chemical properties (because of having the same number of electrons in their shells). So we have not derived a false conclusion from true premises.

Whatever the problems with the actual syllogism presented by Orudzhev, however, let us grant that a contradiction arose in the research in question between a standard interpretation of Mendeleev's periodic law (we may express it more precisely as the interpretation according to which two substances with the same chemical properties must have the same atomic

---

[97]Ibid., pp. 181–182; Orudzhev, "Some Problems," pp. 248–249; Orudzhev, *Dialektika kak sistema*, pp. 223–224.

[98]Orudzhev, "Some Problems," p. 248. "The absence of elementary logic in philosophical works," wrote one Soviet philosopher in 1982, "is a very common disease" ("Materialy soveshchaniia po problemam dialekticheskogo materializma," p. 40).

weight) and the existence of isotopes, which have the same chemical properties but different atomic weights. In Orudzhev's view, the theoretical advance here consisted in taking a comprehensive view of the subject, identifying the contradictory elements, and showing how both of them can be *true* by finding the links that join them. "Bohr discovered a whole set of intermediate links connecting these two contradictory propositions—Mendeleev's law and the independence of the chemical properties of certain isotopes on their atomic weight. The intermediate links were the concepts of the 'positive charge of the nucleus,' the 'neutral heavy particle of the nucleus,' and, finally, the 'electron shell,' which directly conditions the chemical properties of the atom." Many different varieties of inference were required at various points in this work, Orudzhev holds, and the entire system or complex of them constitutes the "logical method of the ascent from the abstract to the concrete."[99] What, we may ask, is wrong with such an account of the situation?

Most generally, what is wrong is that the scientific process of examining an apparent counterexample (the characteristics of isotopes) and reinterpreting a principle (Mendeleev's law) by giving up a less adequate version of it for one that is more adequate, and perhaps making a discovery (neutrons) in the process, is a perfectly familiar process for which the Hegelian "abstract-concrete" terminology seems not only unilluminating but inappropriate. Granting that a "richer" (more "concrete"?) picture of the atom emerged from this research, there was here no inferential process that went *from* a more abstract picture *to* a more concrete one that sublated the former, through intermediate conceptual links between them. The "ascent" was not from a relatively empty concept to a relatively full one but from a proposition not in accordance with the facts (that substances with the same chemical properties have the same atomic weight) to one in accordance with them (that substances with different chemical properties have different atomic weights but not vice versa). Certainly no two *true* but contradictory statements were shown by the discovery of "intermediate links" to be compatible. The contradiction between the two statements mentioned in Orudzhev's passage above is resolved by adopting a new interpretation of Mendeleev's law and rejecting the old one as false. Finally, the contradiction in question is not "in" the chemical substances under investigation but in our thinking about them; we are not even as close to an objective contradiction here as we are with some of Orudzhev's other illustrations, such as that of the "contradictory charges" (positive and negative) of a single atom. It may have been uneasiness about this fact that led Orudzhev, in a recent treatment of this case, to suggest that the

[99]Orudzhev, "Some Problems," p. 248.

"links" exist not between contradictory *propositions* but between the objective *characteristics* of atomic weight and chemical properties: what was
once thought to be a direct connection between the two, he states, has
now been shown to be an indirect one, mediated by the notions of atomic
nucleus, neutrons, electron shell, and so on.[100] But in that analysis, where
is the *contradiction* to begin with? And how can *notions* like 'electron
shell' mediate between *characteristics*?

Orudzhev's unclarity as to whether it is a contradiction in the objects
or in thought about the objects that is mediated in the "ascent from the
abstract to the concrete" once again shows the influence of Hegel's identification of the two realms on the neo-Deborinist dialecticians in Soviet
philosophy, who attempt to make the Hegelian progressive sublation of
concepts (with its resolution of contradictions and increasing concreteness)
describe the actual advance of empirical knowledge in the sciences. It is
of course not Hegel who is to be blamed for this but Marx, who first
conceived the idea of applying the Hegelian method to a scientific investigation. But actually not even Marx is to blame. For Soviet dialectical
logicians not only have eagerly harvested all the fruits of Marx's original
error but also have multiplied them through an ideologically inspired devotion to the Marxian method.

For one thing, they have turned the method of the ascent from the
abstract to the concrete into an a priori standard for the interpretation
and evaluation of all science, natural as well as social. Since, according to
that method, richer, more concrete concepts do not simply succeed less
adequate ones but follow from them by some inner conceptual necessity,
the entire history of science is read in such a way as to find conceptual
links of this sort in every theoretical advance. This yields such artificial
and dubious results as the view that Einstein "inferred" his richer theories
of relativity from the simpler classical (Galilean) version.[101] Not surprisingly the principal objection that Soviet dialecticians have raised to the
widely discussed views of Thomas Kuhn on the development of scientific
knowledge is that the "paradigm shifts" that Kuhn sees as marking revolutionary changes in scientific thinking are viewed by him as unrelated
to each other and essentially unprogressive. "The weakest spot in the
conception of T. Kuhn," writes B. M. Legostaev, "is the denial of the
cumulative character of the development of science."[102] The evolution of
theories in science, according to Orudzhev, consists not in the rejection of

---

[100]Kumpf and Orudzhev, pp. 181–182.
[101]Orudzhev, *Dialektika kak sistema*, p. 282.
[102]V. M. Legostaev, "Filosofskaia interpretatsiia razvitiia nauki Tomasa Kuna," *Voprosy filosofii*, 1972, no. 11, p. 133.

paradigms but "in moving each time to a new scientific category"—specifically, in a logical progression from a poorer category to a richer one.[103]

A second and still more regrettable consequence of Soviet devotion to the Marxian method is that it is held to be capable of providing *conclusive proof* of a scientific theory—the prime example being the Marxian economic theory in *Capital*.

Following Tsereteli, Orudzhev argues that every logic requires a theory of proof, and he devotes considerable attention to producing one for dialectical logic. In his view the kind of proof that is appropriate to the theoretical thinking investigated by dialectical logic is neither inductive nor deductive but consists first and almost exclusively in the act of constructing the theory itself. Every theory begins with an initial idea or concept, according to Orudzhev, and constructing the theory—which is at the same time coming to know the subject theoretically—consists in tracing out the *conceptual* relations (with occasional empirical checking) between the initial concept and what Orudzhev calls the "central" and finally the "culminating" concepts of the theory.[104] This process of substantiating the initial idea by elaborating it into a complete theory is the essence of theoretical proof: "Strictly speaking, what is proved is not the theory but the theoretical idea which is not yet developed into a theory, has not become a theory. In such form the initial theoretical idea has the status of a hypothesis. It loses that status as soon as a theory has been constructed. A theory cannot be a hypothesis. It is the proof of the truth of the initial idea."[105] Since this process takes place by tracing the relations of concepts, Orudzhev contends that "the essence of dialectical logical proof consists in portraying the *transition* from one category to another."[106] This is not quite the whole story, however, for Orudzhev also states that the entire theory is still subject to confirmation by empirical testing—that is, in "practice." Such testing, then, is the concluding stage in the truth process: it is "the final act in the proof of the theoretical proposition, which makes the proof conclusive."[107]

Although Orudzhev does thus acknowledge the value of empirical confirmation, the great bulk of his attention goes to the conceptual elaboration of a theory, and his presentation is suffused with the confidence that an adequately developed theory penetrates to the real "essence" of its subject matter. In his view the concepts of such a theory appear to flow into one another with the necessity Hegel described in his *Science of Logic*, except

---

[103]Kumpf and Orudzhev, p. 208.
[104]Ibid., pp. 203–206.
[105]Ibid., p. 221.
[106]Orudzhev, *Dialektika kak sistema*, p. 219 (italics in original).
[107]Kumpf and Orudzhev, pp. 221–222.

that here the necessity guarantees the correct analysis of a material reality. Orudzhev seems to assume, in other words, that in other subjects, as in Marxian economics, the adroitly chosen initial concept ('commodity'), properly explored in its conceptual linkages, leads inexorably to the correct central concepts ('use value', 'exchange value') and ultimately to the richest and fully concrete culminating concept ('surplus value'), as a result of which the inner nature of the subject matter stands revealed once and for all. Otherwise it is difficult to see how such confidence could be lodged in empirical testing as capping a "conclusive proof." The empirical testing for Orudzhev simply confirms *what is already a proof*, consisting in the conceptual necessity of the theoretical structure itself.

Orudzhev acknowledges that the acceptance by dialectical logic of a doctrine of conclusive proof may raise charges of dogmatism, since, it may be alleged, for any theory facts may come to light that the theory cannot explain. But he rejects these charges by offering in rebuttal a statement from *Materialism and Empirio-Criticism*, through which he shows both his root concern for the authority of Marxian economics and the astounding extremity of dogmatism to which even serious philosophers in the USSR are at times willing to go: "Bogdanov [Lenin wrote] agreed to acknowledge Marx's theory of money circulation as an objective truth 'for our time' only, calling 'dogmatism' the ascription to this theory of 'suprahistorically objective' truth.... This is another muddle. No future circumstances can alter this theory's correspondence with practice, for the same simple reason that makes it *eternally* true that Napoleon died on May 5, 1821."[108] Rejection of the possibility of conclusive proof is relativistic, Orudzhev charges, and one of the services of dialectical logic is to provide what he calls "decisive arguments" against such relativism.[109]

The dialectical logic currently being elaborated in the USSR by moderate neo-Deborinists such as Orudzhev cannot simply be dismissed as a nonfield in the manner common among Western critics.[110] Its subject matter can be seen as a perfectly legitimate and indeed important one, as long as we do not expect it to coincide with traditional Aristotelian or modern mathematical logic. It studies scientific theorizing—the formation, structure, content, proof, and succession of scientific theories—the same thing studied under the headings 'logic of science' or 'philosophy of science' in other philosophical communities. What is distressing is not that dialectical logic lacks a subject but that in dealing with its important subject these Soviet

---

[108]Lenin, *Soch.*, vol. 18, p. 146 (italics in original); Kumpf and Orudzhev, p. 236.
[109]Kumpf and Orudzhev, p. 237.
[110]Blakeley, *Soviet Theory of Knowledge*, p. 144; Richard T. De George, *Patterns of Soviet Thought. The Origins and Development of Dialectical and Historical Materialism* (Ann Arbor, 1966), p. 215.

philosophers exhibit so many weaknesses, including an apparent willingness to tailor a logic to the needs of an "eternally true" Marxist ideology. And while scholarly and sophisticated Soviet work in the logic of science, utilizing the powerful tools of modern mathematical logic, is relegated to isolated research institutes, dialectical logic was in 1979 made a required, seventy-four-hour course for all philosophy students at Moscow State University, taught by Z. M. Orudzhev.

The Concepts of Reflection and Practice in Soviet Epistemology

Epistemology, or the theory of knowledge, though not yet institutionalized as a discipline in the organizational world of Soviet philosophy, has at least been made possible as a distinct subject of study by the now widely accepted interpretation of the "unity" of dialectics, logic, and the theory of knowledge. According to this interpretation, the latter field can have a subject matter of its own—the relation of thinking to being, or of subjective mind to the objective world that it reflects—and hence also laws of its own. Typically, a widely read work in the field such as *The Dialectics of Scientific Cognition* (1979) will contain not only sections devoted to "the general laws of dialectics in their cognitive functions" but far longer sections devoted to "the specific dialectical laws of cognition."[111]

In the past two decades many of the best known and also of the most respected Soviet philosophers have addressed themselves to epistemological questions. They include Kedrov, Rozental', Uemov, Narskii, Gorskii, Tiukhtin, Lektorskii, and above all Pavel Vasil'evich Kopnin (1922–1971), the director of the Institute of Philosophy in Moscow from 1968 until his death, whose serious and undogmatic works raised many questions and inspired much interest in the theory of knowledge among younger scholars.[112] On the surface this extensive and high-level attention would not appear to have made dramatic alterations in Marxist-Leninist doctrines in the theory of knowledge. It has left in place the traditional concepts of *reflection* and *practice* as between them characterizing the essential features of the knower's contact with the known. Yet when we examine the ca-

[111]Voishvillo, Gorskii, and Narskii, p. 476.
[112]A brief biography of Kopnin (pp. 9–16) and a bibliography of his works (pp. 308–316) may be found in P. V. Kopnin, *Dialektika kak logika i teoriia poznaniia. Opyt logiko-gnoseologicheskogo issledovaniia* (Moscow, 1973). For additional information on Kopnin's life, see Werner G. Hahn, *Postwar Soviet Politics. The Fall of Zhdanov and the Defeat of Moderation, 1946–1953* (Ithaca, 1982), pp. 170–171. A respected recent work by another author is V. A. Lektorskii's *Sub"ekt, ob"ekt, poznanie* (Moscow, 1980).

pacious interpretations that are being given these commonplaces of Marx-ist-Leninist thought in current Soviet philosophy, we find that in episte-mology as in other fields, an old vocabulary is being stretched to accommodate new content.

We have already seen the Soviet interest in the relation between the concepts 'reflection' and 'information'—a question regarded as one of the most pressing in recent Soviet epistemology.[113] Of still broader significance, however, are two closely related issues that have persistently generated controversy among Soviet philosophers. They are the questions of the likeness of a cognitive reflection to its original and of the relation between reflection and the creative activity of the human mind.

The metaphorical term 'reflection' used by Engels understandably led his followers to emphasize the close resemblance between ideas and their objects, as witness Lenin's use of the word 'copy' for the relation. But just as understandably, serious attention to epistemology has raised the ques-tion of what this resemblance can be. What exactly does a general idea like 'house' or 'quality' reflect? How can we speak of a *resemblance* be-tween theoretical constructions such as 'electron' and some unseen and perhaps counterintuitive original? Above all, the issue has arisen in Soviet philosophy because of the supposed existence of "objective contradic-tions." The neo-Deborinist purists maintain, as we have seen, that to reflect such contradictions *thought* must itself be contradictory. To maintain the contrary, and assert that contradictions in things are not properly repre-sented by contradictions in thought, other Soviet philosophers have been obliged to promote a general weakening of the "resemblance" between things and thoughts. As V. P. Porus writes, "an adequate image of dia-lectical contradiction can be attained only in coherent and formally non-contradictory systems of knowledge of the object."[114]

Typically this weakening is effected by Soviet philosophers not by openly tampering with the definition of reflection but by quietly reinterpreting the term to include relationships far removed from resemblance or point-to-point correspondence. In speaking of the cognitive reflection of contra-dictions, the term 'image' should be put in quotation marks, Viakkerev says, and we must stress the "nongraphic [*nenagliadnyi*] character of the-oretical reflections of objective contradictions."[115] In this connection a standard formulary expression employed by many Soviet philosophers is found in Kedrov's 1963 book *The Unity of Dialectics, Logic, and the Theory of Knowledge*: the laws of the external world and the laws of its

[113]"Vsesoiuznaia nauchnaia konferentsiia 'Leninskaia teoriia otrazheniia i sovremennye problemy gnoseologii,' " *Filosofskie nauki*, 1980, no. 3, p. 160.

[114]Voishvillo, Gorskii, and Narskii, p. 472.

[115]*Dialekticheskoe protivorechie*, p. 215.

[174]

cognition by man are two different sets of laws, Kedrov writes, which are "identical in content but different in form."[116] The laws are ultimately "about" the same object—the reflected external world; but the dialectics of the reflection takes a different form from the dialectics of the object. Thoughts are not isomorphic with things. Referring once again to the cognition of a "contradictory" reality, Kedrov writes: "To express motion and contradiction in general in concepts is no easy matter, since the ways and means of doing it are not the simple reproduction of what the object itself presents us. In the process of cognition we always coarsen and over-simplify reality, since we cannot reflect it all at once in an exhaustive manner. But in our coarsened, oversimplified image reality itself is contained, and it alone."[117] The "image" is thus not a copy but is related in some looser way to the reality it "contains." When Soviet philosophers working in this spirit hazard actual definitions of reflection in its cognitive application, their statements are commodiously vague; for Kopnin it is "the capacity of the cognition of man to reproduce *in a certain form* and to *a certain degree of fulness and exactness* the object existing outside him."[118]

On the whole, then, Soviet discussions in epistemology are concerned with attempting to determine *what* form and *what* degree of fulness and exactness the cognitive "reproduction" of reality takes. The disputes that arise, such as that between neo-Deborinist literalists and others, which in another philosophical idiom might be called a dispute between copy theorists and their opponents, take place in Soviet philosophy *within* the ample boundaries of reflection theory. Everything from identity to a "coarse," "nongraphic" representation can be accommodated—provided only that the fundamental realism of Marxism-Leninism is observed and the idea is not made a "hieroglyph" or other purely conventional symbol having no relation to "reality itself."[119]

That realism is the core of meaning left to the reflection concept in current Soviet philosophy is made clear by Kopnin: "The concept of reflection does not exhaust all the relations of cognition to the object," he writes; "it characterizes it only from one side: *does the cognition have objective content or not?*"[120] At most, Soviet reflection theory adds to

---

[116]Kedrov, *Edinstvo*, p. 157. For more recent uses of this distinction, see *Dialekticheskoe protivorechie*, pp. 167, 169, 238.

[117]Kedrov, *Edinstvo*, pp. 167–168.

[118]P. V. Kopnin, *Gnoseologicheskie i logicheskie osnovy nauki* (Moscow, 1974), p. 103 (italics added). This posthumously published volume contains complete texts of Kopnin's *Vvedenie v marksistskuiu gnoseologiiu* (1966) and *Logicheskie osnovy nauki* (1968).

[119]Plekhanov's view that sensations are "hieroglyphs" bearing no resemblance to reality was severely criticized by Lenin in *Materialism and Empirio-Criticism* (Lenin, *Soch.*, vol. 18, pp. 244–251).

[120]Kopnin, *Gnoseologicheskie*, p. 107 (italics added).

realism nothing more than a correspondence theory of truth. Kedrov dissolves the reflection relation into an unspecified correspondence when he writes that the materialist theory of knowledge requires simply the "correspondence, the 'coincidence' of our subjective images (concepts, theories, and so forth) with objective reality, *that is, the correspondence of our knowledge with material reality itself.*"[121] At any event, as in so many areas of Soviet philosophy, what once stood for a narrow dogma that allowed for no philosophical debate now functions more as a framework within which disagreements may take place and alternative views may be explored. The term 'reflection' is thus in a sense devalued or debased by assuming an exceedingly broad meaning. But that seems a small price to pay for the renewed vitality of Soviet epistemology.

The breadth allowed 'reflection' has a direct bearing on the other principal issue concerning the concept that has arisen in recent Soviet philosophy—the question of the relation between reflection and the creative activity of the human mind. Discussion of this question was prompted initially by external criticism of the Soviet reflection approach to knowledge, though some Soviet writers joined in the criticism as well. It came from Marxists who saw the notion of reflection as promoting a passive picture of the mind inconsistent with the spirit of Marx's thought. Mihailo Marković, a member of the well-known "*Praxis* group" of Yugoslav Marxist philosophers, made the point succinctly: "The concept 'reflection' is not at all characteristic of the Marxist, active conception of philosophy. It does not sufficiently draw attention to the creative dimension of human consciousness, to the symbolic character of many human creative acts of which we say that they are 'true.'"[122] The most outspoken Soviet critic of the reflection conception was P. M. Egides, who in 1968 attacked it in harsh terms not often applied to an approved concept in Soviet philosophy. Suggesting that it provides a conceptual ground for alienation and even for totalitarianism, Egides wrote that the concept fosters "recognition only of the blind, contemplative reflection of being by an alienated, unfree, timid, dutiful reason, fettered by all sorts of blinders, standards, patterns, and clichés; recognition . . . only of a state of affairs in which reason trudges along behind being, passively photographing it."[123]

The response to such objections generally favored by the Soviet philosophers taking part in these discussions is that inasmuch as reflection is not

---

[121]Kedrov, *Edinstvo*, pp. 81–82 (italics added).
[122]M. Marković, "Osnovi dijalektičko-humanističkoi teorije istine," *Praxis*, 1965, no. 2, p. 179.
[123]P. M. Egides, "K probleme tozhdestva bytiia i myshleniia," *Filosofskie nauki*, 1968, no. 4, p. 106. Egides, whose views will be discussed further in Chapter 7, was forced into emigration in 1980.

a mechanical copying of the object, there is ample room in the notion for the active mind. "Cognition," Kopnin writes, "does not slavishly follow the object, but creatively reflects it." At least two sorts of cognitive creativity are now regularly acknowledged by Soviet philosophers. First, there is the synthesizing activity whereby the mind constructs generalizations, laws, and theories combining separate elements of immediate data. Second, there is imaginative projection from the given, in which the mind's "reflection" of the object, in Kopnin's words, shows us "what it might be as the result of the transformative activity of man."[124]

The recognition of both these varieties of creative contribution by the mind within a reflection framework has been greatly facilitated in recent Marxist-Leninist philosophy by the notion of "anticipatory reflection" (*operezhaiushchee otrazhenie*) advanced by the Soviet physiologist Petr Kuz'mich Anokhin (b. 1898). In an enormously influential article published in *Voprosy filosofii* in 1962, Anokhin used that expression to describe the physiological mechanism whereby, from the earliest stages of the evolution of life, biological organisms have developed the capacity to "anticipate" future developments, such as the ability of some insects to respond to the cooler days of late summer by producing glycerine, which their bodies will need only later as protection against winter's cold. This same capacity to reflect influences not passively but actively and with a future reference, Anokhin argues, at a later stage of evolution makes possible the conditioned reflex and "all higher forms of the anticipation of future events."[125] Soviet philosophers were quick to take up this idea as a valuable addition to the theory of reflection in epistemology, arguing that imagination, prediction, and other aspects of scientific cognition, not to mention the elaboration of ideals for future practical action, are revealingly approached as forms of anticipatory reflection. D. P. Gorskii has argued in an interesting article that scientific cognition is the highest form of such reflection, which takes place, he says, "when glycerine is formed in the body of the parasitic wasp . . . and also when the general theory of relativity is formulated." The justification for introducing abstractions and idealized objects into science, Gorskii writes, is precisely that they are "powerful and effective instruments of advance reflection of reality." Gorskii attempts to frame rules both for the introduction into and the elimination from scientific theories of such theoretical entities—rules that will show that a concept

---

[124]Kopnin, *Gnoseologicheskie*, pp. 105–106. A highly regarded recent book dealing with the relation between reflection and activity is A. M. Korshunov's *Otrazhenie, deiatel'nost', poznanie* (Moscow, 1979).

[125]P. K. Anokhin, "Operezhaiushchee otrazhenie deistvitel'nosti," *Voprosy filosofii*, 1962, no. 7, p. 111.

such as 'electron' is a legitimate reflection of reality, whereas a concept such as 'God' is not.[126]

But whether or not it is linked with the physiology of anticipatory reflection, creativity is widely acknowledged as either an ingredient of or a supplement to reflection in Soviet discussions of the subject-object relation, and most of the discussion now concerns not whether reflection is compatible with creativity but what exactly the relation between them is. Some contend that the two notions are intrinsically related, whether through anticipatory reflection or otherwise.[127] Others, such as Kopnin, argue that reflection and creativity are independent but equally important principles in Marxist-Leninist epistemology—"two concepts," Kopnin writes, "which in equal measure express essential aspects of cognition."[128] It may be noted, however, that none of these views is likely to satisfy the *Praxis* group or others who seek not a position compatible with reflection but a position that approaches cognition with another metaphor entirely, one more in keeping with Marx's stress on the creative nature of human action.

The concept of practice has not received as much critical attention as the concept of reflection in recent Soviet philosophy. In the more popular, ideologically oriented work it is often invoked in philosophically dubious ways, such as when ideas one opposes are said to receive "practical refutation" by decisions of the Communist party.[129] Nonetheless, in the atmosphere of diminished dogmatism that succeeded the Stalin era, it has been possible for some Soviet philosophers to explore the concept of practice in a serious philosophical manner.[130] A sign of this has been their willingness, here as in other areas of Soviet philosophy, to respond to objections to Marxist-Leninist theses made by its Western critics.

A common criticism of the practice criterion is that it is question-begging. Gustav Wetter phrases the objection as follows: "As for the theory of practice as the criterion of truth, it commits the logical fallacy of tacitly assuming the point to be proved. For confirmation in practice (in the shape of an experimental proof, for example) is also supposed to warrant the validity of our sensory knowledge. But . . . the positive (or negative) out-

---

[126]D. Gorsky, "Advance Reflection of Reality at the Level of Human Cognition," in V. Lorentson and B. Yudin, eds., *Materialist Dialectics Today* (Moscow, 1979), pp. 176, 182, 185–191. See also D. Gorskii, "The Meaning of Semiotic Expressions and the Criteria Validating the Introduction of Higher-Level Abstractions (Universals) into Science," in F. J. Adelmann, ed., *Philosophical Investigations in the U.S.S.R.* (The Hague, 1975), pp. 103ff.

[127]"Vsesoiuznaia nauchnaia konferentsiia," p. 160.

[128]Kopnin, *Gnoseologicheskie*, p. 105.

[129]Dudel' and Shtraks, p. 81.

[130]See, for example, E. V. Bezcherevnykh, *Problema praktiki v protsesse formirovaniia filosofii marksizma* (Moscow, 1972), and B. A. Voronovich, *Filosofskii analiz struktury praktiki* (Moscow, 1972).

come of the experiment cannot be perceived except by sensory awareness."[131] P. V. Kopnin addressed Wetter's point directly in his *Introduction
to Marxist Epistemology* (1966), and his reply is provocative because at
first it, too, appears to be question-begging. We need not be concerned
about the trustworthiness of our sensory perception of the results of practical action, Kopnin affirms, because "confidence in the evidence of the
senses lies at the foundation of the materialist theory." If that is the case,
we may be tempted to ask, what is the need for the *practice* in the first
place? Kopnin's answer is in effect that practice is *not* needed when we
are confronted with direct empirical evidence. Given the fundamental realist assumption of "the materialist theory," there is for Kopnin an objective
state of affairs in the material world; and at the sensory level, as Lenin
held, we are in immediate contact with that objective reality. Practice is
needed, according to Kopnin, to test the abstract, general theses in which
scientific or theoretical knowledge consists, for practice is the link between
those theories and the sensory level. "In practice," he writes, "a human
idea *having a general character* acquires the concrete sensory form which
possesses the virtue of certainty [*dostovernost'*]." Thus practice is in fact
(though Kopnin does not draw this conclusion explicitly) not the criterion
of the truth of all beliefs but of general beliefs only, and it operates by
translating them to the level at which another "criterion" operates—the
self-warrant of empirical immediacy. "The testing of the truth of judgments," Kopnin writes, "is in one way or another connected with the
immediate certainty of sensibility."[132]

These references to "certainty" may suggest that, although Kopnin may
have weakened the practice criterion by restricting it to scientific and
theoretical propositions, he has at the same time strengthened it by allow-
ing it to provide absolute truth. Like Orudzhev in another context, Kopnin
talks about "conclusive" proof, as when he speaks of the activities in
which man "materially embodies his ideas . . . and thereby proves 'conclusively' the objective truth of the knowledge which is realized in practice." But for Kopnin the matter is not that simple, as his use of quotation
marks around 'conclusively' suggests. For no single practical act can be
taken as fully trustworthy, Kopnin argues; a particular experiment, for
example, may only partially "embody" the general proposition, may fail
to effect an adequate link between theory and fact. It is only as a continued
process of practical activity that practice can be considered trustworthy,
according to Kopnin. Hence his conclusion: "As a historically undertaken

[131]Wetter, *Dialectical Materialism*, p. 516.
[132]Kopnin, *Gnoseologicheskie*, pp. 164, 163 (italics added), 168.

process, practice is an absolute criterion of truth; as a separate practical act, it is relative."[133]

Kopnin's stress on practice as the never-final translation of theoretical statements into sensory evidence is shared by Narskii, Gorskii, and other representatives of the more scientifically, less dialectically inclined wing of Soviet philosophy that I have called neomechanism, and it goes along with a conception of theoretical thinking that sets these philosophers apart from even moderate neo-Deborinists such as Orudzhev. Orudzhev's emphasis, as we saw, was on the dialectics of theory construction—on the intrinsic conceptual relations among the terms of a given theory—and I argued that for him the conceptual necessities of these relations both rendered the question of empirical support distinctly secondary and encouraged belief in the kind of absolute certainty claimed by Lenin for the Marxian economic theories. The neomechanists' stress on "practice" rather than on the dialectics of theoretical concepts is a commitment to the empirical sciences, for the "practice" they have chiefly in mind is that of empirical confirmation processes: the "active experiment," Gorskii, Narskii, and Oizerman write, is "one of the most effective sorts of practical verification," and where experiment is not possible, "active observation" is second best.[134] These philosophers are principally concerned, in other words, not with the relations of the different concepts in a theory but with the relation of the theory to empirical evidence, and they typically find the empirical object richer than can be handled conclusively by any finite set of tests. "Not even a series of experiments can give a conclusive answer to all the questions of the cognition of a given object," they write. The neomechanists thus generally reject the view that absolute truth is attainable, and ironically they are able to support their position with a quotation from the very same work to which Orudzhev appealed: "The criterion of practice [Lenin wrote in *Materialism and Empirio-Criticism*] can never, by the very nature of the matter, confirm or disconfirm *fully* any human idea whatever. That criterion is also so 'indefinite' that it does not permit the knowledge of man to be turned into an 'absolute.' "[135]

Gorskii and his colleagues quote the continuation of the above passage as well, in which Lenin adds that the criterion of practice "is at the same time so *definite* that it wages a merciless struggle against all varieties of idealism and agnosticism." It is in this qualification that we can see most clearly the source of these Soviet philosophers' opposition to pragmatism. The idea of the active, unending testing of beliefs in material life is certainly

---

[133]Ibid., pp. 171–172, 165.
[134]Mitin, vol. 2, p. 21.
[135]Ibid., p. 23; Lenin, *Soch.*, vol. 18, pp. 145–146 (italics in original).

not incompatible with pragmatism, but Kopnin, Gorskii, and their colleagues are pragmatists only to a point. For in their view all practice seeks "the world as it is"—an objectively given structure directly accessible to sense perception—and when that point is reached, pragmatic standards are no longer relevant. These philosophers are, in other words, realists first and pragmatists second, and so they cannot accept a pragmatic theory of truth as *constituted* by successful practice. Ultimately truth is not what works but what corresponds to objective fact; the job of practice is to effect a contact between our theories and that fact. That we can never be sure the contact is adequately made neither relieves us of the obligation to continue the quest nor shakes the faith that the fact is there.

The ultimate weakening of the practice criterion in contemporary Soviet philosophy consists, then, in using it to mean simply the application of scientific procedures of empirical confirmation against the background assumption of realism. Thomas Blakeley wrote in 1964 that if in Soviet use the practice criterion signifies nothing more than sense contact with an objective world, "a clarification of terminology is in order."[136] This clarification has essentially been carried out by Kopnin, Gorskii, and others. The *vocabulary* of 'practice' has been retained, but that should not cause us to overlook the breadth that has been introduced into it in Soviet philosophical usage. Among the neomechanists, at least, the process of turning dialectical materialism into scientific method is continuing, under a protective mantle of time-honored terms.

[136]Blakeley, *Soviet Theory of Knowledge*, p. 144.

[5]

Philosophy of History

THE previous chapters have been devoted to Soviet Marxist-Leninist philosophy in its broadest dimension—that is, as a general theoretical outlook, labeled "dialectical materialism," which advances doctrines concerning the nature of reality and of human knowledge. In traditional philosophical terms, we have been examining the ontology and the epistemology of Marxism-Leninism.

The name given the entire philosophy in the USSR, however, is "dialectical *and historical* materialism," and in proceeding now to the historical dimension we are taking up another part of Marxist-Leninist theory which, though less cosmic in scope, is held by Soviet philosophers to be equally indispensable to the whole. The exact nature of its relation to dialectical materialism is not unproblematical, and we shall have occasion to discuss the question later in this chapter. But there is no doubt as to what, in bare outline, Soviet philosophers typically claim the connection between dialectical and historical materialism to be: the latter, they hold, results from applying the general principles and methods of the former to the field of social life and its development through time. Historical materialism, according to Soviet Marxist-Leninists, is the dialectical materialist philosophy of society and history.

As such, historical materialism has traditionally been given broad jurisdiction over a range of subjects that in the West are commonly divided among a variety of disciplines. More than a philosophy of history, historical materialism lays claim to cover the concerns of sociology, of social and political philosophy, and even of such (in the Marxist interpretation) socially defined fields as ethics and aesthetics. Only in recent years have the last two fields, and sociology to a degree, been granted disciplinary status in the Soviet academic world; there is still no theoretical recognition of a separate "social philosophy" or "political philosophy," either in the organization of scholarly institutions or in common academic parlance.

When the expression 'social philosophy' is encountered in Soviet philosophical literature, it usually stands for historical materialism itself.[1]

In practice, however, the subject matter of historical materialism has been narrowed in recent years by the establishment of the field called "scientific communism" as a separate academic discipline. Historical materialism and scientific communism are said to be distinguished by their levels of generality: whereas the former deals with the characteristics of societies and their history in all times and places, the latter is charged with developing the theory of the communist order—its beginnings, its present state, and its future.[2] But since Soviet discussions of social and political questions are heavily concentrated on just those topics, the effect has been to restrict historical materialism to theoretical questions concerned with the historical process rather than with present-day society. Unlike the theses of scientific communism, moreover, the strictly historical doctrines of historical materialism have in the past two decades been the subject of remarkably wide-ranging theoretical discussions, which have produced some of the most unorthodox suggestions in recent Soviet philosophy. Hence in the present chapter I shall isolate for study the doctrines appropriate to historical materialism as a theory of history and shall reserve for the next chapter the social and political doctrines now more commonly treated by Soviet philosophers under the rubric of scientific communism. The first section will introduce the traditional elements of the Soviet theory of history as they are presented in textbooks and popular works; the next three sections will follow the reexamination to which those elements have been subjected in the Soviet theoretical literature; and the final section will assess the Soviet theory of history in its current state.

Elements of the Soviet Theory of History

Central to the Marxist-Leninist view of history are two theses that, though said to be empirically provable, are taken as axiomatic in standard expositions. One is that history is what the authors of *The Fundamentals of Marxist-Leninist Philosophy* call "a law-governed process."[3] The other is that the laws that "govern" history are economic in character, or in

[1] "Materialy soveshchaniia po problemam istoricheskogo materializma v redaktsii zhurnala 'Voprosy filosofii,'" *Voprosy filosofii*, 1982, no. 6, pp. 25, 27.

[2] E. A. Anufriev, E. V. Tadevosian, and M. F. Vetrov, eds., *Nauchnyi kommunizm. Opyt razrabotki i chteniia lektsii* (Moscow, 1982), pp. 6–10.

[3] F. V. Konstantinov, ed., *The Fundamentals of Marxist-Leninist Philosophy*, trans. Robert Daglish (Moscow, 1982), p. 201.

other words that economic forces are the motors of significant historical change.

The human past, according to the first thesis, is a series of events that are neither random nor ordered by an outside force such as a divine will. Events in history are linked in regular sequences and patterns that are describable by objective laws, not unlike the laws of the natural sciences; these laws are internal to the process itself, and they hold regardless of anyone's recognition of them or attitude toward them. The presence of these inherent linkages makes the past intelligible, Marxist-Leninists believe; by studying history scientifically, they contend, we can come to understand its laws and gain the ability to make dependable predictions about its future.

What laws govern history? According to the second thesis, the key to the historical process is to be found not in any of the realms favored by pre-Marxist historians, such as politics, law, or religion, but rather in the economic realities of social life. Marx and Engels were profoundly right, the Soviet historical materialist argues, when they wrote in *The German Ideology* that "men must be able to live in order to be able 'to make history.'"[4] And since living requires first of all producing the physical necessities of food, shelter, and clothing, Marx and his colleague were also right in finding a people's social existence to be anchored in the mode of economic production that it has worked out and in accounting for the major shifts in its political, legal, and spiritual life by reference to laws linking those shifts with underlying changes in its mode of production.

In fleshing out these broad theses, Soviet philosophers rely heavily on the writings of Marx himself; the theory of history is one of the few subjects on which they cite Marx more frequently than Engels or Lenin. And in the settled opinion of Soviet philosophers there is no better single statement of historical materialism as a theory of history than the one that Marx presented in his preface to *A Contribution to the Critique of Political Economy*, published in 1859. Its core is the following much quoted passage:

> In the social production of their life, men enter into definite relations that are indispensable and independent of their will, relations of production which correspond to a definite stage of development of their material productive forces. The sum total of these relations of production constitutes the economic structure of society, the real foundation, on which rises a legal and political superstructure and to which correspond definite forms of social consciousness. The mode of production of material life conditions the social, political and intellectual life process in general. It is not the consciousness of men that

[4]L. D. Easton and K. H. Guddat, trans. and eds., *Writings of the Young Marx on Philosophy and Society* (New York, 1967), p. 419.

determines their being, but, on the contrary, their social being that determines their consciousness. At a certain stage of their development, the material productive forces of society come in conflict with the existing relations of production, or—what is but a legal expression for the same thing—with the property relations within which they have been at work hitherto. From forms of development of the productive forces these relations turn into their fetters. Then begins an epoch of social revolution. With the change of the economic foundation the entire immense superstructure is more or less rapidly transformed.[5]

Soviet historical materialists fully accept the "foundation-superstructure" metaphor advanced in Marx's presentation, and they consider the social whole made up of foundation and superstructure to be the central unit of historical analysis. To refer to this unit they use the expression 'socioeconomic formation', a term of art defined in the current edition of the Soviet *Philosophical Dictionary* as "a historical type of society, grounded on a particular mode of production and constituting a stage in the progressive development of the world history of mankind."[6] The "mode of production" of which Marx and the definition speak encompasses, in the Soviet interpretation, not only the economic foundation, or "base" of the social structure, but also the still more fundamental "material productive forces" employed in the production process. These "forces by which society influences nature and changes it," as they are called in *Fundamentals*, are not themselves social phenomena; they are the ultimate material underpinning without which society is impossible.[7]

The "main" productive force, Soviet textbooks ritually affirm, echoing a statement by Marx in another work, is man himself—the laborer who transforms nature in order to live. All other productive forces are called by Soviet writers *means of production*. These include both *objects of labor*—the natural realities that labor is called upon to transform—and the *means of labor* that people employ in the transformative process. The means of labor, finally, are subdivided into *instruments of labor*, or phys-

---

[5]Karl Marx and Frederick Engels, *Selected Works in One Volume* (New York, 1968), pp. 182–183.

[6]I. T. Frolov, ed., *Filosofskii slovar'*, 4th ed. (Moscow, 1980), p. 256. On the history of the use of the term 'formation' by Marx and Engels, see Eero Loone, *Sovremennaia filosofiia istorii* (Tallin, 1980), pp. 201–203.

[7]Konstantinov, *Fundamentals* (1982), pp. 220–221 (italics omitted). For this contrast of 'material' and 'social', see S. V. Mochernyi, "Zakon edinstva i bor'by protivopolozhnostei v politekonomicheskom issledovanii," *Filosofskie nauki*, 1980, no. 2, p. 57; and G. A. Cohen, *Karl Marx's Theory of History. A Defence* (Princeton, 1978), p. 47.

ical equipment such as tools and machines, and other, nonphysical means such as the production techniques associated with a particular technology.[8]

Proceeding "upward" in accordance with Marx's metaphor, we encounter first the lower level of the socioeconomic formation—that is, the economic base on which the remainder of the social edifice rises. This base is for Marx and for Soviet philosophers the economic structure of the society, and it consists in the relationships that have become established among people in that society with respect to the production, exchange, and distribution of the necessities of life—relations of reciprocity or exploitation, of equality or dominance and subordination, as manifested above all in the society's system of ownership of the means of production. But why do some economic relations rather than others arise in a society? The answer is to be found by looking beneath the base, to the character of the productive forces available to that people at that time. "The windmill," Marx asserted in a much-discussed epigram, "gives you society with the feudal lord; the steam mill, society with the industrial capitalist."[9] This statement does not mean that production relations exert no reverse influence on the productive forces; as Marx's summary of his position indicates, the development of the forces may be either "fettered" or promoted by the character of the production relations. But it is essential to historical *materialism*, Soviet philosophers insist, that the primary causal action be the other way around, from the "material productive forces" to the social base. One of the principal laws of historical development, according to *Fundamentals*, is the law of "the determining role of the productive forces with regard to economic relations."[10]

On the foundation of every society's economic order rests its superstructure—an entity concerning which there is some ambiguity in Marx's writing. Is the superstructure identical with the "social, political and intellectual life process in general" that Marx describes in the preface as conditioned by the mode of production of material life? Or is intellectual life something distinct from what he calls in the preceding sentence the "political and legal superstructure?" Soviet philosophers adopt the first interpretation, but they distinguish between an organizational and an ideological stratum within the superstructure, viewing political, legal, and other noneconomic *institutions* as more directly exposed to the determining influence of the

[8]See, for example, G. A. Bagaturiia, "Kategoriia 'proizvoditel'nye sily' v teoreticheskom nasledii Marksa i Engel'sa," *Voprosy filosofii*, 1981, no. 9, p. 107. Some Soviet writers, however, reject the view that objects of labor are to be counted among the productive forces; see "Proizvoditel'nye sily kak filosofskaia kategoriia. Materialy Kruglogo stola," *Voprosy filosofii*, 1981, no. 4, pp. 91, 95, 101–102; no. 9, p. 100.

[9]Easton and Guddat, p. 480.

[10]Konstantinov, *Fundamentals* (1982), p. 204.

base than are political, legal, and other *ideas*. Nonetheless, both strata are said to derive their character, directly or indirectly, from the economic realities that sustain them. The mechanism of this determination is typically illustrated by reference to class societies: a dominant economic class, in the Soviet view, is in a position to impose on society the institutions and ideas that best serve the class's interests. This analysis again implies a reverse influence: the superstructure functions to strengthen and sustain the existing economic order. But the more powerful action is once more conceived as proceeding from the bottom up. A law operating at all stages of social evolution, we read in *Fundamentals*, is the law of "the determining role of the economic basis in relation to the social superstructure."[11]

Thus far we have concentrated on the internal dynamics of a socioeconomic formation in a stable period of its existence. But as Marx's preface indicates, historical materialism is also a theory of broader temporal sweep that seeks to identify epochal changes in the evolution of human society; in Soviet terminology, such changes are transitions from one socioeconomic formation to another. And just as economic factors are basic in the analysis of a society within a given epoch, so, too, in the Marxian analysis accepted by Soviet philosophers, they are the engines of progression from one socioeconomic formation to another. The appearance of a new social order, Marx wrote in the preface, is ultimately traceable to the continuing development of productive forces "in the womb of the old society."[12] Eventually these forces outgrow the relations of production within which they are operating and necessitate a radical restructuring, first of the society's economic base and consequently of its superstructure.

Although Marx himself was concerned above all with the development of the capitalist socioeconomic formation and its revolutionary replacement by communism, he addressed himself to epochal changes in precapitalist society as well. He leaned toward a unilinear conception of development according to which human history is marked by the successive appearance of a relatively small number of distinct socioeconomic formations; in the preface he wrote that "Asiatic, ancient, feudal, and modern bourgeois modes of production" could be called "progressive epochs in the economic formation of society."[13] At the same time, the questions of what formations, in what sequence, could be found in history were not settled dogmatically by Marx. He was unsure about the "Asiatic" formation, and at times he indicated the possibility of alternative routes of

---

[11]Ibid.
[12]Marx and Engels, *Selected Works*, p. 183.
[13]Ibid.

development for different societies.[14] Soviet historical materialism, on the other hand, has been identified since the time of Stalin with a particular historical scenario, according to which a set cast of five socioeconomic formations proceeds in a fixed order across the stage of human history. Although fundamental questions are raised about this scenario in the technical literature of Soviet philosophy, as we shall see below, it is still advanced in most textbooks and reference works with little or no attempt at qualification.[15]

Eliminating Marx's "Asiatic" mode of production altogether, the orthodox Soviet scheme postulates an earliest socioeconomic formation of millennial duration called *primitive communalism*; its paradigm case is the tribal society that lacks the institution of private ownership and provides only a marginal existence for its members because of its low level of economic development. The next stage, *slave society*, is made possible by advances in productive power, but at the same time it introduces private property and the polarization of society into exploiting and exploited classes, slaveowners and slaves; from this point until the eventual establishment of communism, social change follows laws appropriate to class societies, such as the "law of the class struggle as the driving force of history."[16] *Feudalism*, the next advance produced by the development of mankind's productive forces, brings a partial emancipation of the exploited laborer; no longer a mere thinglike possession of a master, the serf is, however, legally deprived of many powers held by the lord who oppresses him. *Capitalism* is the result of the enormous advances in productivity made possible by steam power and other technological innovations, and it also completes the "freeing" of the laborer from the legal disabilities of earlier class societies; but as Marx took pains to point out, the "free" proletarian laborer, himself propertyless, is still at the mercy of the capitalist, who owns the means of production. Capitalism promotes the development of productive forces to the point at which material abundance comes finally within man's grasp. Like previous socioeconomic formations, however, capitalism is ultimately incapable of accommodating the forces it has unleashed. Only *communism*—a classless structure in which property is socialized and labor takes place without exploitation—is capable of providing the needed form for the perfected productive capacity of mankind. In communism the laborer is genuinely and completely liberated

---

[14]See the discussion of these questions in Melvin Rader, *Marx's Interpretation of History* (New York, 1979), pp. 122–130.

[15]See, for example, Frolov, p. 256; V. G. Afanasyev, *Marxist Philosophy*, trans. D. Fidlon, 4th rev. ed. (Moscow, 1980), pp. 209–224.

[16]Frolov, p. 281.

from bondage, and society attains a state of harmony and prosperity stretching indefinitely into the future.

Forces for Change in Soviet Theory of History

Theory of history has been a subject of much discussion in the USSR in recent years, and perhaps greater departures from Stalinist dogmatism have been made in this area than in any other field of Soviet thought. The course of historical revisionism in the USSR has not been smooth, and it has not led thus far to any authoritative or generally accepted restatement of doctrine. But so many questions have been raised by so many Soviet philosophers and historians that the "orthodox" view described in the previous section can be said to exist in textbooks only, not in the minds of specialists in historical materialism.

To list the reasons for deviation from orthodoxy in this area is to catalogue the various and often conflicting forces that have affected Soviet philosophical thought in recent years. One such force is the demands of ideology. The questions of historical materialism are more closely connected with political interests than are the more abstract issues of dialectical materialism, and hence the treatment of the former is more responsive to ideological needs. Such needs often, of course, simply reinforce old dogmas, but they can also promote change. If it is desired to put greater stress on the "leading role" of the Communist party in building communism, for example, emphasis cannot simultaneously be placed on the determination of the political superstructure by the economic base. And if the USSR is to assist Third World countries to move directly to communism untouched by the scourge of capitalism, there must be some flexibility in the epochal scenario.

Another force for change is the desire on the part of some Soviet philosophers to make the theory not more ideological but more Marxian. Marxist-Leninists are committed at least formally to the utterances of Marx himself as the source of historical materialist doctrine; but the available corpus of those utterances has changed significantly in recent decades, through the publication of major works by Marx, unknown to Lenin and unmentioned by Stalin, such as the *Economic and Philosophic Manuscripts* (1844) and the *Grundrisse* (1857–1858).[17] These works, which contain

---

[17]A widely available complete English translation of the *Economic and Philosophic Manuscripts* may be found in Karl Marx, *Early Writings*, trans. R. Livingstone and G. Benton (Harmondsworth, England, 1975), pp. 279–400. For an English translation of the *Grundrisse*, see Karl Marx, *Grundrisse. Foundations of the Critique of Political Economy (Rough Draft)*, trans. Martin Nicolaus (London, 1973).

support for interpretations of historical materialism that are at odds with the essentially technological and deterministic view sketched in the preface, are no longer ignored in the USSR. True, there is a strong tendency among Soviet scholars to regard the earlier works as products of a juvenile, Hegelian Marx who had not yet raised historical materialism to the level of science; and certainly the new publications in general have not created in the USSR the revolution in Marxist scholarship that has taken place in other parts of the world. But they are now issued and read in the Soviet Union; Soviet philosophers cite them frequently, and the ideas found in them generate a certain amount of dissatisfaction with the orthodox view.

A third, less direct source of deviation from historical materialist orthodoxy is the tendency toward "differentiation" in philosophy discussed in Chapter 1. Some Soviet philosophers have become known in recent years for a professional interest in the philosophy of history as a special discipline—that is, they have addressed themselves not directly to the elaboration of historical materialism as a substantive theory of history but to conceptual and methodological problems concerning historical theorizing in general, in the manner of the "analytic" philosophy of history pursued in the West. When in 1963 the Institute of Philosophy in Moscow established the Seminar on Philosophical Problems of the Study of Society, the first years of the seminar's work were devoted to such metaquestions concerning history—what are now typically called by Soviet philosophers questions of "historical cognition" or the epistemology of history rather than history itself. Essays by members of the seminar, including A. V. Gulyga, A. Ia. Gurevich, and Iu. A. Levada, have received much attention, and works in a similar idiom by G. M. Ivanov, Iu. V. Petrov, and others have also been widely read.[18] The significance of this activity for our investigation is that it has encouraged a more reflective and critical attitude toward historical materialism—at the same time that it has been stimulated by the growth of the same attitude.

The final but certainly not the weakest influence for change in the orthodox version of historical materialist theory is the desire to make it a coherent theory that accords with the facts of history. The scholar and the ideologist alike may be moved by this desire. For historical materialism is presented as a science, confirmed by historical data; if there are discrepancies between the data and the theory, both the intellectual substance and the public image of the theory are jeopardized. But Soviet philosophers now openly acknowledge the existence of difficulties with the theory in

---

[18]Many of these essays are reprinted, with an extensive bibliography, in A. V. Gulyga and Iu. A. Levada, eds., *Filosofskie problemy istoricheskoi nauki* (Moscow, 1969). A more recent bibliography of Soviet works in the philosophy of history is found in Loone, pp. 279–293.

its orthodox version. Even some elementary texts admit, for example, that a slavery formation did not occur in the history of the Germanic and Slavic peoples, and some writers have noted that, although slavery existed in the United States, it was not a prelude to feudalism.[19] Hence Soviet scholars have been moved to seek modifications in the theory that will allow it to accommodate such anomalies.

The need to put Marxist-Leninist theory in line with the facts of history is no doubt felt more keenly by historians than by philosophers, and it is among historians that the most vocal and widely discussed dissatisfaction with orthodox historical materialism can be found in the post-Stalin period. Such dissatisfaction was already much in evidence in the early and mid 1960s, at the height of the thaw, when historians including M. Ia. Gefter, I. F. Gindin, N. I. Pavlenko, and L. V. Danilova began, as a contribution to "liquidating the consequences of the cult of personality," to speak out against accepted views on a wide range of historical topics.[20] In 1968, these historians were publicly called champions of a "new current" in Soviet historiography, and there was talk of a "great upsurge" in Soviet historical studies generally.[21]

The new current was not without its dogmatic opponents, however, and when in 1969 Gefter and others produced a book that, among other indiscretions, called openly for "a new reading of the historical conception advanced by Marx, Engels, and Lenin," the movement was widely thought to have gone too far.[22] In early 1971 the Institute of History in Moscow mounted a conference to criticize the volume, at which Academician V. M. Khvostov pronounced an anathema upon probing reconsiderations of historical doctrine. "There is a certain sum of absolutely exact knowledge obtained by the Marxist-Leninist method," Khvostov proclaimed, "a sum of objective, exactly and scientifically established social regularities that are true, and precisely for that reason are not subject to reexamination."[23] Gefter was removed from his administrative position at the Institute of History, though he was not dismissed from the institute. There was further

---

[19]Afanasyev, p. 208; Loone, p. 232.

[20]For description and discussion of these developments, see Arthur P. Mendel, "Current Soviet Theory of History, New Trends or Old?" *American Historical Review* 72 (1966), pp. 50–73; and James P. Scanlan, "From Historial Materialism to Historical Interactionism: A Philosophical Examination of Some Recent Developments," in Samuel H. Baron and Nancy W. Heer, eds., *Windows on the Russian Past. Essays on Soviet Historiography since Stalin* (Columbus, 1977), pp. 3–23.

[21]*Dokumenty sovetsko-ital'ianskoi konferentsii istorikov, 8–10 aprelia 1968 goda* (Moscow, 1970), pp. 224, 227.

[22]M. Ia. Gefter et al., eds. *Istoricheskaia nauka i nekotorye problemy sovremennosti* (Moscow, 1969), p. 6.

[23]G. P. Shurbovanyi, "Obsuzhdenie nekotorykh problem metodologii istorii," *Voprosy istorii*, 1971, no. 10, p. 164.

public criticism as well, which reached a peak with a conference in Moscow in March 1973, at which the "shortcomings and errors" for which the innovators were allegedly responsible were rehearsed by an assemblage of historians, other academic figures, and Party officials. The conference report was explicit in condemning the offenders: "Our duty is not to concoct 'new currents' or demand a 'new reading' of historical materialism," read its concluding paragraph, "not to 'reinterpret' Marxism-Leninism in the light of new data, but on the contrary to interpret the new data of social life in the light of Marxism-Leninism—that is the burning task of historical science."[24] Since 1973 there has been no explicit advocacy of a "new current" in Soviet historiography.

It should not be thought, however, that in post-Stalin Russia the condemned intellectual tendencies vanish without a trace. Their champions, though chastened, are in most cases still active in major scholarly centers and are still known for their unorthodox views, and sympathizers now have some idea of how far they may go and how open they may be in pursuing the questions that have been raised. Thus a tendency may continue to operate in a less visible and less alarming form, and the critique of orthodox historical materialism indeed appears to be doing so. Within the past decade many historians and philosophers have furthered the process of renovating the Marxist-Leninist view of history, but they have furthered it more circumspectly.

The process, from its beginnings after Stalin's death to the present day, has taken place on two distinguishable but related levels. One is the empirical level, on which the particular factors and systems of factors at work in history are identified and analyzed. Here a number of specific innovations have greatly increased the complexity of history as it is viewed by some Soviet scholars and have called into question many of the traditional concepts and assumptions of historical materialist theory, as we shall see in the following section. The other is the theoretical level, on which Soviet philosophers and historians seek to construct a coherent conceptual apparatus for understanding history in general. On this level, to be examined in a later section, there have evolved divergent approaches to the structure of historical materialism as a systematic theory, based upon different views of the nature of history as a "law-governed process."

New Elements in the Historical Process

On the empirical level, the innovations found in Soviet historical writing of recent decades consist either in the acknowledgment of historical cir-

[24]I. I. Mints, M. V. Nechkina, and L. V. Cherepnin, "Zadachi sovetskoi istoricheskoi nauki na sovremennom etape ee razvitiia," Istoriia SSSR, 1973, no. 5, p. 16.

cumstances and influences not recognized earlier or in the reinterpretation of recognized factors in ways that significantly alter their nature and their role in history. Cases of both sorts are included in the survey that follows.

Mnogoukladnost': Mixed Societies

A complication overlooked by orthodox historical materialists but acknowledged by many Soviet writers today is the possibility that a given society may contain elements of more than one socioeconomic formation. Support for this possibility is found in the works of Lenin, who on a number of occasions described the economy of Russia as a complex of what he called different *uklady* ("orders" or "structures"). In a report written in 1921 Lenin identified no fewer than five such uklady still at work in the country—patriarchal, small-scale (*melkotovarnyi*), capitalist, state capitalist, and socialist.[25] The implications of this analysis not only for economics and practical planning (Lenin's interests at the time) but also for the broader historical dynamics of social development were drawn after Stalin's death by a number of new current historians. Thus in 1963 we find I. F. Gindin using the term *mnogoukladnost'* ("multistructured-ness," or the condition of having more than one structure) to describe the economic phenomenon but also indicating its importance for Russian history:

> In Russia significant feudal vestiges were preserved right down to 1917.... The process of the growth of capitalist relations at the expense of precapitalist structures [uklady] continued even into the period of imperialism, and the mnogoukladnost' of the economy was far from overcome at the end of the existence of Russian capitalism.... All this exceedingly deepened the contradictions of the socioeconomic development of Russia at the beginning of the twentieth century and had great influence on the development of the bourgeoisie as well.[26]

Obviously the concept was generalizable, and Soviet historians and philosophers have extended it to other times and places. It has been applied, for example, to the empire of Alexander the Great and to the United States at the beginning of the nineteenth century.[27]

Despite its association with the condemned new current, the term *mnogoukladnost'* continues to be used by many Soviet writers, and the concept

[25]V. I. Lenin, *Polnoe sobranie sochinenii*, 5th ed., 55 vols. (Moscow, 1958–1965), vol. 43, p. 158; see also vol. 3, p. 187 (cited hereafter as *Soch.*).
[26]I. F. Gindin, "Russkaia burzhuaziia v period kapitalizma, ee razvitie i osobennosti," *Istoriia SSSR*, 1963, no. 3, pp. 3, 37.
[27]Loone, p. 220.

for which it stands is invoked by still others who speak, however, of the "combination" or "interweaving" of different formations rather than using the tainted word.[28] Some writers attempt to remove the sting from the notion by assuming that in every "combination" society there is some one predominating structure, so that the traditional historical materialist laws might still be applied with minor qualifications.[29] Others, however, accept the possibility that in some societies the elements of diverse socioeconomic formations are so thoroughly intermixed as to make any causal weighting of them extremely difficult if not impossible.[30] In such cases it is not clear how the orthodox conceptual apparatus could be used to interpret either the short-term or the long-term dynamics of the society's historical development. Gurevich speaks of the "interweaving" of the laws of development of different socioeconomic formations in the case of such a society, but what this might mean in practice is not specified.[31]

Non-Standard Economic Structures

The different economic structures combined in a mixed society might be restricted to those traditionally recognized, but another complicating development in recent Soviet historiography is the identification, by many writers, of new elementary structures. The orthodox view authorized five simple structures—the notorious sequence of primitive communalism, slavery, feudalism, capitalism, and communism, dubbed the *piatichlenka* (five-membered set) by Soviet philosophers. The suggestion that some economic orders cannot be equated either with any element of the piatichlenka or with some combination of them is a major step in the retreat from simplistic dogmatism in Soviet theory of history.

By far the greatest attention in this regard has gone to the "Asiatic mode of production," discussed by Marx in a number of writings but omitted from the piatichlenka. A primitive order found in arid regions of the Orient and elsewhere, "Asiatic" society was characterized by Marx as having a communal style of living and of labor with no private ownership of land but at the same time as marked by the virtual enslavement of laborers to

---

[28]See, for example, G. E. Glezerman et al., eds., *Razvitoe sotsialisticheskoe obshchestvo. Sushchnost', kriterii zrelosti, kritika revisionistskikh kontseptsii*, 2d ed. (Moscow, 1975), pp. 12–13; and A. P. Kazakov et al., eds., *Razvitoe sotsialisticheskoe obshchestvo i obshchestvennyi progress* (Leningrad, 1976), p. 5.

[29]V. V. Dubinin and I. I. Shevchuk, "Uchenie ob obshchestvenno-ekonomicheskoi formatsii i nekotorye voprosy mezhformatsionnogo perekhoda," *Vestnik Moskovskogo universiteta. Seriia 7. Filosofiia*, 1981, no. 6, p. 33.

[30]Loone, pp. 219–221.

[31]Gulyga and Levada, p. 53.

a highly centralized, despotic government; Marx attributed the latter feature to the need for organized large-scale irrigation at a low level of technological development.[32] In Soviet scholarship the question of whether the
Asiatic mode is a variant of either primitive communalism or the slave
system or whether it must be viewed as a separate elementary mode has
generated much dispute, complicated by the perception on the part of
more doctrinaire Soviet theorists that attention to the Asiatic mode is linked
with hostile attacks on Marxism-Leninism. M. Ia. Koval'zon, for example,
stated in 1980 that development of the concept has been connected with
the view that the histories of Asia, Africa, and precolonial America followed paths completely different from that of Europe; and this, Koval'zon
argued, is inconsistent with "the single methodological principle of cognition" of Marxism-Leninism.[33] At the same time, Soviet scholars continue
actively to discuss the Asiatic mode, and many regard it as a sixth elementary formation.[34] The question of the existence of an Asiatic formation
is simply an empirical one, it is now frequently asserted; the Soviet Estonian
philosopher Eero Nikolaevich Loone wrote in 1980 that there are "no
theoretical arguments sufficient to assert that the very idea of the presence
in the past of a special 'Asiatic' formation is anti-Marxist."[35]

Other possible elementary socioeconomic formations are suggested by
individual Soviet scholars. As early as 1965 Iu. I. Semenov identified what
he called the "bondage" (*kabal'naia*) formation, which he characterized
as an ancient exploitative system in which elements later found in slavery,
feudalism, and capitalism existed in an embryonic, not yet differentiated
form.[36] More recently, Eero Loone has discussed a number of additional
possibilities—none of them, he believes, theoretically inconsistent with
Marxism: a "small-scale" (*melkotovarnyi*) formation, grounded on what
Lenin called the "small-scale mode of production"; perhaps a number of
formations that might, with closer historical analysis, be distinguishable
within what is now called simply the "primitive communal" stage; and—
the most intriguing—a future formation *following* communism. Loone
notes that the last possibility is one that specialists usually avoid, and he

[32]See, for example, Marx's article "The British Rule in India," published in the *New York Daily Tribune* for June 25, 1853, reprinted in Karl Marx and Frederick Engels, *Collected Works* (New York, 1975–   ), vol. 12, pp. 125–133.
[33]"Proizvoditel'nye sily," no. 4, p. 90.
[34]"Mezhvuzovskaia nauchnaia konferentsiia 'Osnovnye napravleniia razrabotki marksist-sko-leninskogo ucheniia ob obshchestvenno-ekonomicheskoi formatsii,' " *Vestnik Moskov-skogo universiteta. Seriia 7. Filosofiia,* 1981, no. 3, pp. 49–50.
[35]Loone, p. 261 (italics in original).
[36]For a discussion of Semenov's view, see M. A. Korostovtsev, "O poniatii 'Drevnii vos-tok,' " *Vestnik drevnei istorii,* 1970, no. 1, p. 12.

himself avoids it once he has registered it as an open question.[37] It should be observed, finally, that deviation from the piatichlenka in current Soviet historiography does not always take the form of *increasing* the number of recognized socioeconomic formations. V. P. Illiushechkin, a historian at the Institute of Oriental Studies of the Academy of Sciences, is known for his contentions that there is no "slavery" formation as such and that strictly speaking feudalism is the only socioeconomic formation in the period between primitive communalism and capitalism.[38]

When A. Ia. Gurevich wrote in 1965 of the need to reject "abstract schemes . . . by means of which the course of history is mystified,"[39] there is no doubt that the piatichlenka was one of the schemes he had in mind. This attitude did not escape the notice of the critics who attacked the new current in subsequent years; a charge brought against L. V. Danilova in 1970 was that she denied that the piatichlenka was an integral part of the conception of history developed by Marx, Engels, and Lenin and moreover believed it to be obsolete.[40] And more recently as well there have been suggestions in some historical materialist literature that departing from the five-stage progression is flirting with heresy.[41] But these admonitions have not forestalled continued discussion of possible additions to (or subtractions from) the five-stage scheme in the USSR and did not prevent Loone from writing in 1980 that "Marxism is not wedded to the recognition of a precisely defined number of formations." Loone does grant, however, that at least two formations must be acknowledged by every Marxist—capitalism as a historical fact and communism as a historical possibility.[42]

The Impact of One Society on Another

The foregoing developments in Soviet historiography, however they may complicate the orthodox view of historical progression, are nonetheless consistent with the key historical materialist thesis that the development of a society is determined fundamentally by changes in its mode of production. A more radical innovation would be to accept other factors entirely, such as determinants operating outside the society in question. Soviet

---

[37]Loone, pp. 262–266, 226.
[38]"Proizvoditel'nye sily," no. 9, pp. 97–99; see also Loone, pp. 257–259.
[39]Gulyga and Levada, p. 79.
[40]L. V. Cherepnin et al., eds., *Aktual'nye problemy istorii Rossii epokhi feodalizma. Sbornik statei* (Moscow, 1970), pp. 12–14.
[41]*Historical Materialism. Theory, Methodology, Problems* (Moscow, 1977), pp. 113–114.
[42]Loone, pp. 264, 260.

theorists have always been predisposed to seek internal sources of development, not only because of Marx's assertion that the conditions for a new historical stage mature "in the womb of the old society" but also on the strength of the general philosophical conviction that matter is self-moving and develops through the generation and resolution of "internal contradictions." When external influences are admitted, it has traditionally been only as accelerating or retarding an internal development.[43] In recent years, however, Soviet philosophers and historians have begun to acknowledge that the fate of one society may be determined by the impact of other societies upon it.

A case in point is the treatment by some Soviet writers of the transition from slave societies to feudalism in Western Europe. The traditional view, predictably, is that the feudal order grew out of the slave system of ancient Rome; the slaves are held to constitute the progressive class, and the slave rebellions are seen as destroying the old order and ushering in the new. But a 1964 article by the historian A. R. Korsunskii[44] raised serious questions about this account, and in 1965 A. Ia. Gurevich made explicit some of the theoretical implications of Korsunskii's findings. "It is perfectly obvious," Gurevich wrote, "that the slave uprisings did not lead and by themselves could not have led the Roman social system to destruction, for the slaves were not bearers of new production relations." Rather, Gurevich went on, an external force—the barbarian conquests—was principally responsible for the fall of Rome; this force, he contended, "brought Roman society out of its dead end" and paved the way for the establishment of feudalism.[45] This view, despite its heretical implication that there is no objectively necessary historical progression from slavery to feudalism, continues to attract adherents among Soviet scholars; Eero Loone, for example, endorsed it in 1980.[46]

A second case suggests that external influences not only can precipitate radical changes in a society's course but can alter the fundamental base-superstructure interaction as traditionally understood. This is the case of the analysis of the origins of Russian absolutism. European absolutism in general has long been a problem for Marxist historians because of its seeming inconsistency with the principle that a state serves the interests of a dominant economic class. Engels regarded the absolute monarchies of the seventeenth and eighteenth centuries as exceptional cases in which,

[43]See, for example, G. M. Domrachev, S. F. Efimov, and A. V. Timofeeva, Zakon otritsaniia otritsaniia (Moscow, 1961), p. 28.
[44]A. R. Korsunskii, "Problema revoliutsionnogo perekhoda ot rabovladel'cheskogo stroia k feodal'nomu v Zapadnoi Evrope," Voprosy istorii, 1964, no. 5, pp. 95–111.
[45]Gulyga and Levada, pp. 52–53.
[46]Loone, pp. 229, 232–233.

because the nobility and the bourgeoisie were evenly matched, the state acquired, as he expressed it, "for the moment, a certain degree of independence of both."[47] For Western Europe, Engels's explanation has an element of Marxist plausibility, in that the genesis of the absolutist state can at least be linked with the growing power, if not the dominant power, of the bourgeoisie. In seventeenth- and eighteenth-century Russia, however, there was no nascent bourgeoisie capable of producing political consequences of such magnitude.

At a conference held in Moscow in 1968, several "new current" historians suggested that the solution to the problem of Russian absolutism lay in viewing it as a response to external influences rather than internal economic causes. A. Ia. Avrekh granted that in Russia, absolutism not only antedated the rise of the bourgeoisie but was "one of the most powerful preconditions" for the development of capitalism.[48] It was acknowledged, moreover, that such a situation is a paradoxical reversal of the Marxist principle of the primacy of economic over political factors: "It seems to me," A. D. Lublinskaia stated, "that Russia presents just that interesting case in which the state power as it were ran somewhat ahead of the economy and paved the way for important organizational and administrative measures which made possible the origin of new, capitalist relations, or in any event powerfully promoted them." The problem was how to explain this *operezhenie* (getting ahead, anticipation), as it was called at the conference—no doubt echoing the concept of anticipatory reflection (*operezhaiushchee otrazhenie*) introduced in Soviet epistemology a few years earlier. For many of the speakers, it could be attributed only to the impact of Western states on Russia. Avrekh saw it as the response to a threat: "The fundamental cause of this *operezhenie*," he stated, "was the need to survive in the vicinity of advanced Western European countries." P. V. Volobuev and A. N. Chistozvonov found not only the incentive but the materials for the development of Russian absolutism in the West: Western absolutism, itself a product of developing capitalism, they argued, provided Russia with the bureaucratic, military, and industrial models needed in order to establish an absolutist state before the foundation of capitalism, which it then promoted. Generalizing, Volobuev maintained that influences of this sort are not rare in history and that they make possible the appearance of political institutions in countries in which "it would seem that the internal preconditions for them are lacking."[49]

In more recent years there has not been such explicit discussion of

[47]Marx and Engels, *Selected Works*, p. 588.
[48]*Dokumenty*, p. 222. For a discussion of this conference, see Alexander Gerschenkron, "Soviet Marxism and Absolutism," *Slavic Review* 30 (1971), pp. 853–869.
[49]*Dokumenty*, pp. 175, 222, 197, 194, 218.

historical operezhenie as at the 1968 conference, but Soviet writers are no less ready to acknowledge the significance of external factors on the development of a society's economy. Loone has distinguished between cases of the "self-development" of an economy and cases in which an economy develops because new productive forces are introduced from without.[50] Soviet ideologists can hardly object, committed as they are to the principle of aiding societies less developed than the USSR to make radical economic advances.

The Impact of Economically Neutral Factors

Another, equally unorthodox and theoretically unsettling acknowledgment in recent Soviet historiography is the acceptance of outside historical determinants that come not from other societies but from local influences that are, however, external to the given society's socioeconomic formation or formations. Soviet theorists are finding that the analysis of a society's development, quite apart from its relations with other societies, cannot be carried out without recognizing the powerful operation of factors that are not attributable either to that society's mode of production or to its superstructure. Although no generic name has been given these factors by Soviet writers, we may call them "economically neutral," since they are determined neither directly nor indirectly by the economic system of the society, and in class societies they do not reflect the partisan interests of any economic class.

For many years the possibility of neutral historical factors was not seriously considered by Soviet philosophers, who like most Marxists assumed that the categories of mode of production and superstructure exhausted every aspect of social life, so that if a given phenomenon did not belong to one, it must belong to the other. Ironically it was the chief dogmatist, Stalin himself, who broke this particular mold in Soviet thinking. His 1950 letters on linguistics gave *language* a class-neutral status that in effect removed it from the operating categories and laws of orthodox historical materialism: "Language," Stalin wrote, "cannot be ranked either among bases or among superstructures."[51] This permission for one important element of social life to exist outside the traditional framework of Marxist concepts suggested that others might similarly be understood as insulated from economic class interests. In the ensuing years many candidates were proposed—and soon without invoking Stalin's authority.

---

[50]Loone, p. 251.
[51]Joseph Stalin, *Marxism and Linguistics* (New York, 1951), p. 34.

In history this movement has taken the form of arguing for the inclusion in historical analysis of causal factors either previously rejected or never seriously considered because they were not accommodated or sanctioned by the dogmatic elements of historical materialism. One such is geography, stressed in an earlier day by the pioneering Russian Marxist philosopher George Plekhanov. On Stalin's own authority, geographical factors were explicitly rejected as significant historical forces in the *Short Course*; but subsequently the importance of these factors has been vigorously reasserted in the influential works of M. A. Korostovtsev, V. K. Iatsunskii, and other Soviet historians.[52] Another newly recognized neutral factor is ethnic nationalism, a sensitive topic in the multinational Soviet Union, to which attention was nonetheless urged by P. N. Fedoseev and Iu. P. Frantsev at a 1964 meeting of historians.[53] A third is social psychology, considered either idealistic or simply superstructural by earlier Soviet historical materialists but recommended for separate study as an "extremely important" category by Gurevich and others beginning in the 1960s; Gurevich suggested that the phenomena of social psychology are a kind of transmission belt between the mode of production and the social superstructure, identified with neither but exercising a "colossal influence" upon them.[54] Surveying noneconomic factors as a group, Gurevich in 1965 identified all of the following as among the "most diverse causes" that must find their place in the study of the actual historical life of a people: "natural conditions, national peculiarities, psychology, ideology, external influences and actions, traditions of every sort, level of cultural development, biological and demographic factors, and much else."[55]

Most Soviet theorists now admit at least grudgingly that geography and other "natural conditions" must be accommodated in historical theory. There is considerably less agreement, however, on the question of whether certain *social* phenomena can be economically neutral, in part because there is among Soviet writers no accepted mode of distinguishing conceptually between a society, a base-superstructure ensemble, and a socioeconomic formation. When the latter is defined, as in the *Philosophical Dictionary* quoted above, as a *type* of society (feudal, capitalist, and so forth), a socioeconomic formation is viewed not as a concrete structure but as an abstraction that is instantiated (perhaps never perfectly) in in-

---

[52]Scanlan, "From Historical Materialism," pp. 9, 21.

[53]"O metodologicheskikh voprosakh istoricheskoi nauki," *Voprosy istorii*, 1964, no. 3, p. 7.

[54]A. Ia. Gurevich, "Nekotorye aspekty izucheniia sotsial'noi istorii. (Obshchestvenno-istoricheskaia psikhologiia)," *Voprosy istorii*, 1964, no. 10, p. 68.

[55]Gulyga and Levada, p. 58.

dividual societies. In this view, concrete societies may have features that are independent of their typological characteristics and thus are economically neutral.[56] Many writers, however, resist this view as "idealistic," comparing it with Max Weber's conception of "ideal types," and instead treat a socioeconomic formation as an actual existing society. In this case, to speak of social phenomena "independent" of a socioeconomic formation is without meaning unless it is argued (implausibly) that a socioeconomic formation contains elements that are external to both its mode of production and its superstructure.[57] Still other Soviet writers advance the puzzling view that a socioeconomic formation is *both* an abstract type *and* a concrete structure—"not only a logical concept," Frantsev wrote in 1964, "but a historical period, a concrete manifestation of the unity of the logical and the historical."[58]

In the absence of clarity on the basic concepts, there is understandably much uncertainty and confusion in the Soviet literature concerning neutral social phenomena. The 1963 *Philosophical Dictionary* ascribed not only language but the family and national peculiarities to a category vaguely called "special [*svoeobraznye*] social phenomena which are related neither to the base nor to the superstructure but are vitally important for understanding the concrete course of development of a particular formation."[59] There is no mention of that category, however, in the otherwise virtually identical 1980 text of the same article, which leaves the impression that all social phenomena are either basal or superstructural.[60] The latest (1982) edition of *Fundamentals*, on the other hand, states that "besides the base and superstructure a socio-economic formation includes other elements of social life (everyday affairs, family relations, and so on)."[61] And a recent technical treatment argues that Lenin himself acknowledged the reality of social phenomena that are not part of a socioeconomic formation at all.[62] In this welter of opinions, historians are left largely to their own devices in dealing with "neutral" factors.

[56]V. I. Verezgov, "Znachenie teorii obshchestvenno-ekonomicheskoi formatsii v issledovanii sotsializma," *Vestnik Moskovskogo universiteta. Seriia 7. Filosofiia*, 1981, no. 3, pp. 20–21; Loone, pp. 203–211.

[57]A. P. Sheptulin appears to take this position in his *Marxist-Leninist Philosophy*, trans. S. Ponomarenko and A. Timofeyev (Moscow, 1978), p. 300.

[58]*Istoriia i sotsiologiia* (Moscow, 1964), p. 335.

[59]M. M. Rozental' and P. F. Iudin, eds., *Filosofskii slovar'* (Moscow, 1963), p. 320.

[60]Frolov, pp. 256–257.

[61]Konstantinov, *Fundamentals* (1982), p. 246.

[62]Loone, p. 218.

The Diminished Role of the Economic Base

For all the unsolved theoretical problems created by the foregoing innovations in Soviet historiography, Soviet theorists nonetheless insist that, in general and on the whole, "material," economic causes determine the direction of human history—that alterations in "material productive forces" and subsequently in production relations are the dominant underlying forces in historical change. But even with respect to the interpretation of this fundamental thesis, significant departures from orthodoxy are found in current Soviet historical writing. One of these departures is the now virtually universal tendency to diminish the "dominance" of the economic factors—that is, to reduce their role to whatever minimum level is consistent with the thesis of their supremacy over other factors.

The tendency itself is no novelty in Soviet Marxism-Leninism, having been stimulated from the beginning by the Leninist emphasis on organized political and ideological activity both in making a revolution and in leading the transformation of the economy thereafter. Some early Soviet historians, it is true, did adopt a radical economic determinism that effectively eliminated everything but "material productive forces" as factors in history; but this position, labeled "economic materialism" in the Soviet literature, has long since been rejected in the USSR even by the most dogmatic theorists as inconsistent with the nature of social relations and the power of the institutional and ideological superstructure as conceived by both Lenin and Marx.[63] Stalin provided the most explicit and authoritative recognition of this power in the *Short Course* when he (or his ideologists) wrote of "the tremendous organizing, mobilizing and transforming value of new ideas, new theories, new political views and new political institutions," and his letters on linguistics also stressed the active and relatively independent part played by superstructural forces in social life.[64]

Post-Stalin work in historical materialism, especially work by historians and philosophers most closely associated with the new current, not only continued this downgrading of economic causes but intensified it. No longer interested in quoting Stalin for support, these writers rediscovered the letters in which Engels, after Marx's death, had attempted to correct what he regarded as excessive attention to economics in the interpretation of historical materialism: "According to the materialist conception of history, the *ultimately* determining element in history is the production and reproduction of real life. More than this neither Marx nor I have ever

[63]See, for example, "O metodologicheskikh voprosakh," p. 23.
[64]*History of the Communist Party of the Soviet Union (Bolsheviks). Short Course*, edited by a Commission of the Central Committee of the C.P.S.U.(B.) (New York, 1939), p. 116; Stalin, *Marxism and Linguistics*, p. 13.

asserted. Hence if somebody twists this into saying that the economic element is the *only* determining one, he transforms that proposition into a meaningless, abstract, senseless phrase."[65] Many types of causes are active in history, Engels insisted, and the real situation is one of causal *interaction* in which economic factors prevail in the end.[66] Beginning in the 1960s these and related comments by both Engels and Marx were quoted increasingly by Soviet philosophers, who complained more and more openly that oversimplified schemes amounting essentially to "economic materialism" were still too much a part of the published literature of historical materialism.[67] The extent to which attention to economic forces had declined by 1967 may be judged by a protest voiced in that year by a Soviet economic historian, who lamented the fact that "powerful directors of scholarly institutions and publishing houses" had come to share the "widespread . . . prejudice" that economic subjects are narrow and are lacking in the "overall historical significance" that attaches to political themes.[68]

The campaign against overemphasizing economic factors has clearly been abetted in recent Soviet philosophy by the ever greater ideological stress on the "leading role" of the Communist party—a political, superstructural force rather than an economic one—in building communism. This is one of a number of cases in current Soviet thought in which ideological interests are exploited by scholars in their opposition to oversimplified intellectual schemes.

The Dematerialization of the Economic Base

The final and most debated departure from traditional historical materialism in current Soviet theory consists not in limiting the efficacy of the economic base but in redefining it to include what were previously considered superstructural elements.

The acceptability of this procedure is one of the issues in a lively debate that has taken place among Soviet theorists since the mid-sixties concerning the economic functions of the socialist state. Several Soviet writers, principally economists, have argued that since state planning and organization are essential to the functioning of the economy under socialism, the socialist

---

[65]Engels to Joseph Bloch, September 21[-22], 1890, in Marx and Engels, *Selected Works*, p. 692 (italics in original).
[66]Engels to W. Borgius, January 25, 1894, in ibid., p. 704 (italics in original).
[67]Gulyga and Levada, p. 30.
[68]Quoted in I. F. Gindin, "Problemy istorii fevral'skoi revoliutsii i ee sotsial'no-ekonomicheskikh predposylok," *Istoriia SSSR*, 1967, no. 4, pp. 41–42.

state must be viewed as part of the economic base, or at least as performing what some call "base functions."[69] But such wholesale transportation of a superstructural element into the economic base is unacceptable to many other scholars, who continue to seek alternative analyses; some have attempted, for example, to distinguish between the economic *base* and the economic *system* of a society, ascribing the economic functions of the state to the latter rather than to the former.[70] The issue, which remains unsettled, is widely regarded by Soviet theorists as a critical demonstration of the need for fuller and clearer elaboration of such fundamental categories of historical materialism as 'base' and 'superstructure'.[71]

In another instance, Soviet scholars have succumbed in large numbers to the temptation to introduce "nonmaterial" elements into the economic base, though not without much controversy.

A question long raised by critics of Marxist theory is that of how the historical materialist can relegate the activity of the human mind to a secondary, derivative, "superstructural" status when it seems clear that the level of development of the "material productive forces" in a society, on which the entire socioeconomic formation rests, is itself the consequence of the technological application of science—that is, of the activity of the human mind. Now that such problems are seriously addressed in the USSR, Soviet philosophers are no longer limited to the question-begging reply that science only makes such discoveries as are called for by a given mode of production. Rather, appealing to Marx's references to the function of science in production, many Soviet philosophers now contend that this function has become still more important in the "scientific-technological revolution" of the present day.[72] Science, they argue, must not be considered a superstructural phenomenon; it is itself a "material productive force" and one that has a direct role—indeed a "decisive role"—in the production process.[73]

What makes this intellectual force sufficiently "material" for many Soviet writers is simply the fact that in the form of knowledge relevant to

---

[69]References to the recent debate on the issue are found in Iu. K. Pletnikov and V. N. Shevchenko, "Issledovaniia v oblasti istoricheskogo materializma," *Voprosy filosofii*, 1981, no. 1, p. 32.

[70]Ibid.

[71]Ibid.; V. Zh. Kelle and M. Ia. Koval'zon, "Vazhneishie aspekty metodologii sotsial'no-filosofskogo issledovaniia," *Voprosy filosofii*, 1980, no. 7, pp. 118–119.

[72]For Marx's view, see, for example, Marx, *Grundrisse* (London, 1973), p. 699; *Historical Materialism*, p. 43.

[73]R. G. Vartanov, "Nekotorye problemy dialektiki proizvoditel'nykh sil i proizvodstvennykh otnoshenii razvitogo sotsializma," *Voprosy filosofii*, 1980, no. 11, p. 51. The absence of definite and indefinite articles in the Russian language creates ambiguities that are often exploited by Russian writers to allow for strong commitments without actually making them; here, "*a* decisive role" could just as well be "*the* decisive role."

the production process it is lodged in the actual, physical human beings who engage in that process. Soviet historical materialists, as we have seen, consistently regard the human laborer as a productive force alongside the whole complex of "means of production." This is not an uncontroversial position among Marxists, for although Marx did write in the *Grundrisse* that "the human being himself" is "the main force of production,"[74] he nowhere else called the human laborer a productive force at all, much less the main one. The closest Marx came to a systematic account of productive forces is a list in *Capital* of what he termed the "simple elements" of the labor process, in which he included work *activity* but not the worker himself; and it may be argued that in the *Grundrisse* Marx used 'the human being himself' as shorthand for man's laboring activity or labor power.[75] By fastening on the *laborer* as a productive force, however, Soviet historical materialists are able to include within that category the knowledge that the laborer brings to his work activity, and in this way such knowledge can be said to enter the productive process "in materialized form."[76]

Still, a number of Soviet writers are understandably disturbed by the idealist implications of incorporating a subjective factor such as knowledge in the "material" underpinnings of society. Once knowledge directly related to production is included, other forms of knowledge may qualify as well; in a 1981 article, for example, V. V. Dubinin and I. I. Shevchuk list as productive forces not only technological but *economic* knowledge.[77] The next step is to bring in noncognitive characteristics of the laborer, such as his dedication and enthusiasm; even what I. N. Sizemskaia calls "the creative attitude of the worker to labor" can be included, for it can be said to contribute to the worker's effectiveness in the production process just as his technical knowledge does.[78] Hence it is now not uncommon for Soviet philosophers to recognize as productive forces a whole, ill-defined category of "spiritual qualities" of the individual, in the distinctive Soviet sense of 'spiritual' (*dukhovnyi*) in which the term covers a broad range of subjective traits, moral and affective as well as cognitive but not religious. And this recognition, many think, is going too far. "Certain authors," it was observed at a recent conference, "write of the productive

---

[74]Marx, *Grundrisse* (London, 1973), p. 422 (italics omitted).
[75]Karl Marx, *Capital. A Critique of Political Economy*, vol. 1, trans. Ben Fowkes (New York, 1967), p. 284; cf. Cohen, pp. 42, 45.
[76]"Proizvoditel'nye sily," no. 4, p. 96.
[77]Dubinin and Shevchuk, p. 29.
[78]"Proizvoditel'nye sily," no. 4, p. 105; Vartanov, "Nekotorye problemy," p. 55.

forces in such a way as to create the impression that they have altogether forgotten about materialism."[79]

The question of the place of the laborer and his subjective characteristics in historical materialist theory continues to be a lively one, which some Soviet theorists attempt to resolve by softening the thesis that the laborer is the "main" productive force. M. Ia. Koval'zon has argued that the "main" factor need not be the *determining* material factor required by historical materialist theory. But Koval'zon's effort ends feebly with the declaration that it is an "objective contradiction" (meaning in this case a paradoxical truth that is not yet understood) that among the productive forces, "one element—the material-technical base—is the determining but not the main element; the other—people—is the main but not the determining element."[80] V. G. Marakhov has also found it difficult to explain what he significantly calls "the new form of materialism" required by the changed relations of science and production in the present day.[81] Other writers are seemingly content to accept an idealist heart within the body of historical materialism, and some come close to calling it that. "In the very category of the mode of production," wrote Dubinin and Shevchuk in 1981, "there exists a spiritual factor in the person of the chief productive force."[82]

Alternative Conceptions of the Historical Process

The wealth of complications, "idealist" and otherwise, introduced into historical analysis by the developments described in the previous section has cast serious doubt on the "orthodox" conception of that process, according to which history is viewed, following Marx's preface, as the necessary, law-governed sequence of a small number of discrete socioeconomic formations. There is now virtually unanimous agreement among Soviet philosophers and historians that Marx's preface statement requires correction or at least qualification. But there are marked differences of opinion concerning how far and in what directions the departure from the classic statement must go. There is in Soviet philosophy today, in other words, no accepted description of the historical process and hence no set conception of the content of historical materialism as a theory of history.

Closest to the old orthodoxy are theorists who remain basically loyal to the piatichlenka and to the idea of "necessary laws," but even these

[79]"Proizvoditel'nye sily," no. 9, p. 101.
[80]Ibid., pp. 91–92; see also pp. 101–102.
[81]"Proizvoditel'nye sily," no. 4, p. 96.
[82]Dubinin and Shevchuk, p. 29; see also "Proizvoditel'nye sily," no. 4, p. 95.

theorists now concede that the laws do not apply to every actual society. V. G. Afanasyev in his popular textbook *Marxist Philosophy* admits that not all modern nations have passed through the recognized stages in the established order, but he maintains that this fact does not refute "the *general objective tendency* of mankind's development" through the standard five-stage sequence.[83] Iu. I. Semenov suggests that many Marxists have mistakenly attempted to apply to each society distributively what is true only of all societies taken together—namely, that in their historical progression there is a succession of what he calls "world systems" or groups of societies representing a given socioeconomic formation that are "stages in the evolution of human society as a whole." The career of an individual society is quite beside the point, according to Semenov; indeed he asserts that "there are no social organisms that could be said to have gone through all formations," just as "there are no socio-economic formations through which all social organisms could be said to have gone." Here it must be noted, however, that if it is indeed true of individual societies, as Semenov states, that "formations appear as types of these social organisms, and not as stages of their internal development," then it is no longer clear how we are to understand the mechanics of the process. Unable to appeal, as Marx did, to the internal development of concrete societies to account for the tendency, Semenov provides no substitute for it apart from vague references to "the objective inner necessity of the development of all social organisms taken together."[84]

At the other extreme, furthest from the old orthodoxy, some Soviet writers have questioned the very usefulness of the traditional apparatus of socioeconomic formations and their laws and have emphasized the openness and indeterminateness of the historical process. The clearest presentation of this position, one of the most controversial elements of the new current in the 1960s, remains a 1965 essay by Aron Iakovlevich Gurevich entitled "General Law [*zakon*] and Concrete Regularity [*zakonomernost'*] in History."

According to Gurevich the general laws to which historical materialists traditionally appeal, such as the law of the correspondence of production relations to the level of development of the productive forces, are too abstract to apply to the real historical process without "essential modifications and specifications." History, rather, is an arena of what he calls "concrete regularities," or more specific and detailed patterns that lack the universality of laws of nature and apply only over short stretches of

[83] Afanasyev, pp. 208–209 (italics in original).
[84] *Philosophy in the USSR. Problems of Historical Materialism,* trans. S. Syrovatkin (Moscow, 1981), pp. 51, 45, 46.

time. In part this is attributable, Gurevich believes, to the complexity of historical causation: "Historical phenomena," he writes, "take place as the result of the intersection of many factors, expressing different lines of development, often in opposite directions.... The historical phenomenon ... has no single cause and hence cannot be univocally explained." The concrete regularities to be found in history, Gurevich argues, take shape "on the basis of the totality of the causal and other connections" affecting social development in a particular society at a particular moment.[85]

But another reason Gurevich has for questioning the general-laws approach is that it does not do justice to what he calls "the human content of history." Historical regularities, he argues, are unlike natural laws in that they are manifested through the actions of human beings, who are not "bearers of a law that stands above them." Thus historical circumstances, he writes, though "conditioned" by "the objective situation," are also "to a colossal degree dependent upon the will and the actions of the classes, groups, and individuals who make up society." Furthermore, Gurevich does not regard the subjective elements as fully amenable to scientific analysis and prediction. Through he avoids an outright statement of freedom of the will, he does at one point refer to human action as "autonomous," and he clearly views the resulting historical process as objectively undetermined: "The course of history is not a track or rut laid down beforehand once and for all," he writes. "History is not programmed or predetermined by anyone. Historical development is an open system with the broadest possibilities, with an unlimited 'set' of probabilities and variations."[86] Clearly this open system bears little resemblance to the five-stage process governed by the objective laws of the traditional view.

Denying the importance of the general laws was a major charge against the new current historians in the early 1970s,[87] but this doctrinaire reaction has not kept other writers from entertaining the idea that history is an open process. Even a recent editorial in *Voprosy filosofii* affirms that social development "cannot be set out in linear, uniform models" and that the theory of history must be open to "necessary modifications in conformity with the demands of life."[88] The fullest recent development of this view is provided by the Estonian philosopher Eero Loone in his interesting book of 1980, *Contemporary Philosophy of History*. Loone constructs a number of different models—all of them, he argues, acceptably "Marxist"—for the succession of socioeconomic formations. Among Loone's models are complex ones in which societies are confronted with real choices among

---

[85]Gulyga and Levada, pp. 53–55.
[86]Ibid., pp. 51, 76, 57, 74.
[87]Shurbovanyi, p. 160.
[88]"Za tesnuiu sviaz' teorii i praktiki," *Voprosy filosofii*, 1982, no. 1, p. 7.

alternative paths of development, and it is with these models that his own sympathies clearly lie. In adopting one of them, Loone writes, the theoretician is "renouncing the unilinear conception of social development, which permits only the acceleration or retardation of processes and not a choice among possibilities that are different in principle both from the preceding stage and from each other. All the old terminology, all thought of the old oppositions, proves inadequate.... And gone are the ideas of a necessity that rules out the significance of *choice*."[89] Significantly, Loone does not exclude Marx himself from the scope of his generalization when he asserts that "ideas of linearity (or of essential linearity) came easily to the minds of nineteenth-century historians; but at the end of the twentieth century we can and must pose questions that were not raised in the eighteenth or nineteenth." This is a gentler but an equally unmistakable call for a "new reading" of the historical conception of Marx. Still, Loone does admit that for a Marxist, one transition is "necessary"—the transition from capitalism to communism.[90]

The two extreme positions sketched thus far set the outer limits of the debate, but most of the Soviet discussion since the early 1970s concerning the nature of the historical process has taken place in the broad middle ground between the proclamation of a fixed five-stage cosmic tendency and the affirmation of an open system of historical development. Virtually everyone agrees now that there is a need to accommodate human choice and conscious activity in the theoretical structure of historical materialism; the problem is how to do it without giving up economic determinism. One of the more striking features of Soviet philosophy in the past decade has been the great increase in books and articles devoted to what is sometimes called "the problem of man."[91] What makes man a "problem" for Soviet thinkers is the difficulty of acknowledging the significance of conscious individual activity while at the same time, in the words of one writer, "preserving the value of the Marxist conceptual scheme presented in the famous preface to the work *A Contribution to the Critique of Political Economy*."[92] Some writers still maintain that the preface doctrines themselves, suitably qualified and supplemented, are adequate to the task; whereas others believe that appropriate categories and principles to describe the historical process must be sought elsewhere in the Marxian corpus.

---

[89]Loone, p. 234 (italics in original).

[90]Ibid., pp. 234, 260. For a fuller treatment of Loone's book, see the review-essay by James P. Scanlan in *History and Theory* 22 (1983), pp. 311–317.

[91]See, for example, "Materialy soveshchaniia po probleme cheloveka v zhurnale 'Voprosy filosofii,' " *Voprosy filosofii*, 1980, no. 7, pp. 94–115.

[92]G. G. Filippov, "Konstruktivnoe nachalo," *Voprosy filosofii*, 1981, no. 12, p. 82.

One of the earliest attempts to look beyond the preface for the fundamental concepts of historical materialism was that undertaken in the mid-1950s by V. P. Tugarinov—the same Tugarinov who was also responsible for a number of early innovations in the discussion of dialectical materialism. Seeking to develop the concept of 'social being', to which Marx in the preface subordinated 'social consciousness', Tugarinov argued that the key to its content could be found in the statement in *The German Ideology* that "the existence of men is their actual life-process," and on this basis Tugarinov defined 'social being' as "the entire real practical life and activity of people, including the material, social, and political life of society."[93] Much discussed at the time and subsequently, Tugarinov's analysis suggested that the proper approach to the formulation of historical materialist theory is to begin not with "material productive forces" and relations of production but with the concept of practical activity.[94]

Following Tugarinov's lead, and drawing broadly on the early writings of Marx, a number of other Soviet philosophers (including V. A. Demichev, M. S. Kagan, L. P. Bueva, and I. A. Maizel') have also stressed the active, subjective side of social life, and consequently have become known as proponents of what is called "the activity approach" to the theory of historical materialism. One of the most prominently placed of these writers, Iurii Konstantinovich Pletnikov, head of the Section on Current Problems of Historical Materialism of the Institute of Philosophy, has recently taken the lead in arguing that the concept of *activity* should be the fundamental category by reference to which the system of historical materialism is constructed. The "objectified results of the activity of people" are the only key to social life in the Marxian conception, Pletnikov argues, and therefore the category of activity, itself not defined by any of the other categories of historical materialism, should be "the point of departure for the theoretical reproduction of the historical process." Thinkers who look to objective social relations as the key, he holds, are wrong in that, on Marxian grounds, social relations are simply products of practical life. The fact that activity inescapably has a subjective dimension should not be an obstacle to the primacy of the concept, Pletnikov argues, inasmuch as the creations of this subjective activity, including social relations, have "as much an objective form of being as other objects of the material world."[95]

---

[93]Easton and Guddat, p. 414; V. P. Tugarinov, *Obshchestvennoe bytie* (Leningrad, 1958), p. 9.

[94]For an account of this discussion, with extensive bibliographical information, see G. S. Aref'eva and A. I. Verbin, "Sushchnost' materialisticheskogo ponimaniia istorii," *Filosofskie nauki*, 1978, no. 3, pp. 141–145.

[95]Iu. K. Pletnikov, "Problemy dal'neishei razrabotki teoreticheskoi sistemy istoricheskogo materializma," *Filosofskie nauki*, 1981, no. 4, pp. 15–16, 20.

The nontraditional character of this approach to history is stressed by the Soviet philosopher A. V. Margulis when he writes that what is needed in the last analysis is *not* "an objectivist description of history." Society exists as a system of social activity, Margulis insists, and hence any characterization of it must center on the whole complex set of activities that make up its being.[96] But nontraditional though it may be, the activity approach is not without influence in high places, as witness the publication of Pletnikov's major article advocating it in *Kommunist* in 1978.[97]

Many other equally well-placed Soviet philosophers, however, have been disturbed by what one of them, Matvei Iakovlevich Koval'zon of Moscow State University, *Voprosy filosofii*'s editor for historical materialism, has called "the one-sided position" of recent years that regards activity as "the ultimate determinant of history."[98] Seeking to combat the activity approach in the name of true materialism, Koval'zon in 1980 collaborated with Vladislav Zhanovich Kelle on a major article on the subject that was featured in *Voprosy filosofii* and became the focus of much discussion. The authors acknowledged that Marx's preface cannot stand alone as stating the content of historical materialism, for in it, in their view, Marx abstracted from the individual and his activity in order to highlight "the logic of world history, conditioned by the succession of modes of production, by the dialectics of productive forces and production relations."[99] For a full picture, Kelle and Koval'zon argue, the elements Marx excluded from the preface must be taken into account.

Their proposal is to recognize the existence of three distinguishable and equally legitimate aspects from which history should be viewed. The first they call, echoing a comment of Marx's, the *natural history* (*estestvennoistoricheskii*) aspect, or in other words the respect in which human history, like natural history, is describable by objective laws that do not depend upon the consciousness or will of people.[100] The second is the *activity* aspect, in which history is linked with what the authors call "the creative principle" in that it is seen as "the process and the result of the activity of people." Finally there is the *humanistic* aspect, in which it is acknowledged that man and his development are the objects of historical

---

[96]A. V. Margulis, "K kharakteristike metodologicheskikh aspektov obshchesotsiologicheskoi teorii," *Voprosy filosofii*, 1981, no. 12, p. 81.

[97]Iu. K. Pletnikov, "Nekotorye napravleniia razrabotki teorii istoricheskogo materializma," *Kommunist*, 1978, no. 17, pp. 32–39.

[98]"Proizvoditel'nye sily," no. 4, p. 89.

[99]Kelle and Koval'zon, p. 118.

[100]In a letter to Engels dated December 19, 1860, after reading Charles Darwin's *Origin of Species*, Marx wrote that the book contained "the natural history foundation [*die naturhistorische Grundlage*] for our view" (Karl Marx and Friedrich Engels, *Werke*, 39 vols. [Berlin, 1960–1968] vol. 30, p. 131).

study as well as the agencies of historical change; "in the last analysis," Kelle and Koval'zon write, "the history of society is the development of man himself." In the authors' view, then, history is simultaneously three things: a process conforming to objective laws, a product of the creative activity of individuals, and a record of the development of humanity.[101]

The authors suggest that it is only to be expected and indeed is desirable that these three perspectives appear difficult to reconcile, inasmuch as in real life they are dialectically related and hence "contradictory." In fact, however, for the authors the reconciliation is effected by their interpretation of the three perspectives as *hierarchically* related, and it quickly becomes apparent that the "addition" of elements from which Marx abstracted in the preface produces no major revision of that text. The first or "natural history" approach is primary and determining, they argue; only by pursuing it can we understand "the unity and overall direction of the historical process," "the fundamental stages of historical development," and "the historical necessity of the transition from one formation to another, higher and more progressive one." The "creative principle" is manifestly subordinated to the objective laws for Kelle and Koval'zon; among man's creations, they hold, what actually becomes a factor in the historical process and thus has some enduring historical significance depends upon "the objective conditions and laws of social development." "The basis of departure for social theory," Kelle and Koval'zon write, cannot be subjective activity but must be "something independent of the subject and his consciousness." Marx's pronouncement in the preface that "it is not the consciousness of men that determines their being" must be preserved. Hence their unequivocal conclusion: "First come the objective laws of history. Then and on that basis come the activity of people and the problems of their part in realizing the demands of the laws."[102]

In appearances at conferences discussing their paper subsequently, Kelle and Koval'zon left no doubt that their principal objective in writing the article was to defend materialism in history against what they saw as the idealistic excesses of the "activity" and "humanistic" approaches. Koval'zon's reasoning at a conference in December 1980 is summarized as follows:

> To understand and to present society as an objective process not dependent on consciousness and as a product similar in this respect to nature, it is necessary to view society as a system of impersonal, superindividual, depersonified relations—that is, in a natural history aspect. To regard activity,

[101]Kelle and Koval'zon, pp. 123, 126, 127.
[102]Ibid., pp. 123, 126, 121, 129.

practice, or the concrete man as of paramount importance is without foundation, for then it would be impossible to establish the opposition in principle between materialism and idealism, the material and the ideal.[103]

The reactions of other Soviet theorists to the Kelle-Koval'zon article, as reported in *Voprosy filosofii* in correspondence from its readers and as stated at special conferences on the subject, have been decidedly mixed. Many respondents have expressed general approval of the proposal or of the motivation behind it, but at least an equal number have advocated greater attention to the "human" factors.[104] And a few months after the Kelle-Koval'zon article was featured in *Voprosy filosofii*, the journal *Filosofskie nauki* published both a paper by Pletnikov strongly defending the activity approach and a report of a conference, cosponsored by Pletnikov's division at the Institute of Philosophy, at which his paper was the keynote address. The majority of the speakers at the conference, the journal stated, were in agreement with "the methodological principles" advanced by Pletnikov, and many participants were said to have indicated that the proposals of Kelle and Koval'zon "cannot serve as the basis for the construction of a system of historical materialism."[105]

Faced with this split, it is not surprising that many Soviet writers are now suggesting positions that would in some manner reconcile the activity approach and the "natural history" approach (or "formational" approach, as the latter is sometimes called, in reference to its emphasis on socioeconomic formations and their historical succession). At a recent conference no fewer than eleven different concepts—including 'material productive activity', 'the empirically active individual', and 'human society as a whole'— were proposed by various speakers as the needed "initial category" for historical materialism.[106] V. N. Sagatovskii argues that it is not contradictory to regard *both* human activity *and* objective social relations as primary, inasmuch as each *is* primary at different points in the historical process. An individual's goals and ideals, Sagatovskii writes, are generated by the objective world in which he or she exists; but "once having been formed by *preceding* circumstances, these values *functionally* operate as a relatively independent factor in relation to the objective circumstances *of the present and the future*." Furthermore, these subjective elements may be not only effective but preponderant, he argues: "In those situations in

[103]Filippov, p. 85.
[104]Two conferences at which the paper was discussed are reported in ibid., pp. 82–85, and in A. S. Aizikovich, N. V. Kliagin, and A. A. Orlov, "Vsesoiuznoe koordinatsionnoe soveshchanie po problemam istoricheskogo materializma," *Filosofskie nauki*, 1981, no. 4, pp. 146–150.
[105]Aizikovich, Kliagin, and Orlov, pp. 147–148.
[106]Ibid., p. 149.

which the possibility of choice becomes especially significant, in which the manifestation of an *active vital position* may prove to be the [a?] deciding influence on the outcome of events, the activity approach may come to the forefront." Thus the solution, as Sagatovskii sees it, is to abandon the quest for the absolute subordination of one of these "abstractions" to the other in favor of their "mutual supplementation."[107] For Kelle and Koval'zon, of course, such a solution cannot be satisfactory, precisely because it does not provide for the clear subordination of subjective to objective factors that "materialism" would seem to require.

In summary, Soviet philosophers today are generally agreed that the picture of the historical process drawn in Marx's preface stands in need of correction—that human history cannot adequately be described as simply a succession of socioeconomic formations in accordance with objective laws. But whether the correction is to take the form of supplying secondary elements that complement the preface picture without altering its substance or the form of a fundamental revision of the "natural history" conception in the direction of the subjective concepts stressed by Marx earlier in his career is by no means a settled question. And for this reason there is no consensus among Soviet philosophers as to which concepts to employ as points of departure in constructing the system of historical materialism or as to what is required to make that theory suitably Marxist and materialist.

A Critical Assessment of Soviet Historical Materialism

The fact that the theory of historical materialism remains unsettled suggests that there are deep-rooted obstacles to coherence in this field as in dialectical materialism. Just as dialectics does not sit well with materialism, neither, it seems, does history. In the latter case, unlike the former, however, the theoretical problems have emerged principally in connection with the second half of the conceptual combination—that is, with the concept of materialism itself. Seeking to do justice to the process of history on a materialist basis, Soviet philosophers have experienced great difficulty in fixing the "material" nature of that process in a convincing and productive manner.

The Relation of Historical Materialism to Dialectical Materialism

That the materialist character of historical materialism should pose a problem would come as a surprise to the doctrinaire theorist of the Stalin

---

[107]V. N. Sagatovskii, "Obshchestvennye otnoshenia i deiatel'nost'," *Voprosy filosofii*, 1981, no. 12, pp. 73–75 (italics in original).

period, who held that the theory was a straightforward deductive extension of dialectical materialism to the domain of history.[108] This view, advanced on the authority of Stalin himself in the *Short Course*, was clearly an attempt to take seriously the insistence on the monolithic unity of Marxist philosophy proclaimed by Lenin and still stressed by Soviet philosophers today. Indeed Lenin's assertion that Marxism is "forged from a single piece of steel" was explicitly made in the context of the relation between materialism in general, which in Lenin's words "recognizes objectively real being (matter) as independent of consciousness," and historical materialism, which "recognizes social being as independent of the social consciousness of mankind."[109] The *Short Course* authors were simply following in the spirit of this notion when they affirmed that the relation was one of logical inference:

> If nature, being, the material world, is primary, and mind, thought, is secondary, derivative; if the material world represents objective reality existing independently of the mind of men, while the mind is a reflection of this objective reality; it follows that the material life of society, its being, is also primary, and its spiritual life secondary, derivative, and that the material life of society is an objective reality existing independently of the will of men, while the spiritual life of society is a reflection of this objective reality, a reflection of being.[110]

The belief that truths about society can be deduced from ontological principles has long been abandoned by most philosophers; Bertrand Russell, who ascribed the belief to Marx among others, called it "a proof of logical incapacity."[111] Whatever the general merits of Russell's claim, as an attempt to deduce Marxian economic determinism from philosophical materialism the *Short Course* statement does in fact contain a fatal logical flaw. For to argue as the statement does that, since "the material world is primary" in ontology, therefore "the material life of society" must be primary in history is to equivocate on the term 'material'. In the premise the term is ontologically universal: it means (setting aside the problems discussed in Chapter 2) whatever is objectively real and empirically discernible. In the conclusion, however, the "material" life intended is *economic* life, and the remainder of the material world is excluded. The argument draws plausibility, no doubt, from the popular conception of economic concerns as "materialistic." But in ontological terms, economic

---

[108]G. S. Aref'eva, "V pomoshch' prepodavateliam marksistsko-leninskoi filosofii. Istoricheskii materializm kak nauka," *Filosofskie nauki*, 1982, no. 4, p. 145.

[109]Lenin, *Soch.*, vol. 18, p. 346.

[110]*History of the Communist Party*, p. 115.

[111]Bertrand Russell, *Freedom versus Organization, 1814–1914* (New York, 1934), p. 196.

factors—including the most material of material productive forces—are no *more* "material" than other objectively real and empirically discernible forces in the natural or social worlds. Economic factors have no greater claim to materiality than do sunspot eruptions, sexual impulses, or political power, and theories of history based on any of these noneconomic forces have as much right to the designation 'materialist' as a theory based on forces and relations of economic production.[112] The latter might be a better theory, but if so, not because it is uniquely materialist but because *its* materialist categories best fit the facts of history. Logically, the same is true of the reverse relation, it might be added: one may be a "materialist" in the sense of accepting the primacy of economic factors in history and nonetheless reject ontological materialism as a universal theory of being— by believing in the supernatural but nonprovidential God of the eighteenth-century Deists, for example.

At best, then, the two theories are logically consistent but independent: neither provides the other with deductive support. In this case consistency is not enough for Soviet philosophers, however, and although they no longer repeat the *Short Course* argument in so many words, neither do they renounce it. They continue to make statements suggesting a close logical relation between the two theories and intimating that no other theory of history is compatible with dialectical materialism. "Historical materialism and dialectical materialism are one," wrote A. D. Kosichev, dean of the philosophy faculty of Moscow State University, in *Kommunist* recently; "the former is suffused with the categories of the latter."[113] As to what more exactly the logical relation is, however, there is no further explanation.

The Dilemma of Historical Materialism

A second and more fundamental problem is not whether historical materialism is the only materialist theory of history but whether it is a materialist theory at all. Many of the innovations in historical theory and practice surveyed in the preceding sections appear to be inconsistent with the economic determinism affirmed in Marx's preface. The impact of sci-

---

[112]For a thorough discussion of the equivocations involved in Marxist uses of the term 'material', see George L. Kline, "The Myth of Marx's Materialism," *Annals of Scholarship* 3, no. 2 (October 1984), pp. 1–38.

[113]A. D. Kosichev, "Aktual'nye voprosy podgotovki filosofskikh kadrov," *Kommunist*, 1982, no. 3, p. 63. For recent Soviet discussions, with bibliographical information, of the relation between dialectical materialism and historical materialism, see Aref'eva, "V pomoshch'," pp. 143–149, and Pletnikov and Shevchenko, pp. 26–27.

ence in production, the "leading role" of the Communist party, the influence of economically neutral factors, the creativity of the conscious human subject—all these phenomena are difficult to reconcile with the thesis that the level of development of a society's "material productive forces" determines its character and its future. When recognition of what are generically called "subjective factors" reaches the point at which a Soviet philosopher can assert, as A. F. Tsyrkun did in 1982, that historical materialism itself (a division of Soviet *philosophy*) is becoming a *productive force*, in that it "participates in the formation of social relations and of the chief productive force—man,"[114] the conflation of being and consciousness in current Soviet philosophy seems complete.

For all the qualifications, however, no Soviet philosopher wishes to reject outright what is still considered the fundamental principle of historical materialism—the Marxian thesis that social being determines social consciousness. The issue is rather one of how and in what form that principle can be maintained. In the summary report of a recent conference on the nature of "material productive forces," it was observed that Soviet investigators are faced with "a highly contradictory task": socialism and the modern day require the inclusion of much new content within the category of 'productive forces', but at the same time investigators must keep in mind "the completely indisputable proposition that the acknowledgment of the determining role of productive forces in the development of society remains the unshakeable principle of materialist monism in the understanding of history, and that however the makeup of the productive forces is expanded, this basic methodological position must be preserved."[115] But is every expansion of the category compatible with "materialist monism?" "If one acknowledges that consciousness takes part in the productive process, and, more than that, that productive activity is directed by consciousness," G. S. Aref'eva and A. I. Verbin wondered in 1978, "then how is one to understand the basic thesis of historical materialism concerning the subordination of consciousness and its dependence on the social being of people?"[116]

It seems clear that Kelle and Koval'zon are right when they insist that if activity and consciousness are to be included in historical materialist theory, it cannot be as the principal categories of that theory; they must be subordinated to the objective elements of the mode of production—material forces and production relations—which are independent of human consciousness and will. For it is precisely in this "natural history"

---

[114]"Materialy soveshchaniia po problemam istoricheskogo materializma," no. 7, p. 113.
[115]"Proizvoditel'nye sily," no. 9, p. 101.
[116]Aref'eva and Verbin, p. 145.

dimension of the historical process, as Kelle pointed out in a discussion of their article, that we see the essence of "the materialist understanding of history and its root opposition to the idealist view."[117] To argue (as Soviet proponents of the activity approach do) that activity, despite its inescapably subjective motives and objectives, is sufficiently "material" to be made the point of departure and the focus of the entire theory, appears to conflict with Marx's basic concern in opposing *being* to *consciousness* in the preface.[118]

At the same time it seems equally clear that supporters of the activity approach are right in affirming that developed productive forces and production relations exist only as what Pletnikov calls "the objectified results of the activity of people,"[119] that in general it is the actions of conscious, creative human beings that make history, and that Marx himself affirmed these propositions in no uncertain terms in other writings. Clearly a dilemma or "contradiction" is at hand, aptly described by Sagatovskii as one that pits attention to the "free choice" of the subject against affirmation of the "material being" of social reality as governed by objective necessities.[120] G. S. Aref'eva expresses the predicament of Soviet philosophers in the language of historical laws when she writes that, "although everyone is of course agreed that the laws of society cannot operate apart from people ... , the question of *whether the element of consciousness is included in the very mechanism of a law* or not remains debatable."[121] Is there a dialectical—and materialist—resolution of this predicament?

If history follows objective laws—laws the "mechanism" of which does *not* include consciousness—it is possible to call the doctrine that discovers those laws "materialist" and to invest it with the authority of science, to which historical materialists have always aspired. It is possible to maintain that the transition from capitalism to communism is objectively necessary, regardless of the attitudes toward this fact of any human beings, and hence that the triumph of the proletariat is inevitable—propositions still dear to the hearts of Soviet philosophers. It is not possible, however, to ascribe a significant role in these events to free human choice. For if the events depended on human choice, the objectivity conditions just stated could obtain only if the choice were in its turn necessitated by factors independent of consciousness—that is, only if the choice were not free. Under such circumstances "freedom" could at best be a kind of subjective awareness

---

[117]Filippov, p. 82.
[118]Pletnikov, "Problemy," pp. 15–20.
[119]Ibid., p. 15.
[120]Sagatovskii, p. 71.
[121]"Materialy soveshchaniia po problemam istoricheskogo materializma," no. 6, p. 30 (italics in original).

of the inevitable—the famous "recognition of necessity" endorsed by Engels, Plekhanov, and Lenin—that permits individuals to dispose themselves in harmony with the inexorable course of events.[122] It is worth noting that the conception of freedom as the recognition of necessity *is* compatible with a certain local and inessential freedom of choice and control over events that can give the illusion of significant historical agency. A pilot running low on fuel and recognizing the necessities of aerodynamics and gravity can choose among a range of actions that will hasten or delay as well as establish other conditions for his landing. An analogous set of choices can be allowed individuals on the threshold of communism. But as to the fact of the inevitable outcome, there is no subjective control in either case. In the "natural history" approach, communism must come as surely as the plane must meet the earth.

If, on the other hand, choice is real and free human agency is historically effective, so that genuine alternative possibilities of historical direction exist, it is not possible to conceive of historical "materialism" as materialistic or as a science of general objective laws of the "natural history" variety. For then consciousness would be part of the "mechanism" of the laws, and there would no longer be any "necessity" to recognize, unless it be one so undemanding as that suggested by G. A. Cohen, who has argued that to the extent that the course of history is inevitable for Marx, it is so "because of what men, being rational, are bound, predictably, to do."[123] If historical necessity amounts to no more, it could be defeated by ignorance, miscalculation, irrationality, or sloth, and such a necessity surely does not qualify for "natural history" status. If choice is real, the only laws that could be found in history are statistical laws, and that is presumably not what Marx had in mind in speaking of the inevitable demise of capitalism. Indeed the consequences of the reality of choice for order and predictability in the historical course of human events are so profound that it is not clear that any Soviet Marxist philosopher has genuinely confronted them in public. Loone, as we saw, inconsistently allows the transition from capitalism to communism to be necessary. Even Gurevich, who affirms that in history the determination of human action can never be complete and who warns against "fatalistic, vulgar" interpretations of the notion that freedom is the recognition of necessity,[124] does not actually disavow that formula. Significantly, one of Gurevich's few concrete examples of an "open" historical situation is the position of the Greek defenders under Leonidas at Thermopylae. Granting Gurevich's point that

[122]Engels advanced this view in his *Anti-Dühring. Herr Eugen Dühring's Revolution in Science* (Moscow, 1947), pp. 136–137.
[123]Cohen, p. 147, no. 1.
[124]Gulyga and Levada, pp. 57, 69.

the Greeks were equally free to run or to fight, it must also be noted that the outcome—the eventual triumph of the Persians' overwhelmingly superior forces—was beyond Leonidas's control. If this example is to serve as a historical paradigm, its lesson can only be that there is room for futile gestures within the fixed framework of historical life.[125]

The Retreat from Materialism to Interactionism

Faced with the dilemma of choice versus necessity, of the power of the superstructure against the "primacy" of the base, of social consciousness vying for precedence with social being, a great many Soviet philosophers and historians now typically adopt a methodological stance that permits them to claim the best of both worlds while avoiding the choice between them. That stance is to stress the *interaction* among the various elements of the historical process rather than the subordination of some of them to others. V. N. Sagatovskii's proposal for the "mutual supplementation" of activity and objective social relations is an example of this approach, and it is far from an isolated one. In the recent literature of historical materialism, no terms for the relation of causal factors to each other are encountered more frequently than 'interaction' (*vzaimodeistvie*), 'interrelation' (*vsaimootnoshenie*), 'interconnection' (*vzaimosviaz'*), and related expressions that acknowledge the mutual impact of causal elements without making any commitment as to their relative weight.

From a dialectical standpoint the notion of interaction has excellent credentials. The idea of viewing a thing in its complex interconnections with other things has long been advanced as one of the defining characteristics of a dialectical as opposed to a "metaphysical" outlook. With specific reference to cause-and-effect relations, no less an authority than Frederick Engels affirmed that "they run into each other, and they become confounded when we contemplate that universal action and reaction in which causes and effects are eternally changing places."[126] There is, furthermore, good Engelsian justification for applying the notion specifically to society and its development. In the letters to Franz Mehring and others over the years 1890 to 1894, in which Engels responded to attacks on historical materialism, he faulted his critics for what he called their "total

---

[125]Ibid., p. 70. For a detailed discussion of the Marxist conception of freedom, see James J. O'Rourke, *The Problem of Freedom in Marxist Thought* (Dordrecht, 1974). Pehaps the closest approach to a rejection of the "recognition of necessity" formula in the Soviet philosophical literature is found in A. G. Myslivchenko's *Chelovek kak predmet filosofskogo poznaniia* (Moscow, 1972), pp. 128, 137.

[126]Marx and Engels, *Selected Works*, p. 412.

disregarding of interaction" in failing to see that historical materialism accepts the mutual operation of economic and noneconomic causes upon each other. "It is not that the economic situation is *cause, solely active,* while everything else is only passive effect," Engels wrote. "There is, rather, interaction on the basis of economic necessity, which *ultimately* always asserts itself."[127]

The "basis of economic necessity," of course, for Engels preserves the materialist character of the position. But because this necessity only asserts itself "ultimately," Engels in effect established an indefinitely long term span in which interaction need *not* show an economic bias and could in fact manifest the greater weight of ideal factors. "Once an historic element has been brought into the world by other, ultimately economic causes," Engels wrote, "it reacts, can react on its environment and even on the causes that have given rise to it."[128] If we go back far enough in the causal chain, we shall encounter initiating economic factors. In the short term, however, economics may not provide the key to the historical situation.

A great many Soviet writers have taken advantage of the short term–long term distinction provided by Engels to argue that "subjective," or at least noneconomic, factors may have equal weight or may even predominate in the short term. Approaching society in the light of what Pletnikov and Shevchenko call "the interconnection and interdetermination of its material and spiritual sides," the investigator need only remember that the material side must predominate "in the last analysis" (*v konechnom schete*)[129]—an expression that has become extremely familiar in recent Soviet historical materialist literature. In sum, Engels's distinction has allowed Soviet investigators to be short-term idealists and to stretch the short term to indefinite lengths.

It will readily be seen that the device can be used to legitimize all of the innovative developments in Soviet historiography described earlier in this chapter. Superstructural causes, factors outside both mode of production and superstructure, the impact of other societies, the conscious choices of individuals—all these influences can be considered not only as interacting significantly with economic factors but as prevailing over indefinite periods of time as long as room is left for "determining" economic causes "in the last analysis." It may be noted, too, that this multifactoral, interactionist approach both gains support from and contributes to the vogue for systems theory in the USSR. For many Soviet philosophers, indeed, viewing society as a system of elements in "intrasystemic interaction" is the key to the

---

[127]Engels to Franz Mehring, July 14, 1893, in ibid., p. 701; Engels to W. Borgius, January 25, 1894, in ibid., p. 704 (italics in original).
[128]Ibid., p. 701.
[129]Pletnikov and Shevchenko, p. 29.

development of Marxist social theory. Thus it is argued, for example, that productive forces should be viewed as a subsystem of the social whole that, although having a definite structure of their own, "cannot be viewed outside that whole, outside the connection with the other components of the social system."[130]

Predictably, the interactionist approach has not escaped criticism by Soviet fundamentalists, who see it (correctly) as a departure from historical materialism. The law of the determination of production relations by "material productive forces" is basic to Marxism, writes V. G. Marakhov, and it cannot be "replaced" by "the formulation of dialectical interaction between productive forces and production relations."[131] To dwell on "the fact of the interaction of equal components of the functioning and development of society" is said by V. V. Dubinin and I. I. Shevchuk to be not Marxism but pluralism, for it denies "the leading role of the mode of production in socio-historical development."[132] Ironically, however, the very writers who voice these criticisms can find no better way to characterize this "leading role" than to speak of the dominance of economic factors "in the last analysis."[133]

We have uncovered the ultimate weakness of the "materialist" position to which so many Soviet philosophers and historians have had recourse. Prevented by ideological needs, by the richness of Marx's various analyses of society, and by sound empirical instincts from accepting the unilinear economic determinism suggested in Marx's preface, they postpone that determinism to a more or less distant "last analysis." But they provide no account of it even at that remove—no explanation of what it means to call economic factors dominant "ultimately," no evidence to support it, and no indication of where to look for such evidence. In short, they do not argue for the theory. In the vast Soviet literature on historical materialism, there is not a single effort comparable to that undertaken recently by G. A. Cohen, who has attempted in *Karl Marx's Theory of History* to show to what claims a historical materialist theory is committed and what arguments could be offered in its support. Among the Soviet writers who adopt the systems approach, for example, there is no effort to show how, in a thoroughly interrelated system, some elements can be given greater weight than others—the crucial step in supporting the "material" character

[130]Ibid., p. 31; "Proizvoditel'nye sily," no. 9, p. 101.
[131]*Philosophy in the USSR. Problems of Historical Materialism*, p. 188.
[132]Dubinin and Shevchuk, pp. 28–29.
[133]Ibid.

of the system.[134] In work after work, we learn only that objective, law-governed economic forces prevail "ultimately" and "in the last analysis."

The result is once again the vacuousness of a major theoretical component of Marxist-Leninist philosophy. The "last analysis" declarations are empty, for they make no specific commitment to which a theorist might eventually be held. As in the case of the indefinitely extended "measures" and series of measures discussed in Chapter 3, no evidence of *lack* of economic determination need ever be accepted by Soviet historical materialists, for they may always argue that the long term has not yet arrived. Given the open-endedness of time, the "short term" within which *non*-economic causes may prevail is infinitely extendable, for there is always a more remote past or future to which the long term may be deferred. In history the truly *last* analysis is never reached, and for that reason the appeals to it in historical materialist theory are no more than hollow declarations of faith.[135]

In practice most Soviet historians and philosophers of history are historical interactionists rather than historical materialists, accepting a wide variety of diverse factors, subjective as well as objective, noneconomic as well as economic, and attending to the complex interplay among them. Soviet historical interactionism is surely a more fruitful approach to history than the historical materialism it pretends to be, and we can only regret that Soviet scholars are not at liberty to develop it systematically and consistently. Instead they find themselves presiding over a tangle of unruly contradictions: there are open possibilities in history, but communism is inevitable; the laws of history are independent of human will and consciousness, but conscious human laborers are the main productive force; the economic base determines the political superstructure, but the Communist party directs the construction of communism. Under these conditions it is not surprising that their efforts to construct a "system" of historical materialist doctrine have so long remained fruitless.

[134]It is not only *Soviet* Marxists who have difficulty with the systems approach to historical materialism. Melvin Rader, whose "organic totality" model is another example of the approach, also argues that a hierarchy of importance can be established among the interrelated elements of a system. But Rader's analogical appeal to the human heart as the "most determinant of all the organs" in the biological system of the body (comparable to productive forces in the socioeconomic formation) is quite unconvincing in the face of the critical importance of lungs, kidneys, brain, and other "determinants" of bodily functioning. See Rader, p. 78.
[135]For a fuller presentation of this argument, see James P. Scanlan, "A Critique of the Engels-Soviet Version of Marxian Economic Determinism," *Studies in Soviet Thought* 13 (1973), pp. 11–19.

[6]

Social and Political Philosophy

SOCIAL and political philosophy, the field closest to ideological concerns, is the one fully monolithic and dogmatic field of Soviet philosophy. Whereas in other areas there are opposing schools of thought or at least probing discussions of basic issues, no such openness can be found in this area. There has been no movement to develop an ideologically neutral, analytical approach to theoretical questions analogous to the study of "historical cognition" (as opposed to the substantive theory of historical materialism) mentioned in the last chapter; social and political philosophy in the Soviet Union is the normative, substantive theory of communism. And special authority is given this theory when it is set off from the rest of philosophy as one of the three basic constituents of Marxism-Leninism and is endowed with the weighty title 'scientific communism'.

We should not conclude, however, that Soviet social and political thought persists unchanged, in dogmatic purity, from decade to decade. There have in fact been very significant changes since Stalin's death, concerning questions as important as the nature of Soviet society, the character and role of the Soviet state, and the timetable for the arrival of communism. We should note rather that when novelty comes it comes from the top and not from public discussions among scholars or ordinary citizens. It may, of course, reflect legitimate theoretical interests as well as ideological needs. But any prior debate takes place in inner councils of the Communist party, and the new doctrines are announced in major addresses by the Party head or by a specialist in ideology such as the late Mikhail Andreevich Suslov (1902–1982). Once promulgated, these officially sponsored innovations constitute instant orthodoxy. They quickly find their way into textbooks and popular tracts, and the voluminous discussion of them that ensues in the scholarly literature takes the form, in the approving words of *Voprosy filosofii*, of "following the basic theoretical elaborations given in Party documents and in the works of the leaders of the CPSU."[1] That is, the discussion is after the fact and is limited to second-order questions of interpretation and implementation.

For these reasons a new procedure must be followed in the present chapter. In other areas of Soviet philosophy it has been useful to distinguish between the orthodox, established views expressed in popular works and the post-Stalin developments that are manifested principally in the professional literature, where they receive fundamental discussion. In social and political philosophy, however, the most revealing distinction is that between the classic Marxist-Leninist dogmatism that sufficed for the Stalin era and the significantly altered set of dogmas that is found in Soviet textbooks today. Hence in this chapter the "orthodox" doctrines of Soviet social and political philosophy will be presented in not one but two sections. The first will sketch the standard position inherited from the 1950s and before. The second section will describe the new orthodoxy, expounding its more important elements, examining the subsidiary issues that do arise among Soviet philosophers in interpreting them, and attempting to provide some of the more searching critical analysis that is lacking in the Soviet literature. An overall evaluation of Soviet social and political philosophy will be reserved for the third and final section.

The Original Orthodoxy

The classic Soviet analysis of contemporary society, like the analysis of history, takes its start from Marx's summary of his outlook in the preface to *A Contribution to a Critique of Political Economy*. It consists essentially in the application of Marx's foundation-superstructure model to the understanding of capitalism, communism, and the transition between them.

Capitalist society, in this analysis, is best understood by focusing on its distinctive economic base, which is marked by the institution of private ownership of the means of production, the existence of a free market in commodities, including human labor, and a mode of production that requires the bourgeoisie, or capitalist minority (who own the premises, tools, and materials required for the production process), to suppress and exploit the proletariat or working-class majority (who have nothing but their own labor power to exchange for their subsistence). To compete successfully in a free market, capitalists must buy labor power as inexpensively as

---

[1]V. S. Semenov, "Uchenie o razvitom sotsializme i ego pererastanii v kommunizm," *Voprosy filosofii*, 1980, no. 7, pp. 6–7.

possible and must extract from it what Marx called a "surplus value," not returned to the workers in payment for their services, which permits the capitalists not only to live well but to expand their productive capacity. The workers seek an adequate wage, but the capitalists, who control the means of production, are in a position to set the terms of the labor contract.

This economic dominance, moreover, translates into social, political, and ideological dominance. The capitalists' power permits them to shape the society's superstructure of institutions and ideas—which cannot survive or flourish without economic support—in such a way as best to promote their own class interests. Capitalists will thus provide support for only those social and political institutions that operate to their advantage; but since it is also to their advantage that the true nature of these institutions be hidden from the classes whose interests are harmed, they will also promote ideologies that misdescribe the institutions. Capitalists will, for example, encourage the fiction that individual rights are widely and equally distributed in capitalist society, whereas for the great majority they are in fact mere forms, consisting either in the absence of legal prohibition of an act (which means nothing to the person who lacks the means to undertake the act in the first place) or in "equality before the law" (which is empty without the legal resources to make the formal equality effective). Thus the capitalists are able to deprive the proletarians of rights while at the same time leading them to believe that they possess such rights.

The capitalists' ability to control both appearance and reality in their own favor is nowhere more evident, in the orthodox Marxist-Leninist view, than in connection with the institution of the state. The fiction conveyed by the bourgeoisie and its ideologists is that the state is a protective institution found in every society; standing above individuals and groups, the state is said to defend the interests of all and to adjudicate among them fairly in the name of the common good. But the facts as displayed by Marx and Engels and elaborated by Lenin are quite different, the Marxist-Leninist believes. The state, Engels argued in his *Origin of the Family, Private Property, and the State*, has not always existed but arose under definite historical circumstances—namely, when there first appeared an exploiting class that had need of organized coercion so as to ensure the orderly perpetuation of the status quo against a class irreconcilably hostile to it.[2] In the Marxian analysis, then, as Lenin emphasized in *State and Revolution*, the state does not serve to reconcile opposing class interests but is a product of their irreconcilability;[3] it functions, rather,

---

[2]Karl Marx and Frederick Engels, *Selected Works in One Volume* (New York, 1968), p. 589.
[3]V. I. Lenin, *Polnoe sobranie sochinenii*, 5th ed., 55 vols. (Moscow, 1958–65), vol. 33, p. 7 (cited hereafter as *Soch.*).

as a class weapon—in Engels's much quoted phrase, a "special repressive force" in the hands of a dominant class.[4] However "democratic" a bourgeois state may appear to be, the reality is otherwise: representative institutions and democratic principles such as "one man, one vote" are shams when votes are bought by the wealthy and when parliamentary elections reduce, as Marx wrote, to "deciding once in three or six years which member of the ruling class was to misrepresent the people."[5] A "bourgeois democracy" is in fact a state ruled by the bourgeois minority in its own interest.

Radical social and political change, in the Marxian view, originates in the economic foundation of society. Marx's *Capital* was devoted to revealing the mechanisms whereby a capitalist economic order inexorably digs its own grave—the processes that eventually cause the duped proletariat to awaken and to destroy the capitalist order through revolution (violent revolution, according to the *Communist Manifesto* and Lenin's *State and Revolution*). A new, nonexploitative base and a new superstructure appropriate to it would then be built. But whereas Marx and his immediate followers were clear enough as to the initial economic requisites for the transformation—elimination of the institution of private ownership of the means of production and centralization of economic planning and control—they were far less definite concerning further requirements and especially concerning the superstructural consequences of this fundamental economic alteration. Lenin made a number of suggestions in *State and Revolution*, however, and Soviet theorists have relied heavily upon them in developing the social and political theory of the postrevolutionary period.

In Lenin's view the key to the understanding of this period, and hence of the entire "communist formation" that succeeds capitalism, is that it proceeds through two successive phases or stages. Marx had suggested such a distinction in passing in his *Critique of the Gotha Program*, and Lenin fastened upon it with great emphasis, labeling the earlier phase "socialism" and the later "communism" or "full communism."[6] The rationale for the distinction lies in the need for a period of transition and building between the destruction of the old order and the full establishment of the new. A radically different economic system is required, and constructing it takes time and organization. The material abundance needed for the successful functioning of communism cannot be provided until the new system has been built. And equally important is the character of the citizenry immediately after the revolution: the people, born and bred in a

[4]Marx and Engels, *Selected Works*, p. 430.
[5]Ibid., p. 292.
[6]Ibid., pp. 323–325; Lenin, *Soch.*, vol. 33, pp. 91–102.

grasping, competitive capitalist environment, will not at once be capable of acting as perfect communists. A significant number of them, indeed, will be the dispossessed bourgeoisie, who can be expected to oppose the new order actively, to the point of attempting counterrevolution.

Accordingly the first or socialist phase of the new communist socioeconomic formation must be marked by what Lenin, borrowing a phrase from Marx, called "the dictatorship of the proletariat."[7] The old power relationship will simply be reversed: the proletariat will control the apparatus of coercion, and will use it to suppress the bourgeoisie and build the new society against the determined opposition of its former masters. Politically, then, socialism requires the continued existence of the state and hence of class rule. But Lenin and his followers were quick to note that the proletarian state is qualitatively different from any other, since in it for the first time power is wielded by the majority of people in their own interest, against those who would exploit them. It is, in other words, a *democratic* dictatorship—the first genuinely democratic state in history. Rights and freedoms are provided equally for all working people, and the government is organized on the principle of what Lenin called "democratic centralism": the people elect representatives to the various levels of a pyramid of "Soviets" (councils), and the decisions made by higher Soviets are binding on those below. Of course in Lenin's understanding the workings of the government are firmly guided at every step by the Communist party, but this feature of the political system, too, is viewed as "democratic" by Soviet theorists, since the Party—the "vanguard" of the working class—is held to be broadly based and to represent the true will of the people. "In socialist society the Party and the people are one," we read in a recent work; "the Party does not and cannot have its own special interests apart from the interests of the people."[8]

Economically, the socialist state presides over the nationalization of industry, the collectivization of agriculture, and the establishment of central economic planning. Through these means, and through requiring labor of every able-bodied citizen ("he who does not work, neither shall he eat"), unemployment and the other wastes of capitalism will be eliminated; rational allocation of resources and greater productivity will allow the economy to meet the needs of the people more adequately. But in this earlier

---

[7] The expression was used by Marx both in a letter of 1852 to J. Weydemeyer and in the *Critique of the Gotha Program* (1875); see Marx and Engels, *Selected Works*, pp. 331, 679. In using the term 'dictatorship', Marx was no doubt harking back to the Roman institution of the *dictatura*, under which a leader was temporarily invested with absolute power in a time of crisis.

[8] G. E. Glezerman, M. N. Rutkevich, and S. S. Vishnevskii, eds., *Sotsialisticheskii obraz zhizni* (Moscow, 1980), p. 100.

phase even the inherent economic superiorities of socialism will not suffice to satisfy needs fully, and in fact the new system is not designed to do so. Rather its fruits, according to Lenin, should be distributed in such a way as, while meeting the elementary demands of all, to encourage the greatest productive effort from workers whose mentality is a product of an earlier day. Hence Lenin, echoing Marx, held that in this first phase rewards should be proportional to work performed.[9] Following this lead Soviet policy has consistently regarded both the quality and the quantity of labor as grounds for differential rewards, and Soviet writers continue to argue, against Maoists and other critics, that this appeal to the workers' self-interest is not an obstacle to the development of truly communist attitudes. "Material stimuli," one Soviet economist wrote recently, "have a salutary effect on strengthening the socialist discipline of labor; they promote the development among the workers of love of labor, responsibility for fulfilling the assigned task, thriftiness, economy, etc."[10]

Socially, the early phase of the communist formation is marked by the persistence of group differences that in full communism will be overcome. Lenin foresaw the initial survival of a hostile bourgeoisie, but even after the integration of that minority into the ranks of the toilers other differences may remain. Because collective farms in the USSR are organized as cooperatives that own their instruments of labor and divide their incomes among their members, the collective farm workers (kolkhozniki) are, in the eyes of Soviet theorists, a separate class, distinguishable from ordinary workers (rabochie), who are employed and paid directly by the state. Associated with this distinction is the persistence under socialism of the broad rift, much decried by Marx, between rural and urban life. Still another continuing division is that between mental and physical labor; the intelligentsia, though not economically a distinguishable class, is viewed by Soviet theorists as a third principal component of socialist society, comprising a wide range of intellectuals, party functionaries, and professional people—all, of course, employed by the state but not engaged in economic production. Even the class difference between collective farmers and workers, however, is not seen as an antagonistic one, and all three groups are said to be joined by compelling common interests that override any possible friction among them. "The activities of all the non-proletarian sections of the working people are based on socialist property"—that is, on jointly owned property—write the authors of a recent textbook; "the

[9]Lenin, Soch., vol. 33, pp. 91–95.
[10]M. N. Rutkevich et al., eds., Problemy sotsialisticheskogo obraza zhizni (Moscow, 1977), pp. 64–65.

people rally around the working class, forming a single monolithic force."[11] And through the workings of socialism the surviving differences among them will be diminished, as will acquisitiveness, the influence of religion, and other vestiges of antagonistic class society.

Marx offered no timetable for the advance from the "first" to the "higher" phase of communist society, though given his expectation of a worldwide revolt of the proletariat there is no reason to think that he foresaw any special obstacle to the rapid progress of human history thereafter. Lenin, too, in his prerevolutionary writings such as *State and Revolution* suggested a prompt advance to communism. But when the Bolshevik revolution failed to spark proletarian uprisings in other countries and Lenin was faced with the practical problems not only of transforming Russian society but of doing so in a largely hostile international environment, he began to temporize. In mid-1919 he spoke of Russian society as not yet actually embarked on the *first* phase but rather as struggling to reach it—as, in his words, seeking "to solve the problems of the transition from capitalism to socialism."[12] And none of Lenin's successors has argued that the USSR has yet completed the transition from socialism to communism—though Khrushchev thought that the breakthrough to the higher phase was near. Hence the Marxist doctrine of classless, stateless communism, which originated as a vision of the future, remains a vision of the future for Soviet theorists today; but it continues to be advanced as the "scientific" description of the goal toward which socialist society is inexorably advancing.

The classlessness of communist society will make possible its statelessness, according to Marx, Engels, and Lenin. In the absence of class oppositions the state will have no function, and consequently it is expected to "wither away" or atrophy from disuse. Engels provided the classic formulation in *Anti-Dühring*:

> As soon as there is no longer any social class to be held in subjection; as soon as class rule, and the individual struggle for existence based upon our present anarchy in production, with the collisions and excesses arising from these, are removed, nothing more remains to be repressed, and a special repressive force, a state, is no longer necessary....State interference in social relations becomes, in one domain after another, superfluous, and then withers away of itself....The state is not "abolished." *It withers away.*[13]

[11][F. V. Konstantinov, ed.], *The Fundamentals of Marxist-Leninist Philosophy*, trans. R. Daglish (Moscow, 1974), p. 427.
[12]Lenin, *Soch.*, vol. 39, p. 16.
[13]Frederick Engels, *Anti-Dühring. Herr Eugen Dühring's Revolution in Science* (Moscow, 1947), p. 333 (italics in original).

The Marxist view of statelessness is not an anarchistic one, however. Given that the state is a *repressive* mechanism, its absence need not mean the absence of centralized organization altogether. Significantly, in *Anti-Dühring* Engels also described the withering process as one in which "the government of persons is replaced by the administration of things and by the conduct of processes of production."[14] Engels surely recognized that to administer "things" and guide production one must direct persons as well, but he apparently believed that in the absence of class antagonisms such direction could be carried out without the repression implied by "government." In any event, neither he nor Marx denied that even in communism group life will require management. "An individual violinist directs himself," Marx wrote in *Capital*; "an orchestra needs a conductor."[15]

Also gone in the higher phase are the antisocial attitudes and traits that made it impossible for people to move directly from capitalism to communism. Through the intermediary tutelage of socialism, individuals will have become "new men," free of the selfish and defensive habits of class society. They will have come to regard socially useful labor not as an onerous and disagreeable necessity but as, in Marx's expression, "a primary vital need," and they will eagerly undertake such labor for the good of society no less than for their own fulfillment.[16] As a result it will be possible to adopt for communist society a radically different, more humane principle of distribution, which Lenin, echoing Marx and earlier socialists, proclaimed in *State and Revolution*: "From each according to his ability, to each according to his needs."[17] Reward is thereby disengaged from contribution and is tied instead to personal requirements, the full satisfaction of which, it is assumed, can now be provided by a perfected communist economy.

The early writings in which Marx constructed his now famous image of communist man as the dealienated, rehumanized master of nature had little impact on the orthodox Marxist-Leninist doctrine of communism, which was formulated well before those writings were widely known. Consequently the Soviet account of communist life has traditionally stressed the themes sounded in classic nineteenth-century Marxism: freedom of the individual from exploitation and all forms of tyranny; the equation of personal with social interests, and the elimination from society of all the

---

[14]Ibid.

[15]Karl Marx and Friedrich Engels, *Werke* (Berlin, 1960–1968), vol. 23, p. 350. For a Soviet use of this passage, see E. A. Anufriev, E. V. Tadevosian, and M. V. Vetrov, *Nauchnyi kommunizm. Opyt razrabotki i chteniia lektsii* (Moscow, 1982), p. 225.

[16]Marx and Engels, *Werke*, vol. 19, p. 21.

[17]Ibid.; Lenin, *Soch.*, vol. 33, p. 96.

conflicts historically created by class differences and by the division of labor, and above all by the fundamental disparities between urban and rural labor and mental and physical labor; the elimination of illusion and superstition, including of course religious superstition, and universal provision of the knowledge that allows people to control their destiny; and finally the development of economic productivity to the point where the human needs of everyone can be met. Freedom, harmony, enlightenment, and abundance thus make up the "bright future" that Marxist-Leninist orthodoxy has promised mankind.

The New Orthodoxy

Although many of the foregoing theses are as acceptable to Soviet theorists today as they were in Stalin's time, a number of major changes both in emphasis and in substance have taken place in Marxist-Leninist theory in recent years.

Some of these changes, however interesting they may be as signs of shifts in Soviet policies or attitudes, have little significance theoretically because they are isolated modifications that require a minimum of conceptual adjustment. An example is the thesis, now regularly asserted by Soviet writers in contradiction to both *The Communist Manifesto* and *State and Revolution*, that a proletarian revolution may be nonviolent. In this case Soviet theorists are in fact returning to a view once advanced by Marx himself—that in some developed capitalist countries the proletariat could come to power through peaceful means.[18] A related change in the Soviet view of the modern world is found in the current doctrine that future world wars are not inevitable; contrary to the analysis presented in Lenin's *Imperialism as the Highest Stage of Capitalism*, it is now held that global, "imperialist" wars can be avoided, since the armed might of the socialist bloc can dissuade bourgeois governments from starting them.[19] Dogmatic innovations of this sort may be of the first importance ideologically, but they can be accommodated in Marxist-Leninist philosophy without major dislocation of the elements of "scientific communism."

Other changes, however, are more radical and require the revision of fundamental concepts. Not surprisingly most of these have had to do with the identity and the timing of the progressive social stages from capitalism to communism. Soviet leaders have understandably sought to orient them-

[18]See Marx's Amsterdam speech of September 8, 1872 (Robert C. Tucker, ed., *The Marx-Engels Reader*, 2d ed. [New York, 1978], pp. 522–524).
[19]See, for example, Anufriev, Tadevosian, and Vetrov, p. 39.

selves—or to justify the actual course their society has taken—by reference to the progression called for by the theory. But often they have found themselves in situations not authorized or correctly described by the theory in its original form, and consequently they have been obliged to supplement or alter the projected progression to make it applicable to the actual course of events. Lenin did this in 1919 when he introduced a transitional period between the revolution and the "first phase" of communist society, and every subsequent regime has had to make additional modifications.

Although many of these modifications have been substantial, it was left to the Brezhnev regime to introduce the most far-reaching changes in Soviet social and political theory since Lenin. For under Brezhnev a new conceptual apparatus was devised, and it was used to provide a characterization of present-day Soviet society that differs from earlier accounts at three major points. First, a new and lengthy historical period, called "developed socialism," was interposed between the original first phase and the eventual higher phase of communist society. Second, a new political doctrine, based on the concept of the "all-people's state," was elaborated for this new stage of socialist evolution. Third, the idea was advanced that there is a special "socialist mode of life" appropriate to developed socialism. These innovations, all three of which also received the blessing of Iurii Andropov in his theoretical pronouncements as Brezhnev's successor, will be examined in turn in the sections that follow.

Developed Socialism

The heart of the current Soviet sociopolitical orthodoxy is the thesis that the USSR has reached a milestone in the evolution of the communist socioeconomic formation—the stage of "developed socialism" (*razvitoi sotsializm*). Also called "mature socialism" (*zrelyi sotsializm*), this stage is presented as one that every socialist society must go through on the road to communism, and it is generally held to be both the culminating period of the first or socialist phase of the formation and at the same time the period within which the transition to communism is effected.

Lenin is said to have anticipated this stage when he spoke on a number of occasions of the eventual construction in Russia of a "developed socialist society."[20] No special notice was taken of that expression, however, until the late 1960s, when it began to appear, without elaboration, in Communist party literature, including a 1967 speech by Brezhnev.[21] At the

[20]Lenin, *Soch.*, vol. 36, p. 139; vol. 40, pp. 104, 260.
[21]Leonid I. Brezhnev, *Leninskim kursom. Rechi i stat'i*, 4 vols. (Moscow, 1975), vol. 2, p. 153.

twenty-fourth congress of the Party in 1971, Brezhnev used the term more pointedly in his keynote address: "The selfless labor of the Soviet people," he stated, "has built the developed socialist society"; from that point on, the concept of developed socialism became the subject of intensive elaboration in the theoretical journal *Kommunist* and other Soviet publications.[22] The final step in establishing the concept came in 1977 with the ratification of a new Soviet Constitution designed for the perfected socialist order: "A developed socialist society has been built in the USSR," the Constitution's preamble proclaims.[23] In subsequent Soviet literature, the concept is presented as the centerpiece of a great theoretical advance—"a new chapter in the theory of scientific communism"[24]—and as the key to understanding Soviet socialist reality in the present day. "The most important features of contemporary Soviet society," Iurii Andropov wrote in 1983, "have found reflection in the conception of developed socialism."[25]

The nature of developed socialist society as it is understood in current Soviet theory is best approached by viewing that society in its supposed relation to earlier stages of postrevolutionary history. Marx saw only a single period—his "first phase"—separating the revolution from communism. Lenin added another period—a time of transition before the "first phase" began. The present Soviet theory goes one step further by postulating three separate, qualitatively distinct periods between the revolution and the "higher phase" of communism.

The first of these three periods is identical with Lenin's "transition from capitalism to socialism," and in current Soviet thinking it extended until about 1936. The Constitution of that year is held, as it was by Stalin, to mark a turning point in Soviet development, identified now as then by the expression "the construction of socialism in the main [*v osnovnom*]." Before that time, it is argued, socialism was being built on an alien foundation—that is, on the economic base inherited from the presocialist past. Socialist production relations were developing ab ovo, against hostile in-

---

[22]Ibid., vol. 3, p. 390. For an excellent account of the history and significance of the concept in Soviet ideology, see Alfred B. Evans, Jr., "Developed Socialism in Soviet Ideology," *Soviet Studies* 29 (1977), pp. 409–428.

[23]*Konstitutsiia (osnovnoi zakon) Soiuza Sovetskikh Sotsialisticheskikh Respublik* (Moscow, 1977), p. 4; see also G. L. Furmanov, A. P. Sertsova, and S. S. Il'in, eds., *Dialektika pererastaniia razvitogo sotsialisticheskogo obshchestva v kommunisticheskoe* (Moscow, 1980), p. 34.

[24]V. Medvedev, "Marksistsko-leninskaia kontseptsiia razvitogo sotsializma," *Kommunist*, 1978, no. 17, p. 20. Different stages in the development of the concept are identified in Semenov, "Uchenie," pp. 5–9.

[25]Iu. V. Andropov, *Uchenie Karla Marksa i nekotorye voprosy sotsialisticheskogo stroitel'stva v SSSR* (Moscow, 1983), p. 24. This work by Andropov was published simultaneously as the lead article in both *Voprosy filosofii* (1983, no. 4, pp. 3–16) and *Kommunist* (1983, no. 3, pp. 9–23).

ternal and external opposition; there was, under the circumstances, constant danger of losing the forward thrust of the revolution. Soviet writers are unanimously agreed that roughly two decades were required to assure the victory of socialism within the USSR, by establishing an economy that was fundamentally socialist, in agriculture as well as industry.[26] The only active dispute concerning this period in the current Soviet literature is the academic one of how to label it historically: is it a transitional stage antedating the entire communist socioeconomic formation, is it within that formation but before its "first phase" (socialism), or is it the first stage of socialism?[27]

The second period, which everyone agrees is part of the socialist phase of the communist socioeconomic formation, is said to be the period of the *building* of developed socialist society; it is now dated from about 1936 to the late 1960s. According to the Soviet analysis of this period, the need for additional "building" after 1936 was created by the weak and immature condition of the newly established socialist economy and of its attendant superstructure. Although the exploiting classes had by that time been thoroughly dispossessed and the socialist economy was functioning on its own distinctive basis, productivity was not yet high. There were still pockets of nonsocialist production. The peasantry, though collectivized for the most part, was not yet freed from the grip of a "private-ownership psychology."[28] And political institutions appropriate to socialist society were still in their infancy. 'Strengthening' (*ukreplenie*) is the word regularly used for what socialism needed in that period—strengthening in economic, social, and political respects. Consolidation of the international position of socialism is also said to have been necessary; not until the twenty-first Communist party congress in 1959, Soviet writers point out, was socialism proclaimed to have won "not only a complete, but a final victory," ending all danger of the restoration of capitalism from without by "the forces of international imperialism."[29] Until the mid-1970s, that 1959 declaration was frequently used as a sign that the building of developed socialism had been completed by the late 1950s or early 1960s. More recently, however, it is usually suggested that the period of building lasted into the latter half

[26] Anufriev, Tadevosian, and Vetrov, p. 180; Semenov, "Uchenie," p. 10.

[27] For statements of the opposing positions, see R. I. Kosolapov, *Sotsializm. K voprosam teorii*, 2d ed. (Moscow, 1979), p. 522; Furmanov, Sertsova, and Il'in, p. 193; and V. I. Verezgov, "Znachenie teorii obshchestvenno-ekonomicheskoi formatsii v issledovanii sotsializma," *Vestnik Moskovskogo universiteta. Seriia 7. Filosofiia*, 1981, no. 3, pp. 24–26.

[28] Anufriev, Tadevosian, and Vetrov, p. 180.

[29] G. E. Glezerman et al., eds., *Razvitoe sotsialisticheskoe obshchestvo. Sushchnost', kriterii zrelosti, kritika revizionistskikh kontseptsii*, 2d ed. (Moscow, 1975), p. 16.

of the 1960s, thus bringing the onset of developed socialism closer to Brezhnev's announcements of it.[30]

The third and current period, then, is the stage of developed or mature socialism. In the broad terms in which it is often described in formal documents such as the Constitution of 1977, developed socialism would seem to differ only in degree from the period of building that preceded it. It is called a society with a stronger economy, one the base of which is now strictly socialist and which is far more productive than the fledgling socialist economy of 1936. It is a society of "mature socialist social relations," meaning that with the complete elimination of private ownership of the means of production all citizens are now more firmly bound together by ties of cooperation and mutual benefit.[31] To account for the enormous significance attributed to the new stage in the Soviet literature, however, it is necessary to go beyond these generalities to a few special functions that the concept may be seen to perform in current Soviet ideology.

A point always stressed in the Soviet literature on developed socialism is the intimate connection between the new historical stage and what is called the "scientific-technological revolution"—the rapid modern growth of scientific knowledge and its application to industry. The affinity between developed socialism and the scientific-technological revolution is said to consist in the facts, first, that only at advanced levels of the development of productive forces, such as are found in developed socialism, does it become possible to utilize the results of the revolution effectively; second, that at such levels, exploiting the scientific-technological revolution is necessary for significant further advance; and third, that a developed *socialist* economy can most fully exploit the advances in science and technology for the benefit of all mankind. The last point is heavily emphasized, with a multitude of references to the blessings of centralized planning and the rational satisfaction of needs.[32] Thus the theory of developed socialism provides a conceptual showcase for what is termed the "special role" of the scientific-technological revolution in the Soviet Union, and in this light the theory serves as one more indication of the Brezhnev regime's determination to advance the Soviet economy through massive injections of high technology and thereby "defeat in economic competition the most developed countries of capitalism."[33]

A second aspect of the doctrine of developed socialism that meshes neatly

---

[30]See, for example, A. P. Kazakov et al., eds., *Razvitoe sotsialisticheskoe obshchestvo i obshchestvennyi progress* (Leningrad, 1976). pp. 6–7; Anufriev, Tadevosian, and Vetrov, pp. 180–181; Furmanov, Sertsova, and Il'in, p. 196.

[31]*Konstitutsiia*, p. 4.

[32]See, for example, Anufriev, Tadevosian, and Vetrov, pp. 194–199.

[33]Ibid., p. 194; Glezerman et al., *Razvitoe sotsialisticheskoe obshchestvo*, p. 25.

with Soviet policy interests is the contention that the new level of progress has been reached only in the USSR. On this ground the doctrine provides additional support for the old Soviet claim that the pioneering experience of the USSR entitles it to leadership of the world socialist movement. In the Soviet literature even the more advanced of the other socialist countries are portrayed as still at the level of *constructing* developed socialism. Not until the late 1950s or early 1960s, it is argued, did Bulgaria, Czechoslovakia, East Germany, Hungary, Poland, and Rumania complete the stage passed by the USSR in the mid-1930s—the establishment of socialism "in the main."[34] Thus in relation to those countries the USSR can represent itself as not simply further along on the common path, but as having reached a major plateau from which it can survey the whole long course they have yet to traverse. As for still other socialist countries—China prominently included—the Soviet Union views them as not yet having established socialism "in the main" and thus as lagging two full stages behind.[35]

A third way in which the doctrine of developed socialism performs a valuable service for the Soviet leadership is by allotting the new stage a long historical life. This may be the aspect of the doctrine that is most important for the future of Marxist-Leninist social theory, for it frees that theory from a complication created by Khrushchev and makes possible an era of ideological stability lasting for decades to come. At its twenty-second congress in 1961, the Communist party under Khrushchev for the first time made a definite temporal commitment to the coming of communism: "The present generation of Soviet people," the Party's new program solemnly proclaimed, "shall live under communism!"[36] By interposing developed socialism between Khrushchev's generation and communism, on the other hand, the Brezhnev party removed the pressure of that earlier promise. And it did so, moreover, without substituting any other promise for it. Developed socialism is conceived as no transitory phenomenon but "an independent historical stage" that will endure for half a century or more.[37]

It might be thought that once socialism has developed, communism cannot be far off. But Soviet writers use the terms 'developed' and 'mature' to refer in this case not to the end of a process but rather to the completion

---

[34]Glezerman et al., *Razvitoe sotsialisticheskoe obshchestvo*, p. 14n; Semenov, "Uchenie," p. 4. For good discussions of the doctrine of developed socialism as it applies to other Eastern European countries as well as to the USSR, see Jim Seroka and Maurice D. Simon, eds., *Developed Socialism in the Soviet Bloc. Political Theory and Political Reality* (Boulder, 1982).

[35]Anufriev, Tadevosian, and Vetrov, pp. 168–169.

[36]*The Road to Communism. Documents of the Twenty-second Congress of the Communist Party of the Soviet Union, October 17–31, 1961* (Moscow, n.d.), p. 589.

[37]Semenov, "Uchenie," p. 10.

of its formative stages. V. S. Semenov offers an analogy: the period of building that preceded developed socialism, he states, is like the birth of an organism, whereas developed socialism itself is like the organism's life, in which there must be further development, rising to "ever newer levels of maturity." On this ground Semenov concludes that developed socialism must last longer than the formative period that preceded it—thus longer, presumably, than the half century from 1917 to the late 1960s.[38] Many writers speak of different qualitative levels or substages within developed socialism, though there is yet no settled description of them. R. I. Koso-lapov proposes two principal substages, the first an essentially legalistic one in which, under the influence of the growing "material-technical base" of communism, the distinction between the two existing forms of socialist property—state and cooperative—is gradually eliminated; and the second a longer period in which the broad social consequences of this property change are manifested, including the elimination of all vestiges of the division of labor so that "full social homogeneity" is attained.[39] No Soviet authority now suggests less than an indefinite span of "decades" for this development; the report of the latest, twenty-sixth congress of the Communist Party of the Soviet Union (CPSU) in 1981 speaks simply of "a historically protracted period."[40] Andropov, writing in 1983—some fifteen years after the supposed attainment of developed socialism—identifies the USSR as being "at the beginning of this lengthy historical stage."[41] Of course if we accept Semenov's biological analogy, a life of centuries could be expected for an offspring that was fifty years in the womb.

If it is objected that communism appears forgotten in the preoccupation with the durability of socialism, the Soviet writer has a ready answer: the further maturation of developed socialist society is *at the same time* the construction of communism. There is no difference between the two proc-esses, it is argued.[42] Unlike the building of socialism, which required the elimination of an old, exhausted mode of production and the forging of a new one, the building of communism takes place on a continuing eco-nomic foundation—the single foundation common to the whole com-munist socioeconomic formation. Hence the maturing of society on that foundation at one stage is simultaneously the building of the next, and

[38]Ibid., pp. 13–14.
[39]Kosolapov, pp. 523–524. One maverick Soviet writer publishing in Armenia argues that developed socialism is not the culminating stage of the socialist phase but will be followed by still another stage that he calls "highly developed" or "comprehensively developed" socialism, leading to what Lenin once termed "the middle phase of communism"; see R. G. Vartanov, *Sotsializm. Stupeni razvitiia* (Erevan, 1982), p. 193.
[40]Anufriev, Tadevosian, and Vetrov, pp. 181, 184.
[41]Andropov, *Uchenie Karla Marksa*, p. 25.
[42]Semenov, "Uchenie," p. 8.

progress continues without any strict division between socialism and communism.

Still, there is no question but that the emphasis on—indeed the celebration of—developed socialism in the current Soviet sociopolitical orthodoxy has served to push communism itself ever further from the center of Marxist-Leninist ideological attention. "Our time is the time of mature socialism," one recent work intones, and Soviet writers leave no doubt that they consider it not only an enduring era but a glorious one.[43] The rhetoric once reserved for communism is now lavished on developed socialism. The new stage is described as "the supreme achievement of the social progress of mankind," "the highest attainment of world civilization, a society of full freedom and real democracy," a society "the like of which the peoples of the world have never known," one that evolves continuously and harmoniously, without crises.[44] Developed socialism has become a communism surrogate in current Soviet ideology, and the parallel extends even to the indefinite but ever more blissful future attributed to it.

Khrushchev saw the Soviet Union on the verge of the great historical breakthrough to communism predicted by classic Marxist-Leninist theory. The ideological legacy of the Brezhnev regime is at once more inventive and more cautious: Brezhnev lent his name to a major conceptual innovation, but it is one designed to encourage settling in for a long evolution on the present historical plane. Alluding to the 1961 Party program, which contained Khrushchev's pledge of communism within the generation, *Voprosy filosofii* in a diamond jubilee tribute to Brezhnev in 1981 described the latter's contribution with revealing restraint: in Brezhnev's speeches and reports, the journal stated, "the paths and the timing of the realization of the program goals of the CPSU have been corrected [*utochneny*] and concretized, and strategy and tactics for a prolonged historical period have been defined."[45] These very words were used by Andropov in his first major statement of theory in 1983, though he attributed the contribution not to Brezhnev personally but to "the Party"; the Party, he went on, "has warned against possible exaggerations in understanding the country's proximity to the higher phase of communism."[46] By introducing the concept of developed socialism, Brezhnev and his ideologists created a new theoretical situation that could endure for years to come. The change has been endorsed by his successors, and it now remains only for the Com-

[43]Glezerman et al., *Razvitoe sotsialisticheskoe obshchestvo*, p. 221.
[44]Semenov, "Uchenie," pp. 8, 18; Kosolapov, p. 51.
[45]"Tvorcheskoe razvitie marksistsko-leninskogo ucheniia," *Voprosy filosofii*, 1981, no. 12, p. 5.
[46]Andropov, *Uchenie Karla Marksa*, p. 25.

munist party at its next congress in 1986 to adopt a revised program that formally proclaims this latest and longest deferral of communism.

The All-People's State

Although the concept of developed socialism is the centerpiece of the Brezhnev sociopolitical orthodoxy, this concept is accompanied in the Soviet literature by others that also represent striking departures from classical Marxist ideas. Chief among them is the notion of the *all-people's state* as a new political institution that has arisen in the USSR under conditions of developed socialism.

The idea of an "all-people's state" (the Russian term, *obshchenarodnoe gosudarstvo*, is also sometimes translated "state of the whole people") was first introduced under Khrushchev—a fact that has not been mentioned in the Soviet literature for some twenty years—and thus it actually antedates the identification of developed socialism. The original characterization of the Soviet socialist state as a dictatorship of the proletariat had long seemed unnecessarily harsh to many Soviet ideologists. Even Stalin was moved to exclude the term from the 1936 Constitution, calling the Soviet state instead a "socialist state of workers and peasants." With the end of Stalin's rule Khrushchev saw the opportunity to have done not only with the term but also with the very idea that the Soviet state continues to function as an instrument of class domination. Accordingly, in the Communist party program of 1961 it was announced that "the dictatorship of the proletariat has fulfilled its historic mission" and hence is no longer needed in the USSR and that the Soviet state has become "a state of the entire people, an organ expressing the interests and will of the people as a whole."[47] The new development was immediately taken up in the theoretical literature, where the all-people's state was trumpeted as the first state in history that is not an instrument of coercion used by one class to oppress others but instead represents the entire population.[48]

Following the ouster of Khrushchev in 1964, less attention was paid to the concept of the all-people's state. But the utility of the notion was too great to ignore, and in the 1970s it once again came into the foreground in discussions of political theory, now identified with the Brezhnev leadership. The ultimate authoritative recognition of the concept came with its enshrinement in 1977 in the new Brezhnev Constitution. "Having ful-

---

[47]*Road to Communism*, p. 547.

[48]The introduction of the concept and its uneven career in Soviet ideology are discussed in Roger E. Kanet, "The Rise and Fall of the 'All-People's State': Recent Changes in the Soviet Theory of the State," *Soviet Studies* 20 (1968), pp. 81–93.

filled the tasks of the dictatorship of the proletariat," that document reads, echoing the words of the 1961 Party program, "the Soviet state has become an all-people's state," "a socialist all-people's state which expresses the will and interests of the workers, peasants, and intelligentsia, the working people of all the nations and nationalities of the country."[49] This represents "a development of enormous significance for the political system of socialism," Iurii Andropov wrote in 1983.[50] The new state is now invariably associated with the historical stage of developed socialism marked by the 1977 Constitution and is held to be what distinguishes this stage politically from others.[51]

Although regarded as an unprecedented political system, in which coercion is not employed systematically against any class, the all-people's state is not identified with the "communist public self-administration" expected in postsocialist society. Rather it is viewed as something between statelessness and the dictatorship of the proletariat, neither the one nor the other. To the extent that it has lost its class-coercive features, the socialist state in the USSR is regarded as having already partly "withered away." But Soviet theorists are quick to note that it is still a professionally administered institution that marshals represssive force against both external threats and internal deviants and that in fact has still greater powers of organization, education, and control in the period of developed socialism than it had before.[52] The socialist state is expected to endure throughout the period of developed socialism, or in other words for an indefinitely long time to come. Soviet accounts of all the conditions that must be met for the full withering of the state often seem calculated to remove any expectation of achieving statelessness in anything short of a geological age, as in the following pronouncement by M. N. Perfilyev:

> With respect to internal conditions, the state can wither away only *after* communism *has essentially been built*, i.e., when the following problems are solved: creating the material and technical basis of communism; eliminating the essential differences between town and country and between physical and mental labor; attaining complete unity among the nations [of the USSR]; developing [the] traits characteristic of man in a communist society; developing democracy to the fullest possible extent; increasing the role of mass organizations in the administration of the country; involving all citizens in the job of administering public affairs. As for the external conditions, the Soviet state

---

[49] *Konstitutsiia*, pp. 4, 6.
[50] Andropov, *Uchenie Karla Marksa*, p. 20.
[51] See, for example, Glezerman, Rutkevich, and Vishnevskii, p. 96; Verezgov, p. 22.
[52] M. Perfilyev, *Soviet Democracy and Bourgeois Sovietology*, trans. A. Bratov (Moscow, n.d.), p. 88; V. G. Afanasyev, *Marxist Philosophy*, trans. D. Fidlon, 4th ed. (Moscow, 1980), pp. 299–300.

can wither away fully *only* upon the *disappearance of the imperialist camp* and the consequent *elimination of the danger of aggression* on the part of the imperialist states.[53]

Although no Soviet writer has questioned the theoretical merits of the new political conception, outside the Soviet bloc it has been roundly criticized by Marxists and non-Marxists alike for its manifest deviation from classical Marxist theory. Soviet writers contend that the appearance of an "all-people's state," though a development that may not have been foreseen by Marx, Engels, or Lenin, is nonetheless perfectly consistent with their view of the state in general and of the socialist state in particular.[54] Perhaps in no other instance, however, is a Soviet claim concerning Marxist theory so demonstrably untenable by reference to readily available evidence.

Both Marx and Lenin are on record as holding that the dictatorship of the proletariat is the last historical form of the state—that is, the last state before the advent of classless, stateless communism. "Between capitalist and communist society," Marx wrote in his *Critique of the Gotha Program*, "lies the period of the revolutionary transformation of the one into the other. Corresponding to this is also a political transition period in which the state can be nothing but *the revolutionary dictatorship of the proletariat*."[55] The parallel point in Lenin's *State and Revolution* reads as follows: "The transition from capitalism to communism, of course, cannot but yield a great abundance and diversity of political forms, but their essence will inevitably be the same: the *dictatorship of the proletariat*."[56]

Confronted with these passages, Soviet scholars have adopted the heroic course of arguing that by 'communist society' and 'communism' Marx and Lenin meant not the final, classless society but rather the "communist socioeconomic formation" as it is described in Soviet theory—that is, the entire socialism-cum-communism epoch that the Soviet Union did not reach until the mid-1930s.[57] According to that interpretation, the dictatorship of the proletariat was needed in the true "transition" (that is, pre*socialist*) period in which the remnants of an opposing class still required suppression by the victorious proletariat, but some *other* form of state may still be needed in the first or socialist phase of the communist socioeconomic formation. This argument has proved unconvincing to many

[53]Perfilyev, p. 113 (italics in original).
[54]This argument is forcefully presented in ibid., pp. 80–92. Many Western critics have demonstrated the unsoundness of the position; see (in addition to the sources mentioned by Perfilyev) Kanet, pp. 85–87, and Tamurbek Davletshin, "The Concept of a 'State of All the People'," *Studies on the Soviet Union*, 1964, no. 1, pp. 105–119.
[55]Marx and Engels, *Selected Works*, p. 331 (italics in original).
[56]Lenin, *Soch*, vol. 33, p. 35 (italics in original).
[57]Perfilyev, p. 90.

other Marxists; Marxist-Leninist theoreticians in the People's Republic of China, and others, persist in regarding the dictatorship of the proletariat as the only legitimate socialist state. More to the point, the argument conflicts directly with a still clearer statement of Lenin's that has not yet been squarely faced by Soviet writers: "The essence of Marx's teaching on the state," Lenin wrote in *State and Revolution*, "has been mastered only by someone who has understood that the dictatorship of a *single* class is necessary not only for every class society in general, not only for the *proletariat* which has overthrown the bourgeoisie, but also for the entire *historical period* separating capitalism from 'society without classes,' from communism."[58] It is hard to imagine a more explicit statement to the effect that, short of classless communism, class dictatorship is a fact of life.

Some Soviet writers have attempted to avoid the conceptual problem of accommodating a state that is not an instrument of class coercion by arguing that the all-people's state is strictly speaking not a *state*. In support of this view they cite Lenin's assertion (seconding a point made by Engels) that the Paris Commune was "no longer a state in the proper sense."[59] The difficulty with this approach, however—aside from the fact that it makes the designation 'all-people's state' a misnomer—is that Lenin left no doubt that by "no longer a state in the proper sense" he meant simply that in the Commune it was not a majority but a minority (the former exploiters) that was suppressed. Thus, far from denying that the Commune represented the dictatorship of one class over another, both Engels and Lenin insisted on it. When the state "at last . . . becomes the real representative of the whole of society," Engels wrote in *Anti-Dühring*, "it renders itself unnecessary."[60] The idea of a "people's state," Lenin insisted in *State and Revolution*, is "nonsense" and "a departure from socialism."[61]

Thus there is no question but that Soviet theorists have in effect greatly loosened the original tight Marxist meaning of the term 'state'. To accommodate the new political organism they wish to describe, which is said to represent the interests and will of the entire society, the term 'state' can no longer require class suppression as a necessary condition for its application. A broader generic concept of the state is presupposed, within which class-coercive and non–class-coercive states form separate species.

What is surprising in this light is that for all the emphasis on the new supraclass state in the Soviet ideological and theoretical literature, the actual definitions of the term 'state' that are found in Soviet texts and

---

[58]Lenin, *Soch.*, vol. 33, p. 35 (italics in original).
[59]Ibid., p. 66; Perfilyev, p. 82.
[60]Engels, *Anti-Dühring*, p. 333.
[61]Lenin, *Soch*, vol. 33, p. 66.

reference works still rely on the old, genuinely Marxian formulas, which in fact exclude the new state. The latest (1980) edition of the Soviet *Philosophical Dictionary*, for example, defines 'state' as "the political organization of an economically ruling class which seeks to preserve the existing order and to suppress opposition from other classes."[62] Why, it may be asked, have the dictionaries not simply been rewritten to express the broader concept required for the new, non–class-coercive state? One reason, of course, is that Soviet theorists do not admit that any change has taken place; the all-people's state is not, they insist, a "revisionist" notion. But another reason may be fear of opening a conceptual Pandora's box: general recognition that the state is no longer to be seen as class-coercive by nature might encourage a search for other historical states—or worse, possible future states—to swell the non–class-coercive species, thus overturning the claim of the all-people's state to be its one and only member. Considerations such as these may thus limit the power even of an absolutist ruling body to manipulate meanings by controlling the dictionary. It may be thought preferable to muddle along with the present confused situation, mouthing one definition but thinking another, even though it leads some intrepid Soviet ideologists to make so absurd a claim as the recent one that the new political organ of developed socialism is *both* a class state *and* an all-people's state.[63]

Alternatively it might be asked why the concept of the all-people's state is promoted at all. Why should the Brezhnev regime have so enthusiastically coopted for its own orthodoxy a Khrushchev invention that requires troublesome adjustments in hallowed concepts and that contributes to conflicts among the Communist powers? It is not difficult to find a number of inducements.

First, some sort of major political advance was needed to mark the new historical stage attained in the USSR (and only in the USSR). The progress won in reaching developed socialism is considered so significant that it could hardly lack an accompanying qualitative improvement in the political order. The appearance of the new and superior state, then, heightens the feeling of forward movement; and at the same time, that state itself is given a firmer foundation than it had in Khrushchev's earlier formulation, by being embedded in a special historical era of its own.

Second, the concept of the all-people's state is useful in assuaging the sensitivities of the multitude of national minorities that make up the USSR. Part of the concept's appeal lies in the fact that the Russian expression

[62]I. T. Frolov, ed., *Filosofskii slovar'*, 4th ed. (Moscow, 1980), p. 77.
[63]Glezerman, *Razvitoe sotsialisticheskoe obshchestvo*, p. 31; Anufriev, Tadevosian, and Vetrov, pp. 240–242.

obshchenarodnoe gosudarstvo suggests that it is the state not simply of every individual but of every nationality or folk (*narod*). The interest of the Brezhnev regime in stimulating a sense of solidarity within the multinational Soviet population was demonstrated in 1972 by the introduction of the concept of a single "Soviet people" (*sovetskii narod*), into which, as a "new historical community," the separate Soviet nationalities are said to have merged in the course of building socialism. For the same purpose, the notion of a state common to that compound "people" is undoubtedly welcome.[64]

Turning to considerations of more fundamental theoretical importance, a third attraction of the concept to the Soviet leadership is that it offers a justification for the use of systematic, political coercion against individuals who are not class enemies. This Soviet extension of the potential objects of political coercion to embrace the entire citizenry is a genuine novelty in Marxist political theory. The organized coercive force of the dictatorship of the proletariat was always held by Marxists to be directed, like the force of every state before it, against a hostile class or classes. Marxist theory never recognized a need to use state force against members of one's own class, which was assumed to be so solidary as to require no organized or formal policing. Laws were viewed as designed to control subordinate classes only; precisely for that reason the state was expected to wither away once class domination had disappeared. In developed socialist society, on the other hand, there are no subordinate classes, and yet there is organized coercive force. This force is said to be employed internally not against classes but against deviant individuals—specifically, against individuals who have not yet "become accustomed to observing elementary rules of social intercourse" or who are "wilfully impeding the building of a communist society."[65] But since such benighted creatures may be found anywhere in society, in any stratum or (nonantagonistic) class, laws for the first time have as their rightful scope the entire population. This argument and its theoretical significance are not presented explicitly by Soviet writers, but the importance of "socialist legality" and its universal application is much emphasized. "Socialist democracy presupposes strict discipline and organization, an unfailing adherence to the laws," we read in a recent work; "Soviet socialist discipline is mandatory for all."[66]

Finally, the concept of the all-people's state is valuable to the Soviet leadership because it supports the broad extension of power into whatever

---

[64]Brezhnev, vol. 4, p. 91; note that Brezhnev himself attributes the idea to the twenty-fourth Party congress.

[65]Perfilyev, p. 83.

[66]*Historical Materialism. Theory, Methodology, Problems* (Moscow, 1977), p. 68.

area the state deems necessary. "The Soviet state not only governs all the citizens of the Soviet Union," Perfilyev writes, "it does so along all lines—economic, political, and ideological."[67] The justification for this totalitarian view of state power is that the all-people's state by its very definition expresses "the will and interests" of all the citizens of the land, so that whatever the state dictates must be a legitimate manifestation of popular demand. "These laws and principles reflect the will of the peoples," affirms another writer recently, "and thus their observance meets the vital interests of the whole society and of each of its members."[68] Like Jean-Jacques Rousseau's "general will," the all-people's state *cannot* misrepresent the people. But whereas Rousseau viewed his conception as an ideal construct, difficult if not impossible to embody in actual political institutions, the Soviet leaders contend that the popular will is perfectly expressed by the existing Soviet state. Justifying the further extension of state power is moreover no academic matter for the Soviet leadership, for just such extension is said to be required for the effective building of communism. Only by growing stronger can the state, we are assured, eventually be in a position to wither away.[69]

The Socialist Mode of Life

The Brezhnev regime's final major contribution to the theory of scientific communism is the notion of a special "mode of life" that is said to be characteristic of developed socialism. Introduced and popularized during the 1970s, this notion provides the new stage of history with a distinctive social identity, complementing the political identity supplied by the concept of the all-people's state.

Leonid Brezhnev referred in passing to "our mode of life" at the twenty-fourth Party congress in 1971, but not until 1974 was special theoretical attention devoted either to the notion of a "mode of life" (*obraz zhizni*) in general or to the "socialist mode of life" in particular. Early in that year both *Kommunist* and *Voprosy filosofii* carried major articles on the concepts, and at the end of the year two scholarly conferences on them were held in Moscow.[70] The biggest boost, however, came at the twenty-

---

[67]Perfilyev, p. 89 (italics omitted).
[68]*Historical Materialism*, p. 68.
[69]Afanasyev, pp. 305–306; Perfilyev, p. 108.
[70]Rutkevich, *Problemy*, p. 4. The two articles were G. Glezerman, "Lenin i formirovanie sotsialisticheskogo obraza zhizni," *Kommunist*, 1974, no. 1, pp. 105–118; and S. G. Strumilin and E. E. Pisarenko, "Sotsialisticheskii obraz zhizni: metodologiia issledovaniia," *Voprosy filosofii*, 1974, no. 2, pp. 27–38.

fifth Party congress in 1976, at which Brezhnev proclaimed that with the attainment of developed socialism, there had been formed in the USSR a special "Soviet mode of life." Calling this mode of life one of the principal fruits of six decades of Soviet rule, Brezhnev identified it briefly as marked by true collectivism and comradeship, by the unity and friendship of the various nationalities within the USSR, and by "moral health."[71] In another report presented at the congress, Soviet social scientists were enjoined to develop the theory of the new concept, and they have responded with an outpouring of literature, conferences, and course revisions.[72] In 1977, a reference to "the advantages of the socialist mode of life" was included in the new Soviet Constitution, and Brezhnev continued to stress the concept at his last Party congress, the twenty-sixth in 1981.[73] Andropov signaled his approval of the notion by mentioning it in his theoretical pronouncement of 1983.[74] There is now a broad consensus among Soviet writers not only that the *socialist* (or "Soviet") mode of life is both a theoretical and a practical concern of the first importance but that the generic concept of a mode of life is a major new category of historical materialism.[75]

No definition of the generic concept is contained in Party documents, however, and left to their own devices Soviet theorists have fallen into disagreement on the question. The principal opposing positions mirror the split seen in the previous chapter between theorists who stress the objective conditions of social phenomena and those who stress human social activity. For the former, a mode of life consists in a particular set of objective circumstances—according to one formulation, in "the totality of socio-economic, political, and spiritual conditions of life."[76] The latter, on the other hand, see such an approach as reducing the concept 'mode of life' to the concepts 'socioeconomic formation' or even 'social being'.[77] A practical danger of this approach, A. P. Butenko writes, is that it encourages

[71]*Materialy XXV s"ezda KPSS* (Moscow, 1977), p. 87.
[72]Ibid., p. 214. It was estimated in a Soviet work in 1980 that in the period since the twenty-fifth congress in 1976, Soviet publishing houses had issued approximately 950 titles (with a total circulation of some 22 million copies) devoted to "various aspects of the Soviet mode of life"; see S. D. Laptenok, *Aktual'nye voprosy metodiki prepodavaniia marksistsko-leninskoi etiki* (Minsk, 1980), p. 122. For a brief summary of the Soviet literature on the subject, see Iu. K. Pletnikov and V. N. Shevchenko, "Issledovaniia v oblasti istoricheskogo materializma," *Voprosy filosofii*, 1981, no. 1, p. 34.
[73]*Konstitutsiia*, p. 4; *Documents and Resolutions of the Twenty-sixth Congress of the Communist Party of the Soviet Union* (Moscow, 1981), pp. 74–82.
[74]Andropov, *Uchenie Karla Marksa*, p. 17.
[75]Rutkevich, *Problemy*, p. 3; *Socialist Way of Life. Problems and Perspectives* (Moscow, 1981), p. 43.
[76]Pletnikov and Shevchenko, p. 34; *Socialist Way of Life*, p. 44.
[77]Anufriev, Tadevosian, and Vetrov, p. 156.

the illusion that improving people's living conditions automatically improves their life. For Butenko a mode of life transcends the influence of the socioeconomic formation in which it arises; it consists not in any set of environing conditions but rather in the distinctive activities of people in those conditions.[78]

Supporters of the activity approach can quote on its behalf a passage in the *German Ideology* in which Marx and Engels employed the German equivalent (*Lebensweise*) of the Russian *obraz zhizni*: a society's mode of production, they wrote, "must not be viewed simply as reproduction of the physical existence of individuals. Rather it is a definite form of their activity, a definite way of expressing their life, a definite *mode of life*."[79] With this authoritative backing Butenko defines 'mode of life' as "the sum total of forms of life activity"—a view he sees as gaining ever broader acceptance in the USSR.[80] It is true that many Soviet writers now employ that expression, but there is also much apprehension that it may be interpreted as suggesting that "life activity" is somehow autonomous or independent of objective circumstances. Consequently most theorists who take the activity approach hedge their position by adding to Butenko's formula a phrase that, although meaningless from the point of view of the logical structure of a definition, is a protection against charges of ignoring the objective determination of action. A mode of life, they argue—in a formula that is now repeated almost word for word by many writers—is "the totality of all forms of activity, taken in their indissoluble unity with the conditions of that activity."[81]

As to the concept of the *socialist* mode of life, it does receive explicit treatment in Communist party documents, and the only real disagreement concerning it is whether the notion should be understood descriptively or normatively. In the more heavy-handed ideological literature, the socialist mode of life is sometimes presented simply as an accomplished condition, an actual state of affairs in which Soviet citizens are uniformly blessed with "moral health," "social optimism," "thoroughgoing democratism," and a wealth of other virtues.[82] A number of Soviet theorists, however, regard such statements as idealizations that unjustifiably ignore the dark regions in Soviet life. "Not every living thing under socialism has a socialist

---

[78]*Socialist Way of Life*, pp. 66, 72.
[79]L. D. Easton and K. H. Guddat, trans. and eds., *Writings of the Young Marx on Philosophy and Society* (New York, 1967), p. 409 (italics in original).
[80]*Socialist Way of Life*, p. 65.
[81]Glezerman, Rutkevich, and Vishnevskii, p. 11; Pletnikov and Shevchenko, p. 34; Rutkevich, *Problemy*, pp. 14, 221.
[82]Kosolapov, p. 52; Glezerman, Rutkevich, and Vishnevskii, pp. 38–39.

nature," Butenko has written.[83] He and others have suggested that a distinction must be drawn between "the socialist mode of life," as an ideal to be worked for, and "the mode of life of socialist society," as the actual situation in an imperfect society still bearing the birthmarks of capitalism.[84] This distinction now enjoys wide currency, and although Soviet leaders and propagandists often still speak of "the socialist mode of life" as if it were a descriptive category, they actually use it as an ideal: they rely on it to recommend and promote the traits they would like to see more widespread in the Soviet citizenry. This point becomes clear when we delve beneath the clouds of "moral health" and "social optimism" to the earthly features actually ascribed to the socialist mode of life in Soviet writings.

First, the socialist mode of life is invariably said to be a life of industrious labor. Eventually, in the fully developed economy of communism, it is argued, free time will exceed working time and greater attention can be given to social and cultural activity. In the meantime, however, labor must take precedence; and hence according to Butenko the socialist mode of life is one in which, among the various forms of life activity, labor "occupies the dominant place with respect to time."[85] It is, in a brief formula often encountered, "first of all a *laboring* mode of life."[86] Psychologically, however, labor has not yet become, as it will become under communism, "a primary vital need." Consequently the external stimulus of differential rewards remains necessary, and a feature of the socialist mode of life is what E. I. Kapustin calls "the personal material interest of the worker in the results of his labor."[87] But in present-day Soviet society it is clear that the external stimulus itself stands in need of further reinforcement, as witness the hortatory repetition of maxims such as "he who wishes to live better must work more and better" and the frequent attacks on worker apathy, absenteeism, and such manifestations of *uravnilovka* (egalitarianism in a pejorative sense) as paying workers simply for being present at the workplace and distributing bonuses regardless of achievement.[88] A principal function of the concept of the socialist mode of life in current Soviet ideology, then, is to advance and buttress the ideal of productive labor based on the personal ambition for a better life.

Second, the socialist mode of life is presented as one marked by the closest unity of all the members of society, "the unity of all classes and

---

[83]A. P. Butenko, *Sotsialisticheskii obraz zhizni i formirovanie novogo cheloveka* (Moscow, 1975), p. 28.
[84]Rutkevich, *Problemy*, pp. 24, 51–52; *Socialist Way of Life*, p. 160.
[85]Rutkevich, *Problemy*, p. 47.
[86]Glezerman, Rutkevich, and Vishnevskii, p. 29 (italics in original); Pletnikov and Shevchenko, p. 34 (italics added).
[87]Rutkevich, *Problemy*, p. 64.
[88]Anufriev, Tadevosian, and Vetrov, pp. 162–163.

social groups, of all nations and nationalities, of all generations of Soviet society."[89] Actually, 'uniformity' would be a better word than 'unity' for what is intended, however, for at a more concrete level the *likenesses* of socialist citizens in economic, political, social, and cultural respects are stressed. Thus Semenov in a prominent recent article on developed socialism praises as unifying features the "social homogeneity" of workers, peasants, and intelligentsia and the "intellectual-moral unity" that consists in a uniform devotion to Marxism-Leninism.[90] N. M. Keizerov has argued that those Western writers who pretend to find pluralism and conflicting interest groups in Soviet society are seeking to "cast doubt on the spiritual principles of the socialist mode of life."[91] Fundamental to that life, in the current interpretation, is social solidarity based on a commonality of status, ideas, and interests.

A third recurrent theme in Soviet presentations of the socialist mode of life is the need for externally imposed norms of behavior. What is called "the planned improvement of the socialist mode of life" presupposes the observance by individuals of "social parameters" established by the planners with an eye to "the harmonious development of all spheres of social life and the formation of the new man." It is often emphasized that such planning does not exclude individual life styles as long as they are chosen "within the framework of existing conditions."[92] But there is no doubt that the Soviet socialist ideal stresses the acceptance of external direction and close adherence to it not only in the economic sphere but in other areas of life as well. G. S. Batishchev, by contrast, is on record as protesting that under socialism people should develop to the point where they no longer need to have norms dictated to them from outside; but his view has been vigorously attacked by other writers who argue that even in developed socialist society individuals must be subjected to external direction backed by force.[93]

Finally, a feature that is heavily stressed in all accounts of the socialist mode of life is the large and growing role in that life of the Communist party. The unity and direction already mentioned are not seen as haphazard consequences of spontaneous development; rather it is argued that "the

[89]Furmanov, Sertsova, and Il'in, p. 269.
[90]Semenov, "Uchenie," p. 12.
[91]Rutkevich, *Problemy*, p. 2.
[92]Glezerman, Rutkevich, and Vishnevskii, p. 261.
[93]Kazakov, p. 111. Batishchev's unorthodox views, much indebted to the writings of the young Marx, are well presented in his essay entitled "Deiatel'nostnaia sushchnost' cheloveka kak filosofskii printsip," in I. F. Balakina et al., eds., *Problema cheloveka v sovremennoi filosofii* (Moscow, 1969), pp. 73–144. For a discussion of Batishchev's views and an account of official criticism of them, see Zeev Katvan, "Reflection Theory and the Identity of Thinking and Being," *Studies in Soviet Thought* 18 (1978), pp. 102–107.

leading and directing activity of the Communist party" is "the guiding force of the whole social structure and political system of developed socialism, cementing all its links and all its activity."[94] Furthermore there is said to be a need to strengthen and increase this force. "The growth of the leading role of the CPSU," we read, "is both an objective law of the construction of socialism and communism and an unalterable principle of the truly democratic development of society."[95] Politically, this increase in the role of the Party goes along with the increased role of the state in developed socialist society, since it is taken as a matter of course that the Party is the nucleus of the socialist political system. "Democracy without the leading role of the Communist party is anarchy," a recent text affirms.[96] But it is made abundantly clear in the Soviet social and political literature that the same principle applies in other areas of life as well. Developed socialist society is described as marked by "the furthest growth of the role of the Party in the direction of all aspects of the life of society."[97] The socialist citizen, then, welcomes and abides by the Party's guidance in whatever sphere it is offered. "An important feature of the socialist mode of life," the Soviet people are informed, "is loyalty and devotion to the Communist party."[98]

The fact that many Soviet citizens are deficient in such loyalty and devotion only serves to point up the status of the concept of the socialist mode of life as an ideal, designed (at least in internal use) not so much to report the present situation of the Soviet people—who after all know better—as to show them the state to which their life should be brought. As such the concept, it will be noted, serves to project an image of an existence strikingly different from any Karl Marx imagined for mankind. The socialist mode of life as elaborated in current Soviet ideology is the life of citizens who are personally ambitious, eager to gain greater economic rewards and willing to work hard to do so; who seek to be like their fellows in intellectual and moral as well as social respects; who submit to the discipline of externally imposed norms in every area of their social and cultural activity; and who place boundless trust in the wisdom of the Communist party. For Marx, the very idea of defining a settled "socialist mode of life" of indefinite but very long duration is of course out of keeping with the transitory character he attributed to the first phase of communism. But still more out of keeping with Marx's thought are the attributes of

[94]Glezerman, Rutkevich, and Vishnevskii, p. 100.
[95]"Za tesnuiu sviaz' teorii i praktiki," *Voprosy filosofii*, 1982, no. 1, p. 14.
[96]Glezerman, *Razvitoe sotsialisticheskoe obshchestvo*, p. 33.
[97]Ibid., p. 271.
[98]Anufriev, Tadevosian, and Vetrov, p. 160.

acquisitiveness, conformity, docility, and loyalty to a ruling elite that Soviet theorists now recommend for the socialist citizen.

Thus to accompany the new social order that is its communism surrogate, the Brezhnev regime also advanced a new ideal of humanity. Soviet Marxists are often chided for failing, after more than six decades, to produce the fabled "new man" fit for communism—the self-governing, internally motivated transformer of nature whose labor is as free and creative as any artist's. But producing *that* new man is not on the agenda. Instead the Brezhnev ideology, through the concept of the socialist mode of life, introduced a forerunner—a socialist new man, whose traits differ sharply from those of his eventual communist descendant. All efforts are now concentrated on producing this newer new man, and he is provided with a lengthy era in which to flourish before yielding the historical stage to the kind of man envisaged by Marx.

An Assessment of Soviet Social and Political Philosophy

The current sociopolitical orthodoxy of Marxism-Leninism is obviously open to fundamental criticism from the standpoint of other values and other philosophical perspectives. But such criticism is beyond the scope of the present investigation, which seeks to judge Soviet Marxism-Leninism as far as possible in its own terms, without importing principles or standards from other intellectual systems. Internally, Soviet social and political theory is subject to evaluation of two sorts. As an integral part of Marxist-Leninist philosophy, it should be consistent with the general principles of that philosophy. And as supposedly "scientific," like Marxist-Leninist philosophy as a whole, it should be conformable to the actual state of the world. Whether it meets these two requirements is the subject of this concluding section.

Consistency with Dialectical and Historical Materialism

A surprising feature of the immense Soviet literature on "scientific communism" is that it contains few references to the laws of dialectics. The advancement of society from the proletarian revolution to the construction of socialism "in the main," then to developed socialism, and ultimately to classless, stateless communism is for Marxist-Leninists a clear and momentous case of a progressive developmental process and one that we now know to be protracted and complex. As such it would seem to be just the sort of process to which the laws of dialectics are applicable. But aside

from a controversy concerning the "basic contradiction" of socialist society, there is scarcely any mention of the laws in the standard treatises
of scientific communism. Books with titles such as *The Dialectics of the
Growth of Developed Socialist Society* discuss the process, but not in terms
of the classic laws.[99]

Although developed socialism is considered a great historical advance
and an independent stage in the career of the communist socioeconomic
formation, no effort is made either to exhibit it as a case of the operation
of the law of the transformation of quantity into quality or to explain why
the law does not apply to it. Quantitative changes in socialist society are
certainly noted—growing economic productivity and greater application
of science to industrial processes, for example—but there is no attempt to
find "nodes" at which these developments precipitate a qualitative advance
or to identify the "leap" in which such an advance consists. The same may
be said for the change from the dictatorship of the proletariat to the all-
people's state. When the former, having "fulfilled its historic mission,"
gave way to the latter, a new kind of state was born; but the event is not
analyzed in terms of quantity and quality. And in neither of these two
cases is any evidence presented of a return to a previous condition on a
higher level, such that the law of the negation of the negation might be
invoked.

One way to justify this silence would be to argue that the basic laws of
dialectics have so broad a sweep that they abstract from such relatively
short-term events as the stages within the communist socioeconomic formation; that entire formation, it might be maintained, forms a single
qualitative level for purposes of the basic laws. Some Soviet writers have,
in fact, contended that there is no qualitative difference between the dictatorship of the proletariat and the all-people's state.[100] But this contention
is implausible in light of the great significance attributed to this political
advance by Soviet writers, and indeed Iurii Andropov may have put the
claim to rest by explicitly calling the change "qualitative" in his first major
theoretical pronouncement as head of the Communist party.[101] It would
surely be a devastating indictment of the basic laws of dialectics to say
that they are too abstract to describe the principal stages of the most
important developmental process in human history.

There have been attempts by Soviet philosophers to apply the law of
the unity and struggle of opposites to the development of the communist
formation, but these attempts can only be called half-hearted and uncon-

[99]See, for example, Furmanov, Sertsova, and Il'in.
[100]Afanasyev, *Marxist Philosophy*, p. 299; see also Kanet, pp. 88–90.
[101]Andropov, *Uchenie Karla Marksa*, p. 20.

vincing. The theoretical problem to which they have been addressed is real enough. With the establishment of socialism "in the main" there is no longer a struggle among antagonistic classes in socialist society; what "opposites," then, account for the further advance of society?[102] Among theoreticians who have addressed themselves to this question of the motive force of socialist society the issue has become known as that of finding the "basic contradiction" of socialism, and a large number of candidates has been suggested. For some writers, the basic contradiction consists in a disproportion between the levels of development of the productive forces and the production relations. Others point to the fact that in socialism all workers have the same relation to the means of production but receive different rewards. Still others see the contradiction as consisting in the fact that whereas laborers are rewarded according to their work, they labor according to their ability. And a not inconsiderable number fasten on the contrast between the growing needs of the population and the inadequate level of development of production.[103] What is striking about each of these suggestions, however, is that it is simply an abstract statement of some disproportion existing in socialist society without any indication of a mechanism whereby the disproportion might operate as a motive force. In no case is the supposed "contradiction" analyzed in such a way as to demonstrate an actual causal linkage between it and concrete social progress.

Why do Soviet writers in the area of "scientific communism" give so little attention to the basic laws of dialectics and present so unpersuasive a case for the operation of the laws when they do appeal to them? The answer would seem to be that they in fact subscribe to an account of social change not only different from but inconsistent with the account provided by the basic laws. For according to the doctrines of scientific communism as we have examined them above, it is not contradictions that move socialist society forward but the Communist party. The enormous emphasis placed on the Party as the leading and directing force not only of the political system but of every aspect of Soviet life is simply incompatible with the view that objective contradictions within the society provide the fundamental forward impetus. Productive forces must develop, to be sure; but the Party plans and directs their development. Science must progress

[102]Some prominent Soviet ideologists have suggested that recent events in Poland show that *antagonisms* may still exist in socialist society even after antagonistic *classes* have been eliminated; but of course the antagonisms that these writers have in mind are viewed by them as grave obstacles to progress, not as what moves society forward (see "Materialy soveshchaniia po problemam istoricheskogo materializma," no. 5, p. 38; "Materialy soveshchaniia po problemam dialekticheskogo materializma v redaktsii zhurnala 'Voprosy filosofii,' " *Voprosy filosofii*, 1982, no. 5, p. 28).

[103]For a comparison of these positions, see V. S. Semenov, "Problema protivorechii v usloviiakh sotsializma," *Voprosy filosofii*, 1982, no. 7, pp. 18–25.

and must be applied to industry; but the Party prompts, nurtures, and channels the process.[104] No genuine causal efficacy could be attributed to "contradictions" without diminishing the contribution of the Party, and so none is found. And the other basic laws, too, are irrelevant for the same reason. Since the Party's wisdom and determination bring about qualitative changes in society, it cannot be argued that objective quantitative accumulations generate them. As for the law of the negation of the negation, there is certainly no ground for thinking that the Party is constrained to lead society in circles, even ascending ones; surely by conscious and deliberate guidance it can accomplish what Rutkevich called "straightening the spirals of social development."[105]

If the doctrine of the leading role of the Communist party conflicts with basic principles of dialectical materialism, it also creates problems for the materialist theory of history. For in Marxian terms it means the dominance of consciousness over being in determining the course of history—the supremacy of superstructural, subjective factors over the objective economic conditions that orthodox Marxists see as the determinants of social progress. Many Soviet historians, as we found in the last chapter, operate as historical interactionists rather than historical materialists, tacitly including subjective factors as coequal strands in the web of historical explanation. By contrast, many writers on scientific communism operate as full-blown (though not as declared) historical idealists, stressing and glorifying the conscious direction of socialist society. According to a recent editorial in *Voprosy filosofii*, "the activization in every way of the subjective factors of social development has enormous significance for the ever fuller realization of the possibilities and advantages of mature socialism. Such subjective factors include first of all the leading role of the Communist party in the construction of the new society."[106] With the victory of the proletarian revolution, another source affirms, the superstructure of society "reveals its creative force, its rational, creative direction in relation to the basis of socialist society." In the Soviet literature the "primacy" and "supremacy" of politics, guided by the Communist party, are reiterated on all sides, with the explicit assurance that they apply in relation to economics as to "every other sphere of social life."[107]

By way of excusing these departures from economic determinism, Soviet

---

[104]R. G. Vartanov, "Nekotorye problemy dialektiki proizvoditel'nykh sil i proizvodstvennykh otnoshenii razvitogo sotsializma," *Voprosy filosofii*, 1980, no. 11, p. 51.

[105]F. V. Konstantinov et al., eds., *Dialektika i logika nauchnogo poznaniia. Materialy soveshchaniia po sovremennym problemam materialisticheskoi dialektiki, 7–9 aprelia 1965 g.* (Moscow, 1966), p. 223 (italics omitted).

[106]"Za tesnuiu sviaz'," p. 15.

[107]Furmanov, Sertsova, and Il'in, pp. 31–32; Medvedev, "Marksistsko-leninskaia kontseptsiia," p. 29.

writers repeat the familiar "in the last analysis" qualifications examined in the previous chapter. There is no "Maoist subjectivism" here, we are assured, because in the Soviet interpretation politics is *ultimately* an "expression of economics."[108] It is in the exceptional circumstances of the "revolutionary situation" following the overthrow of capitalism, Soviet writers assert, that politics and "the creatively constructive function of the superstructure" come into the foreground.[109] But they have remained in the foreground for well over sixty-five years now, with no retreat in sight; and the Leninist idea of the primacy of politics, we are told, "fully preserves its force under conditions of developed socialism."[110] Consequently, given the protracted career now envisaged for developed socialism, we are confronted with a "revolutionary situation" that is conceived as lasting well over a century. The operation of the central principle of historical materialism—the determination of the superstructure by the economic base—is suspended for the entire socialist past and the foreseeable future of Soviet society in order to make room for the political forces in which Soviet theorists actually believe.

Conformity with the Real World

Whether or not Soviet social and political doctrines are consistent with the more general principles of Marxist-Leninist philosophy, we may also ask whether they are consistent with reality. Does the sociopolitical orthodoxy we have been examining accurately reflect the current state of Soviet socialist society?

To some extent at least the theoretical changes introduced or endorsed by the Brezhnev regime can be viewed as forms of coming to grips with reality and thus as representing a healthy impulse in Soviet social thought. By any objective indications communism is not just over the horizon in the USSR, and the theory of developed socialism provides for a lengthy future without it. The state has not withered away, and the doctrine of the all-people's state acknowledges this fact. The Communist party is the overwhelmingly dominant force in Soviet society, and the concept of the socialist mode of life admits it. Such tailoring of Marxist-Leninist theory to fit the real world would appear to be openly encouraged in the Soviet scholarly literature; it is what the editors of *Voprosy filosofii* have in mind when they call for "the continual deepening and correlating of the scientific,

[108]Medvedev, "Marksistsko-leninskaia kontseptsiia," p. 29.
[109]Furmanov, Sertsova, and Il'in, p. 32.
[110]Medvedev, "Marksistsko-leninskaia kontseptsiia," p. 29.

theoretical model [*obraz*] of developed socialism with the actual social reality of mature socialism."[111] The same kind of impulse is at work when Soviet theorists adjust their view of the social ideal to correspond more closely with the actual foreseeable future, as we have seen in the transformation of developed socialism into a communism surrogate.[112] It is a sign of realism when Soviet authorities, eschewing the term 'communism', now solemnly proclaim that "the future belongs to socialism."[113]

At the same time, not all the seemingly factual claims advanced by Soviet social and political theorists can be seen as concessions to the actual state of social life, and in general the "realism" of their orthodoxy is more apparent than genuine. On many topics the vagueness and flexibility of the concepts employed and the distance of these concepts from concrete social reality allow Soviet theorists to choose among a wide range of theses without fear of contradiction by facts. As a result, the Soviet doctrines are often more stipulative than descriptive, and they depend more on perceived ideological needs than on the objective state of the world. Fastening on the late 1960s as the time of arrival of developed socialism may be considered a case of such stipulative determination of doctrine. Earlier, the late 1950s were considered the starting date with equal plausibility, and there is no objective reason why socialism could not have been declared "developed" in the 1940s or 1930s; indeed Stalin must have thought he *was* declaring it developed in the Constitution of 1936.

The possibilities for stipulative truth making are greatest where there is some normative, ideal element concealed in the presumably factual assertion, as there frequently is in Soviet doctrines. Among the central theses of current Soviet ideology are the contentions that the Soviet state represents the will of the entire population and that the Communist party has no interests apart from the interests of the people. Although both theses are seemingly intended to describe the real world, the existence of evidence against them does not appear to be a matter of concern to Soviet philosophers. It is not considered relevant that the will of religious minorities and political dissidents is thwarted rather than represented by the Soviet state or that some Party members are more attached to power and privilege than to promoting the interests of the public. Why are these phenomena not taken into account? Because, I suggest, they are viewed as reflecting not the "true" will and interests of the individuals involved but rather some pathological condition that is a throwback to a presocialist era. The *genuine* will of the citizen is to build communism in accordance

[111]"Za tesnuiu sviaz'," p. 12.
[112]This point is well made in Evans, p. 414.
[113]*Documents and Resolutions*, p. 108; Y. V. Andropov, *Speech at the CPSU Central Committee Plenary Meeting, June 15, 1983* (Moscow, 1983), p. 29.

with the state program, and the *genuine* interest of the Party member is to direct that endeavor for the good of all. Here the fact-value ambiguity of expressions like 'true will' and 'genuine interest' is exploited to pass off as straightforward fact what is actually a decision concerning what people *ought* to will and what their interests *ought* to be. The supposedly factual theses about government and Party are based not on an examination of the empirically expressed desires and motives of people but on a stipulation concerning their ideal desires and motives. This normative variety of stipulative truth making gives ideologists a broad field for operation because it employs ideal standards that they can manipulate almost at will.

To see the full potential of this technique we need only consider the possibility of determining stipulatively the advent of communism. At first glance it seems obvious that the Soviet Union is a long way from achieving the promised communist society and that it is a mark of realism on the part of contemporary Soviet theorists to acknowledge this fact. But on closer examination the situation is far less straightforward.

A precondition for communism is the development of the socialist economy to the point where it can provide what is called "material abundance." But what constitutes material abundance? Clearly, enough to satisfy fully the needs of the society. What are those needs? They must not, of course, be fanciful or extravagant ones; whatever the level of social wealth, a recent Soviet work argues, the principle of rationality must prevail: society must be satisfied with "consumption within the bounds of necessity and knowing no wastefulness."[114] Nor can selfishness on the part of any members of the society be condoned. "Abundance," then, must be considered enough to provide for what Soviet writers now call "needs that are reasonable and preclude elements of self-interest and individualism," the needs of "people of high culture and consciousness"—in other words, the needs people *ought* to have as determined by communist principles.[115] Thus material abundance can be said to be at hand when the actual output of the economy matches a normative decision concerning what the society should need. Within broad limits, the Soviet leadership can set the level of need at whatever point it chooses and thus can establish the presence of "material abundance" by fiat.

In communism, the output must not only be equal to the society's needs as a whole, its distribution to individuals must be determined by their separate needs. But it can be argued that such a system of distribution already exists in Soviet society. Low-cost public transportation, the assignment of living space in accordance with family size, and the provision

---

[114]*Socialist Way of Life*, p. 169 (quoting a statement by the Polish sociologist Jan Szczepański).

[115]Glezerman, Rutkevich, and Vishnevskii, p. 313; *Socialist Way of Life*, p. 148; Anufriev, Tadevosian, and Vetrov, p. 311.

of as much free medical care as an individual's state of health requires can all be considered forms of distribution according to need. As for the fact that people receive unequal salaries, it must be remembered that neither Marx nor his Soviet followers ever intended distribution according to need to be an egalitarian standard. Just as under socialism the person who works more gets more, so under communism the person who needs more gets more. But who is to say that an individual who works harder, or works in remote areas or under difficult conditions—all circumstances that are currently held to justify differential wages according to the *work* standard—does not *need* more to replenish body and spirit? Who is to say that the Communist party member, with his onerous special duties and responsibilities, does not need more in the way of leisure opportunities and everyday conveniences? The point is that whether any particular distribution of rewards matches individuals' needs depends entirely, again, on a decision as to what those needs "really" are. And this decision is a normative one that the Soviet leadership has wide latitude in making.

But communism, it may be objected, also requires the withering away of the state, and the Soviet state seems a long way from withering. Although there is here no normative element for the Soviet theorist to exploit, the indeterminateness of the relevant concepts still makes possible a withering by stipulation. The present Soviet socialist political system, it might be argued, is a far cry from the dictatorship of the proletariat, and even the latter was not a "state" in the full sense of the term. Class antagonisms are gone forever. The people's delegates to the Soviets are ordinary citizens, not professional bureaucrats. More and more administrative functions are performed by volunteers—Comrade's Courts, People's Control Committees, the Voluntary People's Militia, and the like. A centralized government and Party leadership persist, but of course it was never expected that communism could do without central direction, without Engels's "administration of things"; the orchestra will always need a conductor. In short, there is nothing in the logic of these concepts to prevent the next regular Communist party congress in 1986 from proclaiming that the all-people's state has fulfilled its historic mission and that communist public self-administration has arrived. It need not be perfect or even "mature" at first, of course; the establishment of "communism in the main" could be said to be followed by a long period of "building developed communism." Khrushchev may have had such a proclamation in mind when he made his famous promise in 1961.

It is sometimes assumed that the failure of communism to arrive after so many decades of Soviet rule is a source of embarrassment to ideologists in the USSR. But the real problem for them is not how to explain the tardiness of communism but when to declare that it has come. The concepts of "scientific communism" are so pliant that with a little ingenuity communism can be either postponed indefinitely or welcomed tomorrow. Brezhnev and his successors have opted for the former course, preferring the familiar ground of socialism to the uncharted waters of communism. It is in this ability to "establish" truths by stipulation that we see the remarkable ideological flexibility, but at the same time the fundamental theoretical weakness, of Soviet social and political doctrine. For despite an occasional nod to realism, its theses ultimately hinge not on objective social facts but on conceptual decisions prompted by political circumstances.

[7]

Philosophy of Morality

To many observers—supporters and critics alike—the Soviet conception of morality is wholly contained in a notorious statement made by Lenin in the formative years of the Soviet state. "Morality," the Bolshevik leader told the Young Communist League in 1920, "is what serves to destroy the old exploiting society and to unite all toilers around the proletariat, which is building a new, communist society."[1] Some supporters, including most of the early Bolsheviks, have seen the statement as a fitting revolutionary rejection of the oppressive moralism through which exploiting classes have sought to strengthen their dominance over the people. Critics, on the other hand, have pointed to it as evidence of the Machiavellian amoralism of Soviet Marxism, a proclamation of the right to employ any means, however vile, to attain the goal of worldwide communism; it is this view, critics maintain, that is so regularly manifested in the brutal actions of the state that Ronald Reagan has called "the focus of evil in the modern world." And neither side has felt any need for further explanation of the position. Marxist-Leninist "morality," in this view, reduces simply to whatever promotes the cause of communism.[2]

Although Soviet philosophers in the present day by no means disavow Lenin's statement—indeed they quote it sympathetically and often—they no longer believe that it tells the whole story. The statement, they hold, is only a capsule summary of a complex Marxist approach to morality; behind it is said to be not only a positive moral position but one that represents the highest advance of the moral consciousness of mankind. A new subdivision of Soviet philosophy—"Marxist-Leninist ethics"—has been

[1]V. I. Lenin, *Polnoe sobranie sochinenii*, 5th ed., 55 vols. (Moscow, 1958–1965), vol. 41, p. 311.
[2]The principal Western studies of Soviet ethics are Richard T. De George, *Soviet Ethics and Morality* (Ann Arbor, 1969); Peter Ehlen, *Die philosophische Ethik in der Sowjetunion. Analyse und Diskussion* (Munich, 1972); and Philip T. Grier, *Marxist Ethical Theory in the Soviet Union* (Dordrecht, Holland, 1978).

established to elaborate this position, and a voluminous literature has been produced in the field. Instruction in ethics has become a prominent part of Soviet education, from primary schools to the universities. The public media, too, now spend much time discussing moral topics and purveying moral lessons—to the point where a Bolshevik Rip van Winkle would surely be astonished at the rampant moralism of Soviet popular culture.

On the theoretical level, Marxist-Leninist ethics is, after social and political theory, the most dogmatic and ideologically controlled field of Soviet philosophical thought. Explicit Communist party pronouncements on the subject in the post-Stalin period have given clear direction to doctrinal developments, with the result that a definite and virtually unquestioned orthodoxy now prevails in the field. Still, there has been some discussion of significant theoretical issues in the professional philosophical literature, especially in the 1960s and early 1970s; and even as the orthodoxy has hardened in more recent years, Soviet philosophers have at least provided further material for the assessment of their views by continuing to respond to Western criticisms. The ultimate aim of this chapter is to judge the strengths and weaknesses of those views—a task that will be undertaken in the final section. The first two sections will be devoted to a brief exposition of the current Soviet orthodoxy in ethics and a history of the disputes and decrees surrounding its establishment.

Elements of the Soviet View of Morality

In the Soviet philosophical literature, ethics is defined as the "science" or study of morality, and morality is viewed as a social phenomenon of broad significance, not a mere matter of individual conscience. Marx's thesis that morality is a form of social consciousness generated by social being is accepted by Soviet philosophers, and in this light they see morality as a superstructural product of the economic base of society and more specifically an expression of economic class interests. The words of Frederick Engels in *Anti-Dühring* are frequently cited: "Men, consciously or unconsciously, derive their ethical ideas in the last resort from the practical relations on which their class position is based—from the economic relations in which they carry on production and exchange." One's class situation, then, determines the morality one espouses. "Morality has always been class morality," Engels went on; "it has either justified the domination and the interests of the ruling class, or, ever since the oppressed class became powerful enough, it has represented its indignation against this domination and the future interests of the oppressed."[3] A corollary

---

[3]Frederick Engels, *Anti-Dühring. Herr Eugen Dühring's Revolution in Science* (Moscow, 1947), pp. 114–115.

of this view is that morality changes as class configurations change, and Soviet philosophers have enthusiastically endorsed Marx's and Engels's view that morality is inescapably historical in character.

At the same time, Soviet philosophers today do not overlook the fact that Engels qualified his historicism significantly by contending that "proletarian morality" is a positive advance over all others and a step toward a future "really human morality which stands above class antagonisms."[4] Soviet philosophers follow Engels in thus accepting a notion of moral *progress*, and consequently they accept the existence of objective standards against which the value of moral change can be gauged. Indeed they vigorously oppose the theory of ethical relativism as a prime example of the unprincipled subjectivism and moral nihilism of bourgeois culture. History, they claim, demonstrates that the morality of the working class has progressively incorporated moral norms of enduring value; the textbook *Fundamentals of Marxist-Leninist Philosophy* calls them "simple standards of human morality" that arise in the process of mankind's historical development.[5] These standards are seen as flowing from the basic requirements of community life, such as the need to be honest and truthful, to aid others in distress, to refrain from harming others—none of which appears clearly connected with class position. "It is hard to say," A. I. Titarenko writes, "what class interest guides a man who carries a child from a burning building."[6] Communist morality, it is argued, takes these standards seriously by virtue of the fact that in representing the interests of the radically dispossessed proletariat it speaks for mankind rather than for property and privilege, and hence communist morality is said to be the closest approximation yet known to the "really human morality" beyond class distinctions that was foreseen by Engels.

Until such time as full communism arrives and is no longer beset by external foes, however, "communist morality" must remain an approximation and must be oriented toward helping to bring about the desired "really human" condition. It must be, in other words, a morality for builders and defenders of communism rather than members of a full-fledged communist community. The principles of this morality were formulated on the highest authority as part of the Communist party program adopted at the twenty-second Party congress in 1961, and this formulation has been regarded as canonical ever since. Under the title of "The Moral

[4]Ibid., p. 115.
[5]F. V. Konstantinov, ed., *The Fundamentals of Marxist-Leninist Philosophy*, trans. R. Daglish (Moscow, 1982), p. 347 (italics omitted).
[6]A. I. Titarenko, *Nravstvennyi progress* (*Osnovnye istoricheskie cherty nravstvennogo progressa v dokommunisticheskikh obshchestvenno-ekonomicheskikh formatsiiakh*) (Moscow, 1969), p. 146.

Code of the Builder of Communism," it is the unquestioned basis of every presentation of communist morality to be found in the Soviet philosophical and ideological literature. It reads as follows:

> The Party holds that *the moral code of the builder of communism* should comprise the following principles:
>
> devotion to the communist cause; love of the socialist motherland and of the other socialist countries;
>
> conscientious labor for the good of society—he who does not work, neither shall he eat;
>
> concern on the part of everyone for the preservation and growth of public wealth;
>
> a high sense of public duty; intolerance of actions harmful to the public interest;
>
> collectivism and comradely mutual assistance; one for all and all for one;
>
> humane relations and mutual respect between individuals—man is to man a friend, comrade and brother;
>
> honesty and truthfulness, moral purity, modesty, and unpretentiousness in social and private life;
>
> mutual respect in the family, and concern for the upbringing of children;
>
> an uncompromising attitude to injustice, parasitism, dishonesty, careerism and money-grubbing;
>
> friendship and brotherhood among all peoples of the USSR; intolerance of national and racial hatred;
>
> an uncompromising attitude to the enemies of communism, peace and the freedom of nations;
>
> fraternal solidarity with the working people of all countries, and with all peoples.[7]

Soviet philosophers make no apologies for the militant tone of this code, nor do they strive to qualify its powerful stress on service to a social cause. Due note is taken of the "universal" elements contained in those clauses that call for honesty, mutual respect, and the like; by virtue of their inclusion in the code these elements are acknowledged as moral values and can be cited by Soviet philosophers as evidence that their view should not be considered a Machiavellian rejection of common human standards of morality. At the same time, however, no doubt is left by Soviet commentators that the code's first principle is its governing one, and the syllabus for every course in Marxist-Leninist ethics taught in Soviet schools begins

[7] *The Road to Communism. Documents of the Twenty-second Congress of the Communist Party of the Soviet Union. October 17–31, 1961* (Moscow, n.d.), pp. 566–567 (italics in original).

its treatment of communist morality with some equivalent of the statement that "devotion to the cause of communism is [the] supreme principle of communist morality." That principle, it is frequently added, has "determining significance for the other principles and norms."[8]

The same pattern of the dominance of the communist social cause is carried through in the standard Soviet treatments of all the concepts traditionally found in moral theories. The good as a category of ethics, writes L. B. Volchenko, embraces everything that promotes "the struggle for the strengthening and perfection of communism."[9] Duty is seen as a bond of obligation between individuals and social entities, provided that the latter are "progressive": a 1980 work defines duty as "the profoundly felt and recognized personal need of a man to fulfill the historically necessary, progressive demands of society, class, social group, and social organization."[10] Individual happiness is not rejected as a desideratum by Soviet philosophers, but in analyzing it they resort once more to the concept of social service: "the entire essence of happiness," wrote one Soviet philosopher in 1967, "is fulfilling one's *duty* to society."[11] Even the concept 'the meaning of life', despite its possibly idealistic and even religious overtones, is claimed as a fundamental category of "materialist" Marxist-Leninist philosophy through the mediation of the service ethic: "The foundation of ethical philosophy," students at Moscow State University are told, resides in "ideas of the meaning of life as service to the social interests of progress and of social and legal justice."[12]

The ethical philosopher is himself not exempt, of course, from the general obligation to serve the cause of communism, and in his professional capacity he has the special duty of helping to instill proper moral notions in others. An essential feature of the conception of moral philosophy in the USSR is the ascription to the discipline of a major educative function—a critical role in what is called "the formation of the communist consciousness."[13] A current standard textbook, *Marxist Ethics* (1976), asserts that the task of ethical science is not only to describe and explain morality but to *teach* it, and the author adds that "an ethics that does not help

[8]S. F. Anisimov and B. O. Nikolaichev, eds., *Programma kursa marksistsko-leninskoi etiki dlia studentov Filosofskogo fakul'teta i plany seminarskikh zaniatii* (Moscow, 1978), p. 16. See also A. I. Titarenko, ed., *Marksistskaia etika* (Moscow, 1976), p. 187.

[9]L. B. Volchenko, *Marksistsko-leninskaia etika. Kurs lektsii. Chast' III. Sistema obshchikh kategorii etiki* (Moscow, 1978), p. 30.

[10]S. D. Laptenok, *Aktual'nye voprosy metodiki prepodavaniia marksistsko-leninskoi etiki* (Minsk, 1980), p. 138.

[11]G. D. Bandzeladze, ed., *Aktual'nye problemy marksistskoi etiki (sbornik statei)* (Tbilisi, 1967), p. 472 (italics in original).

[12]Volchenko, p. 61.

[13]Laptenok, p. 3.

people to become better and purer is as useless as a medicine that cannot heal."[14] Thus identified as a physician of the human soul, the ethical philosopher is charged with treating the moral ills of the populace, and the great attention devoted to moral education in the USSR today is evidence of his industrious compliance.

Development of Ethics in the Post-Stalin Period

Both the precise content of the view of morality just sketched and the great attention paid to the subject in Soviet thought and public life are products of the post-Stalin era, during which marked changes have come about in the Soviet approach to ethical philosophy. How the present orthodoxy emerged from the interplay of philosophical, ideological, and political forces affecting Soviet thinking about morality in this period is the topic of the present section.

The Exploratory Decade of the 1960s

Through the Stalin era, Soviet thinking on ethics was dominated by the same "vulgar sociologism" that characterized Soviet social thought generally in the early decades after the revolution. The dependence of morality on the economic and specifically the class structure of society was heavily stressed, with the result that old notions of ethics as the study of universal moral standards were widely dismissed as the dispensable legacy of a classbound past. Ironically, two earlier Russian Marxist philosophers, Georgii Valentinovich Plekhanov (1856–1918) and Liubov' Isaakovna Aksel'rod (1868–1946), had developed more sophisticated and sympathetic approaches to traditional philosophical ethics and had argued for the existence of what (borrowing a phrase from Marx) they called "simple laws of morality and right" that, having universal validity, bind the proletariat as well as other men.[15] The political identification of these thinkers with Menshevism, however, caused their independent philosophical efforts to be rejected wholesale; they were attacked as Kantians in ethics, and the very expression "simple laws of morality and right" acquired what one

<hr>

[14]Titarenko, *Marksistskaia etika*, p. 12.
[15]For a good exposition of their views by V. S. Shtein, see Bandzeladze, *Aktual'nye problemy*, pp. 128–145. Marx had invoked "simple laws of morality and right" (*die einfachen Gesetze der Moral und des Rechts*) in 1864 in his "Inaugural Address of the International Working Men's Association" (Karl Marx and Friedrich Engels, *Werke* [Berlin, 1960–1968], vol. 16, p. 13).

Soviet observer termed "an odious character," as synonymous with the anti-Marxist denial of the class nature of morality.[16] More than that, *all* talk of moral norms became suspect, however respectable its source. When the Russian educational pioneer A. S. Makarenko spoke in 1927 of the need to imbue Soviet young people with a sense of duty to their class, he was told that 'duty' is a "bourgeois category" that cannot form part of Soviet education. Whenever anyone begins to talk of norms of social morality, said the old Bolshevik M. I. Kalinin in 1928, "we pull him up at once: don't moralize, morality is a bourgeois characteristic."[17]

What is now often called this "nihilistic attitude" toward ethics persisted in Soviet thought until the beginning of the 1960s, though grounds for overcoming it were laid somewhat earlier. Stalin's doctrine of the relative independence of the superstructure, stressed in his 1950 letters on linguistics, was a blow to "vulgar sociologism" generally; on its authority superstructural phenomena of all sorts could lay claim to independent treatment, and in 1955 Aleksandr Fedorovich Shishkin (1902–1977), soon to become one of the chief academic spokesmen for Soviet ethics, published a work entitled *Principles of Communist Morality*.[18] After Khrushchev's denunciation of Stalin at the twentieth Party congress in 1956, ethics participated in the widespread rejuvenation of scholarship in the Soviet Union. In 1959 the first course specifically devoted to ethics was introduced in some Soviet institutions of higher learning, and in 1960 the Central Committee issued a decree instructing pedagogical, medical, and agricultural institutes as well as universities to make available an optional course in "Principles of Marxist-Leninist Ethics."[19] The year 1960 also saw the publication of V. P. Tugarinov's *On the Values of Life and Culture*, the first Soviet work devoted to philosophical questions of value theory.[20]

There can be no doubt, however, that the new Party program adopted at the twenty-second Party congress in 1961 both established ethics firmly in the circle of Marxist-Leninist concerns and put an end to the long-standing view that morality is a purely class phenomenon. For the program at one stroke effected three significant innovations. First, it legitimized the notion of "communist morality" and specified the principles of that morality in the Moral Code of the Builder of Communism. Second, it returned to the long-scorned ideas of Plekhanov and Aksel'rod and accepted the existence of what it termed "elementary standards of morality and justice."

[16]Bandzeladze, *Aktual'nye problemy*, p. 138.
[17]Ibid., p. 487.
[18]A. F. Shishkin, *Osnovy kommunisticheskoi morali* (Moscow, 1955).
[19]S. Utkin, *Ocherki po marksistsko-leninskoi etike* (Moscow, 1962), p. 7; "Vsesoiuznaia nauchnaia konferentsiia po etike," *Filosofskie nauki*, 1975, no. 4, p. 157.
[20]V. P. Tugarinov, *O tsennostiakh zhizni i kul'tury* (Leningrad, 1960).

Communist morality, the program reads, "encompasses the fundamental norms of human morality which the masses of the people evolved in the course of millenniums as they fought against vice and social oppression." Third, it explained the political reason for the renewed official concern with morality—a reason that is the key to the broad and deep interest in the subject that continues to mark Soviet philosophy and ideology today. "In the course of [the] transition to communism," the program reads, "the moral principles of society become increasingly important; the sphere of action of the moral factor expands and the importance of the administrative control of human relations diminishes accordingly. The Party will encourage all forms of conscious civic self-discipline leading to the assertion and promotion of the basic rules of the communist way of life."[21] In other words, the effort is to be made as far as possible to replace legal compulsion with moral suasion as the regulator of behavior in Soviet society. Morality, it was decided, is the appropriate instrument of social control in a socialist order, and hence every effort must be made to strengthen its influence. Clearly the leadership recognized that the utility of concepts such as duty is too great to dismiss them as "bourgeois."

However narrowly functional this conception of morality, the importance it ascribes to the phenomenon provided the impetus and the opportunity for relatively lively and fertile development of ethical theory in the 1960s and early 1970s. An institutional understructure for work in the field was created by the establishment of a separate department (*kafedra*) of Marxist-Leninist ethics at Moscow State University and a corresponding section of ethics at the Institute of Philosophy of the Academy of Sciences. Much attention had to be devoted at first to locating the new branch of learning on the Marxist philosophical landscape and especially to distinguishing ethics as a "philosophical science" from the everyday morality that it proposed to study. A major part in this effort was played by a series of articles on the nature of ethics as a theoretical discipline published in *Filosofskie nauki* between 1961 and 1965; the series began with an article by Leonid Mikhailovich Arkhangel'skii (1925–1982) on the fundamental concepts of ethical philosophy, subsequently expanded into his influential book, *The Categories of Marxist Ethics* (1963).[22] Of course, substantive attention was given to the characteristics of morality as well; an early and enduring interest was the attempt to characterize the distinctive features of the *moral* consciousness as opposed to other forms of consciousness produced by social being. Concerning both these ques-

---

[21]*Road to Communism*, pp. 565–566.
[22]L. M. Arkhangel'skii, "Sushchnost' eticheskikh kategorii," *Filosofskie nauki*, 1961, no. 3, pp. 117–125; L. M. Arkhangel'skii, *Kategorii marksistskoi etiki* (Moscow, 1963).

tions—the nature of ethics and the nature of morality—disputes arose among Soviet philosophers as they groped for appropriately Marxist-Leninist analyses of the newly approved topics.[23]

Some of these analyses went remarkably far in testing the limits of the Marxist-Leninist tolerance of an independent ethics and of fundamental moral norms that are not class-based. For some writers, interested in the philosophy of Immanuel Kant or in the early writings of Marx, the identification of ethics as a separate study was an opportunity to recognize the autonomous demands of morality and to assert the supremacy of universal norms over all partisan or other socially imposed standards. The more adventurous and controversial philosophical productions of this first decade of ethical exploration in the USSR included a volume of essays edited by the Soviet Georgian philosopher Gela Doment'evich Bandzeladze in 1967. Entitled *Current Problems of Marxist Ethics*, the work brought together a number of lesser known ethical writers from various regions of the Soviet Union. V. S. Shtein contributed a detailed and sympathetic history of the concept of simple laws of morality and right, in which he vigorously defended Plekhanov and Aksel'rod against their detractors. P. M. Egides developed an analysis of Marxist morality in terms of the young Marx's concept of alienation; rejecting the official view that Soviet socialist society is free of alienation, Egides vigorously condemned as morally alienated themselves those "dogmatists [who] call their position partisan" as well as those who, although they claim to be against alienation and against a life lived "according to algorithms," are "afraid to come forward, afraid to open their mouths against the specific perpetrators of the algorithmization of man and against specific algorithms."[24]

From the point of view of basic ethical theory, however, the most unorthodox contributions to the Bandzeladze volume were those of Iakov Abramovich Mil'ner-Irinin, an older but previously unpublished philosopher who was the chief philosophy editor for the Nauka (Science) Press in Moscow, the publishing arm of the Soviet Academy of Sciences. In 1963 the Academy had distributed for purposes of discussion some sixty copies of a book-length manuscript by Mil'ner-Irinin entitled *Ethics; or, The Principles of True Humanity*; the manuscript was widely read and hotly debated by scholars, winning many partisans as well as many critics. When in the end the work was rejected for publication, Bandzeladze resolved to provide Mil'ner-Irinin with an outlet in the form of his 1967 volume, which was published in Tbilisi, Georgia. Calling Mil'ner-Irinin's work unparalleled in the Marxist ethical literature for "depth of thought, breadth

---

[23]For a detailed account of these discussions, see Grier, especially pp. 86–97.
[24]Bandzeladze, *Aktual'nye problemy*, pp. 106–107.

of erudition, comprehensiveness of exposition, and logical rigor of argumentation,"[25] Bandzeladze opened the volume with a lengthy essay by Mil'ner-Irinin and also included one chapter from the suppressed book.

For Mil'ner-Irinin, ethics is not a descriptive but a purely normative or prescriptive science—the "science of what ought to be" (*nauka o dolzhnom*), as his 1967 essay is titled. He presents his ethical system in the form of a set of ten principles or imperatives, which he considers to be absolute, categorical commands, valid throughout the universe, and which express what he describes alternatively as the essence of morality or the "principles of true humanity." There is little in common between Mil'ner-Irinin's principles and the Moral Code of the Builder of Communism, for instead of a teleological social service ethic Mil'ner-Irinin presents a Kantian, deontological ethic of conscience concerned not with the social consequences of actions but with the moral worth of their motives. Hence his first principle is not "devotion to the cause of communism" but rather what he calls "the principle of conscience," which requires a person always to be true to his or her own moral convictions. This fundamental command is supplemented by such other imperatives as "the principle of self-perfection," which requires the individual to become a person ("for man is not born ready-made but forms himself all his life"); "the principle of good," which requires the individual to create value in both the natural and the social worlds; and "the principle of nobility," which commands the individual to use only worthy means in the pursuit of worthy ends.[26] Mil'ner-Irinin does not entirely ignore the building of communism, for he includes among his principles the duty to labor and the duty to fight for and to protect "social ownership of the means of production"; he even goes so far as to say that the working class is "the only bearer and creator of a consistently revolutionary, universally human morality in the present day."[27] Furthermore, he purports to derive his imperatives not directly from man's rational nature (as Kant did) but from man's social nature.[28] But despite these concessions to orthodox Marxist ideas, Mil'ner-Irinin's uncompromising insistence on the categorical authority of the personal conscience and his refusal to subordinate individual autonomy to any social goal were bound to evoke official disapproval. Nowhere in the Moral Code of the Builder of Communism is there anything resembling Mil'ner-Irinin's "principle of freedom," which requires each person to preserve

---

[25]Ibid., p. 11.
[26]Ibid., pp. 43, 45, 50.
[27]Ibid., pp. 47, 36.
[28]Ibid., p. 20.

inner, spiritual independence; "there is no viler crime against human conscience," he writes, "than spiritual (moral) slavery."[29]

The storm of controversy created by the contributions of Mil'ner-Irinin
and others to the Bandzeladze volume culminated in a two-day "discussion" in Moscow in February 1968 designed to allow the ethics establishment of the Institute of Philosophy to rein in the outsiders. Mil'ner-Irinin
was subjected to the most severe attacks, being accused not only of heresy
but of philosophical incompetence, religious leanings, and a literary style
borrowed from Ecclesiastes. But Egides, Shtein, and Bandzeladze himself
were also castigated for seeking to present a "new direction" in ethical
thought based on Mil'ner-Irinin's conceptions—this at about the same
time, it will be remembered, that the "new current" in historiography was
being discussed in other philosophical circles in the USSR. A few of the
conference participants defended the authors, but most agreed with M. G.
Zhuravkov, head of the institute's Section of Ethics, that the accused had
presented views that were not simply questionable but also egregiously
non-Marxist and that therefore must be opposed "militantly, from Party
positions."[30]

The crux of the doctrinal critique, as Zhuravkov summarized it, consisted in the fact that the champions of the new direction treated the simple,
common norms of morality "abstractly" and in so doing departed from
Marxism on two counts. First, they ignored the class character of morality.
"Marxism considers that the proletariat works out its own, historically
higher type of morality," Zhuravkov is reported as saying; "whereas Mil'ner
considers the proletariat only a 'bearer' of a universal, timeless, and 'eternal' morality, intended for all rational creatures of all worlds." "Such
fantasies," Zhuravkov went on, "can bring nothing but harm." Second,
the new direction was said to contradict Marxist historicism, which demands "historical concreteness" in the treatment of all concepts. Conscience, for example, can be dealt with only in particular historical contexts;
there is no such thing as "an autonomous conscience dependent on nothing."[31] As for Egides's comments about alienation and the "algorithmization" of man, A. F. Shishkin complains that they could be interpreted
as implying that alienation will persist under socialism as long as "discipline" is present. But since discipline will always be necessary in society,
Shishkin asserts, Egides's conception is a misunderstanding of the Marxist
view of alienation, "a confusion that only disorients the reader." Critic
after critic expressed righteous horror at the departures from Marxist

[29]Ibid., p. 49.
[30]N. A. Golovko and V. S. Markov, "Za nauchnost' i konkretnost' v razrabotke problem
etiki," *Voprosy filosofii*, 1968, no. 8, p. 148.
[31]Ibid., p. 155.

"methodological unity" exhibited in the Bandzeladze volume. "The right to seek is the right of every scholar," stated one speaker; "but apparently not everyone looks where he should and finds what he should."[32]

Clearly the question of the relation of the classless "simple norms" to the Marxist class conception of morality could not be approached with the freewheeling preference for the former that had been displayed by some of the Bandzeladze volume authors. Timing was also significant in deciding their fate, as in 1968 it could not have escaped notice that some of their ideas paralleled those of the "Prague spring." Indeed Shtein was speaking in the very idiom of the Czech liberals when he wrote that the simple moral norms must be acknowledged by "everyone who wishes to preserve his human face," and there was little doubt whom Egides had in mind when he praised "creative Marxists" and called for "the deepest and broadest democracy in all spheres of our life."[33] Greater caution was needed, with less enthusiasm for the simple norms.

Dogmatism and the Turn to Practice in the 1970s

Condemnation of the Bandzeladze volume did not cut off theoretical development in Soviet ethics; the importance attributed to the field was by then too great. But after 1968 two different but often intersecting trends are observable in Soviet ethical philosophy. On the one hand, the continuing specialization in ethics on the part of some Soviet philosophers and their increasing knowledge of the world literature in the field made possible the appearance of sophisticated theoretical studies. Among the more impressive are the influential works produced in the short career of Oleg Grigor'evich Drobnitskii (1933–1973), whose studies in the logical structure of the moral consciousness contain echoes of Hegel's *Phenomenology of Mind*.[34] On the other hand, there were continuing and increasing efforts in the Soviet philosophical and ideological communities to tie Marxist-Leninist ethics more firmly to the principles of the social service morality enunciated in the Moral Code of the Builder of Communism, and in this connection greater attention was urged to the practical aspects of ethics

[32]Ibid., pp. 149, 151.
[33]Bandzeladze, *Aktual'nye problemy*, pp. 156, 106, 105.
[34]O. G. Drobnitskii's essays on the moral consciousness, as well as other writings, are collected in the posthumous volume *Problemy nravstvennosti* (Moscow, 1977). For discussions of Drobnitskii's ethical theory, see Grier, especially pp. 86–97 and 191–213; and Peter Ehlen, "Emancipation through Morality: New Paths of Ethical Thought in the Soviet Union," *Studies in Soviet Thought* 13 (1973), pp. 210–216.

and the function of morality in contemporary socialist life. Ironically, Drobnitskii's own theoretical work fell in with this practical spirit. For Drobnitskii, who opposed the "reflection" orthodoxy according to which morality is simply a form of consciousness derivative from social being, laid great stress on the active role of morality as a regulator of behavior—"one of the basic methods for the normative regulation of the actions of man in society," in his words.[35] And although Drobnitskii himself, like Mil'ner-Irinin, sought a basis for moral imperatives in the essential nature of man, apart from the actual standards of any particular social order, his conception of morality as a regulating force has been welcomed by those concerned with the uses of morality as an instrument of social control in Soviet society.[36]

Another theorist whose works are valued for the same reason is Aleksandr Ivanovich Titarenko, head of the Department of Marxist-Leninist Ethics at Moscow State University, who, with the passing of Shishkin, Drobnitskii, and most recently Arkhangel'skii, has become the most prominent ethical philosopher in the USSR. Titarenko, like Drobnitskii, has devoted much attention to the analysis of moral consciousness, but his study has concentrated on the use of historical and anthropological data as opposed to the primarily conceptual analysis of Drobnitskii; Titarenko has, in other words, stressed more the second half of the Hegelian "unity of the logical and the historical." In this connection he has written extensively on the topic of moral progress.[37] With regard to the nature of morality, Titarenko borrows an expression from Marx's *Grundrisse* and defines morality broadly as a method of "appropriating the world" practically and spiritually; he emphasizes the many functions that morality performs in human society: it is educative, motivational, communicative, and much else.[38] Basic to all these functions, however, is the regulative role of morality: distinguishing it from scientific and artistic ways of dealing with the world, Titarenko writes that morality is "an evaluative-imperative mode of appropriating reality that *regulates* the behavior of people from the point of view of the opposition of *good* and *evil*."[39] Hence Titarenko's

---

[35]Drobnitskii, *Problemy nravstvennosti*, p. 17.

[36]See, for example, V. T. Ganzhin and Iu. V. Sogomonov, "Sotsial'noe upravlenie i moral'. Issledovatel'skie perspektivy," *Filosofskie nauki*, 1980, no. 5, pp. 11–12; and V. I. Bakshtanovskii et al., eds., *Nauchnoe upravlenie nravstvennymi protsessami i etiko-prikladnye issledovaniia* (Novosibirsk, 1980), pp. 11–14, 17.

[37]Titarenko, *Nravstvennyi progress*; A. I. Titarenko, *Struktury nravstvennogo soznaniia. Opyt etiko-filosofskogo issledovaniia* (Moscow, 1974). For a discussion of Titarenko's ethical theory, see Grier, especially pp. 95–97 and 163–166.

[38]Titarenko, *Marksistskaia etika*, pp. 90, 93; for the source of the expression in Marx, see Karl Marx, *Grundrisse. Foundations of the Critique of Political Economy (Rough Draft)*, trans. Martin Nicolaus (London, 1973), p. 101.

[39]Titarenko, *Marksistskaia etika*, p. 90 (italics in original).

conception, too, lends itself to practical application in the work of social control. One recent writer recommends Titarenko's model of morality for its applicability to "formulating general social codes of morals, planning societywide ideological activities, and in general all those social influences on man that carry a charge of evaluative conviction."[40]

The views of philosophers, of course, are not the principal stimuli for what Arkhangel'skii called in 1981 the "development of the applied regions of ethical knowledge" in the contemporary period.[41] Political, not theoretical, developments initiated and have sustained the new emphasis, prompted by the increasing official desire to mobilize the resources of morality to support public policy and encourage productive labor. The proceedings of Communist party congresses tell the story here as in the even more sensitive area of social and political thought. "It has become a tradition," Arkhangel'skii remarked ingenuously in 1981, "that Party congresses determine the basic landmarks for the development of Soviet social science, and this applies fully to ethical science."[42] The twenty-fourth congress in 1971 gave explicit attention to moral aspects of the "molding of the new man"; a prime task of the Party, Brezhnev affirmed, was to continue improving the "moral atmosphere" and to make ideology active to the point that it "determines the norms" of people's everyday behavior; particularly must it foster a communist attitude toward labor.[43] At the twenty-fifth congress five years later, Brezhnev inveighed against "scholastic theorizing" and stressed the urgent need to "raise the effectiveness of science" by linking it more closely with practice. He singled out moral education for special attention, assigning it the specific task of producing what he called "an active life position" on the part of individuals—meaning a condition in which people not only recognize the demands of communist morality (always including the demand to *labor*) but actually carry them out.[44] Given these prominent "landmarks," it is not surprising that Soviet ethical philosophers have busied themselves with the practical concerns of moral training and have adopted functional conceptions not only of morality but of ethics itself. Soviet ethics in the 1970s, in other words, was presented with a demand for "the unity of theory and practice" not unlike the demand presented to philosophy in general by Stalin in the 1930s.

On the theoretical side this situation has meant retreat into the conven-

---

[40]Bakshtanovskii, *Nauchnoe upravlenie*, p. 17.

[41]L. M. Arkhangel'skii, "Aktual'nye problemy marksistskoi etiki," *Voprosy filosofii*, 1981, no. 1, pp. 39–40.

[42]Ibid., p. 39.

[43]*Report of the CPSU Central Committee to the Twenty-fourth Congress of the Communist Party of the Soviet Union* (Moscow, 1971), pp. 97, 99.

[44]*Materialy XXV s"ezda KPSS* (Moscow, 1977), pp. 73, 77.

tional, trustworthy conceptions of class morality and socioeconomic determination. The notion that there are moral norms that are valid in all
community life is not rejected; but neither is it emphasized, and great care
is taken in discussing it. Characteristically, Titarenko criticizes Bandzeladze
for giving too much attention to the common norms in his discussion of
moral progress, and Shishkin in turn finds even Titarenko's conception
too "abstract."[45] Any suggestion that the common norms—or any other
moral values or traits—may be genetically rather than socially based is
vigorously opposed; in a kind of latter-day Lysenkoism, modern theories
of bioethics are rejected out of hand by Marxist-Leninist ethical philosophers. Early in the 1970s some Soviet scientists created a stir by arguing
that there is natural selection in human populations for humane characteristics such as altruism and that criminal tendencies may have genetic
roots.[46] But at a conference in 1972 designed to quell such notions, the
philosophers gave familiar dogmatic responses: the biogenetic account of
moral traits, several affirmed, is a mere "hypothesis," whereas the social
determination of morality is "a theory advanced by Marxism and confirmed by history."[47]

Nor can it be said that feminist conceptions—to take another example
of new developments in world ethics—have penetrated the shell of Soviet
moral philosophy. Inconsistently with their opposition to genetic determinism (but in deep accordance with conservatism of another kind) Soviet
philosophers assume that there are biological grounds for morally relevant
differences between the sexes. The current most widely used Soviet textbook in ethics, Titarenko's *Marxist Ethics*, mentions not only physical
strength but "strength of will" as among the "advantages given by nature"
to males, and the book counts as appropriately feminine such virtues as
modesty and the avoidance of "undue familiarity" (*razviaznost'*).[48]

In practice, the energies of Soviet ethical philosophers have been ab-
sorbed increasingly by the effort to popularize and to promote the effectiveness of the social service ethic as enunciated in the Moral Code of the
Builder of Communism. Much of this activity is devoted to moral education
in its traditional form—that is, in the form of instruction in academic
institutions. The course "Fundamentals of Marxist-Leninist Ethics" is now
obligatory in higher educational institutions in a number of Soviet repub-

---

[45]Titarenko, *Nravstvennyi progress*, p. 150; A. F. Shishkin, "On Some Problems of Research in the Field of Ethics (Reflections on Reading the Literature on Ethics)," *Soviet Studies
in Philosophy* 12 (Winter 1973–1974), pp. 25–26.
[46]See, for example, V. P. Efroimson, "Rodoslovnaia al'truizma (Etika s pozitsii evoliu-
tsionnoi genetiki cheloveka)," *Novyi mir*, 1971, no. 10, pp. 193–213.
[47]"Vstrecha etikov i genetikov v MGU," *Vestnik Moskovskogo universiteta. Seriia 8.
Filosofiia*, 1972, no. 5, p. 98.
[48]Titarenko, *Marksistskaia etika*, pp. 267–268.

lics, including Georgia and Belorussia, and formal moral training has also been introduced experimentally in many middle and elementary schools throughout the USSR.[49] Attention is also given to extending moral instruction beyond the schools to other institutions, from the Young Pioneers to the Red Army. Special efforts are made to reach workers on the job, where it is hoped that moral improvement will be manifested in the growth of a communist attitude toward labor; in 1979, the first secretary of the Stavropol' district committee of the Communist party reported that in the course of two years, some five thousand lectures on moral themes had been delivered to the toilers at various workplaces in his district.[50] All Soviet philosophers are expected to take part in this work of raising the communist consciousness of the laboring masses, but the obligation presently lies most heavily on the ethical philosophers, in view of the great importance attributed by the leadership to the internalization of moral norms. Attention to this special responsibility, no doubt, accounts for the fact that, since 1974, when "socialist competition" in extracurricular lecturing and other public service activities was first instituted among the fourteen departments of the philosophy faculty of Moscow State University, the Department of Marxist-Leninist Ethics has won the competition in every year but 1975, when it slipped to second place.[51]

More than instruction, however, is included in the practical work of forming the communist moral consciousness. Within the past few years Soviet ethical philosophers have developed the notion of moral "management" (upravlenie) or "regulation" (reguliatsiia) as a broader strategy of which moral education is only a part. Morality, a social regulator, is itself subject to regulation by social means, Titarenko affirms, and he argues that it behooves society—led by the Communist party, of course—to make conscious and "scientific" use, for the purpose of moral betterment, of all "institutions, organizations, and persons" that can contribute to such betterment.[52] "The science of management," another author writes recently, is called upon to "establish a system of the most effective mechanisms which can, by influencing the moral life of society and the individual under definite circumstances, impart to that life the needed parameters and characteristics."[53]

Such statements may suggest a more thoroughgoing control than is in

[49]Ibid., p. 247; "Vsesoiuznaia nauchnaia konferentsiia po etike," p. 161.

[50]V. N. Sevruk, ed., Voprosy partiinogo rukovodstva nravstvennym vospitaniem (Moscow, 1979), p. 70.

[51]S. F. Anisimov and B. O. Nikolaichev, "Moscow University's Department of Marxist-Leninist Ethics: A Decade of Teaching and Socio-political Activity," Soviet Studies in Philosophy 19 (Spring 1981), p. 98.

[52]Titarenko, Marksistskaia etika, pp. 242–243.

[53]L. M. Arkhangel'skii, ed., Metodologiia eticheskikh issledovanii (Moscow, 1982), p. 331.

fact envisaged by Soviet theorists, however, for the "mechanisms" actually discussed in the growing literature in this field are relatively benign. One that is receiving major attention currently is the promulgation of codes of professional ethics for different occupational groups.[54] By far the principal concern in this literature is the question of how to generate an "active life position" in the quite specific sense of how to make people work harder. Thus a book with the sweeping title *Problems of the Party Management of Moral Training* (1979) is devoted almost entirely to the relative merits of different systems of worker competition ("a moral stimulus to labor") and of different types of rewards for successful performance; it conveys such information as the fact that the title "Shock Worker of Communist Labor," which workers in Tula consider the highest honor, ranks only seventh among effective stimuli in Turkmenia, where being featured on the Honor Board as a "Victor of Socialist Competition" is much preferred.[55] This is not to say, of course, that other forms of moral management are ruled out, for the same book recommends using "all the means at our disposal, including the public opinion of the collective, the critical voice of the press, methods of persuasion, and the force of law" to correct moral shortcomings.[56]

Thus although ethics is now firmly established as a separate philosophical discipline in the USSR, dogmatism reigns in the field and concern for questions of basic theory has largely given way to preoccupation with the social management of morality and to the actual conduct of such management through educative and other practical activities. Unlike the situation in Soviet philosophy of history, where the "new current" remains clearly discernible in a number of studies, in ethics the "new direction" sought by some philosophers in the 1960s has all but disappeared amid the intense official concern for the authority and the functional role of communist morality in developed socialist society. When a heretical view does surface, as still happens from time to time, it comes from someone outside the ethics establishment and is quickly put down. A striking instance occurred in 1982 when a highly unorthodox book on moral philosophy was published by Iurii Nikolaevich Davydov, a writer noted for his studies in the philosophy of culture and in contemporary Western, "bourgeois" philosophy. Entitled *The Ethics of Love and the Metaphysics of Self-Will* and issued in an edition of 50,000 copies by the Molodaia Gvardiia (Young Guard) publishing house, Davydov's book entirely ig-

---

[54]See, for example, "Issledovaniia v oblasti marksistsko-leninskoi etiki," *Voprosy filosofii*, 1977, no. 8, p. 140; and "Ethics and Morality Studies: A Soviet Discussion," *Soviet Studies in Philosophy* 21 (Fall 1982), p. 18.

[55]Sevruk, p. 188.

[56]Ibid., p. 5.

nores the commonplaces of Marxist-Leninist ethics and urges its young readers to seek the answer to their search for the meaning of life in the moral values defended by Dostoevskii and Tolstoi. Davydov argues not only for the importance of acknowledging moral absolutes in general but for the specific absolutes of love and self-sacrifice advanced by the great Russian novelists, despite the standard Soviet rejection of their ethical views as religious and perniciously utopian.

> Is the "moral idealism" of Tolstoi and Dostoevskii really so impractical, so fantastic, and so divorced from life? [Davydov writes] Does not this "idealism" contain far more real knowledge of man, of human nature, and of history than that Nietzschean "realism" that could only have been a product of madness?...Against this background, does not Russian moral philosophy, with its "idealistic" faith in the immutability of moral absolutes, appear not only reasonable but far more realistic?[57]

The Communist party journal *Kommunist* replied promptly with a blistering attack on Davydov, to whom it attributed a litany of offenses including "utterly abandon[ing] the class approach to morality," failing to note "the untenability of the religious understanding of morality," and presuming to write a book of moral philosophy containing "not one word about the communist ideal or communist morality." Publication of the work by Molodaia Gvardiia, the journal concluded, was "a serious ideological error"[58]—the like of which, we may venture, will not soon happen again.

Critical Questions in Soviet Ethical Theory

The great emphasis on the inculcation of communist morality does not, of course, alter the fact that the basic theory behind it—the theory of Marxist-Leninist ethics as expounded in the first section of this chapter—continues to be taken seriously by Soviet philosophers, who offer it as an objectively grounded, philosophically defensible account of morality. Ever since the promulgation of the Moral Code of the Builder of Communism, however, certain questions have persistently been raised about this theory by Western critics. One question is made all the more pressing by the stress

---

[57]Iu. Davydov, *Etika liubvi i metafizika svoevoliia (problemy nravstvennoi filosofii)* (Moscow, 1982), p. 262.

[58]R. Petropavlovskii, "Po povodu odnoi knigi," *Kommunist*, 1983, no. 8, pp. 106, 112, 114.

on moral engineering in recent years: Are not individuality and personal freedom sacrificed when devotion to a social cause is made the supreme principle of morality? The contention that individuals may be "managed" to make them put the interests of society above their own interests strikes many observers as an assault on morality, not its highest expression. A second question has to do with the relation between "devotion to communism" and other moral values. Despite the official recognition of standards common to all community life, such as truth-telling and refraining from injuring others, does not the great emphasis placed on the "cause" of social transformation mean that no other values may stand in its way? Is not the Soviet philosopher, then, still committed to the maxim that the end justifies the means? Third, on what ground is the supreme value of "devotion to communism" established? Soviet philosophers contend that "communist morality" is objectively superior to any other, but what is the proof of that contention?

Soviet philosophers in the post-Stalin period have generally recognized their intellectual obligation to respond to such questions, and indeed they are constantly urged by political leaders to do so as part of the "ideological struggle" with the West. An appropriate way to evaluate current Marxist-Leninist ethical theory, then, is to consider the reasonableness and the adequacy of the responses that Soviet philosophers make to these crucial questions.

Is the Individual Enslaved to Society?

Soviet writers now frequently acknowledge that an apparent problem does exist with respect to the relations of society and the individual in Marxist-Leninist ethics, given the talk of social management of the standards and behavior of the individual.[59] But the appearance is deceiving, we are told: there is actually no conflict between the communist social service ethic and the legitimate moral demands of the individual.

A facile "resolution" of the apparent problem consists in the contention that there can be no subjection of the individual to society inasmuch as the interests of the individual, correctly understood, are identical with those of society.[60] This response is now rarely given by Soviet writers, who generally agree that although such an identity is a desirable future condition, it does not prevail in the imperfect present. It is acknowledged, for

[59]Titarenko, *Marksistskaia etika*, pp. 242–243.
[60]See, for example, S. F. Anisimov, "O kriterii kommunisticheskoi nravstvennosti," *Vestnik Moskovskogo universiteta. Seriia 8. Filosofiia*, 1966, no. 6, p. 28.

one thing, that individuals may well fail to understand that their "true" interests coincide with society's; and some theorists go further and suggest that the two sets of interests can never coincide fully.[61] In either case a gap between individual and society is admitted, and the question arises of how it may be overcome morally.

A few Soviet philosophers simply dismiss the question with the pronouncement that the individual must yield to society because the latter has greater moral worth. S. F. Anisimov minced no words in 1966 when he wrote that "in the hierarchy of values, the existence of human society has a higher value than that of the separate individual."[62] Even a writer with the independent inclinations of a Bandzeladze was willing in his textbook *Ethics* to call the individual a *means* to the well-being of society:

> The Soviet citizen sees the happiness of society as the highest goal of his life, and that does not mean that he considers concern for society's happiness to be a means of achieving his own. If my highest ideal is the happiness of society, then that is my *goal, not a means*.... The recognition of society as a goal implies regarding oneself as a means. Moral duty requires the subordination of personal interests to society. In relation to society, the individual cannot but regard himself as a means.[63]

Statements like these, of course, provoke the critical questions in the first place, and most Soviet philosophers do not regard them as adequate responses.

The great majority of ethical writers in the Soviet Union, although fully accepting what Arkhangel'skii calls "the principle of the priority of social over personal interests,"[64] argue not that individuals are subordinate instruments of lesser value than society but that individuals are free and morally worthy agents who have, however, a moral obligation to make the interests of society their own. In this view, promoting the well-being of society is an objective duty that individuals can be educated to recognize and to fulfill voluntarily, and it is no diminution of their moral stature or their freedom to be aided in this endeavor by social agencies. The important distinction, it is said, is not between freedom and moral management—which are considered to be fully compatible—but between both and *ma-*

[61]Titarenko, *Marksistskaia etika*, pp. 220–221.
[62]Anisimov, "O kriterii," p. 28.
[63]G. D. Bandzeladze, *Etika. Opyt izlozheniia sistemy marksistskoi etiki*, 2d ed. (Tbilisi, 1970), pp. 229–230 (italics in original).
[64]Arkhangel'skii, *Metodologiia*, p. 362.

nipulation (manipul'iatsiia). Although no ready definition of 'manipulation' is provided by those who urge this distinction, it is typically coupled in Soviet writings with the control of behavior by *command*, as presumably a mode of influence that operates against the will of the subject.[65] Management, on the other hand, is presented as merely a deliberate means of guiding what takes place informally in any event; all social changes create changes in moral consciousness, Titarenko asserts, and through moral management it is possible to plan such changes as are morally desirable.[66] Furthermore, management is conceived as a mode not so much of operating on individuals directly as of altering the circumstances in which they exist and act. Titarenko in *Marxist Ethics* provides a characterization that has won wide acceptance among Soviet philosophers: moral management, he writes, means "the development of the conditions needed for the free moral creativity of the individual."[67]

Lest this apparent concern for the autonomy of the moral person remove the sting from moral management altogether, however, it is well to remember what the term 'freedom' means to the Marxist-Leninist philosopher. As the recognition of necessity, freedom does not require the existence of a range of alternatives among which individuals choose in accordance with their inclinations or convictions; it consists, rather, in the acknowledgment of an objective standard and the putting of one's own desires and actions in line with that standard. "Freedom of moral choice," Titarenko writes, "is the capacity to make a decision on conduct in accordance with recognized historical necessity, which takes the form of moral necessity."[68] Hence freedom and the acceptance of objective, morally relevant standards are one and the same thing: "Man is morally right *and free*," we read in a recent work, "only when the direction of his thoughts and acts coincides with the objective logic of social development."[69] Nor should Titarenko's use of the term 'creativity' be taken too seriously, given that the moral values that the individual is obliged to acknowledge are set independently of his will and consciousness. Creating the conditions for "free moral creativity," then, comes down to creating conditions not for autonomous choice but for the recognition and acceptance of the prescribed morality, and hence moral management is clearly compatible with heavy doses of indoctrination and in general a wide variety of social influences aimed at producing moral rectitude. In effect Soviet philosophers resolve the ques-

[65]Titarenko, *Marksistskaia etika*, p. 243; Sevruk, p. 107.
[66]Titarenko, *Marksistskaia etika*, p. 243.
[67]Ibid.; see also Ganzhin and Sogomonov, p. 5.
[68]Titarenko, *Marksistskaia etika*, p. 128 (italics omitted).
[69]N. M. Kozhanov, *Nravstvennye printsipy kommunista* (Moscow, 1979), p. 7 (italics added).

tion of the subjection of the individual to social control by employing a conception of freedom that not only permits but requires such subjection.

The best that can be said for the Soviet conception of moral freedom is that it preserves the element of *voluntariness* essential to standard non-Marxist definitions of freedom and presupposes that the "conditions" moral management seeks to bring about are *social* in character. Not simply the *doing* of what is right but the recognition *that* it is right and the consequent voluntary decision to do it are needed before morality can function as a social regulator that will replace the force of law. Thus, contrary to an otherwise analogous notion of moral freedom advanced by Jean-Jacques Rousseau, in the Soviet conception I cannot be forced to be free; I can only be strongly urged to choose freedom—that is, to accept my moral duties to society—voluntarily. Furthermore, in keeping with the broader principles of historical materialism, the mechanisms employed for encouraging that voluntary acceptance are limited to *social* influences and conditions. Thus when we read such chilling assertions as that moral management must be "comprehensive, systematic, and grounded on scientific principles" and that the Communist party must seek "optimal means for the subjection of personal to social interests,"[70] we can be assured that Soviet *philosophers*, at least, are not referring to genetic engineering or chemical treatment of the water supply.

Of course the yoke of society is yoke enough, particularly since it seeks to effect the acceptance not only of moral duties but of a corresponding conception of individual happiness as well. "Society tells the individual in what it is necessary to see happiness," students at Moscow State University are informed in their lectures in ethics.[71] Perhaps the most dangerous aspect of the notion of freedom that permits such statements is that it defines no sphere of individual life to which the influence of society must *not* extend. It identifies no realm of freedom *apart* from society and its norms, no preserve for individual privacy, or what Richard De George has called "interiority."[72] It is a telling fact that, for all its emphasis on moral duties, Marxist-Leninist ethics contains no mention of duties *to oneself*. References to individual "rights" in the Soviet literature are seldom found, and where they do occur they are invariably canceled out by reminders of social duties.[73]

Only a conception of moral freedom that disengaged freedom from socially defined obligations could allow a real sphere of individual rights and hence provide some assurance that the individual is not in fact enslaved

---

[70]Titarenko, *Marksistskaia etika*, pp. 243–244 (italics omitted).
[71]Volchenko, p. 67.
[72]De George, *Soviet Ethics and Morality*, pp. 101–103.
[73]See, for example, Sevruk, p. 107.

to social interests. Such an alternative view has rarely been expressed in the Soviet philosophical literature, however. Mil'ner-Irinin suggested one in the 1960s. Egides, too, was appealing to another conception of freedom when, contrasting creative with dogmatic Marxism, he wrote that "the crying, unmitigated contradiction of the dogmatists consists in their desire to create a free society with spiritually and politically unfree people."[74] But neither writer was permitted to explore these alternatives further. It is ironic that when Egides was dismissed from his academic position, arrested, and forced to emigrate in 1980, the charge against him was that he had performed the "amoral act" of resorting to an underground journal to press his case for freedom and democratic reforms.[75]

Does the End Justify the Means?

Heavy emphasis on devotion to the cause of communism, coupled with Lenin's pronouncements on revolutionary morality, has left Soviet ethics open in the past to the charge of disregarding basic moral norms in the relentless pursuit of a social goal. Is this charge still legitimate, now that Soviet orthodoxy recognizes not only the moral value of communism but also "elementary standards of morality and justice"? Soviet philosophers say no, claiming that the identification of Marxist-Leninist ethics with the view that the end justifies the means is "a favorite subject of anticommunist fabrication."[76]

On its face, Lenin's dictum that what serves to destroy the old order and promote communism is moral would appear to mean that the very fact of serving to advance the communist cause *makes* a course of action moral, or in other words that *any* means found effective in promoting the goal are morally permissible. Soviet philosophers today, however, reject the notion that a worthy end justifies *whatever* means may be used in its service—a notion that, following Plekhanov, they call "jesuitism."[77] Anisimov, indeed, has argued that some means—an example he offers is that of nuclear war—are unconditionally unacceptable and hence could not be redeemed by any end whatever.[78] Although most Soviet philosophers are unwilling to go so far, there is seemingly unanimous agreement among them that the morality of means as well as of ends must be considered in making moral decisions and that the immorality of the means employed

[74]Bandzeladze, *Aktual'nye problemy*, p. 106.
[75]*A Chronicle of Current Events* 53 (1980), p. 68.
[76]"Vsesoiuznaia nauchnaia konferentsiia po etike," p. 162.
[77]G. V. Plekhanov, *Sochineniia*, 24 vols. (Moscow, 1923–1927), vol. 15, p. 127.
[78]S. F. Anisimov, *Moral' i povedenie* (Moscow, 1979), p. 66.

can diminish the moral value of an end in view to the point of destroying it.[79] As a general principle, then, Soviet philosophers no longer subscribe to the Leninist maxim if the latter is taken to signify that the morality of means may simply be disregarded as long as they are effective in promoting a worthy goal.

At the same time, Soviet philosophers also reject what they consider to be the error at the other extreme from jesuitism—namely, the view that means immoral in themselves may never be used for any end, however important. Calling this view "abstract humanism," they denounce not only the most illustrious example of it in Russian thought—Leo Tolstoi's doctrine of nonviolence—but also any more modern teaching that limits the choice of means to those that are moral in abstraction from the uses to which they are put, such as Mil'ner-Irinin's "law of nobility."[80] To adopt such a limitation, they argue, would be to give up the good that can on balance be achieved, under certain circumstances, by accepting departures from ordinary morality. Thus, Titarenko maintains, there are situations in which violence is the only appropriate moral response, for to renounce it would "destroy the possibility of good and bring about evil."[81]

The path between the two extremes of jesuitism and abstract humanism, according to Soviet philosophers, lies in recognizing the interdependence of means and ends in actual situations and in specifying what an appropriate relationship between them is. The ethical inseparability of the two categories must be acknowledged, it is held; Titarenko, recasting an epigram of Kant's, writes, "Ends without means are empty, means without ends are blind."[82] But what is a morally appropriate relationship between the two? The end must be a morally good one, of course, and the means must be effective—that is, they must be sufficient to produce the desired end. But in the event that these effective means are in themselves morally bad—because, for example, they contravene one or more of the "simple standards of human morality" such as truth-telling or respect for others— Soviet philosophers are now generally agreed that an additional test must be applied: are the means indispensable for the production of a balance of good in the situation? Is the agent confronted with the choice of either renouncing his moral goal or employing the means in question? Evil means, in other words, must be unavoidable as well as adequate in order to be morally permissible. The simple question to be asked of every means then,

---

[79]Ibid.; Titarenko, *Marksistskaia etika*, pp. 141–143.
[80]Bandzeladze, *Aktual'nye problemy*, p. 50.
[81]Titarenko, *Marksistskaia etika*, p. 144.
[82]Ibid.

according to V. I. Bakshtanovskii, is this: "Is it *necessary* and *sufficient* for the attainment of the moral end?"[83] As applied to the end of communism, the principal difference between this test and the original Leninist formula is that the latter required only sufficiency: whatever was effective in promoting communism was thereby declared moral. By adding the requirement of necessity, Soviet philosophers have adopted a weaker, less Machiavellian formula.

We may well wonder, however, whether the practical significance of this change is as clear-cut as the theoretical distinction. For everything now depends on what is considered necessary for the promotion of communism. Soviet writers regularly and loudly disclaim the use of murder, treachery, sabotage, and other terrorist tactics either domestically or in international relations; such "unprincipled" means are said to be incompatible with "proletarian morality."[84] Anisimov is even on record as asserting that "only morally valuable behavior can serve the cause of building communism."[85] These statements are invariably qualified, however, by acknowledgments that violence and deception, for example, are not unconditionally prohibited and that their use is sometimes unavoidable. The workers and their parties must not be "excessively delicate and overscrupulous," Anisimov himself goes on to state, when a reactionary force "comes forth against the achievements of the revolution with weapon in hand and resorts to terror and repression against the people."[86] Because communism is, as Titarenko writes, "the objectively highest aim,"[87] other values may be sacrificed to it so long as that is necessary. Titarenko makes the point by drawing a distinction between moral *norms*, which have "no independent sense" and the binding force of which depends upon circumstances, and moral *principles*, which are unconditionally obligatory:

> In virtue of the concrete character of norms, deviation from them in certain situations is not only permissible but necessary. For example, the demand to tell the truth does not mean that we must reveal secrets to an enemy. Moral principles, on the other hand, because of their generalized form, have a relative independence in relation to the diversity of empirical situations. It is impossible, for example, under any circumstances to justify departure from a moral principle such as devotion to the cause of communism.[88]

---

[83]Bandzeladze, *Aktual'nye problemy*, p. 243 (italics in original); see also Titarenko, *Marksistskaia etika*, p. 143.

[84]Anisimov, *Moral' i povedenie*, p. 73; see also A. F. Shishkin, *Osnovy marksistskoi etiki* (Moscow, 1961), p. 195.

[85]Anisimov, *Moral' i povedenie*, p. 135.

[86]Ibid., pp. 73–74.

[87]Titarenko, *Marksistskaia etika*, p. 141 (italics omitted).

[88]Ibid., p. 184.

Despite the moral primacy thus given to the promotion of communism, it would be a mistake to conclude that Soviet philosophers attribute no real significance to the "simple standards" or any other moral values. Some writers, it is true, do suggest that the worth of the ultimate goal is so great that it can transform means that would otherwise be evil into positive goods. When there is no alternative but abandoning the valuable end, Bakshtanovskii writes, then the available means is "necessary, moral, and man is obliged to use it."[89] Other writers, however, stress the notion that a morally bad means remains an evil, albeit a necessary one, and that its use is regrettable and fraught with danger. When we must use bad means we are forced, Titarenko writes, to make a "moral compromise," and he warns that then the risks of becoming immoral are very great. He argues that it is essential under such circumstances to remain aware of the fact that our moral choice has required "the suspension of a certain value in the name of a higher value," so that we will be alive to the need to limit the negative consequences of such a choice to a minimum. "The role of the 'least evil' in such situations," he writes, "is to eliminate the necessity of resorting to it in the future."[90] Clearly, Titarenko and others are aware of the possible abuse of the "necessity" requirement.

In summary, Soviet philosophers do not accept the maxim that the end justifies the means if that maxim is taken to signify that *any* course of action that serves to promote the cause of communism is thereby considered morally acceptable. In the Soviet view there are standards of morality other than what promotes communism, and in accordance with those standards a course of action may independently be judged morally impermissible. At the same time, the promotion of communism is regarded as the highest moral aim, and in the event that a person *must* choose between promoting that aim and observing a lesser value, communism should prevail. Other values may be suspended if that is necessary for the promotion of the chief aim. But as some Soviet philosophers are themselves aware, the determination of what is necessary in a particular situation is a question rife with moral hazards, and in practice it will be answered by people whose judgment may not be aided by generous inclinations or humane sensibilities. Stalin is reported to have told Lady Astor in 1931 that his extermination policies were necessary for the transformation of Soviet society to communism.[91] And even in the absence of a Stalin, there is no assurance in Marxist-Leninist theory that the question of means will

[89]Bandzeladze, *Aktual'nye problemy*, p. 243.
[90]Titarenko, *Marksistskaia etika*, pp. 144–145 (italics omitted).
[91]Christopher Sykes, *Nancy. The Life of Lady Astor* (New York, 1972), p. 339.

always be taken seriously, given the extreme moral importance attributed to the end, or that the determination of what means are necessary will be free of the peculiar blend of arrogance and paranoia with which Soviet leaders have habitually confronted both their own subjects and the world.

How Is the End Justified?

The third question commonly addressed to Soviet philosophers by their critics concerns the grounds on which communism is declared to be the highest end. For the Marxist-Leninist, the thesis that devotion to communism is the supreme moral principle is an objective, "scientific" truth; but what is the objective basis of that supposed truth? Clearly this is the key point in the case for the Marxist-Leninist ethical position, for without an adequate answer to this question the Soviet defense of communist morality on the two issues discussed above remains unsupported. Moral freedom can be given no content if the moral necessity it must recognize has not been established; and unless the ultimate aim is itself justified, there is no ground for suspending other values in its pursuit.

Despite the central importance of the question, it is not easy to find a developed answer to it in the Soviet literature. On one level, the position taken by Soviet philosophers is clear: it is *history*, they affirm, that grounds all values. "It makes no sense to seek extrahistorical criteria of evaluation," Drobnitskii wrote in 1969, "inasmuch as all questions concerning values arise only within the framework of the historical development of mankind and conceal real social problems."[92] When it comes to explaining *how* history demonstrates the validity of moral principles, however, it is far less clear what Soviet philosophers wish to argue. Most, in fact, do not argue the position at all but simply assume that what Drobnitskii calls "the derivation of ideals from objective laws of history" is a legitimate application of historical materialist science. Drobnitskii, reporting on extended discussions with a number of British ethical philosophers in 1968, 1969, and 1970, found it necessary to inform his countrymen that the British asked for proof of the Marxist ethical theses. "What is obvious to us seems to these people highly debatable," he wrote; "our basic principles are, to them, hypotheses in need of verification."[93] This statement is particularly true, of course, of the principle of the historical validation of

---

[92]O. G. Drobnitskii, "Diskussiia po problemam etiki mezhdu sovetskimi i britanskimi filosofami," *Voprosy filosofii*, 1969, no. 2, p. 145.
[93]Ibid., p. 144.

ideals; explaining how such validation is possible has been called by Philip Grier "the central task and challenge of Marxist-Leninist ethical theory."[94]

Critics sometimes think that Soviet philosophers are appealing to historical inevitability for the grounding of moral values. According to the "objective laws of history" to which Drobnitskii refers, communism is the goal of the future in that it is the condition toward which history is inexorably advancing. Is the Soviet philosopher, then, saying nothing more than that communism is valuable because it is inevitably coming? Perhaps when Titarenko writes that "scientific understanding of the laws of social development has permitted us to put forward the new 'ultimate goal' of our time"—that is, communism—what is being asserted is that the warrant for the goal derives from our knowledge of the fact that its coming is assured.[95] But of course from the point of view of common logic this will not do. There is no connection between the inevitable approach of something—a person's death, for example—and the attribution of positive value to it.

Although Soviet philosophers may at times tacitly rely on inevitability as a ground of value, they do not in fact offer it as an explicit argument. Rather, those who directly confront the question of the justification of communist morality contend that communism is the supreme value not because history shows it to be inevitable but because history shows it to be the goal of a progressive development. The laws of history as discovered by Marxist science, it is argued, disclose not a neutral, valueless movement but an advance—a positive movement toward a better future. The science of history demonstrates that the course of human events has direction and that its direction is forward. On this basis Drobnitskii can write that ultimately the establishment of moral standards hinges on "acknowledgment of the overall progressive movement of history."[96] And since communism is the condition toward which that movement is advancing, communism is the supreme moral value for mankind.

Logically, however, this argument would appear to be on no better footing than a response based on inevitability. Even if there were evidence to show that history is moving in a certain direction, how could that evidence establish that the direction is a *good* one? The events of history simply are what they are; they cannot be self-warrant for their own worthiness. To call the movement of history "forward" is to assume that history is moving not merely in a particular direction but in the *right* direction; progress is not any change but change from a state of lesser

[94]Grier, p. 100.
[95]Titarenko, *Marksistskaia etika*, p. 168.
[96]Drobnitskii, "Diskussiia," 1970, no. 5, p. 139.

value to one of greater value. The only way in which history can be shown to be "advancing" is by smuggling into it value notions that are independent of the historical facts investigated. The Marxist-Leninist, it would appear, is simply *presupposing* certain value notions; he is bringing values to history, not deriving them from it. For this reason the Soviet philosopher's attempt to infer values from facts has consistently been rejected by Western critics on grounds of circularity.[97]

There is very little in the way of focused response to this objection in the Soviet philosophical literature. Perhaps the most frank and thoughtful reply to it came in the 1970s from Drobnitskii, whose reflections on the matter may be taken as the best attempt to date on the part of Soviet philosophers to cope with the theoretical questions raised by the thesis that history proves the supreme value of communism.

First, Drobnitskii contends that a fixation on the established techniques of formal logic and what he calls "scientistic pedantry" have prevented Western philosophers from taking a sufficiently broad view of the matter. He admits that in present-day logic there is no accepted method of deducing moral propositions from factual ones, but he asserts that morality has "its own logic" and "its own methods of substantiation." These methods are essentially historical: "History, in its own way," he writes, "confirms the 'truthfulness,' progressiveness, validity, 'justifiability' of certain ideals." History is now in the process of confirming, he argues, "moral demands that have taken shape among the laboring masses in the course of millennia." And history also *disconfirms* proposed ideals: it denies justification to "those ideals that have revealed their limited character and have proved to be merely a basis for caste and class privileges and for the defense of transient and obsolescent conditions." As to what exactly is the ground for these conclusions, however, Drobnitskii once again acknowledges that there are no "formal laws" governing them.[98]

Drobnitskii does suggest, however, the direction in which he thinks the "logic" of substantiating moral notions should go. He believes that although there are no formal ties between value judgments and statements of fact, it is nonetheless possible to find a correspondence "in content" between certain ideals and the laws of humanity's "historical ascent." The ideals in question are those that together define the nature of social man— those that make up, in other words, a conception of "the human essence," or what man can and should be in society. These are the "humanistic ideals to which Marx was true," according to Drobnitskii, and he contends that all moral judgments ultimately appeal to them. The implication of

[97]Ibid., 1969, no. 2, p. 145.
[98]Ibid., 1970, no. 5, pp. 139–140.

these statements, though never made quite explicit by Drobnitskii, would appear to be that what history "confirms" is an ideal picture of the human being and that that picture serves in turn as the ground of all moral assessments. "Logical analysis of the derivation of moral ideas," he writes, "must lie on the plane of the interrelation between moral judgments and the 'essential' judgments that define the essence of a human existence."[99] A further implication, of course, is that for communism to be the "supreme value," it must be identified with this ideal condition of humanity—a condition in which the ideal human essence is realized.

The notion that communism is justified as the fulfillment of the human essence appears in many forms in current Soviet ethical writing. Not only Drobnitskii and heretics like Mil'ner-Irinin and Egides but many other writers have stressed the humanistic values they see in communism. "Man must be the highest value for man," Bandzeladze writes, and he proceeds to link this highest value with communism by invoking Marx's authority for the thesis that humanism is "the real content of communism."[100] Frequent reference is made by Soviet writers to the line in the Party program that reads, "Everything for man, everything in the name of man," and the historical movement to communism is characterized in such ways as an increase in "level of humanization," "the growth of humaneness in the relations among people," and the like.[101] Many Soviet writers now use the terms 'communism' and 'humanism' more or less interchangeably, speaking of now one and now the other as the "criterion" and "ultimate aim" of human progress.[102] 'Communism' in this sense is taken to be an ideal situation in which human needs are fully met, individual capacities are developed to the full, and—for those partial to the language of the young Marx—alienation has been overcome in a rehumanized mankind.

The ultimate resort, then, on the part of Drobnitskii and some other Soviet philosophers is to a kind of self-realization ethics in which communism is linked with the attainment of humane ideals. But however attractive these ideals may be, the appeal to them does not provide the Marxist-Leninist with the needed theoretical assistance. In the first place, it does not answer the question with which we began: how does *history* "confirm" and "disconfirm" moral principles? If the argument is that history displays a trend toward the fuller and deeper implementation of these ideals in human life, we may even wish to question the factual accuracy of the contention: what exactly is the evidence of an increasing

---

[99]Ibid., p. 140.
[100]G. D. Bandzeladze, "O tvorcheskom kharaktere nravstvennosti," *Voprosy filosofii*, 1981, no. 6, pp. 119–120.
[101]Titarenko, *Nravstvennyi progress*, p. 172; Laptenok, p. 82.
[102]Bandzeladze, "O tvorcheskom kharaktere nravstvennosti," p. 120.

"level of humanization," in this world beset by continuing hunger, strife, and tyranny? But even if it could be established that certain forms of human experience and activity are on the ascendant, we would not have resolved the logical question as to how history *establishes* the *value* of those experiences and activities—that is, as to how history gives them the status of *ideals* in the first place. Nothing in the recourse to a true "human essence" facilitates an inference from is to ought, for the human essence to which Drobnitskii and the others appeal is already a normative conception concerning what man *ought* to be, and this conception is brought *to* historical investigation rather than deduced *from* it. Hence the circularity of the Soviet argument is not overcome by the devices of Drobnitskii's new "logic" of the historical substantiation of moral principles.

But there is still another reason why an appeal to humanistic ideals is not sufficient to establish the supreme value of "communism" as it is understood in Marxist-Leninist ethics. The "devotion to communism" required by the Moral Code of the Builder of Communism is not simply allegiance to a certain set of ideals, it is also allegiance to the actual institutions and policies of the USSR as presumably engaged in the construction of the communist order. That devotion of communism is indistinguishable from devotion to the USSR is a familiar refrain in Soviet theoretical and ideological literature. It is built into the Moral Code in its very first principle, which links "devotion to communism" with "love of the socialist motherland," thus identifying the highest moral value with Soviet patriotism. In Soviet textbooks and course syllabi in ethics, patriotism is always presented as one of the most important of the moral virtues, and it is invariably viewed in a narrow sense as signifying unquestioning obedience to state authority. Soviet students are told that it is always their moral duty to obey the law of the land; there is no recognition of the possible moral worth—much less the moral duty—of civil disobedience under certain circumstances.[103] Nor are students left in any doubt that the "public wealth" that the Code requires to be preserved and increased is the wealth of the USSR or that the "enemies of communism" who are to be uncompromisingly opposed are the enemies of the USSR. In this way existing Soviet reality becomes "communism" for ethical purposes, and the humanistic value attributed to communism as a set of ideals is claimed for actual Soviet institutions and policies as well.

Yet surely this extension of the ideal humanistic content of communism to Soviet reality is illegitimate. Even if we ignore the specific acts of repression, aggression, and barbarism of which Soviet authorities have been guilty in recent years, the very existence of a moral code that requires love

[103]V. I. Bakshtanovskii, ed., *Praktikum po etike*, 2d ed. (Tiumen', 1979), p. 50.

toward one part of humanity and hostility toward another is ample evidence of an antihumanist spirit in contemporary Soviet society, however noble may be the humanist ideals to which some Soviet philosophers appeal. Love of others, the Soviet citizen reads in *Kommunist*, is a quality that must be expressed "with great discrimination" and must be accompanied by "hatred for social enemies."[104] The systematic and vigorous dissemination of a point of view that divides mankind into friends to be loved and enemies to be hated is the manifestation of an ethical provincialism that is utterly inconsistent with the attribution of moral worth to every person. George Kline has argued that Marx himself, although he advanced a humanist ideal for the future, lacked humanist principles for the present;[105] Soviet theorists, far from making up that lack, have institutionalized in the Moral Code of the Builder of Communism an inhumane distinction between "us" and "them." If the supreme value of communism cannot be considered established by history even when 'communism' is taken to mean a set of humanistic ideals, far less can that value be called proved when the meaning of the term is extended to cover the supposed Soviet implementation of those ideals. For the "implementation" contradicts the ideals.

It is simply by fiat that support for the actual institutions and policies of the Soviet state is equated with devotion to communism. Once dignified as "communist," however, those institutions and policies assume the mantle of supreme moral authority in Marxist-Leninist ethics. What they require becomes "morally necessary," and hence they are taken to define the content of moral freedom, which consists in the recognition of moral necessity. Whatever means are considered essential for promoting Soviet institutions and policies are deemed morally permissible, even if they require the violation of universally acknowledged norms of common human morality. Yet by the basic epistemological principles of Marxist-Leninist philosophy itself, these attempted resolutions of the problems of individual freedom and the relation of means and ends cannot be considered successful. For the objective, "scientific" truth of the two theses on which the resolutions depend—that devotion to communism is the supreme moral principle and that devotion to the USSR is devotion to communism—has in no way been established by Soviet philosophers.

---

[104]Petropavlovskii, p. 109; see also A. F. Shishkin, *Osnovy marksistskoi etiki*, p. 198.
[105]George L. Kline, "Was Marx an Ethical Humanist?" *Studies in Soviet Thought* 9 (1969), p. 100.

[8]

Philosophy of Art

AMONG the fields of Soviet philosophy that have acquired a separate identity in the decades since Stalin's death, one of the more active and disputatious has been the philosophy of art. Originally assigned, like ethics, to the broad jurisdiction of historical materialism, philosophical thinking about art in the USSR has found a home of its own in the discipline called "Marxist-Leninist aesthetics," to which a separate department at Moscow State University, a separate section at the Institute of Philosophy, and a large and growing literature are devoted. Unlike ethics, however, the discipline of aesthetics has won not only an administrative identity but a modicum of intellectual independence as well. Because the aesthetic side of human life is not regarded as quite so crucial for the proper functioning of developed socialist society, aesthetic topics have not been stressed so urgently in Communist party pronouncements; there is no "Aesthetic Code of the Builder of Communism" comparable to the Moral Code that is enshrined in the Party program and in the Soviet educational system. And for this reason aestheticians have had more room to examine fundamental issues concerning art.

I do not say that aesthetics is now a hotbed of radical dispute among Soviet philosophers; on a good many basic points, they profess unanimous or near-unanimous agreement. Nor do I say that the hoary doctrine of Socialist Realism has lost its backing. The role of Socialist Realist art as the model and the engine of Soviet aesthetic culture is trumpeted in an unending stream of authoritative publications addressed to every segment of the Soviet population. A current textbook for a course in "Foundations of Marxist-Leninist Aesthetics" portrays the world of Soviet art as a joint venture between, on the one hand, artists who adopt "the position of Socialist Realism" and, on the other hand, the Communist party and the

Soviet state, whose task it is to "evaluate and direct the development of socialist art."[1]

At the same time, the official support enjoyed by Socialist Realism has not prevented some Soviet philosophers from raising basic questions concerning aesthetics or from suggesting alternative conceptions of art. Lively discussions have been generated by these deviations from established dogma, and it is in the content and the consequences of those discussions that we shall find the material for assessing the current state of Soviet philosophy of art. But first it will be useful to sketch the background of orthodoxy against which the discussions have taken place.

Basic Dogmas in Soviet Philosophy of Art

The elements of orthodoxy on which Marxist-Leninist aestheticians are generally agreed were aptly summarized by A. F. Eremeev in a book published in the USSR in 1980. The consensus, as Eremeev presented it, consists of four points: that art is a form of social consciousness, that it seeks both to obtain knowledge of the world and to transform that world, that it is capable of providing an accurate picture of the world, and that Socialist Realism gives the artist the best opportunities for constructing such a picture.[2] These are the elements around which the customary presentation of aesthetic theory in Soviet texts and reference works is built.

The description of art as a form of social consciousness harks back to the famous preface to *A Contribution to the Critique of Political Economy*, in which Marx assigned aesthetics to the ideological superstructure of society. To the economic relations of production in any society, according to Marx, there correspond "definite forms of social consciousness"; we must distinguish sharply, he stated, between the underlying economic changes in society such as those that create class conflict and the "legal, political, religious, aesthetic or philosophic—in short, ideological forms in which men become conscious of this conflict and fight it out."[3] Given that little else was said about aesthetics by Marx (or Engels or Lenin) in the works available to pre-Soviet and early Soviet Marxist philosophers, this remark in the preface became the classic Marxist text for the analysis of

[1] M. F. Ovsiannikov, ed., *Osnovy marksistsko-leninskoi estetiki*, 3d rev. ed. (Moscow, 1978), pp. 75, 144.

[2] I. S. Kulikova and A. Ia. Zis', eds., *Marksistsko-leninskaia estetika i khudozhestvennoe tvorchestvo* (Moscow, 1980), p. 169.

[3] Karl Marx and Frederick Engels, *Selected Works in One Volume* (New York, 1968), pp. 182–183.

art, and it provided the basis for convictions that Marxist-Leninist aestheticians have continued to defend to the present day.

Most obvious is the conviction that art must be approached by examining the socioeconomic environment from which it springs. This tenet has meant to Marxist philosophers that in class societies art is linked with the class position of the artist and hence that it can be seen to express and promote particular economic interests. Soviet philosophers, especially in the present day, stress that art is not related to its economic underpinnings as simply and directly as are other superstructural phenomena such as politics and law; "there are many intermediate links," write the authors of *The Fundamentals of Marxist-Leninist Philosophy*, "between the situation and the interests of a given class and their artistic reflection."[4] Nonetheless the understanding of art as an ideological manifestation of economics that in class societies embodies class interests is basic to the Soviet aesthetic creed. The difference between "bourgeois" art and "socialist" art is both clear and important to the Soviet philosopher.

But if art, determined by social realities, is a form in which people become *conscious* of those realities, then it is more than simply an expression of class interests: it is also a kind of awareness or knowledge of the world. Stress on the cognitive character of art is powerfully encouraged in Soviet philosophy by the Leninist theory of reflection, according to which all consciousness more or less passively reproduces the structure of the objective reality to which it is addressed. Of course, this reproduction, mediated by class interests, does not always reflect its object directly or with perfect accuracy. Art may deliberately or unconsciously misrepresent reality—may pervert, distort, or conceal it—for economic or other reasons: the art of "bourgeois formalism," in the Soviet view, serves to distract attention from the bitter facts of modern capitalist life. But art properly motivated and skillfully executed is also capable of providing a correct picture of life, and to do so is considered by the Marxist-Leninist one of art's most important functions.

Emphasis on the cognitive or knowledge-purveying role of art creates a problem for the Soviet aesthetician: if the job of art is to provide us with truth about the world, how does art differ from science? Various answers to this question have been suggested in recent years, but orthodox Soviet philosophers of art still generally rely on a distinction that evolved in the 1930s. This distinction draws on the writings of the nineteenth-century Russian thinker Vissarion Belinskii, who under the inspiration of Hegel described art as "thinking in images," as opposed to thinking in discursive

[4]F. V. Konstantinov, ed., *The Fundamentals of Marxist-Leninist Philosophy*, trans. Robert Daglish (Moscow, 1982), p. 350.

concepts.[5] In this view, art and science may both be called reflections, and they may be said to have the same object—the real world. But whereas science reflects the world through the use of abstract, general notions, art employs individualized, sensory images. The two cognitive enterprises differ not in their content—both economics and literature can present the truth about capitalism, for example—but in the form in which that truth is conveyed.

Eremeev, it will be remembered, spoke not only of the cognition but of the transformation of reality, and here the social, ideological, and epistemological aspects of art come together in the concept of Socialist Realism. The class interest of the proletariat, as we saw in Chapter 1, is held by Marxist-Leninists to motivate that class to seek an objective, unbiased assessment of the reality it is destined to change. No less is this considered true with respect to the *art* of the proletariat, which thus must reflect the world accurately or realistically. But art must also promote the needed change in society, and in the Soviet view it may do so most effectively by informing, educating, and inspiring the class that is the agent of the change. Although no explicit doctrine of Socialist Realism can be found in the writings of Marx, Engels, or Lenin, the basic tenets of the doctrine are a natural extension of the Leninist theory of reflection in combination with revolutionary activism. Hence no great break with the past was required when in 1934 the Soviet Union of Writers formally endorsed the statement that was to become an aesthetic canon in the USSR for decades to come: "Socialist realism," the Union's congress proclaimed, "demands of the artist the truthful, historically concrete portrayal of reality in its revolutionary development. The truthfulness and historical concreteness of the artistic portrayal must be in harmony with the objective of the ideological alteration and education of the workers in the spirit of socialism."[6]

Although this formula does not go unchallenged in contemporary Soviet aesthetics, as we shall see, the contention remains prominent in orthodox writing that Socialist Realist art constitutes the highest aesthetic achievement of the human race and is "the leading direction and the main line of development of contemporary artistic culture."[7] The conception of the nature of art on which Socialist Realism is based has been the subject of probing theoretical discussions among Soviet philosophers; but at the level of popular culture and mass education, unquestioning emphasis is placed on the epistemological and ideological features of art identified above.

[5]James M. Edie et al., eds., *Russian Philosophy* (Chicago, 1965), vol. 1, p. 285.
[6]*Pravda*, May 6, 1934. For a recent Western study of Socialist Realism, see C. Vaughan James, *Soviet Socialist Realism. Origins and Theory* (London, 1973).
[7]A. G. Dubrovin, ed., *Kommunisticheskoe mirovozzrenie i iskusstvo sotsialisticheskogo realizma* (Moscow, 1977), p. 26.

"First and foremost art is a reflection of reality in artistic images," the students in Communist party training schools are told, and the principal functions this reflection serves are identified as those of providing knowledge of the world and of preparing people ideologically to change it.[8]

The Rediscovery of Beauty in the Post-Stalin Era

There was a time when views such as the foregoing exhausted the content of Soviet philosophy of art. The three decades since Stalin's death, however, have seen a wealth of developments that, although they have not dislodged the above conceptions from Communist party ideology, have supplemented them in such a way as to bring greater depth and scope to Soviet discussions of art and its place in human life. At their most general level, these developments may be described as a turning of attention to the beautiful and to other strictly aesthetic categories.

Although a concern with aesthetic categories may seem an elementary requirement for any philosophy of art, it came as a distinct novelty in Soviet philosophy. The earliest period of Soviet aesthetic thought, extending from the Bolshevik revolution to the mid-1930s, had been dominated by a narrow sociological approach—the same "vulgar sociologism" we have observed in other areas—that concentrated on the class derivation and consequent ideological tendency of the work of art. At its most extreme this approach was manifested in the Proletkult view that a new socialist culture must be created by the efforts of the proletariat alone, with no reliance on the aesthetic notions of the bourgeois past. The idea of art as creating beauty was taken to be such a bourgeois notion, and hence traditional aesthetics, with its debates concerning such matters as the objectivity of beauty, was impatiently dismissed: "Our proletarian present day," wrote N. Iezuitov in the journal *Proletarskaia literatura* in 1931, "rejects both objective and subjective criteria of beauty, for it...is *against beauty altogether.*"[9]

By the time of the proclamation of Socialist Realism in the mid-1930s, however, a new interest in the development of aesthetic theory was discernible in the USSR, linked with the elaboration of the Leninist theory of reflection and with such events as the publication of Engels's letters on realism in art. Soviet philosophers and critics began to speak less of the social origins of the artist and more of the truthful reflection of life in his consciousness and thence in his works. The art work came to be viewed

[8]Ovsiannikov, p. 86.
[9]N. Iezuitov, "Konets krasote," *Proletarskaia literatura*, 1931, no. 4, p. 148.

chiefly as a means for knowing the world rather than as an expression of class interest, and the principal criterion of its value became not its partisanship but its realism, in the sense of its accuracy as a reflection of life.[10] But although the strident antiaestheticism of the earlier period was significantly moderated along with this change, concentration on the cognitive characteristics of art did not stimulate the investigation of specifically aesthetic values. What happened in the mid-1930s, in the words of one present-day Soviet philosopher, was the replacement of "vulgar sociologism" by "vulgar cognitivism [vul'garnyi gnoseologizm]."[11]

There is more to art, many were convinced, than either the expression of class interests or the mirroring of reality. When in the mid-1950s this conviction was allowed expression, it fueled the third and present phase—what may, with suitable qualifications to follow, be called the "aesthetic" phase—in the development of Soviet thinking about art.

Like so many of the post-Stalin developments in Soviet intellectual life, this shift toward aesthetics can be traced to earlier influences, including once again the famous letters on linguistics published under Stalin's name in 1950. These letters, as we have seen, ascribed to the "superstructural" aspects of society greater independence of economic conditions than had often been suggested by Soviet theorists. They also provided an authoritative text for those interested in the uniqueness of particular superstructural elements such as art: "Social phenomena," Stalin wrote, "besides what they have in common, have their own specific characteristics which distinguish them from one another and which are the most important of all for science."[12] This statement was much quoted by the more adventurous Soviet aestheticians, and new energies were devoted to the establishment of aesthetics as a separate field of investigation. Soon this trend was abetted by the broad loosening of intellectual constraints that followed the death of Stalin in 1953 and the condemnation of the "cult of personality" in 1956.[13]

Critically important in the development of Soviet aesthetics in the 1950s and 1960s was the increased availability of theoretical literature outside the dogmatic Marxist-Leninist framework. Beginning in the mid-fifties the writings of an older generation of Russian theorists and critics, including Mikhail Bakhtin and A. F. Losev, were once again published in the USSR.

[10]V. A. Razumnyi, ed., Esteticheskoe. Sbornik statei (Moscow, 1964), p. 177. See also V. P. Krutous and A. S. Migunov, "Osnovnye napravleniia esteticheskikh issledovanii v SSSR za 60 let (1917–1977)," Vestnik Moskovskogo universiteta. Seriia 7. Filosofiia, 1978, no. 1, p. 45.
[11]L. N. Stolovich, Priroda esteticheskoi tsennosti (Moscow, 1972), p. 13.
[12]I. Stalin, Marksizm i voprosy iazykoznaniia (Moscow, 1950), p. 74.
[13]Iu. Riurikov, "The Individual, Art, and Science," Soviet Studies in Literature, Spring 1965, p. 6.

The Russian translation in 1957 of an anthology compiled by the American philosopher Melvin Rader, *A Modern Book of Esthetics*, exposed eager Soviet readers to the same range of theoretical work in aesthetics that was being studied on American university campuses. The publishing event with the greatest portent for Soviet aesthetics, however, was undoubtedly the appearance in 1956 of the first complete Russian-language edition of Karl Marx's *Economic-Philosophic Manuscripts* of 1844; many Soviet philosophers, especially those of the younger generation, were struck by the attention Marx gave in that work to the aesthetic sensibilities and creative powers of man.[14] The Soviet Ukrainian poet Maksim Ril'skij has neatly dramatized the return to aesthetic values in the USSR in the mid-fifties, capped by the rediscovery of the young Marx:

> Suddenly someone blurted out the word 'beauty', and somehow everyone began to stir. It was as if we had forgotten the word, as if we had forgotten that it is not enough for a novel, a poem, a piece of music, a picture, or a statue to express the progressive ideas of its time and serve the people: it must also be *beautiful*. And so a heated discussion of beauty commenced. We were delighted when we remembered Marx's famous statement that man creates in accordance with the laws of beauty.[15]

In the philosophical community, the heated discussion to which Ril'skij refers was initiated largely by one writer, Aleksandr Ivanovich Burov, whose book *The Aesthetic Essence of Art* (1956) was the first full-scale Soviet treatment of art to stress specifically aesthetic values. Without denying that art is a form of consciousness and a reflection of reality, Burov argued that art's *aesthetic* nature has been overlooked: "All the specific aspects and laws of art," he wrote, "are aesthetic aspects and laws, and for that reason the qualitative distinctiveness of art, its essence, is an aesthetic distinctiveness and essence." What is distinctive, moreover, is not simply the form or manner in which art reflects reality—the "thinking in images" of the traditional view; forms of consciousness, according to Burov, are distinguished from each other "in everything, beginning with object and ending with function." Art, then, has an aesthetic subject matter and an aesthetic role—novel and exciting theses in Soviet philosophy, despite the fact that in fleshing them out Burov adhered closely to familiar realist and socialist themes. He still looked to "reality" for the subject matter of art, though he specified that in the case of art this reality is

---

[14]K. Marx and F. Engels, *Iz rannykh proizvedenii* (Moscow, 1956).
[15]Maksim Ril'skij, *Nasha krovna sprava. Statti pro literaturu* (Kiev, 1959), p. 11.

human and social: it is the reality of "social man in the living unity of the social and the personal, in the unity that is characteristic of him in accordance with his objective human essence." The aesthetic function, for Burov, is not radically different from the function Stalin envisaged for his "engineers of the human soul" (an expression that Burov, in fact, quoted sympathetically): it is to present an ideal of human social life and to fight to implement that ideal, to create the "beautiful, full-valued, harmonious man and truly human relationships." Burov defended this view as a general aesthetic theory, despite the admitted fact that in its terms architecture and other creative activities that do not portray or idealize social man cannot be considered genuine arts.[16]

Burov's book was widely read, and although almost everyone found something in it to dislike, the notion that art serves a realm that may legitimately be called "aesthetic" stimulated much discussion and won wide acceptance.[17] The next question, of course, concerned the exact nature of the realm. Few could accept Burov's hazy designation of it as the "living unity" of social man. But in attempting to determine the essence of the aesthetic on acceptably Marxist and materialist grounds, Soviet theorists found themselves divided into two schools by the deep-rooted tension, which we have noted in other areas as well, between ontological materialism on the one hand and historical materialism on the other.

For the Soviet traditionalist who abides by the broad materialist ontology outlined by Engels and Lenin, "being" determines "consciousness" in the sense that physical, empirical objects with their various properties are the sources of our mental perceptions. The Leninist theory of reflection provides a model of the relation between matter and mind according to which mind reflects objective characteristics that exist in nature quite apart from man and human society, and the traditionalist sees no reason to exempt *aesthetic* perception from this principle: "When we define the beautiful object as that which generates in us a sense of rapture and joy," P. Ivanov wrote in 1967, "we wish by that to say that there are in the world, independently of man and of humanity, objects and phenomena that by their material structure are bearers of aesthetic properties capable of arousing a sense of the beautiful."[18] Because they thus anchored aesthetic characteristics in the natural world, those who advanced this view in the discussion prompted by Burov's book came to be called "naturalists" (*prirodniki*); prominent among their early number were G. A. Nedoshivin,

---

[16]A. I. Burov, *Esteticheskaia sushchnost' iskusstva* (Moscow, 1956), pp. 11, 9, 136, 280.

[17]Riurikov, p. 8; for a detailed critical discussion of these developments, see Edward M. Swiderski, *The Philosophical Foundations of Soviet Aesthetics. Theories and Controversies in the Post-War Years* (Dordrecht, Holland, 1979).

[18]P. Ivanov, *O sushchnosti krasoty* (Moscow, 1967), p. 25.

I. B. Astakhov, and G. N. Pospelov. For the naturalists, beauty is decidedly *not* in the eye of the beholder.

The naturalists have been less definite and like-minded, however, when it comes to identifying the "aesthetic properties" that the natural world supposedly possesses. The task, as they see it, is to discover the "laws of beauty" to which Marx merely alluded in the *Economic-Philosophic Manuscripts*,[19] and on naturalist premises the science of aesthetics must seek those laws by investigation of the "material structure" on which the perception of beauty depends. Many believe that the *harmony* of nature in one or more of its manifestations—symmetry, rhythm, unity in diversity, the agreement of form and content—is fundamental to the perception of things as beautiful, but there is no agreement on a formula that would capture these characteristics in a systematic and discriminating manner (so as to rule out, for example, negative aesthetic objects that may also be characterized by harmony of some sort). And some Soviet writers look to other natural features entirely for the "material structure" behind the perception of beauty; the evolutionary process, the approach of an entity to perfection of its kind, the universal interconnection of nature, and simply "the power of nature" have all been invoked by naturalists in their quest for the objective ground of beauty.[20]

The Leninist theory of reflection in its broad ontological application is not the only model available in Soviet philosophy for the analysis of aesthetic perception, however. Not simply art but aesthetic awareness in general may be regarded in Marxist theory as a form of *social* consciousness and thus as governed by the laws of *historical* materialism. In this domain, as we have seen above, the Soviet philosopher wishes to maintain that consciousness is determined not simply by "being" in its ontologically materialist sense but by "social being"—that is, by the social structures and relations within which the consciousness arises. Among the less doctrinaire Soviet aestheticians—those more interested in the writings of the young Marx and in the specifically "aesthetic" essence of art as championed by Burov—the sociohistorical approach to art and the aesthetic consciousness appeared the most promising. These philosophers looked not to nature but to society for the ground of beauty and other aesthetic categories and hence came to be called "societalists" (*obshchestvenniki*). Their principal theoretical spokesman has been Leonid Naumovich Stolovich (b. 1929), a philosopher at the University of Tartu in Estonia, whose book *The Aesthetic in Reality and in Art* (1959) was an early major

[19]K. Marx and F. Engels, *Collected Works* (New York, 1975–), vol. 3, p. 277.
[20]L. N. Stolovich, "O dvukh kontseptsiiakh esteticheskogo," *Voprosy filosofii*, 1962, no. 2, pp. 113–114; Swiderski, pp. 96–101.

statement of the position.[21] Other prominent societalists have been S. S. Gol'dentrikht, Iu. B. Borev, and V. V. Vanslov.

The societalists do not deny that aesthetic judgment begins with perception of the material world, but they argue that its specifically aesthetic character is a function of complex social influences. The "immediate sensory image" of an object, Stolovich writes, is not yet its "aesthetic image"; "the aesthetic in nature," he goes on, "exists as refracted through social reality." The results of such refraction are what Stolovich and other societalists call the "aesthetic properties" of reality—properties of a special sort that are shaped by "sociohistorical practice" and include "sociohistorical relations" in their content. If the naturalists were right, Stolovich argues, a given color would always yield the same aesthetic response; but do the redness of a rose and the redness of blood, he asks, really possess the identical aesthetic property?[22] The societalists generally trace the sociohistorical practice that gives content to aesthetic properties to human labor activities in confronting and transforming nature and society in accordance with human needs and to the human relations and attitudes that the labor engenders. Gol'dentrikht argues, for example, that scenes of untamed nature are aesthetically appealing to humans not because the colors and lines are pleasing but because in dealing with nature over the centuries humans have "acquired the capacity to create a new, human reality."[23] Even aspects of the world not subject to our control are perceived aesthetically through their relation to "social man," Stolovich argues: our response to thunderstorms and to the Aurora Borealis, he contends, hinges on "their place in human life under definite, concrete historical circumstances."[24]

To the naturalists, on the other hand, this appeal to social relations and attitudes to explain aesthetic reactions is a dangerously idealist departure from the theory of reflection. The societalists' view, Pospelov argues, is incompatible with materialism because it traces aesthetic cognition not to the objective properties of things but to mere associations and the "ideological-emotional evaluation" that flows from them. Social relations and attitudes differ from society to society and change over time, Pospelov states; in relating aesthetic properties to them, the societal school, in his words, "builds its 'aesthetic' house on the shifting sands of subjectivity."[25]

By way of countering these objections, the societalists point first of all to the fact that aesthetic experience begins with straightforward perception

[21]L. N. Stolovich, *Esteticheskoe v deistvitel'nosti i v iskusstve* (Moscow, 1959).
[22]Stolovich, "O dvukh kontseptsiiakh," p. 114.
[23]S. S. Gol'dentrikht, *O prirode esteticheskogo tvorchestva* (Moscow, 1977), p. 72.
[24]Stolovich, "O dvukh kontseptsiiakh," p. 114.
[25]Razumnyi, pp. 210–211, 202.

of natural, material objects. But they also defend as "material" the specifically *social* components of the "aesthetic property," employing the
extended, "realist" sense of the term 'material' so often resorted to by
Soviet philosophers. Because the social features of aesthetic properties exist
apart from individual human consciousness, they are held to be as "material" (that is, objective) as the phenomena of nature. This tacit identification of materiality with objectivity is evident in Stolovich's description
of his approach: "In my works," he writes, "I have proceeded from the
thesis that social relations and sociohistorical practice must be understood... from the position of historical materialism. From the point of
view of the materialist understanding of history, the laws of social development, sociohistorical practice, and the social relations of people are
without doubt objective." According to Stolovich it is because the naturalists believe that objectivity is characteristic only of nature that they
reject as idealist and subjectivist any sort of connection between the beautiful and society. "Do they really have a monopoly on materialism?" he
asks—a question that, in the context of Soviet philosophy, amounts to
asking whether they really have a monopoly on truth.[26]

Although the confrontation between naturalists and societalists in Soviet
aesthetics was sharpest and most conspicuous during the ten years immediately following the publication of Burov's book in 1956, it continues
in various forms to the present day. The dispute persists because there is
in Marxist-Leninist philosophy no logical way to resolve it, since it strad-
dles a deep rift in Soviet philosophy—the rift between a focus on physical
nature and its reflection in the human mind and a focus on the social
world as shaped by human labor practice. On balance the positions of
greater institutional authority in Soviet philosophical aesthetics are held
by naturalists such as Mikhail Fedotovich Ovsiannikov (b. 1915), who
concurrently heads the two most important research centers—the Department of Marxist-Leninist Aesthetics at Moscow State University and
the Section of Aesthetics of the Institute of Philosophy. Ovsiannikov advocates the development of experimental aesthetic science in the USSR—
a development that would counter what he considers the excessive pro-
pensity to "sociologize" in aesthetics and would seek the inherent natural
bases of such purported facts as that primitive people unexposed to Western culture respond favorably to the music of Bach but not to the modern
twelve-tone scale.[27] The major societalists—Borev, Gol'dentrikht, and Stolovich—also remain active and productive, however, defending what
Gol'dentrikht recently called "the correct thesis of the objectivity and the

[26]Stolovich, "O dvukh kontseptsiiakh," p. 115.
[27]Interview with M. F. Ovsiannikov, Moscow, April 4, 1978.

sociohistorical essence of the aesthetic" against the "manifestly archaic ideas" of the naturalists.[28]

The dispute between naturalists and societalists, though it lingers on, is no longer the single focus of Soviet aesthetic discussions, however. Disagreements have arisen within each school, and an atmosphere of relative openness has permitted the appearance of other issues and of points of view more or less indirectly connected with the original opposition. The quest for beauty has produced a broad diversity of positions in contemporary Soviet aesthetics. Although this diversity cannot be examined here in all its details, it is well displayed in the range of views that have been advanced on a central question in aesthetics—the question of the nature of art. The following section will seek to identify the principal positions on this question that are defended by Soviet writers and to relate those positions to the original naturalist-societalist controversy.

Conflicting Views of Art in Current Soviet Aesthetics

Four distinguishable conceptions of art have been prominent in the Soviet aesthetics discussions of recent years. We shall begin with the conception most in keeping with traditional Marxist-Leninist notions and proceed from there to increasingly venturesome departures from orthodoxy.

The Ideological Conception of Art

The coming of the "aesthetic" period in Soviet philosophy of art does not mean that older conceptions of the nature of art have been forgotten, and indeed the most doctrinaire group among Soviet aestheticians stands in essential opposition to the "aesthetic" movement and defends the view that art, as a form of social consciousness, is simply a species of ideology. Known as "the ideological conception of art" to supporters and opponents alike, this view draws inspiration from the same Engels-Lenin stress on the theory of reflection that we saw at work in inclining many Soviet theorists toward naturalism. Hence it is not surprising that the most extreme naturalist in Soviet aesthetics—Gennadii Nikolaevich Pospelov, a professor at Moscow State University—should also be the greatest champion of an approach to art that identifies it with an ideologically oriented awareness of objective reality and rejects the idea, put forward by Burov

[28]Gol'dentrikht, p. 50.

and promoted most actively by the societalists beginning in the mid-1950s, that art has an "aesthetic essence."

The "innovators," as Pospelov disapprovingly calls them, were in his view overreacting to the excesses of the older Soviet theories by seeking to reduce both the cognitive and the ideological aspects of art to derivative or accidental features. But these are just the features that are essential to art, Pospelov argues. The source of art's content, he writes, is "an ideological perception of the world, the immediate ideological cognition of life."[29] The aesthetic, he contends, has no existence in works of art "apart from connection with the true, ideological direction of their content and with its cognitive objectivity." Thus despite the "innovators' " conviction that *their* views constitute Marxist-Leninist aesthetics ("at least," Pospelov says, "that is what they keep stressing in their works"), to his mind they have departed from the Marxist-Leninist theory of knowledge. Pospelov assumes the task of overcoming what he calls their "subjectivist" excesses—a task that, consistently, he justifies by *its* ideological importance: "At the present time," he wrote in 1964, "when the question of the ideological significance of art has again been raised in all its sharpness, and when a struggle is being waged against those movements...that deny this significance, the theory of the 'aesthetic essence' of art can only disorient those who take part in this struggle."[30]

Although Pospelov, M. P. Baskin, A. P. Belik, and some others openly counterpose their ideological conception of art to the "aesthetic" approach, essentially the same conception is adopted even by many Soviet writers who appear to acknowledge a distinctively "aesthetic" element in art. M. F. Ovsiannikov, for example, agrees with most Soviet writers in the present day that art plays a number of different roles in human life, and he includes among them a special "aesthetic" role: "Art forms aesthetic feelings, tastes, interests, ideals," we read in a textbook prepared in 1978 under Ovsiannikov's direction; "art brings people joy, aesthetic pleasure." As Ovsiannikov and his collaborators proceed, however, it becomes clear that they relegate the aesthetic to a catchall category of "other functions" which they clearly subordinate to the cognitive and ideological functions of art. What most interests Ovsiannikov and his colleagues is the role of art in shaping and preserving the correct ideological consciousness of the artistic public, not its role in bringing joy and aesthetic pleasure. Advocating the control of art by the Communist party, they insist on the need to "eliminate the possibility of the appearance in our society of artistic

---

[29]G. N. Pospelov, *Esteticheskoe i khudozhestvennoe* (Moscow, 1965), p. 213.
[30]Razumnyi, pp. 218, 183, 218 (italics in original), 217.

works the content of which distorts socialist reality or propagandizes views or ideas that are alien to socialist ideology."[31]

Furthermore it is not only naturalists such as Pospelov and Ovsiannikov whose approach to art is fundamentally ideological. Even some who consider themselves societalists, and who appear to be speaking for the "aesthetic" movement, advance what in the end can only be called an ideological conception. Avner Zis', for example—a Communist party stalwart who heads the Section of Aesthetics of the Institute of Art Studies in Moscow—has criticized Pospelov for inadequate appreciation of aesthetics and has seemed to suggest that judgments of art cannot be based on cognitive and ideological considerations alone. At the same time the latter considerations constantly occupy Zis's attention, and a principal theme of his writing is that undervaluing the cognitive significance of art leads to negation of its all-important ideological role. When neo-Marxists such as Ernst Fischer and Roger Garaudy reject the theory of reflection, Zis' contends, the result is a blow to Communist partisanship: "The anti-Marxist wave of de-epistemologization of art is intrinsically bound up with efforts to separate art from ideology; both are aimed at refuting the fundamental tenet of Marxist-Leninist aesthetics according to which the social nature of art is inextricably bound up with its ideological functions." In the end the aesthetic as such recedes from view in Zis's presentation; it is simply dissolved in the ideological. For him as for Pospelov, the ideological content of a work *becomes* its aesthetic character, as Zis' makes clear when he writes that political commitment in art is itself "an aesthetic principle." Like much other Soviet philosophical work that is translated and widely distributed abroad by Soviet publishing houses, Zis's writings combine a suggestion of broad-mindedness with what proves to be an extremely dogmatic, politically oriented position.[32]

The Conception of Art as Practical-Spiritual Appropriation

Although some societalists in Soviet aesthetics are satisfied with a thoroughgoing cognitivist and ideological conception of art, the stress on sociohistorical practice that the original societalists introduced has found expression in the USSR in a new conception of art as a form of creative aesthetic activity. Through the efforts of Stolovich, Gol'dentrikht, and other "innovators" criticized by Pospelov, this conception has gained con-

---

[31]Ovsiannikov, pp. 67, 86, 76, 143, 141.
[32]Avner Zis', *Foundations of Marxist Aesthetics*, trans. Katharine Judelson (Moscow, 1977), pp. 10–13, 51 (italics in original), 56, 287.

siderable popularity among Soviet aesthetic philosophers, and a classical justification has been found for it by identifying it with what Marx called in the *Grundrisse* "the practical-spiritual appropriation of the world."[33]

The advantage of using Marx's term 'appropriation' (*Aneignung*) in this context is that, like the Russian *osvoenie*, which translates it, it suggests a more active role for the individual creative artist than did the older "reflection" terminology. The aesthetic innovators, concerned as they were to combat a narrow emphasis on the theory of reflection, attacked the reduction of art to the cognitive that had dominated Soviet aesthetics in the preceding period. They insisted that in artistic creation the artist makes the world his own by actively reshaping it in accordance with the laws of beauty. "Not by cognition alone" is the suggestively biblical slogan used by Stolovich in his book *The Nature of Aesthetic Value* (1972).[34] Gol'dentrikht invokes a more orthodox authority in defending the position: Lenin, he writes, did not

see the essence of art only in the reflection of reality in artistic images. The artist not only knows reality, he transforms it. In external, sensory material— marble, wood, stone, colors, sounds, words—he creates a new, aesthetic reality of artistic works....

For Lenin, just as for Marx, art is a special type of practical-spiritual appropriation of the world—that is, a type of comprehension and alteration of reality for the sake of the greatest possible development of the creative potentialities and capacities of people and of the enjoyment of the might of the cognitive and creative powers of man.[35]

This shift from a passive to an active focus in art generated considerable excitement among some Soviet aestheticians in the 1960s, when it was seen as heralding a new artistic era. "This approach," wrote one enthusiast in 1964, "takes art out of the narrow confines of things subsidiary, secondary.... Art now emerges as an independent sphere of life, as a distinct

[33]In the Soviet literature the Russian expression 'prakticheski-dukhovnoe osvoenie' is used to translate Marx's 'praktisch-geistigen Aneignung' (Karl Marx, *Grundrisse der Kritik der politischen Ökonomie. [Rohentwurf.] 1857–1858* [Berlin, 1953], p. 22.) An English version more in keeping with Marx's original meaning might be 'practical-cultural appropriation', but 'practical-spiritual appropriation' will be used here because in addition to being the customary literal rendering of the Russian expression it reflects this Soviet conception's emphasis on art as a form of mental activity.
[34]Stolovich, *Priroda*, p. 20.
[35]Gol'dentrikht, pp. 151–152.

human function, full-blooded and rich. . . .Without ceasing to be a reflection of practical life, art becomes a sovereign region."[36]

The notion of art as a "sovereign region" or as existing for the sake of the development and enjoyment of "creative powers" has understandably disturbed the defenders of the ideological conception, for whom art must always be subservient to partisan interests. One tactic they have employed in response is to appropriate Marx's "appropriation" terminology for themselves, exploiting the fact that the word is vague enough to be applied simply to the cognitive "grasp" of reality and thus to signify nothing more than 'consciousness' or 'reflection'. In this weak sense the word 'appropriation' (osvoenie) has gained broad currency in Soviet philosophy, being often appended to purely cognitive terms with little if any added meaning. Thus when in the most recent Russian edition of The Fundamentals of Marxist-Leninist Philosophy we find a reference to art as "consciousness and appropriation [osvoenie] of reality," the context gives no indication that the two terms conjoined are not simply synonyms, and indeed the Soviet translator of the English-language edition renders the expression as "consciousness and perception of reality."[37] But of course the weak sense does not satisfy those who champion the view of art as "practical-spiritual appropriation"; for what distinguishes this view, Gol'dentrikht argues, is precisely that it regards cognition as insufficient to capture the essence of art and requires the creation of "a new, aesthetic reality."[38]

The substantive attacks on the view have centered on its supposed departure from materialism and lack of ideological content. According to the "practical-spiritual" conception, Pospelov writes, what is actually reflected in art is not the material world but merely the contents of the artist's consciousness. Certainly this conception leaves realism without foundation, he contends; instead it supports "the possibility of art that is unrealistic and subjectivist in its approach to the reproduction of life in images." Still less is socialist realism supported, and in general Pospelov finds that the partisan, ideological side of art is grossly neglected by the proponents of the conception. Stolovich, he finds, "fears like fire" such notions as 'class' and 'ideology'. It is no accident, Pospelov states, that Stolovich mentions Socialist Realism only in the last paragraph of his book The Aesthetic in Reality and in Art (1959) and then "apparently out of politeness."[39]

To maintain their Marxist-Leninist respectability, proponents of the

[36]Riurikov, p. 26.
[37]F. V. Konstantinov, ed., Osnovy marksistsko-leninskoi filosofii, 4th rev. ed. (Moscow, 1978), p. 339; Konstantinov, Fundamentals (1982), p. 352.
[38]Gol'dentrikht, p. 152.
[39]Razumnyi, pp. 214–216.

view of art as practical-spiritual appropriation have been obliged in their more recent works to pay greater attention to Socialist Realism and to give assurances of their devotion to cognitivism and to communist partisanship.[40] But they have also taken pains to develop and exploit the thesis, now grudgingly accepted even by most traditionalists, that art is polyfunctional and hence must be approached from various angles. For thinkers such as Zis' and Ovsiannikov, this thesis is little more than a declaration of open-mindedness that is contradicted by their dogmatic concentration on cognitive and ideological functions. For Stolovich and his associates, on the other hand, it has been a vehicle for exploring other aspects of art without openly renouncing the functions stressed by the more orthodox view. Stolovich in a 1982 article argues that the artist is simultaneously engaged in a number of activities, the blending of which constitutes the distinctiveness of art: "The work of art is a unity of four processes," Stolovich writes; "in it there is *created* a new reality, which *reflects* objective reality, *expresses* the subjective, personal world of the artist, and *transmits* its spiritual content to the recipient."[41] "Reflection" is acknowledged, but Stolovich's emphasis throughout the article is on the work of art as a "new reality" linking the subjective world of the artist with that of his public.

The Practical-Productive Conception of Art

The official world of Soviet aesthetic theory—the world of philosophy faculties, research institutes, and major publications—is populated almost exclusively by defenders of the two conceptions of art just discussed. But champions of still other conceptions have played a significant part in the aesthetics discussions of the post-Stalin period, and despite their failure to establish or maintain themselves in seats of philosophical authority, their unorthodox views of art remain well known and influential, out of all proportion to their number. Of these views the closest to true Marxian principles—closer, many would say, than the current Soviet orthodoxy—is what is called the "practical-productive" conception.

This conception is not a theory of "art" in the conventional sense but a theory of aesthetic creation that takes in the whole range of products of human labor. Whereas the view of art as practical-spiritual appropriation still focuses on art as a realm of consciousness or spirit—albeit *active*

[40]See, for example, Kulikova and Zis', p. 260.
[41]L. N. Stolovich, "Khudozhestvennaia deiatel'nost' kak sub"ektno-ob"ektnoe otnoshenie," *Filosofskie nauki*, 1982, no. 2, p. 103.

spirit—the practical-productive view seeks the aesthetic in the very material practice in which people engage in their everyday working lives. It is sometimes regarded as the logical extreme of the societal approach to the aesthetic, for whereas more moderate societalists such as Stolovich posit the existence of "aesthetic properties" that, for all their human, social content, are still anchored in the perception of external objective nature, the champions of the practical-productive conception trace the aesthetic entirely to the expression of human creative powers as they are developed and applied in social production. Burov, a critic of the conception, formulated the matter succinctly in this description of 1975: "The only source of beauty and of the aesthetic in general is found by this theory's adherents in the essential powers of man, in the creative capacities that are displayed in productive practice. The richer the essential powers of man and the more fully and clearly they are displayed in the labor process, the more beautiful are the objects created and is labor itself. In a word, the aesthetic here is the self-expression of the creative wealth of the individual in all his life activity."[42]

The obvious resemblance of this view to the idea of the transformation of nature by creative man contained in Marx's *Economic-Philosophic Manuscripts* of 1844 is by no means accidental, for that work inspired the first proponents of the view in post-Stalin Russia—young scholars affiliated with the Institute of Art History in Moscow, including Boris Iosifovich Shragin (b. 1926), Iurii Davydov, L. Pazhitnov, and Karl Moiseevich Kantor. Eager Marxists and Communist party members all, these scholars saw in Marx's emphasis on creative human labor and the fundamentally aesthetic nature of dealienated man the key to overcoming the impoverished aesthetic conceptions of the Marxist-Leninist past, and they explored such topics actively in a series of volumes entitled *Questions of Aesthetics*.[43] Their campaign was also fueled by the increased interest in architecture, industrial design, and other applied or useful arts that accompanied the massive rebuilding effort in the years after World War II. To these arts the commonplaces of orthodox Marxist-Leninist aesthetics appeared to have little application; a lathe, it seemed, could not be "socialist," any more than a building could be "realist." The conceptual apparatus of reflection, partisanship, and ideology was out of place in reference to these nonrepresentational arts, and speculation about them raised questions therefore about the nature of 'art' as a genus of which they were species. Some traditionalists responded by denying them mem-

---

[42]A. I. Burov, *Estetika: problemy i spory. Metodologicheskie osnovy diskussii v estetike* (Moscow, 1975), p. 23.

[43]*Voprosy estetiki*, 9 vols. (Moscow, 1958–1971).

bership in the genus, but the admirers of the young Marx persisted in stressing the similarities between "artistic" creation and the creation of physical objects for use.[44] Further opportunities for discussion arose with the establishment of the journal *Dekorativnoe iskusstvo* (Decorative art) in 1957; this journal provided an outlet for innovative ideas through its sponsorship of debates on such questions as "Can a machine be a work of art?"[45] Another important institutional development was the establishment in 1963 of the All-Union Research Institute of Technical Aesthetics, which publishes the journal *Tekhnicheskaia estetika* (Technical aesthetics), in which questions of design are examined on theoretical and historical as well as applied industrial levels.

Intellectual influences on the supporters of the practical-productive conception have included not only Marx but also earlier generations of Russian thinkers. The ideas of the Constructivists and other avant-garde design enthusiasts have had an impact through sympathetic articles in *Tekhnicheskaia estetika*. An important representative of an older generation who remains a living influence is Aleksei Fedorovich Losev (b. 1893), the distinguished classicist, philosopher, and historian of aesthetic thought who is known as an advocate of an expression theory of the aesthetic based on human productive activity.[46] Although Losev's view is developed principally through discussion of the society and culture of the ancient world, its implications for the present day have not been lost on either supporters or critics. Avner Zis', contesting what he calls this "so-called practical-productive conception," writes of both Losev and Losev's colleague the historian Iu. N. Borodai, that "their ideas in a number of cases may be viewed as a conception pretending to disclose the nature of art in other epochs as well."[47]

Among Marxist-Leninist traditionalists in aesthetics the opposition to the practical-productive conception has much in common with the opposition to the conception of art as practical-spiritual appropriation, inasmuch as both are said to fasten attention on "subjective" factors. But the opposition to the practical-productive conception is considerably more intense, in view of what is seen as the more thoroughgoing abandonment of objective reality by the proponents of that conception and their unwillingness to acknowledge the cognitive and ideological functions of art.

[44]Riurikov, pp. 25–26.
[45]*Dekorativnoe iskusstvo*, 1961, nos. 3–7, 11, 12; 1962, nos. 2, 3, 6, 10.
[46]For a discussion of Losev's views, see James P. Scanlan, "A. F. Losev and the Rebirth of Soviet Aesthetics after Stalin," in J. J. O'Rourke, T. J. Blakeley, and F. J. Rapp, eds., *Contemporary Marxism. Essays in Honor of J. M. Bocheński* (Dordrecht, Holland, 1984), pp. 221–235.
[47]A. Zis', *Iskusstvo i estetika. Traditsionnye kategorii i sovremennye problemy*, 2d rev. ed. (Moscow, 1975), p. 28; see also Burov, *Estetika*, p. 147.

According to the practical-productive conception, Burov wrote in 1975, "the nature of the aesthetic... is wholly determined by the essential powers of man, for it is just these powers that make any object aesthetic. In other words, on this theory the subjective principle is presented as absolutely active and the objective as absolutely passive." The proponents of the view, he states, "deliberately cast aside the objective determination of the aesthetic relation of man to reality."[48] To Avner Zis's mind the practical-productive conception, in dispensing with the reflection of an external reality and equating art with "the fashioning of things," is no improvement over the old conception of art as *zhiznestroenie* ("life-building") advanced by A. A. Bogdanov, N. F. Chuzhak, and others in the 1920s.[49]

Defenders of the practical-productive conception are also criticized for holding that there is no legitimate ground for the separate existence of "art" in the traditional sense as a spiritual enterprise. One of them, K. M. Kantor, suggested in his book *Beauty and Utility* (1967) that art as an activity engaged in by a special class of people who are divorced from productive labor is a product of a divided class society and will not exist under communism. Even in socialism, Kantor implied, aesthetic activity and material productive activity should be one.[50] However defensible this view may be from the standpoint of Marx's early writings, the more doctrinaire Soviet aestheticians vigorously oppose it and insist that the significance of art as a special cognitive and ideological activity not only remains but increases under socialism and communism. I. F. Smol'ianinov calls Kantor a "recidivist" who seeks to return to the discredited ideas of the Proletkult. Art will always exist as a work of "spiritual production" distinct from material production, Smol'ianinov argues, and he affirms that as such it will always have the Communist leadership as (quoting Lenin) its "client and defender." Clearly Smol'ianinov, like many other Soviet philosophers, is unwilling to give up the use of art as an ideological instrument of public policy, even to move closer to the original communist vision of Karl Marx. Not Marx but Brezhnev is Smol'ianinov's final authority, and he closes his critique of Kantor with a statement from the Communist party leader to the effect that as Soviet society moves along the path of communist construction, art has a growing role in forming the intellectual and moral makeup of Soviet man. Indeed the theoretical issue itself is made an ideological one by Smol'ianinov, who asserts that any

[48]Burov, *Estetika*, pp. 23–24.
[49]Zis', *Iskusstvo*, p. 28.
[50]K. M. Kantor, *Krasota i pol'za. Sotsiologicheskie voprosy material'no-khudozhestvennoi kul'tury* (Moscow, 1967), pp. 81, 127, 195, 199.

view that leads to "the denial or extreme depreciation of art as a spiritual, ideological, or world-view force" is "bourgeois in character."[51]

Over and above criticism of their philosophical views, the innovative aestheticians associated with the Institute of Art History were also subjected to pressures of a directly political kind. As a result of vocal support for the dissidents Aleksandr Ginzburg and Iurii Galanskov in 1967 and 1968 a number of them, including Pazhitnov and Shragin, lost their positions, their Party membership, or both, and others such as Davydov received severe Party reprimands. Only one more volume of *Questions of Aesthetics* appeared after 1968, and most of its former contributors were thenceforth unable to publish in the field.[52] At present, questions of the aesthetics of industry and design are explored less adventurously by scholars affiliated with the All-Union Research Institute of Technical Aesthetics and especially by L. I. Novikova, whose popular textbook *Art and Labor* was published in 1974.[53] Not even these more cautious scholars are immune from ideological criticism, however. In 1977 the Academician L. F. Il'ichev attacked the institute's journal, *Tekhnicheskaia estetika*, for "forgetting the principles of Marxist aesthetics" and preaching an "artistic-technical world view" that opens the way for an "unscientific ideology."[54]

The Structural-Semiotic Conception of Art

The approach to the theory of art that is furthest from orthodox Marxism-Leninism and from the naturalist-societalist dispute is one promoted by a group of Soviet scholars who, inspired by modern developments in structural linguistics, have applied semiotics—the theory of signs—to the study of language, folklore, literature, and other arts. Some of these scholars, such as B. A. Uspenskii, work in Moscow, but the principal center of the movement since the mid-1960s has been Tartu State University in Estonia, where Iurii Mikhailovich Lotman (b. 1922) presides over an active and productive group of specialists; Lotman is also the member of the group who has gone furthest beyond his own particular interests (literature and cinema) to enunciate a general theory of art on a structural-semiotic basis. Now generally called "the Moscow-Tartu school of semioticians," these scholars have contributed significantly to Soviet aesthetics discussions

[51]I. F. Smol'ianinov, *Problema cheloveka v marksistsko-leninskoi filosofii i estetike* (Leningrad, 1974), pp. 191–193.
[52]Interview with Boris Shragin, New Haven, Connecticut, October 12, 1979; Shragin emigrated from the USSR in 1974.
[53]L. I. Novikova, *Iskusstvo i trud* (Moscow, 1974).
[54]L. F. Il'ichev, *Filosofiia i nauchnyi progress* (Moscow, 1977), p. 260.

and have won international acclaim for the novelty and power of their views, despite heavy criticism from their traditionalist colleagues at home.

Lotman and his associates see art as a language and each work of art—verbal or nonverbal—as a "text" to be read by those who understand its vocabulary and syntax. All languages, for these writers, are "modeling systems"—structures of signs that in virtue of their meanings are said to "model" the world to which they refer. The natural languages such as English and Russian are prime examples. But in addition to these familiar and relatively straightforward languages, there are "secondary modeling systems," or languages of a more complex and abstract nature that are built upon the materials of primary systems but introduce new signs and rules of their own. Myth, it is argued, is a secondary modeling system superimposed upon natural languages, and religion is a still more complex and abstract semiotic superstructure rising on the base of myth. Similarly the arts are regarded by Lotman and his colleagues as secondary modeling systems, each with its vocabulary and grammar, producing texts that may have multiple levels and orders of meaning. Thus a work of art is a complex communicative structure linking artist and public through the shared languages of a particular culture.[55]

On its face this approach to art is not totally at odds with the Marxist-Leninist notion of art as an ideological reflection of reality that conveys knowledge of the world, and in his earlier theoretical writings Lotman stressed the fact. In *Lectures on Structural Poetics* (1964), he wrote that he wished to present a genuinely Marxist, materialist aesthetics, and he affirmed that "art cognizes life by serving as a means of portraying it."[56] Lotman also has sought to distance himself from the earlier Russian formalist theories that are consistently condemned by Marxist-Leninist philosophers. At the same time, non-Marxist as well as Soviet commentators have noted a tension in Lotman's work between, on the one hand, the impulse to relate the artistic work to its cultural and physical surroundings as Marxist theory demands and, on the other hand, an impulse to view it as an autonomous structure of artistic signs constituting a world of its own, with its own meaning and rationale. The latter impulse appears increasingly prominent in Lotman's later writings. In *The Structure of the Artistic Text* (1970), for example, the protestations of loyalty to Marxist aesthetics are gone, and there is no mention of a cognitive function in any way parallel to that of science. Scientific truth, Lotman asserts, "exists in a single semantic field"—the field, we may assume, of the relation between

---

[55]For a survey of Soviet work in semiotics, see Daniel P. Lucid, ed., *Soviet Semiotics. An Anthology* (Baltimore, 1977), pp. 1–20.

[56]Iu. M. Lotman, *Lektsii po struktural'noi poetike. Vvedenie, teoriia stikha* (Providence, 1968), p. 14.

the scientific text and the external reality it purports to describe. Artistic truth, on the other hand, is said to be found in the "mutual interrelation" of several semantic fields simultaneously—a notion that suggests an internal standard of truth comparable to that advanced by formalism rather than a standard dependent upon reference to an external reality.[57]

The tension between viewing artistic signs as subsidiary to an outside referent and viewing them as ends in themselves is both expressed and concealed in the writings of Soviet semioticians by the use of the single term 'model' to signify different relations between the art work and reality. Although for some purposes the term is used to mean a copy or reflection, so that 'modeling the world' means depicting or portraying an external reality, the term is increasingly used rather to signify a *reconstruction* of reality, so that 'modeling the world' means molding or shaping it. As early as the *Lectures* of 1964 Lotman spoke of the artist as "recreating" his surroundings,[58] and in later writings it is clear that this recreation may involve considerable departure from the original. The art work, he writes in *Structure*, is not a copy but a "translation"; the horizons of art have been significantly expanded, Lotman states, by twentieth-century painting with its "combinations forbidden by everyday consciousness."[59] Furthermore the primacy of active modeling is enhanced by the persistent suggestion that artistic signs not only reconstitute reality but mold the *consciousness* of those human agents who use them. "The ultimate implication of Soviet semiotics," observes the American scholar Daniel P. Lucid, "is that human beings not only communicate with signs but are in large measure controlled by them.... A sign system possesses the capacity literally to mold or 'model' the world in its own image, shaping the minds of society's members to fit its structure."[60]

This tendency to view the artistic sign not as a derivative, shadow entity that copies reality but as an aesthetic end in itself that transforms our perception of the world is the major target of the criticism of the structural-semiotic conception by Marxist-Leninist traditionalists. Other elements of the conception are of course criticized as well. Its opponents reject as ahistorical the assumption that there are "semantic universals," such as the binary oppositions of up-down, light-dark, life-death, and the like, that cross cultural borders and are permanent features of a culture's history.[61] But the point to which orthodox Soviet critics continually return

[57]Iu. M. Lotman, *Struktura khudozhestvennogo teksta* (Providence, 1971), p. 301.
[58]Lotman, *Lektsii*, p. 15.
[59]Lotman, *Struktura*, pp. 256, 342.
[60]Lucid, p. 20.
[61]A. Ia. Zis', "Marksistskaia-leninskaia teoriia iskusstva i ee burzhuaznye kritiki," *Voprosy filosofii*, 1980, no. 12, p. 159.

[315]

is that the semiotician's view is inconsistent with the theory of reflection and hence is "subjectivist." According to the Academician Mikhail Borisovich Khrapchenko—a major force for dogmatism in Soviet literary aesthetics and a persistent foe of Lotman—the semiotician simply rejects the idea that the artist is engaged in a process of reproducing an external reality. Lotman's "artistic 'model,' " Khrapchenko writes, "functions not as a system that reveals the structure of the world but as a set of subjective notions about it, or in other words as a projection of categories of 'pure' consciousness."[62] Another prominent opponent—Iurii Iakovlevich Barabash, director of the Gor'kii Institute of World Literature in Moscow and an early critic of Solzhenitsyn—states that modeling can make sense only if it is based on faithfulness to life; but Lotman's attention, Barabash argues, is focused principally on "the model's *dissimilarity* with reality." "The basis of structuralism," he writes, "is the contention that there is an unconscious, concealed, abstract structure that is determined by purely abstract relations among elements, whereas the elements themselves, which reflect various aspects of reality, are of no significance."[63] In this same connection much critical note has been taken of a 1962 statement by Uspenskii in which the Moscow semiotician compared an art work as a structure of signs with a religious sermon and with the performance of a fortuneteller.[64] Such a likening of art to what they consider the realm of the fantastic is regarded by doctrinaire Marxist-Leninist critics as proof that in the structural-semiotic view the artistic model is, as Khrapchenko says, "not only divorced from reality but largely opposed to it."[65]

On the whole the members of the Moscow-Tartu school have avoided open responses to these charges, so that no sustained polemic has developed between them and the orthodox Soviet Marxist-Leninist aestheticians. They have devoted themselves, rather, to substantive studies in the arts—especially literature, cinema, and painting—in which they have applied and developed the structural-semiotic conceptual apparatus imaginatively and in great detail. This work has won them high praise from scholars in other countries. L. M. O'Toole has called them a "brilliant, dynamic, and immensely productive group of scholars...who are forging a new and revolutionary scientific paradigm." For Ann Shukman their work constitutes "an intellectual flowering of enormous significance not only in the intel-

---

[62]M. Khrapchenko, "Semiotika i khudozhestvennoe tvorchestvo. Stat'ia pervaia," *Voprosy literatury*, 1971, no. 9, p. 78.

[63]Iurii Barabash, *Voprosy estetiki i poetiki*, 3d ed. (Moscow, 1978), pp. 238 (italics in original), 242.

[64]See, for example, M. B. Khrapchenko, "Literatura i modelirovanie deistvitel'nosti," in *Kontekst. 1973. Literaturno-teoreticheskie issledovaniia*, ed. A. S. Miasnikov et al. (Moscow, 1974), p. 16; and Yuri Barabash, *Aesthetics and Poetics* (Moscow, 1977), p. 228.

[65]Khrapchenko, "Literatura," p. 18.

lectual life of the Soviet Union, but on a world scale."[66] Within the USSR, however, this flowering is still met with intense suspicion and hostility. The intellectual level of much of the orthodox opposition to the Moscow-Tartu school is perhaps best suggested by the statements of a senior scholar in the Aesthetics Section of the Institute of Philosophy in Moscow, who when asked about the merits of Lotman's views replied that Lotman is "not one of us" and that "when someone spends thirty pages analyzing a very short poem that is perfectly clear to begin with, you can see that something is wrong."[67] It is a sad irony that a group of scholars of whom, as O'Toole remarks, the Soviet Union should be proud is instead the target of denunciation and scorn. The group has already been damaged significantly by the inhospitable atmosphere; B. L. Ogibenin, A. M. Piatigorskii, and D. M. Segal have emigrated. The group's most esteemed scholars, however—including V. V. Ivanov and V. N. Toporov as well as Lotman and Uspenskii—continue to write and publish in the USSR under difficult conditions.

An Appraisal of Current Soviet Aesthetic Philosophy

It cannot be denied that the world of Soviet thinking about art and the beautiful has expanded considerably in the post-Stalin period. No longer is philosophical aesthetics regarded as simply identical with the theory of Socialist Realism. All styles and schools of art are considered open to aesthetic analysis, and the interest of many Soviet philosophers extends as well to the question of aesthetic values in nature and in productive labor. Almost everyone agrees at least in principle that art in general, including Socialist Realist art, is polyfunctional and thus that its role in human life cannot be reduced entirely to that of expressing and promoting partisan class interests. In short, it is widely acknowledged by Soviet philosophers that there is more to aesthetics than art, more to art than Socialist Realism, and more to Socialist Realism than ideology.

There is, moreover, as we have just seen, a significant degree of basic theoretical diversity in recent Soviet aesthetics. To the fundamental question of the nature of art, different answers have been given by different groups of writers. Most of these answers are in some recognizable sense

[66]For a listing of over two thousand works by scholars associated with the Moscow-Tartu school, see K. Eimermacher and S. Shishkoff, *Subject Bibliography of Soviet Semiotics. The Moscow-Tartu School* (Ann Arbor, 1977). The comments by O'Toole and Shukman may be found in reviews of this book in *The Slavonic and East European Review* 56 (1978), p. 616; and 57 (1979), p. 115.
[67]Interview with N. L. Leizerov, Moscow, February 27, 1978.

"Marxist," though they range from the highly doctrinaire application of the Marxist-Leninist theory of reflection to the exploration of the practical-productive suggestions concerning human creativity found in the writings of the young Marx. And one—the structural-semiotic conception—owes more to Ferdinand de Saussure and Roman Jakobson than to Karl Marx, despite its proponents' occasional appeals to the permissive terminology of a broadly conceived Marxism.

At the same time it is abundantly clear that the traditional Marxist-Leninist approach to art summarized in the first section of this chapter, which highlights the cognitive and ideological features of art and affirms the importance of Socialist Realism for contemporary socialist culture, remains the standard against which other attitudes toward art in the USSR are measured. It is the approach taken by those in the positions of greatest authority in Soviet scholarly institutions, and it forms the basis of popular texts and university course syllabi. It provides the theoretical justification for the persistent attacks to which deviant approaches are subjected. Most at home with the ideological conception of art, proponents of the traditional approach can tolerate the conception of art as practical-spiritual appropriation as long as those who support the latter are careful to affirm also that art copies reality and expresses class interests. But they cannot tolerate the other conceptions discussed above, and these are vigorously combated. The idea of theoretical pluralism in the philosophy of art is a bourgeois notion, according to Avner Zis', and to it must be opposed "the Marxist theory," as "a unitary and integral conception of artistic creation" based on the theory of reflection.[68]

One unfortunate consequence is that the deviant views that are voiced are not explicitly or adequately elaborated. They are understated and hedged with qualifications; important theoretical issues are deliberately avoided for fear of calling too much attention to heretical positions. The many gaps and apparent inconsistencies in the theoretical statements of the structural-semiotic conception, for example, have been noted even by its most sympathetic Western supporters; in particular, the epistemological issues raised by the notion of modeling the world have not been adequately explored or even directly stated.[69] "Further expansion of Soviet semiotic research," Lucid writes, "depends in large part on confronting the question of the genesis of sign systems and their relation to external reality."[70] But of course this question would touch on one of the most sensitive articles of the orthodox aesthetic creed—the reflection of reality in art.

[68]Zis', "Marksistskaia-leninskaia teoriia," pp. 152, 154.
[69]For an excellent critical study of Lotman's views, see Ann Shukman, *Literature and Semiotics. A Study of the Writings of Yu. M. Lotman* (Amsterdam, 1977).
[70]Lucid, p. 5.

The problem, as in many other areas of Soviet philosophical thought, is that although the only way to clarify and elaborate alternative views thoroughly is to *contrast* them with existing dogmas as sharply as possible, they must instead be expounded in such a way as to minimize or conceal that contrast. Incompatible with the orthodoxy, they must be presented in language that somehow makes them appear compatible while preserving if possible their theoretical bite. If the writer fails to achieve that appearance, he knows that a gauntlet of "editors" stands ready to aid him in effecting the required compatibility. Most writers prefer to make their own adjustments in advance, thus confirming M. F. Ovsiannikov's statement that in the field of aesthetics (as in Soviet philosophy generally) there is now very little formal censorship of manuscripts once they have been submitted.[71] But whether the censorship is external or internal, its effect cannot but be to mask differences, dull contrasts, and avoid intellectual confrontations, to the detriment of substantive theoretical development.

On the other hand not even the orthodox view of art is well developed theoretically in current Soviet aesthetics, despite having at its disposal all the resources of the Soviet research and publishing empires and being free from the restraints of censorship. The view that art is an ideological reflection of reality raises certain theoretical questions, as we have seen. But most of these questions receive no systematic or penetrating treatment by Soviet philosophers of art. They remain open, half acknowledged and halfheartedly discussed, with no consensus on how to approach them.

The chief unanswered question in orthodox Soviet philosophy of art is undoubtedly the question of how to identify the specifically "aesthetic" characteristics of art. Although virtually everyone now wishes to say that art works are appropriately described by the application of aesthetic predicates such as 'beautiful', it is by no means clear how these predicates are to be defined. Some writers wish to tie them so closely to ideology that even political commitment is an "aesthetic" principle, as we have seen. Others, like Stolovich, find the aesthetic in the joint fulfillment of cognitive, expressive, communicative, and other functions. But neither in these cases nor in others is it made clear what is aesthetic about the features mentioned, and among most orthodox philosophers of art the question is not even discussed. It may not be surprising that Marx's "laws of beauty" remain elusive, but it is remarkable that traditionalists make very little overt effort to find them. Although now seemingly committed to the pursuit of Beauty as well as Truth and Goodness, the orthodox philosophers remain more interested in what makes art cognitively true and ideologically good than in what makes it aesthetically beautiful.

[71]Interview with M. F. Ovsiannikov, Moscow, April 4, 1978.

The absence of a specification of the aesthetic is nowhere more evident in Soviet philosophy than in recent discussions of Socialist Realism. It is now widely held that the original 1934 statement of that doctrine does not adequately distinguish art from nonaesthetic activities: "There is nothing specifically aesthetic in it," Iurii Borev writes; "nothing properly relating to art. It may be applied with equal success to art, propaganda, history, and a number of other social phenomena."[72] Soviet philosophers are agreed that the original formula requires revision, but since it is not known how to identify the "aesthetic" there is no consensus as to a formula to replace it. Hence there is no longer in Soviet philosophy an accepted, standard definition of Socialist Realism.

Soviet philosophers, rather, present a variety of modifications of the original formula in the attempt to accommodate the aesthetic dimension. The most recent (1980) edition of the Soviet *Philosophical Dictionary* defines Socialist Realism as "an artistic method, the essence of which consists in the truthful, historically concrete reflection of reality in its revolutionary development *in the light of the communist aesthetic ideal.*"[73] But since there is no indication of what "the communist aesthetic ideal" is, the addition of the last phrase to the 1934 formula is not very helpful. Still less informative is the definition in the new *Encyclopedic Dictionary of Philosophy* (1983), which identifies Socialist Realism as "the aesthetic expression of a socialistically understood conception of the world and of man."[74] Until "the aesthetic" is itself defined, the accommodation of the aesthetic nature of art in the doctrine of Socialist Realism will remain purely verbal.

A second important theoretical question that goes unresolved in current Marxist-Leninist aesthetics (despite assurances to the contrary) is the question of the relation of the work of art to reality. The orthodox Soviet aesthetician is committed to the theses that all art is a reflection of reality and that good art is a *correct* reflection—one that is realistic, accurate, "true to life." The work of art, then, must bear a particular relation to reality in order to have aesthetic value. But what exactly are the features of this relation? How do we know which works of art are "realistic" and which are not?

What is *not* required for realism, every Soviet writer insists, is the close photographic reproduction of detail; art, it is said, should portray the characteristic, the typical—not surface phenomena but the *essence* of the subject or process. Furthermore, it soon becomes evident in reading Soviet

[72]Iurii Borev, *Estetika*, 2d ed. (Moscow, 1975), p. 225.
[73]I. T. Frolov, ed., *Filosofskii slovar'*, 4th ed. (Moscow, 1980), p. 341 (italics added).
[74]L. F. Il'ichev et al., eds., *Filosofskii entsiklopedicheskii slovar'* (Moscow, 1983), p. 633.

discussions of realism that the "reality" to be captured is not limited to what now exists or has existed. Through the use of anticipatory reflection, we are told, the artist may portray a reality yet to come; hence he may project ideals, so long as they are the ideals that *will* be realized with the historical advance of mankind toward its bright communist future.[75] On this ground, Soviet writers continue to insist, with Maksim Gor'kii, that romanticism and realism are not opposed. Indeed a wide variety of genres and styles is available to Socialist Realist artists, we are assured: they are said to have at their disposal a "most broad artistic palette."[76]

Soviet philosophers effect still further extension of the concepts 'reflection' and 'realism' in order to give Marxist-Leninist aesthetic theory sufficient scope to cover all the arts. Although it is recognized that the "reflection" apparatus is most directly applicable to the analysis of literature, painting, and other representational arts, orthodox Soviet aestheticians are unwilling to say that any art as practiced in a developed socialist society requires fundamentally different theoretical treatment. "The aesthetics of Socialist Realism," Iu. A. Lukin writes, "is the universal, comprehensive conception of all Soviet art in general and of each of its species in particular."[77] The required scope is achieved by arguing that supposedly "nonrepresentational" arts also make use of "artistic images" that derive from the experience of real life and can be said to reflect that life veridically. In dance and in music, it is argued, there is still what V. V. Vanslov calls "likeness and resemblance in form with the phenomena of life"; this resemblance, it is said, has simply taken on a more "mediated" character. Dance movements, for example, "embody" certain emotional states. In music, we find "the rhythms and intonations of life."[78]

Just how far this "mediation" can go is best seen in recent discussions of architecture by Marxist-Leninist traditionalists. "There is faithfulness to life even in architecture," N. L. Leizerov writes, and he points to solidity, balance, and other architectural desiderata in a building as representing "the materialization of particular laws of nature."[79] Vanslov, too, speaks of the rhythm and symmetry of structural elements as reflecting "the laws of the compositional organization of space."[80] The position of these writers is apparently that buildings have a likeness or resemblance to the natural world to the extent that they embody the "regularities" found in the latter. The architect of Lenin's Tomb, according to Leizerov, "drew from objec-

---

[75]N. L. Leizerov, *Obraznost' v iskusstve* (Moscow, 1974), p. 46.
[76]Dubrovin, pp. 29, 34.
[77]Ibid., p. 34.
[78]Kulikova and Zis', pp. 318–320.
[79]Leizerov, p. 159.
[80]Kulikova and Zis', p. 320.

tive reality the rhythmic material organization of architectural forms he needed."[81] Leizerov indeed goes still further when he argues that another aspect of faithfulness to life in an architectural structure consists in its accordance with "the historically changeable, utilitarian, purely aesthetic, and of course ideological demands of a given socioeconomic formation." Thus he argues that in Gothic architecture a particular organization of elements is used to "reflect" a particular religious consciousness. And the same is true, he suggests, of Lenin's Tomb, which he describes as "programmed" by its architect with "the richest associations"—associations that in this case, of course, reflect a socioeconomic formation that makes socialist and atheistic instead of religious demands.[82]

At this point the notion of the reflection of reality in art seems clearly to have been stretched beyond all reasonable bounds. If faithfulness to life can be found in the relation between Lenin's Tomb and the ideological demands of socialism, then it can be found anywhere, and the criterion of verisimilitude or "truth to life" has lost all its discriminating power. At the very least it is no longer possible to make a distinction between realistic representation (which requires a resemblance or likeness between the art work and what it represents) and expressiveness (which does not require resemblance)—a distinction of the first importance for aesthetic theory in general and for realism in particular. In Leizerov's view simple suggestiveness or association appears to take the place of likeness, to the point where anything that has served as a causal element in the artist's mind or environment may be said to be "reflected" in his art, whether or not there is any actual resemblance between that element and the artistic product. But in the context of a realist theory of art, to be true to life cannot mean simply to be caused by life, for then *all* art would be "realistic."

The breadth allowed the terms 'reflection' and 'realism' in orthodox Soviet aesthetics is not without its usefulness to unorthodox philosophers, for the latter can sometimes exploit it to justify the investigation of sensitive subjects. What might otherwise appear to be purely formal aspects of art may be examined, so long as it is maintained that some "mediated" relation of resemblance exists between these aspects and objective reality. A subject such as expressiveness in art may be discussed, so long as the vocabulary of 'image', 'representation', and other "reflection" terms is employed to discuss it. Beyond question some writers use the honorific labels 'reflection' and 'realism' to legitimize the study of phenomena to which, objectively speaking, these labels in no way apply. Thus in a 1978 article on monumental art in the journal *Dekorativnoe iskusstvo*, A. V. Vasnetsov seeks

[81]Leizerov, p. 160.
[82]Ibid., pp. 159–160.

a word for the ideal toward which the monumental artist should strive, and he writes as follows: "I shall find no better term than 'realism', understanding this term in the present case simply as an ideal of perfection contained in the truthfulness—that is, in the appropriateness and proportionality—of all the parts (ideas, material, vital and integral pictorial vision, architectural surroundings, and so on)."[83] In such a definition, wherein 'truthfulness' means not the accuracy with which a representation portrays reality but rather the cohesion of the various elements of a work, even the most abstract creation could be called "realist." Vasnetsov is in effect using the term 'realism' to stand for purely formal values, but under contemporary Soviet conditions it is difficult to fault him for asserting that he can find "no better term" for those values.

The keepers of Marxist-Leninist orthodoxy in aesthetics do not encourage the innovative extension of their basic concepts by other thinkers, and in fact they vigorously oppose the suggestion made by some non-Soviet Marxists that Socialist Realism should be considered an open aesthetic system capable of accommodating ever newer varieties of art.[84] At the same time, these Soviet theorists have provided no philosophically defensible outer limits for the application of the "reflection" apparatus, so that the points at which they do close it are arbitrary from an aesthetic point of view. Leizerov, for example, having lauded dance movements and architectural forms for "faithfulness to life," proceeds a few pages later to reject the "pseudoart" of the "nonobjectivist-abstractionist."[85] As to why the latter artist may not be interpreted as following the same natural "regularities" to which the architect of Lenin's Tomb supposedly adhered, Leizerov is silent. Surely as a product of human aesthetic creativity Lenin's Tomb has greater likeness to a work of "pseudoart" by Piet Mondrian than it has to the ideological demands of a socialist socioeconomic formation. The designs produced by the "nonobjectivist-abstractionist" are rejected by Soviet traditionalists as "modernism," whereas the designs in movement and sound created by the choreographer and composer are welcomed as faithful to life. The distinction between them, however—despite the great energies devoted to attacking modernism in Soviet aesthetics—is given no coherent philosophical basis.

Yet we cannot say that orthodox Soviet philosophers have no touchstone for identifying an acceptable reflection of reality. The touchstone, however, is provided not by philosophy but by ideology, which in turn is periodically fixed by Communist party pronouncements. A resolution of the Central

---

[83] A. V. Vasnetsov, "Kriterii samotsennosti i iskus stilizatorstva," *Dekorativnoe iskusstvo,* 1978, no. 1, p. 15.
[84] See, for example, Zis', *Foundations,* p. 277.
[85] Leizerov, p. 166.

Committee published on July 30, 1982, for example, makes clear to Soviet artists what Socialist Realism demands under present conditions: the resolution exhorts artists to "compose materials in favor of ending the arms race," to oppose the "consumer mentality" among Soviet citizens, and to "poeticize service to the homeland and to the Party's cause"; in addition, artists are told that new generations of Soviet people "need a positive hero who is close to them in spirit and time and who would be perceived as an artistic revelation." Works fulfilling these desiderata are set off against certain unnamed other works that are said to be "biased" and "superficial" and to contain "serious deviations from the truth of life."[86] By implication what is ideologically desirable in Soviet society is what is true to life, whereas what fails to serve the homeland as understood by the Party deviates from realism.

Even if 'truth to life' were taken more defensibly to signify not service to but correspondence with reality, the "realism" of art would still be subject to ideological fixation in the Soviet setting. For Marxist-Leninist ideology itself defines the "reality" with which correspondence is necessary. Iurii Barabash's central charge against Solzhenitsyn when that writer was still published in the USSR was that he did not correctly portray present-day Soviet life; Solzhenitsyn's story "For the Good of the Cause," for example, was said to lack "truth to life" because it represents honest and upright Soviet citizens as helpless in the face of an oppressive social force. Since according to Barabash such a situation is untrue to Soviet socialist reality, Solzhenitsyn is condemned for lacking "a knowledge and deep understanding of the laws governing the movement of the real world."[87] What Barabash meant, of course, is that Solzhenitsyn disagreed with the description of the world provided by Marxism-Leninism. The ultimate control on realist art in Soviet ideology is a control on the reality to which that art must correspond. By maintaining their monopoly on the description of the "movement of the real world," Marxist-Leninists are ready to condemn as unrealistic any art that avoids or distorts what they proclaim to be reality.[88]

From a philosophical point of view the problem with orthodox Marxist-Leninist philosophy of art is not that central terms such as 'realism', 'reflection', 'image', and the like are given narrow and unyielding definitions as part of a fixed philosophical dogma. The problem is that in philosophy

---

[86]"Greater Activism Asked of Literary Press," *Current Digest of the Soviet Press* 34, no. 30 (August 25, 1982), p. 10.

[87]Quoted in Leopold Labedz, ed., *Solzhenitsyn. A Documentary Record* (New York, 1970), pp. 45–46.

[88]For further development of this point, see James P. Scanlan, "Can Realism Be Socialist?" *British Journal of Aesthetics* 14 (Winter 1974), pp. 41–55.

they are given no definitions at all but are allowed to shift with the changing winds of art policy and perceived ideological needs. They are not constants but variables—blank checks that can be filled with a wide and contradictory variety of values, depending on the situation. They can be expanded to accommodate architecture and music, contracted to reject modernism and Solzhenitsyn; loosened to take in romanticism and anticipatory reflection, tightened to exclude the semiotician's modeling of reality. Although this flexibility can at times be used by a clever innovator to permit the insinuation of unorthodox views, it can be used more easily and with less personal risk by political authorities and their ideologists to structure the world of Soviet art in accordance with their perceptions of social and moral need. And there is no sign that Soviet leaders have any intention of relinquishing this power so as to allow the post-Stalin turn to beauty to seek its own accommodation with reality. "The Party cannot be indifferent to the ideological content of art," Iurii Andropov told the Central Committee on June 15, 1983; "it will always direct the development of art so that it serves the interests of the people."[89]

[89]Y. V. Andropov, *Speech at the CPSU Central Committee Plenary Meeting. June 15, 1983* (Moscow, 1983), p. 22.

Conclusion

As applied to Soviet philosophy, the expression 'Marxism-Leninism' is commonly thought to be the name of a single, unified theory to which philosophers in the USSR unanimously subscribe and the integrity of which is preserved by the vigilance of the Communist party. The evidence of the foregoing investigation, however, suggests that in the Soviet Union today 'Marxism-Leninism' names not an integrated philosophical theory but a collection of diverse and sometimes contradictory doctrines, distributed among a set of loosely related disciplines and advanced by thinkers whose Party membership does not prevent them from holding fundamentally opposed positions on many issues. Behind its facade of dogmatic uniformity, Soviet Marxism-Leninism harbors a plurality of intellectual interests and convictions.

In some areas, of course, the official philosophy of the USSR does live up to its stereotype. The field of social and political thought, as we have seen, is ideologically the most sensitive area of Marxism-Leninism and is therefore the area that receives the closest political scrutiny. In this field philosophers take their cue directly from authoritative pronouncements such as the Party program and the reports of the quinquennial Party congresses, and there is no room for independent investigation or the development of conflicting schools of thought. When the next Party program (the third since the Bolshevik revolution and the first since 1961) is announced as scheduled at the twenty-seventh Party congress in 1986,[1]

---

[1] By a resolution of the twenty-sixth Communist party congress dated February 26, 1981, the Central Committee was instructed to prepare the draft of a new Party program to be presented at the next Party congress; see *Documents and Resolutions. The Twenty-sixth Congress of the Communist Party of the Soviet Union. Moscow, February 23–March 3, 1981* (Moscow, 1981), p. 105. Iurii Andropov made many explicit suggestions concerning the content of the new program in his *Speech at the CPSU Central Committee Plenary Meeting. June 15, 1983* (Moscow, 1983), pp. 6–31.

the social and political doctrines that it endorses will undoubtedly set the course of Soviet philosophy in this area for many years to come. Not far behind in degree of dogmatic rigidity is the philosophy of morality; in that field some tentative theoretical explorations were quickly halted in the 1960s, and subsequently the attention of philosophers has been strongly channeled in the direction of the social service ethic championed by the Party leadership.

In other areas, however, we see more room for original inquiry and the development of alternative positions. Even in a field as close to traditional orthodoxy as the philosophy of art, we have not found the undivided sway of Socialist Realism that might have been expected; on the basic question of the nature of art, several conflicting views are defended by different Soviet writers. And when we come to fields more distant from public policy concerns, such as the philosophy of history and the epistemology and ontology of dialectical materialism, we find Soviet philosophers still more broadly and deeply divided. The question of the nature of the historical process—a matter of prime theoretical importance for any Marxist phi- losopher—is not a question on which Soviet philosophers advance a common doctrine. Equally unsettled, as we have seen, are such fundamental questions as the meaning of the term 'matter', the nature of dialectical contradiction, and the content and scope of the basic laws of dialectics.

Ironically, dogmatism itself has contributed to the pluralism we have found in current Soviet philosophy. The dogmatist who takes his dogma seriously wishes to defend its truth, or at least to give it every appearance of truth, and for that reason he must take into account the facts of the world to which it supposedly applies. If those facts appear to conflict with his dogma, he has two choices: either he can dismiss the supposed facts as illusory or unimportant, or he can seek a new interpretation of his dogma that allows it to be consistent with them. The first alternative was often chosen by Soviet thinkers during the Stalin era; but that way madness lies, and no culture can long pursue a course of deliberate schizophrenia. A sane dogmatism seeks rather to accommodate its theses to the world and hence is in a curious sense self-correcting. In the three decades since Stalin's death the second path has increasingly been chosen, and in pursuing it Soviet philosophers have constructed interpretations of doctrine that differ not only from the old orthodoxy but from each other.

One consequence of this drive for accommodation is important quite apart from the question of pluralism. In the attempt to fit them to the world, Marxist-Leninist theses are often diluted or weakened to the extent that they become vacuous—as we have observed in connection with several major articles of the Soviet philosophical creed, including the law of the transformation of quantity into quality and the fundamental thesis of economic determinism in history. Soviet philosophers rescue their theses from empirical refutation by interpreting them in such a way that they are consistent with every eventuality; it was observed by H. B. Acton as early as 1955 that in Soviet philosophy the basic laws of dialectics had become "formulae which may be used to express any state of affairs that it is desired to bring within their ambit."[2] But in that case the truth of such doctrines is trivial, for they are robbed of all specifiable content.

Not every Marxist-Leninist thesis is weakened to the point of emptiness, however, and another consequence of the effort to reinterpret doctrines in order to make them true is simply a diversity of philosophical views. Although the verbal form of a thesis ('there are real contradictions', 'the world is infinite', 'the basis determines the superstructure') may be fixed by tradition or by current ideology, Soviet philosophers may have no settled understanding of those words. And in seeking an understanding that upholds the truth of the thesis, different thinkers (in the absence of direct political pressure) may take different paths. We saw just such a situation in the Soviet discussion of infinity examined in Chapter 2. When G. I. Naan writes, "We know that the material world is infinite, but we never know in precisely what sense," he is both accepting the dogma of infinity and announcing that its meaning is an open question.[3] And the different conceptions of infinity that are advanced by Soviet philosophers, in the relatively apolitical forum of materialist ontology, represent different efforts to find a sense in which the world may plausibly be said to be infinite. Much of the energy of Soviet philosophers is thus expended on seeking truth not directly but through the attempt to forge appropriately truth-preserving interpretations for doctrines the truth of which must not be questioned.

A final source of the pluralism in Soviet philosophy today lies in the fact that Soviet thinkers are burdened with philosophical positions that are at bottom inconsistent. I have noted a lack of logical coherence at a number of critical points in Marxist-Leninist philosophy. In some cases this is simply a matter of the *absence* of logical connections that Soviet philosophers claim to be present. Thus dialectical materialism and historical materialism, I have argued, are not logically interdependent, as Soviet philosophers contend; either theory may be held without the other. At other points, however, Soviet philosophy is marked by direct and fundamental contradictions. Dialectical categories and principles cannot be grounded in a materialist philosophy. The individual can have no free

[2]H. B. Acton, *The Illusion of the Epoch. Marxism-Leninism as a Philosophical Creed* (London, 1955), p. 101.

[3]G. I. Naan, "Poniatie beskonechnosti v matematike i kosmologii," in V. V. Kaziutinskii et al., eds., *Beskonechnost' i Vselennaia* (Moscow, 1969), p. 77.

agency and the process of social development can include no real alternatives if there are necessary, objective laws of history. And the doctrine of the "leading role" of the Communist party is at odds with the basic principle of Marxist economic determinism—that the economic base determines the political superstructure.

On many such points, doctrinal diversity results when different Soviet philosophers are drawn toward different sides of the contradiction. No one, of course, can reject the doctrine of the leading role of the Communist party, but on less sensitive questions each side may have its champions. Thus we have seen the reappearance in post-Stalin Soviet thought of the old dispute between "mechanistically" or positivistically inclined materialists (those who are polarists on the question of the nature of contradiction) and "Deborinist" dialecticians (those who defend antinomism). Similarly grounded in root inconsistencies in Soviet thought are, first, the dispute in the philosophy of history between those who favor the "formational" approach stemming from Marx's preface to *A Contribution to the Critique of Political Economy* and the advocates of the "activity" approach suggested by the earlier writings of Marx; and, second, the divisions in aesthetic theory that are fueled by the same disjunction between Marxist-Leninist and early Marxist ideas.

The pluralism discernible in Soviet philosophy today must not be exaggerated, however. Striking though it may be when contrasted with the stereotype of a monolithic Marxism-Leninism, the variety of views defended by Soviet philosophers is nonetheless severely confined within a framework of dogma that is imposed by political authority. No Soviet writer, no matter how carefully he qualifies his terms, is allowed to call into question—much less to argue against—such fundamental tenets of Marxist-Leninist orthodoxy as the theses that God does not exist; that the material world is the only world there is; that both the world and our knowledge of it develop dialectically; that human societies and human nature change radically over time; that economics is the key to understanding history; that philosophies and moral systems reflect economic class interests; that proletarian revolution is inevitable and capitalism historically doomed; that socialism is both economically and humanly superior to capitalism; and that communism is the eventual future condition of all mankind. The fact that the exact meaning of many of these statements is a subject of controversy does not remove the Soviet philosopher's obligation to avoid every assertion that might appear to conflict with them.

Furthermore even *within* this framework the disagreements that arise among Soviet philosophers cannot function in the way in which disagreements function in other philosophical communities. For a further element of the dogmatic framework is the thesis that Soviet Marxism-Leninism *is* in fact monolithic, and as a result the genuine doctrinal differences that do exist within it are slighted and are prevented from evolving naturally and constructively. Issues are joined but often not sharply and clearly; contradictions appear, but often they are not squarely faced. Because these issues and contradictions arise within a structure that political authorities insist is *not* incoherent but rather "forged from a single piece of steel," they cannot be pursued to their foundations. In Hegelian terms, the contradictory elements cannot be sublated in some further and richer philosophical synthesis, because it cannot be admitted that a basic contradiction exists. A new synthesis, moreover, would constitute a genuine innovation at the heart of Soviet philosophy, and still another prominent feature of the dogmatic framework is the view that radical innovation cannot be necessary, since on the whole the truth is in. The truth, that is, is held to be established in all its fundamental outlines in the system of Marxism-Leninism, which incorporates harmoniously all of the world-revealing insights of the two greatest thinkers of all time (disregarding, as Soviet philosophers invariably do, the fact that it was not Marx or Lenin but Engels who first formulated the materialist ontology and the epistemology of "reflection" on which that system is based).

In general, then, the pluralism that we have seen in Soviet thought is not a productive clash of opinions that might lead to new principles and a new understanding of the world. Rather it is the result of diverse efforts to link a mandated but unruly conceptual apparatus with reality. In the post-Stalin period these efforts have been carried on with considerably greater attention to facts, and with a corresponding increase in the philosophical interest and value of the work. Indeed in the late 1950s and 1960s, in the immediate aftermath of Stalinist oppression, there were in many fields promising movements in the direction of genuinely creative philosophical work. Even today, although the excitement of release from the Stalinist terror has faded and "Communist party discipline" once more prevails, Soviet philosophy in some areas is marked by genuine accomplishments. In formal logic, significant advanced work is being done. Soviet semioticians, and to a lesser extent Soviet systems theorists, are at the cutting edge of their disciplines. The monumental studies of A. F. Losev in the history of thought—especially aesthetic thought—are unparalleled in world literature. Soviet research in the history of Russian philosophy also makes a contribution to international scholarship, despite the heavily doctrinaire and jingoistic spirit in which it is conducted. On the whole, however, far too much of the energy of Soviet philosophers is spent in a dogged campaign to impart sense and relevance to an assortment of time-worn theses, many of which can be made plausible only by stretching them into vacuousness.

Perhaps what should be considered surprising in all this, however, is not that Soviet Marxism-Leninism fails to occupy the front line of world philosophical progress but that philosophy in the USSR is alive at all. The Orwellian assumptions with which we tend to approach Soviet intellectual life suggest a poverty and a torpor that we have not found in most fields of Soviet philosophy. The classic Orwellian devices of thought control, assumed to have their paradigm expression in the USSR, have not in fact been employed in that country with anything like the effectiveness and calculating thoroughness imagined by George Orwell.

An example is the Soviet use of what Orwell called "doublethink," or the propagation of directly and deliberately contradictory theses such as 'freedom is slavery' and 'war is peace'.[4] Although no one could deny the presence of contradictions in Soviet Marxism-Leninism, on the whole Soviet philosophers attempt to minimize or to disguise those contradictions rather than to exalt them. The one case of authoritatively promoted doublethink that we have found in the foregoing examination of Soviet thought had to do with the Soviet concept of the state; Soviet philosophers, as we saw in Chapter 6, wish to hold both that all states are instruments of class coercion and that the Soviet socialist state is not such an instrument. Even in this case, however, the conclusion that the Soviet state is not a state is not paraded on street signs or in textbooks. Rather it appears to be tolerated, somewhat reluctantly, for lack of any better way to accommodate the conflicting demands of classical Marxism on the one hand and contemporary Soviet statism on the other. Whatever else we may think of its merits, Soviet Marxism-Leninist philosophy does not in general rely on the propagation of doublethink for its effectiveness.

Indeed it would appear, contra Orwell, that in the tangled world of Soviet thought the device of doublethink—or at least doubletalk—is used as much by independently minded writers *against* Marxist-Leninist dogmatism as it is by Soviet authorities in the name of that dogmatism. When Vasnetsov takes an accepted, honorific term such as 'realism' in aesthetics and uses it to signify formal values, he is employing a kind of defensive or liberating doublethink; the unexpressed contradiction that realism is formalism is a device for legitimizing and recommending values that might otherwise go unacknowledged. When Batishchev turns his praise of Communist "partisanship" into a brief for "objective partisanship" as consisting in a devotion to logic and to facts, the tacit conclusion is that objective partisanship is not partisan; and Batishchev's readers are quite capable of finding the moral in that paradox. When Losev recommends the study of Plato on the ground that the ancient Greeks were materialists

[4]George Orwell, *1984* (New York, 1961), p. 32.

at heart, the contradictory equation of materialism with Platonic idealism need not be drawn explicitly, but it functions to justify respectful consideration of Platonism.[5] In all these cases, defensive doublethink is a means of enlisting the approbative force of authorized terms—'realism', 'partisanship', 'materialism'—behind sympathetic attention to the exact opposite of what they stand for officially.

Perhaps the single most important respect in which the Soviet intellectual scene differs from Orwell's imaginative picture consists in what might be called the continued toleration of ambiguity in Soviet thought. A principal feature of Orwell's "Newspeak"—the imposed language of the controlled society—is its attempt to strip authorized words of unwanted meanings, so that the words cannot be used to entertain or to express unwanted thoughts.[6] It is indisputable that efforts of this sort do take place in the Soviet Union—efforts not only to limit the lexicon of acceptable terms but to impose a single desired meaning upon each of the words that remain. But in Soviet practice these efforts have in no way produced a philosophical discourse that is perfectly unambiguous or incapable of heterodoxy. The continued ability of Soviet thinkers to entertain and to employ different and sometimes contradictory meanings for the same "approved" term is another form of liberating doublethink in Soviet society.

In field after field of philosophy we have observed that even the more orthodox Soviet philosophers engage in exploring, and in many cases in expanding, the variety of meanings that still attaches to the most hallowed and elementary terms in the Marxist-Leninist vocabulary. Does the term 'matter' mean the whole of objective reality, or does it name a particular class of ontological entities with specific properties? Does 'infinity' signify spatio-temporal endlessness, the unceasing variety of material forms, or the epistemological inexhaustibility of the universe? Does 'logic' stand for the study of formal relationships or of "dialectical" connections among things? Is what is called a 'real contradiction' a logically consistent physical opposition in the material world (such as the antagonism of economic classes), or is it an antinomian, formally contradictory relationship among real things? Does the expression 'economic base' extend to intellectual and emotional forces (such as science and the morale of the socialist worker), or is it limited to strictly "material" factors? Is 'art' a name for a particular ideological reflection of economic interests, for the workings of productive labor, or for a special kind of sign system? Each of the alternative answers to each of these questions has champions among Soviet philosophers, and

[5]A. F. Losev et al., *Antichnaia literatura*, ed. A. A. Takho-Godi, 2d rev. ed. (Moscow, 1973), p. 186. Losev's own monumental study of Plato may be found in his *Istoriia antichnoi estetiki. Sofisty. Sokrat. Platon* (Moscow, 1969), pp. 143–681.

[6]Orwell, *1984*, pp. 246–247.

for that reason we cannot say that the semantic usages of Soviet Marxism-Leninism have been reduced to Newspeak poverty. If anything they are marked by a laxity that allows the kind of imprecision in discourse about which Kedrov complained when he said that some Soviet philosophers deliberately use terms in such a way that the reader may invest them with whatever meaning he or she pleases.

Furthermore, even when Marxist-Leninist theorists do generally agree upon a single meaning, unless the term in question is a purely invented or technical one with little if any bearing on the lives of the great mass of people, the meaning promoted by the theorists (and the ideologists behind them) must still compete against the other meanings associated with the term in the culture at large. Any term in common usage—'matter', 'logic', 'art', or any other—brings with it from the broader culture and especially from the past a rich content of meaning. Its semantic freight is bound up not only with everyday activities and concerns but with a literary, artistic, and scientific heritage that Soviet Marxists have not rejected, despite certain tendencies in that direction among the early Bolsheviks. The term 'freedom' (*svoboda*) is a prime example, and there is perhaps no clearer, more characteristic, or more significant case of the persistent toleration of ambiguity in Soviet intellectual culture than the failure of Soviet authorities to reduce the term 'freedom' to a Newspeak uniformity of content that would preclude subversive and antitotalitarian thoughts.

A single sense of the term 'freedom' is advanced in the Soviet philosophical literature, as we have seen. Freedom is defined in every text and reference work as consisting in "the recognition of necessity"—the acknowledgment of, and the acquiescence in, the objective inevitabilities that structure the world around us. With regard to history, freedom in this conception consists in the acceptance of the objective laws of social change, in accordance with which society marches unswervingly toward communism; the free individual is the one who marches along, not the one who ignores or resists the laws. In the context of ethics, freedom is the recognition of the communist moral norms, which are more and more disclosed as mankind progresses from the hell of class conflict through the purgatory of revolution toward the classless paradise. The ideological usefulness of this conception to Soviet authorities should be evident. The idea that there are inescapable external standards to which the individual's behavior must conform would appear to be just the sort of meaning that a totalitarian order would seek to give to the word 'freedom', assuming that the word is to be retained at all.

When we turn to a current standard Soviet dictionary of the Russian language, however, we find no such univocal definition. Assuredly, a version of the prescribed sense is given pride of place as the first entry under the heading 'Freedom'. But its domain is explicitly restricted to "Philosophy," and thus limited, the orthodox meaning yields immediately to a long list of conflicting meanings that reflect the full range of senses in which the term 'freedom' is actually used in Soviet society, as it was in earlier Russian society as well:

> FREEDOM ... 1. *Philos.* The ability to realize one's goals and aspirations on the basis of knowledge of the laws of development of nature and society. "Freedom is not arbitrariness, but agreement with the laws of necessity." Belinsky ... 2. The condition of one who is not a slave or serf ... 3. The absence of political and economic oppression ... 4. The condition of one who is not imprisoned or in captivity ... 5. Personal independence, the absence of dependence on something or someone ... 6. ... The ability to act in some area without limitations or prohibitions, without hindrance ... 7. Easiness, the absence of difficulties ... 8. Noncompulsoriness, the absence of constraint.[7]

Why, we may ask, have Soviet authorities not exercised their manifest power to control the dictionary and simply eliminated all meanings after the first? No doubt because they realize that such a tactic would not prevent people from *using* the word in the other senses as long as those senses are alive in the broader culture and are appropriate responses to the events of intellectual and practical life. To strip the word of those other meanings it would be necessary, for one thing, to suppress all of the Oldspeak literature in which the term 'freedom' appears and is defined explicitly or contextually in any of the alternative senses. But Soviet Russian communists have shown themselves unwilling to take so drastic a step. They have not turned their backs on Russian folk literature or on the great Russian novelists, poets, and essayists of the nineteenth and early twentieth centuries but instead have resolved to tolerate the semantic diversity their rich national heritage contains. Since alternative and conflicting meanings are thus allowed to live, the controllers of the dictionary may reason that those meanings may at least be kept within bounds by clearly subordinating them to the prescribed philosophical definition in the dictionary listing.

But of course people do not learn their basic vocabulary from dictionaries or philosophy books, and in the everyday life in which their language is formed, the alternative senses of 'freedom' are everywhere. They abound in the most formulaic of Socialist Realist literature. Soviet leaders unwittingly employ them in their public pronouncements, as in their continued references to "free time" (*svobodnoe vremia*) as opposed to working time.[8]

---

[7] S. G. Barkhudarov et al., eds., *Slovar' russkogo iazyka v chetyrekh tomakh* (Moscow, 1957–1961), vol. 4, p. 73.
[8] Andropov, *Speech*, p. 14.

And the alternative senses are of course prominently and deliberately displayed in *samizdat* writings; when in 1971 the authors of *The Sower* demanded "intellectual freedom and freedom of information" in the USSR, they were not asking for permission to acknowledge supposed historical or moral laws.[9] No doubt the most influential uses of 'freedom' to mean personal independence, the absence of restraints, and the like, however, are found in the writings of Pushkin, Tolstoi, Dostoevskii, and the other prerevolutionary authors whose works are treasured by the Soviet public as great products of the Russian national genius. To that literature, above all, contemporary Soviet intellectual culture is indebted for the vitality that it retains. Largely thanks to that literature Soviet students are still capable of the liberating doublethink that allows them to give one definition of 'freedom' in a philosophy examination and to assume another in the events of daily life.

On a snowy November afternoon in Moscow not long ago, a group of Russian schoolchildren, released at last from a regimented tour of the Tret'iakov Art Gallery, burst out the door with gleeful shouts of "Freedom!" Had these young people been thoroughly imbued with the Marxist-Leninist notion of freedom as the recognition of necessity, they would have exclaimed "Freedom!" when they were trooped into the museum, not when they were let out. But surely no such cries of acquiescence in the inevitable have ever been heard in those halls. And that is a fact full of hope. As long as there are Soviet children who proclaim their freedom when they are released from restraints rather than when restraints are imposed upon them, there will be Soviet philosophers who know the difference between free thought and intellectual regimentation and who understand the importance of striving to find, for whatever words are permitted them, the meanings that those words must have if they are to describe the world correctly and fruitfully. The work those thinkers produce, including that examined in the present volume, may fail to make a major contribution to world philosophy, but it will stand as a monument to the resourcefulness of the human spirit in pursuing significance and truth under the most trying of circumstances.

[9] "Samizdat. *Sotsial-demokraticheskaia partiia*. From 'The Sower.' A Call for a Liberal Opposition Party in the Soviet Union," *Intellectual Digest*, January 1973, p. 16.

Bibliography

Acton, H. B. *The Illusion of the Epoch. Marxism-Leninism as a Philosophical Creed.* London: Cohen and West, 1955.

Afanasyev, V. G. *Marxist Philosophy.* Translated by D. Fidlon. 4th rev. ed. Moscow: Progress Publishers, 1980.

Aizikovich, A. S., N. V. Kliagin, and A. A. Orlov. "Vsesoiuznoe koordinatsionnoe soveschchanie po problemam istoricheskogo materializma." *Filosofskie nauki,* 1981, no. 4, pp. 146–150.

Aktual'nye problemy istorii Rossii epokhi feodalizma. Sbornik statei. Moscow: Nauka, 1970.

Aleksandrov, A. D. "Space and Time in Contemporary Physics in the Light of Lenin's Philosophical Ideas." *Soviet Studies in Philosophy* 10 (Winter 1971–1972), pp. 257–262.

Aleksandrov, G. G., ed. *Dialekticheskii materializm.* Moscow: Gos. izd. politicheskoi literatury, 1953.

Alekseev, I. S. *Kontseptsiia dopolnitel'nosti. Istoriko-metodologicheskii analiz.* Moscow: Nauka, 1978.

Alekseev, P. V. *Predmet, struktura i funktsii dialekticheskogo materializma.* Moscow: Izd. Moskovskogo universiteta, 1978.

Andropov, Y. V. [Andropov, Iu. V.]. *Speech at the CPSU Central Committee Plenary Meeting. June 15, 1983.* Moscow: Novosti Press Agency, 1983.

——. *Uchenie Karla Marksa i nekotorye voprosy sotsialisticheskogo stroitel'stva v SSSR.* Moscow: Izd. politicheskoi literatury, 1983.

Anisimov, S. F. *Moral' i povedenie.* Moscow: Mysl', 1979.

——. "O kriterii kommunisticheskoi nravstvennosti." *Vestnik Moskovskogo universiteta. Seriia 8. Filosofiia,* 1966, no. 6, pp. 23–29.

—— and B. O. Nikolaichev. "Moscow University's Department of Marxist-Leninist Ethics. A Decade of Teaching and Sociopolitical Activity." *Soviet Studies in Philosophy* 19 (Spring 1981), pp. 89–98.

Anokhin, P. K. "Operezhaiushchee otrazhenie deistvitel'nosti." *Voprosy filosofii,* 1962, no. 7, p. 97–111.

Anufriev, E. A., E. V. Tadevosian, and M. V. Vetrov. *Nauchnyi kommunizm. Opyt razrabotki i chteniia lektsii.* Moscow: Izd. Moskovskogo universiteta, 1982.

Aref'eva, G. S. "V pomoshch' prepodavateliam marksistsko-leninskoi filosofii. Istoricheskii materializm kak nauka." *Filosofskie nauki*, 1982, no. 4, pp. 143–153.

—— and A. I. Verbin. "Sushchnost' materialisticheskogo ponimaniia istorii." *Filosofskie nauki*, 1978, no. 3, pp. 141–154.

Arkhangel'skii, L. M. "Aktual'nye problemy marksistskoi etiki." *Voprosy filosofii*, 1981, no. 1, pp. 39–50.

——. *Kategorii marksistskoi etiki*. Moscow: Sotsekgiz, 1963.

——. "Sushchnost' eticheskikh kategorii." *Filosofskie nauki*, 1961, no. 3, pp. 117–125.

——, ed. *Metodologiia eticheskikh issledovanii*. Moscow: Nauka, 1982.

Aver'ianov, A. N., and Z. M. Orudzhev. "Dialectical Contradiction in the Evolution of Knowledge." *Soviet Studies in Philosophy* 18 (Winter 1979–1980), pp. 63–82.

Ayer, A. J. "Philosophy and Science." *Soviet Studies in Philosophy* 1 (Summer 1962), pp. 14–19.

Bagaturiia, G. A. "Kategoriia 'proizvoditel'nye sily' v teoreticheskom nasledii Marksa i Engel'sa." *Voprosy filosofii*, 1981, no. 9, pp. 103–116.

Bakhtomin, N. K. *Praktika-Myshlenie-Znanie. K probleme tvorcheskogo myshleniia*. Moscow: Nauka, 1978.

Bakradze, K. S. "K voprosu o sootnoshenii logiki i dialektiki." *Voprosy filosofii*, 1950, no. 2, pp. 198–209.

——. *Sistema i metod filosofii Gegelia*. Tbilisi: Izd. Tbilisskogo gosudarstvennogo universiteta, 1958.

Bakshtanovskii, V. I., ed. *Praktikum po etike*. 2d ed. Tiumen': Tiumenskii industrial'nyi institut, 1979.

—— et al., eds. *Nauchnoe upravlenie nravstvennymi protsessami i etiko-prikladnye issledovaniia*. Novosibirsk: Nauka, Sibirskoe otdelenie, 1980.

Bandzeladze, G. D. *Aktual'nye problemy marksistskoi etiki (sbornik statei)*. Tbilisi: Izd. Tbilisskogo gosudarstvennogo universiteta, 1967.

——. *Etika. Opyt izlozheniia sistemy marksistskoi etiki*. 2d ed. Tbilisi: Sabchota sakartvelo, 1970.

——. "O tvorcheskom kharaktere nravstvennosti." *Voprosy filosofii*, 1981, no. 6, pp. 119–123.

Barabash, Yuri [Barabash, Iurii]. *Aesthetics and Poetics*. Moscow: Progress Publishers, 1977.

——. *Voprosy estetiki i poetiki*. 3d ed. Moscow: Sovetskaia Rossiia, 1978.

Barkhudarov, S. G., et al., eds. *Slovar' russkogo iazyka v chetyrekh tomakh*. 4 vols. Moscow: Gos. izd. inostrannykh i natsional'nykh slovarei, 1957–1961.

Batishchev, G. S. "Deiatel'nostnaia sushchnost' cheloveka kak filosofskii printsip." In I. F. Balakina et al., eds., *Problema cheloveka v sovremennoi filosofii*, pp. 73–144. Moscow: Nauka, 1969.

Bazhenov, L. B. "Nekotorye zamechaniia po povodu publikatsii V. V. Orlova." *Filosofskie nauki*, 1974, no. 5, pp. 74–77.

—— and N. N. Nutsubidze. "K diskussiiam o probleme beskonechnosti Vselennoi." In V. V. Kaziutinskii et al., eds., *Beskonechnost' i Vselennaia*, pp. 129–136. Moscow: Mysl', 1969.

Bender, Frederic L. "Marx, Materialism and the Limits of Philosophy." *Studies in Soviet Thought* 25 (1983), pp. 79–100.

Bezcherevnykh, E. V. *Problema praktiki v protsesse formirovaniia filosofii marksizma*. Moscow: Vysshaia shkola, 1972.

Blakeley, Thomas J. *Soviet Theory of Knowledge*. Dordrecht: D. Reidel, 1964.

Blauberg, I. V., P. V. Kopnin, and I. K. Pantin, eds. *Kratkii slovar' po filosofii*. 2d ed. Moscow: Izd. politicheskoi literatury, 1970.

Blauberg, I. V., V. N. Sadovsky, and E. G. Yudin, eds. *Systems Theory. Philosophical and Methodological Problems*. Translated by S. Syrovatkin and O. Germogenova. Moscow: Progress Publishers, 1977.

Bocharov, V. A., et al. "Nekotorye problemy razvitiia logiki." *Voprosy filosofii*, 1979, no. 6, pp. 102–114.

——. "On Problems of the Evolution of Logic." *Soviet Studies in Philosophy* 18 (Spring 1980), pp. 31–52.

Bocheński, J. M. "Philosophy Studies." *Soviet Survey* 31 (1960), pp. 64–74.

——. "Soviet Logic." In J. M. Bocheński and T. J. Blakeley, eds., *Studies in Soviet Thought*. I, pp. 29–38. Dordrecht: D. Reidel, 1961.

——. *Soviet Russian Dialectical Materialism [Diamat]*. Translated by Nicolas Sollohub. Revised by T. J. Blakeley. Dordrecht: D. Reidel, 1963.

—— and T. J. Blakeley, eds. *Studies in Soviet Thought*. I. Dordrecht: D. Reidel, 1961.

Bogomolova, T. V., and V. I. Kirillov. "Problema vzaimosviazi kategorii dialektiki (obzor literatury)." *Filosofskie nauki*, 1981, no. 2, pp. 43–55.

Borev, Iurii. *Estetika*. 2d ed. Moscow: Izd. politicheskoi literatury, 1975.

Brezhnev, Leonid I. *Leninskim kursom. Rechi i stat'i*. 4 vols. Moscow: Progress Publishers, 1975.

Brutian, G. A. "K voprosu o prirode filosofskogo znaniia." *Filosofskie nauki*, 1976, no. 5, pp. 33–40.

Burov, A. I. *Esteticheskaia sushchnost' iskusstva*. Moscow: Iskusstvo, 1956.

——. *Estetika. Problemy i spory. Metodologicheskie osnovy diskussii v estetike*. Moscow: Iskusstvo, 1975.

Calder, Nigel. *Einstein's Universe*. New York: Viking Press, 1979.

Chudinov, E. M., ed. *Einshtein. Filosofskie problemy fiziki XX veka*. Moscow: Nauka, 1979.

Cohen, G. A. *Karl Marx's Theory of History. A Defence*. Princeton: Princeton University Press, 1978.

Davletshin, Tamurbek. "The Concept of a 'State of All the People.'" *Studies on the Soviet Union*, 1964, no. 1, pp. 105–119.

Davydov, Iu. *Etika liubvi i metafizika svoevoliia (problemy nravstvennoi filosofii)*. Moscow: Molodaia gvardiia, 1982.

De George, Richard T. *Patterns of Soviet Thought. The Origins and Development of Dialectical and Historical Materialism*. Ann Arbor: University of Michigan Press, 1966.

——. *Soviet Ethics and Morality*. Ann Arbor: University of Michigan Press, 1969.

D'Espagnat, Bernard. "The Quantum Theory and Reality." *Scientific American* 241 (November 1979), pp. 158–160+.

Dialekticheskoe protivorechie. Moscow: Izd. politicheskoi literatury, 1979.

"Diskussiia o predmete filosofii." *Vestnik Moskovskogo universiteta. Seriia 8. Filosofiia*, 1971, no. 2, pp. 96–101.

Dobrynina, V. I. "Voprosy formirovaniia kommunisticheskogo mirovozzreniia studenchestva." *Filosofskie nauki*, 1976, no. 2, pp. 35–42.

Documents and Resolutions. The Twenty-sixth Congress of the Communist Party of the Soviet Union. Moscow: Novosti Press Agency, 1981.

Dokumenty sovetsko-ital'ianskoi konferentsii istorikov. 8–20 aprelia 1968 goda. Moscow: Nauka, 1970.

Domrachev, G. M., S. F. Efimov, and A. V. Timofeeva. *Zakon otritsaniia otritsaniia*. Moscow: Vysshaia shkola, 1961.

Drobnitskii, O. G. "Diskussiia po problemam etiki mezhdu sovetskimi i britanskimi filosofami." *Voprosy filosofii*, 1969, no. 2, pp. 143–147; 1970, no. 5, pp. 137–141; 1971, no. 4, pp. 132–135.

——. *Problemy nravstvennosti*. Moscow: Nauka, 1977.

Dubinin, V. V., and I. I. Shevchuk. "Uchenie ob obshchestvenno-ekonomicheskoi formatsii i nekotorye voprosy mezhformatsionnogo perekhoda." *Vestnik Moskovskogo universiteta. Seriia 7. Filosofiia*, 1981, no. 6, pp. 28–37.

Dubrovin, A. G., ed. *Kommunisticheskoe mirovozzrenie i iskusstvo sotsialisticheskogo realizma (sbornik)*. Moscow: Znanie, 1977.

Dudel', S. P., and G. M. Shtraks. *Zakon edinstva i bor'by protivopolozhnostei*. Moscow: Vysshaia shkola, 1967.

Dutt, Clemens, ed. *Fundamentals of Marxism-Leninism. Manual*. 2d rev. ed. Moscow: Foreign Languages Publishing House, 1963.

Easton, L. D., and K. H. Guddat, trans. and eds. *Writings of the Young Marx on Philosophy and Society*. New York: Doubleday, Anchor Books, 1967.

Edie, J. M., et al., eds. *Russian Philosophy*. 3 vols. Chicago: Quadrangle Books, 1965.

Egides, P. M. "K probleme tozhdestva bytiia i myshleniia." *Filosofskie nauki*, 1968, no. 4, pp. 103–113.

Ehlen, Peter. "Emancipation through Morality. New Paths of Ethical Thought in the Soviet Union." *Studies in Soviet Thought* 13 (1973), pp. 203–217.

——. *Die philosophische Ethik in der Sowjetunion. Analyse und Diskussion*. Munich: Anton Pustet, 1972.

Eimermacher, Karl, and Serge Shishkoff. *Subject Bibliography of Soviet Semiotics. The Moscow-Tartu School*. Ann Arbor: Michigan Slavic Publications, 1977.

Engels, Frederick. *Anti-Dühring. Herr Eugen Dühring's Revolution in Science*. Moscow: Progress Publishers, 1947.

——. *Dialectics of Nature*. Translated and edited by Clemens Dutt. New York: International Publishers, 1940.

——. *Ludwig Feuerbach and the Outcome of Classical German Philosophy*. Edited by C. P. Dutt. New York: International Publishers, 1941.

"Ethics and Morality Studies. A Soviet Discussion." *Soviet Studies in Philosophy* 21 (Fall 1982), pp. 3–73.

Evans, Alfred B., Jr. "Developed Socialism in Soviet Ideology." *Soviet Studies* 29 (1977), pp. 409–428.

Feyerabend, Paul K. "Dialectical Materialism and the Quantum Theory." *Slavic Review* 25 (September 1966), pp. 414–417.

Filippov, G. F. "Konstruktivnoe nachalo." *Voprosy filosofii*, 1981, no. 12, pp. 82–85.

Fleischer, Helmut. "The Materiality of Matter." *Studies in Soviet Thought* 2 (1962), pp. 12–20.

———. "Open Questions in Contemporary Soviet Ontology." *Studies in Soviet Thought* 6 (1966), pp. 168–184.

Fock, V. A. "Nil's Bor v moei zhizni." *Nauka i chelovechestvo* 2 (1963), pp. 518–519.

———. "Ob interpretatsii kvantovoi mekhaniki." In P. N. Fedoseev et al., eds., *Filosofskie problemy sovremennogo estestvoznaniia. Trudy Vsesoiuznogo soveshchaniia po filosofskim voprosam estestvoznaniia*, pp. 212–236. Moscow: Izd. Akademii nauk, 1959.

———. "Quantum Physics and Philosophical Problems." In M. E. Omelyanovsky, ed., *Lenin and Modern Natural Science*, pp. 205–224. Moscow: Progress Publishers, 1978.

———. "Quantum Physics and Philosophical Problems." *Soviet Studies in Philosophy* 10 (Winter 1971–1972), pp. 252–256.

Frolov, I. T., ed. *Filosofskii slovar'*. 4th ed. Moscow: Izd. politicheskoi literatury, 1980.

Furmanov, G. L., A. P. Sertsova, and S. S. Il'in, eds. *Dialektika pererastaniia razvitogo sotsialisticheskogo obshchestva v kommunisticheskoe*. Moscow: Izd. Moskovskogo universiteta, 1980.

Ganzhin, V. T., and Iu. V. Sogomonov. "Sotsial'noe upravlenie i moral.' Issledovatel'skie perspektivy." *Filosofskie nauki*, 1980, no. 5, pp. 3–14.

Gefter, M. Ia., et al., eds. *Istoricheskaia nauka i nekotorye problemy sovremennosti*. Moscow: Nauka, 1969.

Gerschenkron, Alexander. "Soviet Marxism and Absolutism." *Slavic Review* 30 (1971), pp. 853–869.

Gindin, I. F. "Problemy istorii fevral'skoi revoliutsii i ee sotsial'no-ekonomicheskikh predposylok." *Istoriia SSSR*, 1967, no. 4, pp. 30–49.

———. "Russkaia burzhuaziia v period kapitalizma, ee razvitie i osobennosti." *Istoriia SSSR*, 1963, no. 2, pp. 57–80; no. 3, pp. 37–60.

Ginzburg, V. L. "Astrofizika. Dostizheniia i perspektivy." *Kommunist*, 1965, no. 4, pp. 56–64.

———. *Key Problems of Physics and Astrophysics*. Translated by Oleg Glebov. Moscow: Mir Publishers, 1976.

Glazunov, I. G. "O razvitii dvukhstupenchatykh gnoseologicheskikh struktur vo mnogostupenchatye." *Vestnik Moskovskogo universiteta. Seriia 7. Filosofiia*, 1981, no. 5, pp. 14–23.

Glezerman, G. "Lenin i formirovanie sotsialisticheskogo obraza zhizni." *Kommunist*, 1974, no. 1, pp. 105–118.

Glezerman, G. E., et al., eds. *Razvitoe sotsialisticheskoe obshchestvo. Sushchnost', kriterii zrelosti, kritika revizionistskikh kontseptsii.* 2d ed. Moscow: Mysl', 1975.

Glezerman, M. N., M. N. Rutkevich, and S. S. Vishnevskii, eds. *Sotsialisticheskii obraz zhizni.* Moscow: Izd. politicheskoi literatury, 1980.

Gol'dentrikht, S. S. *O prirode esteticheskogo tvorchestva.* 2d rev. ed. Moscow: Izd. Moskovskogo universiteta, 1977.

Golovko, N. A., and V. S. Markov. "Za nauchnost' i konkretnost' v razrabotke problem etiki." *Voprosy filosofii*, 1968, no. 8, pp. 148–155.

Gorsky, D. "Advance Reflection of Reality at the Level of Human Cognition." In V. Lorentson and B. Yudin, eds., *Materialist Dialectics Today*, pp. 174–191. Moscow: "Social Sciences Today" Editorial Board, USSR Academy of Sciences, 1979.

Gott, V. "Material'noe edinstvo mira i edinstvo nauchnogo znaniia." *Voprosy filosofii*, 1977, no. 12, pp. 24–33.

——. *This Amazing, Amazing, Amazing But Knowable Universe.* Translated by John Bushnell and Kristine Bushnell. Moscow: Progress Publishers, 1977.

——, E. P. Semeniuk, and A. D. Ursul. "O spetsifike filosofii i ee otnoshenii k drugim naukam." *Filosofskie nauki*, 1982, no. 4, pp. 13–23.

Graham, Loren R. "Quantum Mechanics and Dialectical Materialism." *Slavic Review* 25 (September 1966), pp. 381–410.

——. *Science and Philosophy in the Soviet Union.* New York: Alfred A. Knopf, 1972.

"Greater Activism Asked of Literary Press." *Current Digest of the Soviet Press* 34, no. 30 (August 25, 1982), p. 10.

Gribanov, D. P. "The Philosophical Views of Albert Einstein." *Soviet Studies in Philosophy* 18 (Fall 1979), pp. 79–94.

Gribanov, N. I., and S. A. Lebedev. "Aktual'nye voprosy teorii materialisticheskoi dialektiki." *Vestnik Moskovskogo universiteta. Seriia 7. Filosofiia*, 1981, no. 4, pp. 74-77.

Grier, Philip T. *Marxist Ethical Theory in the Soviet Union.* Dordrecht: D. Reidel, 1978.

Gritskov, Iu. V. "Problema utochneniia statusa obshchei teorii sistem." *Vestnik Moskovskogo universiteta. Seriia 7. Filosofiia*, 1981, no. 5, pp. 49–57.

Gulyga, A. V., and Iu. A. Levada, eds. *Filosofskie problemy istoricheskoi nauki.* Moscow: Nauka, 1969.

Gurevich, A. Ia. "Nekotorye aspekty izucheniia sotsial'noi istorii. (Obshchestvenno-istoricheskaia psikhologiia)." *Voprosy istorii*, 1964, no. 10, pp. 51–68.

Hahn, Werner G. *Postwar Soviet Politics. The Fall of Zhdanov and the Defeat of Moderation, 1946–53.* Ithaca: Cornell University Press, 1982.

Hänggi, Jürg. *Formale und dialektische Logik in der Sowjetphilosophie.* Dissertation zur Erlangung der Doktorwürde von der philosophischen Fakultät der Universität Freiburg in der Schweiz. 2 vols. Zurich: P. Schmidberger, 1971.

Hegel, G. W. F. *Enzyklopädie der philosophischen Wissenschaften im Grundrisse (1830).* Hamburg: Meiner, 1969.

*Hegel's Science of Logic.*Translated by W. H. Johnson and L. G. Struthers. 2 vols. London: George Allen and Unwin, 1929.

Historical Materialism. Theory, Methodology, Problems. Moscow: "Social Sciences Today" Editorial Board, USSR Academy of Sciences, 1977.

History of the Communist Party of the Soviet Union (Bolsheviks). Short Course. Edited by a Commission of the Central Committee of the C.P.S.U. (B.). New York: International Publishers, 1939.

Ianovskaia, S. A. "Matematicheskaia logika i osnovaniia matematiki." In *Matematika v SSSR za sorok let 1917–1957,* vol. 1, pp. 13–120. Moscow: Gos. izd. fiziko-matematicheskoi literatury, 1959.

——. "Osnovaniia matematiki i matematicheskaia logika." In *Matematika v SSSR za tridtsat' let 1917–1947,* pp. 11–45. Moscow-Leningrad: Gos. izd. tekhnichesko-teoreticheskoi literatury, 1948.

Iezuitov, N. "Konets krasote." *Proletarskaia literatura,* 1931, no. 4, pp. 122–159.

Il'ichev, L. F. *Filosofiia i nauchnyi progress.* Moscow: Nauka, 1977.

——, ed. *Materialisticheskaia dialektika kak obshchaia teoriia razvitiia.* 3 vols. to date. Moscow: Nauka, 1982–1983.

—— et al., eds. *Filosofskii entsiklopedicheskii slovar'.* Moscow: Sovetskaia entsiklopediia, 1983.

Ilyenkov, E. V. [Il'enkov, E. V.]. *Dialectical Logic. Essays on Its History and Theory.* Translated by H. C. Creighton. Moscow: Progress Publishers, 1977.

——. *Dialektika abstraktnogo i konkretnogo v "Kapitale" Marksa.* Moscow: Izd. Akademii nauk SSSR, 1960.

"Issledovaniia v oblasti marksistsko-leninskoi etiki." *Voprosy filosofii,* 1977, no. 8, pp. 133–143.

Istoriia i sotsiologiia. Moscow: Nauka, 1964.

Ivanov, P. *O sushchnosti krasoty.* Moscow: Prosveshchenie, 1967.

James, C. Vaughan. *Soviet Socialist Realism. Origins and Theory.* London: Macmillan, 1973.

Jensen, Kenneth M. *Beyond Marx and Mach. Aleksandr Bogdanov's Philosophy of Living Experience.* Dordrecht: D. Reidel, 1978.

Jeu, Bernard. *La philosophie soviétique et l'Occident. Essai sur les tendances et sur la signification de la philosophie soviétique contemporaine (1959–1969).* Paris: Mercure de France, 1969.

Jordan, Z. A. "The Dialectical Materialism of Lenin." *Slavic Review* 25 (June 1966), pp. 259–286.

"K itogam obsuzhdeniia voprosov logiki." *Voprosy filosofii,* 1951, no. 6, pp. 143–149.

Kanet, Roger E. "The Rise and Fall of the 'All-People's State'. Recent Changes in the Soviet Theory of the State." *Soviet Studies* 20 (1968), pp. 81–93.

Kantor, K. M. *Krasota i pol'za. Sotsiologicheskie voprosy material'no-khudozhestvennoi kul'tury.* Moscow: Iskusstvo, 1967.

Kapustin, A. P. "Spory o putiakh izlozheniia dialektiki (Obzor)." *Voprosy filosofii,* 1979, no. 6, pp. 161–169.

Karmin, A. S. "Kosmologicheskie predstavleniia o konechnosti i beskonechnosti

Vselennoi i ikh otnoshenie k real'nosti." *Filosofskie nauki*, 1978, no. 3, pp. 13–22.

———. *Poznanie beskonechnogo.* Moscow: Mysl', 1981.

Katvan, Zeev. "Reflection Theory and the Identity of Thinking and Being." *Studies in Soviet Thought* 18 (1978), pp. 87–109.

Kazakov, A. P., et al., eds. *Razvitoe sotsialisticheskoe obshchestvo i obshchestvennyi progress.* Leningrad: Izd. Leningradskogo universiteta, 1976.

Kaziutinskii, V. V., et al., eds. *Beskonechnost' i Vselennaia.* Moscow: Mysl', 1969.

Kedrov, B. M. *Edinstvo dialektiki, logiki, i teorii poznaniia.* Moscow: Gos. izd. politicheskoi literatury, 1963.

———. "Lenin's Plans for Elaborating the Theory of Materialist Dialectics." In V. Lorentson and B. Yudin, eds., *Marxist Dialectics Today*, 2d ed., pp. 48–82. Moscow: "Social Sciences Today" Editorial Board, USSR Academy of Sciences, 1979.

———. "Leninskii vzgliad na elektron i sovremennaia fizika." *Bol'shevik*, 1948, no. 2, pp. 44–61.

———. "Marksistskaia filosofiia. Ee predmet i rol' v integratsii sovremennykh nauk." *Voprosy filosofii*, 1982, no. 1, pp. 53–62.

———. "Marx and the Unity of Science—Natural and Social." *Soviet Studies in Philosophy* 7 (Fall 1968), pp. 3–14.

———. "Philosophy as a General Science." *Soviet Studies in Philosophy* 1 (Fall 1962), pp. 3–24.

——— and G. Gurgenidze. "Za glubokuiu razrabotku leninskogo filosofskogo nasledstva." *Kommunist*, 1955, no. 14, pp. 45–56.

Kelle, V. Zh., and M. Ia. Koval'zon. "Vazhneishie aspekty metodologii sotsial'no-filosofskogo issledovaniia." *Voprosy filosofii*, 1980, no. 7, pp. 116–129.

Kharin, Yu. A. *Fundamentals of Dialectics.* Translated by Konstantin Kostrov. Moscow: Progress Publishers, 1981.

Khasanov, I. A. "Dve kontseptsii prostranstva i vremeni." *Voprosy filosofii*, 1966, no. 2, pp. 59–67.

Khlyabich, I. *An Outline History of Philosophy.* Moscow: Progress Publishers, n.d.

Khrapchenko, M. B. "Literatura i modelirovanie deistvitel'nosti." In A. S. Miasnikov et al., eds., *Kontekst. 1973. Literaturno-teoreticheskie issledovaniia*, pp. 11–33. Moscow: Nauka, 1974.

———. "Semiotika i khudozhestvennoe tvorchestvo. Stat'ia pervaia." *Voprosy literatury*, 1971, no. 9, pp. 69–95.

Kline, George L. "The Myth of Marx's Materialism." *Annals of Scholarship* 3, no. 2 (October 1984), pp. 1–38.

———. *Religious and Anti-Religious Thought in Russia.* Chicago: University of Chicago Press, 1968.

———. "Was Marx an Ethical Humanist?" *Studies in Soviet Thought* 9 (1969), pp. 91–103.

Kol'man, E. "O konechnosti i beskonechnosti Vselennoi." In V. V. Kaziutinskii et al., eds., *Beskonechnost' i Vselennaia*, pp. 143–151. Moscow: Mysl', 1969.

——. "The Philosophical Interpretation of Contemporary Physics." *Studies in Soviet Thought* 21 (1980), pp. 1–14.

Kondakov, N. I. *Logicheskii slovar'*. Moscow: Nauka, 1971.

——. *Vvedenie v logiku*. Moscow: Nauka, 1967.

Konkin, M. I. *Problema formirovaniia i razvitiia filosofskikh kategorii*. Moscow: Vysshaia shkola, 1980.

[Konstantinov, F. V., ed.] *The Fundamentals of Marxist-Leninist Philosophy*. Translated by Robert Daglish. Moscow: Progress Publishers, 1974.

Konstantinov, F. V., ed. *The Fundamentals of Marxist-Leninist Philosophy*. Translated by Robert Daglish. Moscow: Progress Publishers, 1982.

——. *Osnovy marksistskoi filosofii*. Moscow: Gos. izd. politicheskoi literatury, 1959.

——. *Osnovy marksistsko-leninskoi filosofii*. 4th rev. ed. Moscow: Izd. politicheskoi literatury, 1978.

—— and V. G. Marakhov, eds. *Materialisticheskaia dialektika v piati tomakh*. 3 vols. to date. Moscow: Mysl', 1981–1983.

—— et al., eds. *Dialektika i logika nauchnogo poznaniia. Materialy soveshchaniia po sovremennym problemam materialisticheskoi dialektiki. 7–9 aprelia 1965 g.* Moscow: Nauka, 1966.

——. *Filosofskaia entsiklopediia*. 5 vols. Moscow: Sovetskaia entsiklopediia, 1960–1970.

Konstitutsiia (osnovnoi zakon) Soiuza Sovetskikh Sotsialisticheskikh Respublik. Moscow: Izd. politicheskoi literatury, 1977.

Kopnin, P. V. *Dialektika kak logika i teoriia poznaniia. Opyt logiko-gnoseologicheskogo issledovaniia*. Moscow: Nauka, 1973.

——. *Gnoseologicheskie i logicheskie osnovy nauki*. Moscow: Mysl', 1974.

——. "O prirode i osobennostiakh filosofskogo znaniia." *Voprosy filosofii*, 1969, no. 4, pp. 123–133.

Korostovtsev, M. A. "O poniatii 'Drevnii vostok.' " *Vestnik drevnei istorii*, 1970, no. 1, pp. 3–18.

Korshunov, A. M. *Otrazhenie, deiatel'nost', poznanie*. Moscow: Politizdat, 1979.

Korsunskii, A. R. "Problema revoliutsionnogo perekhoda ot rabovladel'cheskogo stroia k feodal'nomu v Zapadnoi Evrope." *Voprosy istorii*, 1964, no. 5, pp. 95–111.

Kosichev, A. D. "Aktual'nye voprosy podgotovki filosofskikh kadrov." *Kommunist*, 1982, no. 3, pp. 59–68.

Kosolapov, R. I. *Sotsializm. K voprosam teorii*. 2d ed. Moscow: Mysl', 1979.

Kozhanov, N. M. *Nravstvennye printsipy kommunista*. Moscow: Izd. politicheskoi literatury, 1979.

Kozlovskii, V. E. "XXVI s"ezd KPSS i problemy materialisticheskoi dialektiki." *Filosofskie nauki*, 1981, no. 5, pp. 3–13.

Krechetovich, L. M. *Voprosy evoliutsii rastitel'nogo mira. Sbornik statei*. Moscow: Izd. Moskovskogo obshchestva ispytatelei prirody, 1952.

Krutous, V. P., and A. S. Migunov. "Osnovnye napravleniia esteticheskikh issledovanii v SSSR za 60 let (1917–1977)." *Vestnik Moskovskogo universiteta. Seriia 7. Filosofiia*, 1978, no. 1, pp. 41–54.

Kulikova, I. S., and A. Ia. Zis', eds. *Marksistsko-leninskaia estetika i khudozhest-vennoe tvorchestvo*. Moscow: Progress Publishers, 1980.

Kumpf, F., and Z. M. Orudzhev. *Dialekticheskaia logika. Osnovnye printsipy i problemy*. Moscow: Izd. politicheskoi literatury, 1979.

Küng, Guido. "Bibliography of Soviet Work in the Field of Mathematical Logic and the Foundations of Mathematics, from 1917–1957." *Notre Dame Journal of Formal Logic* 3 (January 1962), pp. 1–40.

———. "Mathematical Logic in the Soviet Union (1917–1947 and 1947–1957)." In J. M. Bocheński and T. J. Blakeley, eds., *Studies in Soviet Thought*. I, pp. 39–43. Dordrecht: D. Reidel, 1961.

Kuzmin, V. P. *Printsip sistemnosti v teorii i metodologii K. Marksa*. 2d ed. Moscow: Izd. politicheskoi literatury, 1980.

Kuznetsov, I. V. "But Philosophy Is a Science." *Soviet Studies in Philosophy* 1 (Summer 1962), pp. 20–36.

Labedz, Leopold, ed. *Solzhenitsyn. A Documentary Record*. New York: Harper and Row, 1970.

Laptenok, S. D. *Aktual'nye voprosy metodiki prepodavaniia marksistsko-leninskoi etiki*. Minsk: Izd. BGU im. V. I. Lenina, 1980.

Lebedev, V. P. *Beskonechna li Vselennaia?* Minsk: Nauka i tekhnika, 1978.

Legostaev, V. M. "Filosofskaia interpretatsiia razvitiia nauki Tomasa Kuna." *Voprosy filosofii*, 1972, no. 11, pp. 129–136.

Lektorskii, V. A. *Sub"ekt, ob"ekt, poznanie*. Moscow: Nauka, 1980.

Lenin, V. I. *Materialism and Empirio-Criticism. Critical Comments on a Reactionary Philosophy* [1909]. New York: International Publishers, 1927.

———. *Polnoe sobranie sochinenii*. 5th ed. 55 vols. Moscow: Izd. politicheskoi literatury, 1958–1965.

Lobkowicz, N. "Materialism and Matter in Marxism-Leninism." In Ernan McMullin, ed., *The Concept of Matter in Modern Philosophy*, pp. 154–188. Notre Dame: University of Notre Dame Press, 1978.

Loone, Eero. *Sovremennaia filosofiia istorii*. Tallin: Eesti raamat, 1980.

Lorentson, V., and B. Yudin. *Marxist Dialectics Today*. Moscow: "Social Sciences Today" Editorial Board, USSR Academy of Sciences, 1979.

Losev, A. F. *Dialektika mifa*. Moscow: Izd. avtora, 1930.

———. *Istoriia antichnoi estetiki. Sofisty. Sokrat. Platon*. Moscow: Iskusstvo, 1969.

——— et al. *Antichnaia literatura*. Edited by A. A. Takho-Godi. 2d rev. ed. Moscow: Izd. Ministerstva prosveshcheniia, 1973.

Lotman, Iu. M. *Lektsii po struktural'noi poetike. Vvedenie, teoriia stikha*. Intro. by Thomas G. Winner. Providence: Brown University Press, 1968.

———. *Struktura khudozhestvennogo teksta*. Intro. by Thomas G. Winner. Providence: Brown University Press, 1971.

Lucid, Daniel P., ed. and trans. *Soviet Semiotics. An Anthology*. Baltimore: Johns Hopkins University Press, 1977.

Maksimov, A. A. "Marksistskii filosofskii materializm i sovremennaia fizika." *Voprosy filosofii*, 1948, no. 3, pp. 105–124.

——— et al., eds. *Filosofskie voprosy sovremennoi fiziki*. Moscow: Izd. Akademii nauk SSSR, 1952.

Marcuse, Herbert. *Soviet Marxism. A Critical Analysis*. London: Routledge and Kegan Paul, 1958.

Marek, Jiři, and L. E. Musberg. "Matter in Its 'Infinity.' " *Studies in Soviet Thought* 27 (1984), pp. 25–31.

Margulis, A. V. "K kharakteristike metodologicheskikh aspektov obshchesotsiologicheskoi teorii." *Voprosy filosofii*, 1981, no. 12, pp. 76–81.

Marko, Kurt. "No Juvenal of Bolshevism." *Studies in Soviet Thought* 22 (1981), pp. 147–149.

Markov, M. A. "O prirode fizicheskogo znaniia." *Voprosy filosofii*, 1947, no. 2, pp. 140–176.

Marković, M. "Osnovi dijalektičko-humanističke teorije istine." *Praxis*, 1965, no. 2, pp. 178–192.

Marx, Karl. *Capital. A Critique of Political Economy*. Vol. 1. Translated by Ben Fowkes. New York: Random House, Vintage Books, 1977.

——. *Capital. A Critique of Political Economy*. Vol. 1. Translated by Samuel Moore and Edward Aveling. Edited by Frederick Engels. New York: International Publishers, 1967.

——. *Early Writings*. Translated by Rodney Livingstone and Gregor Benton. Harmondsworth, England: Penguin Books, 1975.

——. *Grundrisse der Kritik der politischen Ökonomie. (Rohentwurf) 1857–1858*. Berlin: Dietz Verlag, 1953.

——. *Grundrisse. Foundations of the Critique of Political Economy (Rough Draft)*. Translated by Martin Nicolaus. London: Penguin Books, 1973.

—— and Frederick Engels. *Collected Works*. New York: International Publishers, 1975–.

——. *Iz rannykh proizvedenii*. Moscow: Gos. izd. politicheskoi literatury, 1956.

——. *Selected Works in One Volume*. New York: International Publishers, 1968.

——. *Sochineniia*. 2d ed. 50 vols. Moscow: Gos. izd. politicheskoi literatury, 1954–1981.

——. *Werke*. 41 vols. Berlin: Dietz Verlag, 1960–1968.

Maslin, M. A. "Nauchnye issledovaniia na Filosofskom fakul'tete MGU v desiatoi piatiletke. Ot XXV k XXVI s"ezdu KPSS." *Vestnik Moskovskogo universiteta. Seriia 7. Filosofiia*, 1981, no. 3, pp. 3–12.

Materialy XXV s"ezda KPSS. Moscow: Izd. politicheskoi literatury, 1977.

"Materialy soveshchaniia po problemam dialekticheskogo materializma v redaktsii zhurnala 'Voprosy filosofii.' " *Voprosy filosofii*, 1982, no. 4, pp. 30–40; no. 5, pp. 17–34; no. 6, pp. 16–22; no. 7, pp. 85–98.

"Materialy soveshchaniia po problemam istoricheskogo materializma v redaktsii zhurnala 'Voprosy filosofii.' " *Voprosy filosofii*, 1982, no. 5, pp. 35–51; no. 6, pp. 23–33; no. 7, pp. 99–117.

"Materialy soveshchaniia po probleme cheloveka v zhurnale 'Voprosy filosofii.' " *Voprosy filosofii*, 1980, no. 7, pp. 94–115.

Matveev, M. N. "Analiz razvitiia. Deistvitel'nye trudnosti i mnimye paradoksy." *Filosofskie nauki*, 1973, no. 5, pp. 61–69.

Mayr, Ernst. "Evolution." *Scientific American* 239 (September 1978), pp. 47–55.

Medvedev, Roy A. *Let History Judge. The Origins and Consequences of Stalinism.* Translated by Colleen Taylor. Edited by David Joravsky and Georges Haupt. New York: Alfred A. Knopf, 1972.

Medvedev, V. "Marksistsko-leninskaia kontseptsiia razvitogo sotsializma." *Kommunist*, 1978, no. 17, pp. 20–31.

Meliukhin, S. T. "Filosofskie osnovaniia idei beskonechnosti Vselennoi." *Filosofskie nauki*, 1978, no. 1, pp. 101–105.

——. *Materiia v ee edinstve, beskonechnosti i razvitii.* Moscow: Mysl', 1966.

——. *O dialektike razvitiia neorganicheskoi prirody.* Moscow: Gos. izd. politicheskoi literatury, 1960.

——. *Problema konechnogo i beskonechnogo.* Moscow: Gos. izd. politicheskoi literatury, 1958.

——. "Problemy filosofskoi teorii materii." *Filosofskie nauki*, 1974, no. 5, pp. 57–67.

Mendel, Arthur P. "Current Soviet Theory of History. New Trends or Old?" *American Historical Review* 72 (1966), pp. 50–73.

Metodicheskoe posobie po dialekticheskomu materializmu. Dlia slushatelei ZVPSh pri TsK KPSS. Moscow: Mysl', 1977.

"Mezhvuzovskaia nauchnaia konferentsiia 'Osnovnye napravleniia razrabotki marksistsko-leninskogo ucheniia ob obshchestvenno-ekonomicheskoi formatsii.' " *Vestnik Moskovskogo universiteta. Seriia 7. Filosofiia*, 1981, no. 3, pp. 48–51.

Minasian, A. M., ed. *Dialektika sotsializma.* Rostov-on-Don: Knizhnoe izd., 1971.

Mints, I. I., M. V. Nechkina, and L. V. Cherepnin. "Zadachi sovetskoi istoricheskoi nauki na sovremennom etape ee razvitiia." *Istoriia SSSR*, 1973, no. 5, pp. 3–16.

Mitin, M. B., et al., eds. *Marksistsko-leninskaia dialektika v vos'mi knigakh.* 1 vol. to date. Moscow: Izd. Moskovskogo universiteta, 1983.

——. *Sovremennye problemy teorii poznaniia dialekticheskogo materializma. Tom 2. Istina, poznanie, logika.* Moscow: Mysl', 1970.

Mochernyi, S. V. "Zakon edinstva i bor'by protivopolozhnostei v politekonomicheskom issledovanii." *Filosofskie nauki*, 1980, no. 2, pp. 53–61.

Morozov, K. E. "Model' sviazi informatsii s dvizheniem." In L. Ia. Stanis et al., eds., *Novye filosofskie voprosy fiziki (Materialy konferentsii 1973–1975 gg.)*, pp. 39–40. Moscow: Nauka, Glavnaia redaktsiia vostochnoi literatury, 1977.

Moskovskii universitet. 1977–1978 uchebnyi protsess. Katalog-spravochnik. Gumanitarnye fakul'tety. Moscow: Izd. Moskovskogo universiteta, 1977.

Müller-Markus, Siegfried. *Einstein und die Sowjetphilosophie.* 2 vols. Dordrecht: D. Reidel, 1960.

——. "Soviet Philosophy in Crisis. The Unity of Science and Ideology." *Cross Currents* 14 (Winter 1964), pp. 35–61.

Myslivchenko, A. G. *Chelovek kak predmet filosofskogo poznaniia.* Moscow: Mysl', 1972.

Naan, G. I. "Poniatie beskonechnosti v matematike i kosmologii." In V. V. Kaziutinskii et al., eds., *Beskonechnost' i Vselennaia*, pp. 7–77. Moscow: Mysl', 1969.

Narskii, I. S. "Eshche raz o probleme tozhdestva logiki, dialektiki, i teorii poznaniia." *Filosofskie nauki*, 1981, no. 5, pp. 44–55.

Novik, I. V. "Some Aspects of the Interrelation of Philosophy and Natural Science." *Soviet Studies in Philosophy* 8 (Winter 1969–1970), pp. 295–310.

Novikova, L. I. *Iskusstvo i trud*. Moscow: Vysshaia shkola, 1974.

"O metodologicheskikh voprosakh istoricheskoi nauki." *Voprosy istorii*, 1964, no. 3, pp. 3–68.

"O predmete marksistsko-leninskoi filosofii." *Filosofskie nauki*, 1980, no. 2, pp. 142–151.

"O sostoianii i napravleniiakh filosofskikh issledovanii." *Kommunist*, 1979, no. 15, pp. 66–79.

Oizerman, T. I. "Filosofiia, nauka, ideologiia." In L. N. Mitrokhin et al., eds., *Filosofiia v sovremennom mire. Filosofiia i nauka. Kriticheskie ocherki burzhuaznoi filosofii*, pp. 95–145. Moscow: Nauka, 1972.

——. "O smysle voprosa 'Chto takoe filosofiia?' " *Voprosy filosofii*, 1968, no. 11, pp. 134–144.

——. *Problemy istoriko-filosofskoi nauki*. Moscow: Mysl', 1969.

Okulov, A. F. *Sovetskaia filosofskaia nauka i ee problemy. Kratkii ocherk*. Moscow: Mysl', 1970.

Omelyanovsky, M. E. [Omel'ianovskii, M. E.]. *Dialectics in Modern Physics*. Translated by H. C. Creighton. Moscow: Progress Publishers, 1979.

——. *Filosofskie voprosy kvantovoi mekhaniki*. Moscow: Izd. Akademii nauk SSSR, 1956.

—— ed. *Lenin and Modern Natural Science*. Translated by S. Syrovatkin. Moscow: Progress Publishers, 1978.

Orlov, V. V. "K voprosu o filosofskom poniatii materii." *Filosofskie nauki*, 1970, no. 4, pp. 123–132.

——. "O nekotorykh voprosakh teorii materii, razvitiia, soznaniia." *Filosofskie nauki*, 1974, no. 5, pp. 47–56.

O'Rourke, James J. *The Problem of Freedom in Marxist Thought*. Dordrecht: D. Reidel, 1974.

Orudzhev, Z. M. *Dialektika kak sistema*. Moscow: Izd. politicheskoi literatury, 1973.

——. "Some Problems of Dialectical Logic." In *Philosophy in the USSR. Problems of Dialectical Materialism*, translated by R. Daglish, pp. 235–257. Moscow: Progress Publishers, 1977.

——, S. Rodriges, and B. Rote. "O strukture dialekticheskoi logiki kak nauchnoi distsipliny." *Filosofskie nauki*, 1980, no. 5, pp. 37–45.

Orwell, George. *1984*. New York: New American Library, 1961.

Ovsiannikov, M. F., ed. *Osnovy marksistsko-leninskoi estetiki*. 3d rev. ed. Moscow: Mysl', 1978.

Perfilyev, M. *Soviet Democracy and Bourgeois Sovietology*. Translated by A. Bratov. Moscow: Progress Publishers, n.d.

Petropavlovskii, R. "Po povodu odnoi knigi." *Kommunist*, 1983, no. 8, pp. 102–114.

Philipov, Alexander. *Logic and Dialectic in the Soviet Union.* New York: Research Program on the U.S.S.R., 1952.

Philosophical Concepts in Natural Science. Moscow: "Social Sciences Today" Editorial Board, USSR Academy of Sciences, 1977.

Philosophy in the USSR. Problems of Dialectical Materialism. Translated by Robert Daglish. Moscow: Progress Publishers, 1977.

Philosophy in the USSR. Problems of Historical Materialism. Translated by S. S. Syrovatkin. Moscow: Progress Publishers, 1981.

Planty-Bonjour, Guy. *The Categories of Dialectical Materialism. Contemporary Soviet Ontology.* Translated by T. J. Blakeley. New York: Frederick A. Praeger, 1967.

Platonov, G. V. "Protivorechiia i ikh rol' v razvitii zhivoi prirody." *Vestnik Moskovskogo universiteta. Seriia 7. Filosofiia,* 1981, no. 5, pp. 3–13.

———, G. M. Shtraks, and V. N. Demin, eds. *Marksistsko-leninskaia filosofiia kak sistema (predmet, struktura i funktsii).* Moscow: Izd. Moskovskogo universiteta, 1981.

Plekhanov, G. V. *Selected Philosophical Works in Five Volumes.* Moscow: Foreign Languages Publishing House, n.d.

———. *Sochineniia.* 24 vols. Moscow: Gosudarstvennoe izd., 1923–1927.

Pletnikov, Iu. K. "Nekotorye napravleniia razrabotki teorii istoricheskogo materializma." *Kommunist,* 1978, no. 17, pp. 32–36.

———. "Problemy dal'neishei razrabotki teoreticheskoi sistemy istoricheskogo materializma." *Filosofskie nauki,* 1981, no. 4, pp. 12–22.

——— and V. N. Shevchenko. "Issledovaniia v oblasti istoricheskogo materializma." *Voprosy filosofii,* 1981, no. 1, pp. 23–38.

Popper, Karl R. "What Is Dialectic?" In *Conjectures and Refutations. The Growth of Scientific Knowledge,* 3d ed., pp. 312–335. London: Routledge and Kegan Paul, 1969.

Pospelov, G. N. *Esteticheskoe i khudozhestvennoe.* Moscow: Izd. Moskovskogo universiteta, 1965.

Prat, Naftali. "Diamat and Contemporary Biology." *Studies in Soviet Thought* 21 (1980), pp. 181–209.

"Proizvoditel'nye sily kak filosofskaia kategoriia. Materialy Kruglogo stola." *Voprosy filosofii,* 1981, no. 4, pp. 87–105; no. 9, pp. 89–102.

"Protiv putanitsy i vul'garizatsii v voprosakh logiki." *Voprosy filosofii,* 1955, no. 3, pp. 158–171.

Rader, Melvin. *Marx's Interpretation of History.* New York: Oxford University Press, 1979.

"Razrabotka teorii dialektiki v vuzovskikh kollektivakh." *Filosofskie nauki,* 1982, no. 1, pp. 159–162.

Razumnyi, V. A., ed. *Esteticheskoe. Sbornik statei.* Moscow: Iskusstvo, 1964.

Report of the CPSU Central Committee to the Twenty-fourth Congress of the Communist Party of the Soviet Union., Moscow: Novosti Press Agency, 1971.

Ril'skij, Maksim. *Nasha krovna sprava. Statti pro literaturu.* Kiev: Derzhavne vidavnitstvo khudozhn'oj literaturi, 1959.

Riurikov, Iu. "The Individual, Art, and Science." *Soviet Studies in Literature* 1 (Spring 1965), pp. 3–40.

The Road to Communism. Documents of the Twenty-second Congress of the Communist Party of the Soviet Union. October 17–31, 1961. Moscow: Foreign Languages Publishing House, n.d.

Rosenthal, M., and P. Yudin, eds. *A Dictionary of Philosophy.* Moscow: Progress Publishers, 1967.

Rozental', M. M., and P. F. Iudin, eds. *Filosofskii slovar'.* Moscow: Izd. politicheskoi literatury, 1963.

——. *Kratkii filosofskii slovar'.* 4th rev. ed. Moscow: Gos. izd. politicheskoi literatury, 1955.

Rozental', M. M., and G. M. Shtraks, eds. *Kategorii materialisticheskoi dialektiki.* Moscow: Gos. izd. politicheskoi literatury, 1956.

Rozhin, V. P., et al., eds. *Marksistsko-leninskaia filosofiia. Uchebnoe posobie.* 2d ed. Moscow: Izd. politicheskoi literatury, 1966.

Russell, Bertrand. *The ABC of Relativity.* New York: Harper and Brothers, 1925.

——. *Freedom versus Organization. 1814–1914.* New York: W. W. Norton, 1934.

Rutkevich, M. N. *Dialekticheskii materialism. Kurs lektsii dlia estestvennykh fakul'tetov.* Moscow: Izd. sotsial'no-ekonomicheskoi literatury, 1959.

—— et al., eds. *Problemy sotsialisticheskogo obraza zhizni.* Moscow: Nauka, 1977.

"S pozitsii partiinosti." *Voprosy filosofii,* 1974, no. 1, pp. 47–56.

Sadovskii, G. "Logika revoliutsionnogo myshleniia i klassovyi podkhod v logike." *Kommunist,* 1979, no. 11, pp. 63–75.

Sagatovskii, V. N. "Obshchestvennye otnosheniia i deiatel'nost'." *Voprosy filosofii,* 1981, no. 12, pp. 69–75.

"Samizdat. *Sotsial-demokraticheskaia partiia.* From 'The Sower.' A Call for a Liberal Opposition Party in the Soviet Union." *Intellectual Digest,* January 1973, pp. 15–18.

Scanlan, James P. "A. F. Losev and the Rebirth of Soviet Aesthetics after Stalin." In James J. O'Rourke, Thomas J. Blakeley, and Friedrich J. Rapp, eds., *Contemporary Marxism. Essays in Honor of J. M. Bocheński,* pp. 221–235. Dordrecht: D. Reidel, 1984.

——. "Can Realism Be Socialist?" *British Journal of Aesthetics* 14 (Winter 1974), pp. 41–55.

——. "A Critique of the Engels-Soviet Version of Marxian Economic Determinism." *Studies in Soviet Thought* 13 (1973), pp. 11–19.

——. "From Historical Materialism to Historical Interactionism. A Philosophical Examination of Some Recent Developments." In Samuel H. Baron and Nancy W. Heer, eds., *Windows on the Russian Past. Essays on Soviet Historiography since Stalin,* pp. 3–23. Columbus: American Association for the Advancement of Slavic Studies, 1977.

Semenov, Iu. I. "Problema sotsial'no-ekonomicheskogo stroia drevnego Vostoka." *Narody Azii i Afriki,* 1965, no. 4.

Semenov, V. S. "Problema protivorechii v usloviiakh sotsializma." *Voprosy filosofii,* 1982, no. 7, pp. 17–32; no. 9, pp. 3–21.

———. "Uchenie o razvitom sotsializme i ego pererastanii v kommunizm." *Voprosy filosofii*, 1980, no. 7, pp. 3–18.

Seroka, Jim, and Maurice D. Simon. *Developed Socialism in the Soviet Bloc. Political Theory and Political Reality.* Boulder: Westview Press, 1982.

Sevruk, V. N., ed. *Voprosy partiinogo rukovodstva nravstvennym vospitaniem.* Moscow: Izd. politicheskoi literatury, 1979.

Sheptulin, A. P. *Dialekticheskii materializm.* Moscow: Vysshaia shkola, 1965.

———. *Marxist-Leninist Philosophy.* Translated by S. Ponomarenko and A. Timofeyev. Moscow: Progress Publishers, 1978.

———. *Osnovnye zakony dialektiki.* Moscow: Nauka, 1966.

———, ed. *Materialisticheskaia dialektika kak nauchnaia sistema.* Marksistsko-leninskaia dialektika v vos'mi tomakh, edited by M. B. Mitin et al., vol. 1. Moscow: Izd. Moskovskogo universiteta, 1983.

Shinkaruk, V. I., et al., eds. *Dialekticheskii i istoricheskii materialism. Filosofskaia osnova kommunisticheskogo mirovozzreniia.* Kiev: Naukova dumka, 1977.

Shishkin, A. F. "On Some Problems of Research in the Field of Ethics (Reflections on Reading the Literature on Ethics)." *Soviet Studies in Philosophy* 12 (Winter 1973–1974), pp. 3–26.

———. *Osnovy kommunisticheskoi morali.* Moscow: Gospolitizdat, 1955.

———. *Osnovy marksistskoi etiki.* Moscow: Izd. IMO, 1961.

Shtraks, G. M., et al., eds. *Osnovnye napravleniia raboty kafedr filosofii.* Moscow: Vysshaia shkola, 1969.

Shukman, Ann. *Literature and Semiotics. A Study of the Writings of Yu. M. Lotman.* Amsterdam: North-Holland Publishing, 1977.

Shurbovanyi, G. P. "Obsuzhdenie nekotorykh problem metodologii istorii." *Voprosy istorii*, 1971, no. 10, pp. 159–166.

Sistemnye issledovaniia. Ezhegodnik. 1978. Moscow: Nauka, 1978.

Smol'ianinov, I. F. *Problema cheloveka v marksistsko-leninskoi filosofii i estetike.* Leningrad: Izd. Leningradskogo universiteta, 1974.

Socialist Way of Life. Problems and Perspectives. Moscow: "Social Sciences Today" Editorial Board, USSR Academy of Sciences, 1981.

Solopov, E. F. *Predmet i logika materialisticheskoi dialektiki.* Leningrad: Nauka, 1973.

———. *Vvedenie v dialekticheskuiu logiku.* Leningrad: Nauka, 1979.

Somerville, John. *Soviet Philosophy. A Study of Theory and Practice.* New York: Philosophical Library, 1946.

——— and Howard L. Parsons, eds. *Dialogues on the Philosophy of Marxism. From the Proceedings of the Society for the Philosophical Study of Dialectical Materialism.* Westport: Greenwood Press, 1974.

Spirkin, A. "Filosofiia." In F. V. Konstantinov et al., eds., *Filosofskaia entsiklopediia*, vol. 5, pp. 332–347. Moscow: Sovetskaia entsiklopediia, 1960–1970.

Stalin, Joseph [I. Stalin]. *Marksizm i voprosy iazykoznaniia.* Moscow: Gos. izd. politicheskoi literatury, 1950.

———. *Marxism and Linguistics.* New York: International Publishers, 1951.

Stolovich, L. N. "Khudozhestvennaia deiatel'nost' kak sub"ektno-ob"ektnoe otnoshenie." *Filosofskie nauki*, 1982, no. 2, pp. 99–106.

——. "O dvukh kontseptsiiakh esteticheskogo." *Voprosy filosofii*, 1962, no. 2, pp. 110–120.

——. *Priroda esteticheskoi tsennosti*. Moscow: Izd. politicheskoi literatury, 1972.

Strumilin, S. G., and E. E. Pisarenko. "Sotsialisticheskii obraz zhizni: metodologiia issledovaniia." *Voprosy filosofii*, 1974, no. 2, pp. 27–38.

Sviderskii, V. I. *O dialektike elementov i struktury v ob"ektivnom mire i v poznanii*. Izd. sotsial'no-ekonomicheskoi literatury, 1962.

Swiderski, Edward M. *The Philosophical Foundations of Soviet Aesthetics. Theories and Controversies in the Post-War Years*. Dordrecht: D. Reidel, 1979.

Sykes, Christopher. *Nancy. The Life of Lady Astor*. New York: Harper and Row, 1972.

Teilhard de Chardin, Pierre. *The Phenomenon of Man*. Translated by Bernard Wall. 2d ed. New York: Harper and Row, Harper Torchbooks, 1965.

Titarenko, A. I. *Nravstvennyi progress. (Osnovnye istoricheskie cherty nravstvennogo progressa v dokommunisticheskikh obshchestvenno-ekonomicheskikh formatsiiakh)*. Moscow: Izd. Moskovskogo universiteta, 1969.

——, ed. *Marksistskaia etika*. Moscow: Izd. politicheskoi literatury, 1976.

Tiukhtin, V. S. "K sootnosheniiu obraza, znaka i struktury." *Filosofskie nauki*, 1974, no. 5, pp. 68–73.

——. "Perekhod kolichestvennykh izmenenii v kachestvennye." In F. V. Konstantinov et al., eds., *Filosofskaia entsiklopediia*, vol. 4, pp. 239–241. Moscow: Sovetskaia entsiklopediia, 1960–1970.

Tsekhmistro, I. Z. Review of V. P. Lebedev, *Beskonechna li Vselennaia?* (Minsk: Nauka i tekhnika, 1978). *Filosofskie nauki*, 1979, no. 5, pp. 157–158.

Tselishchev, V. V., et al., eds. *Logika i ontologiia*. Moscow: Nauka, 1978.

Tsereteli, S. B. *Dialekticheskaia logika*. Tbilisi: Metsniereba, 1971.

Tucker, Robert C., ed. *The Marx-Engels Reader*. 2d ed. New York: W. W. Norton, 1978.

Tugarinov, V. P. *O tsennostiakh zhizni i kul'tury*. Leningrad: Izd. Leningradskogo universiteta, 1960.

——. *Obshchestvennoe bytie*. Leningrad: Obshchestvo po rasprostraneniiu politicheskikh i nauchnykh znanii RSFSR, 1958.

——. *Sootnoshenie kategorii dialekticheskogo materializma*. Leningrad: Izd. Leningradskogo gosudarstvennogo universiteta, 1956.

"Tvorcheskoe razvitie marksistsko-leninskogo ucheniia." *Voprosy filosofii*, 1981, no. 12, pp. 5–9.

Utkin, S. S. *Ocherki po marksistsko-leninskoi etike*. Moscow: Izd. sotsial'no-ekonomicheskoi literatury, 1962.

Vartanov, R. G. "Nekotorye problemy dialektiki proizvoditel'nykh sil i proizvodstvennykh otnoshenii razvitogo sotsializma." *Voprosy filosofii*, 1980, no. 11, pp. 50–59.

——. *Sotsializm. Stupeni razvitiia*. Erevan: Aiastan, 1982.

Vasnetsov, A. V. "Kriterii samotsennosti i iskus stilizatorstva." *Dekorativnoe iskusstvo*, 1978, no. 1.

Verezgov, V. I. "Znachenie teorii obshchestvenno-ekonomicheskoi formatsii v issledovanii sotsializma." *Vestnik Moskovskogo universiteta. Seriia 7. Filosofiia*, 1981, no. 3, pp. 18–27.

Viakkerev, F. F., and V. V. Il'in, eds. *Problemy dialektiki. Vypusk III. Voprosy dialektiko-materialisticheskoi teorii protivorechiia*. Leningrad: Izd. Leningradskogo universiteta, 1973.

Viakkerev, F. F., et al., eds. *Edinstvo dialekticheskogo i istoricheskogo materializma*. Leningrad: Izd. Leningradskogo universiteta, 1978.

———. *Materialisticheskaia dialektika v piati tomakh. Tom I. Ob"ektivnaia dialektika*. Moscow: Mysl', 1981.

Voishvillo, E. K., D. P. Gorskii, and I. S. Narskii, eds. *Dialektika nauchnogo poznaniia. Ocherk dialekticheskoi logiki*. Moscow: Nauka, 1978.

Volchenko, L. B. *Marksistsko-leninskaia etika. Kurs lektsii. Chast' III. Sistema obshchikh kategorii etiki*. Moscow: Izd. Moskovskogo universiteta, 1978.

Volkov, G. A. "Konferentsiia po voprosam protivorechii." *Voprosy filosofii*, 1958, no. 12, pp. 163–173.

Voprosy estetiki. 9 vols. Moscow: Iskusstvo, 1958–1971.

Vorob'ev, M. F. "O soderzhanii i formakh zakona otritsaniia otritsaniia." *Vestnik Leningradskogo universiteta*, 1956, no. 23, pp. 57–66.

Voronovich, B. A. *Filosofskii analiz struktury praktiki*. Moscow: Mysl', 1972.

"Vsesoiuznaia nauchnaia konferentsiia 'Leninskaia teoriia otrazheniia i sovremennye problemy gnoseologii.' " *Filosofskie nauki*, 1980, no. 3, pp. 159–163.

"Vsesoiuznaia nauchnaia konferentsiia po etike." *Filosofskie nauki*, 1975, no. 4, pp. 157–162.

"Vstrecha etikov i genetikov v MGU." *Vestnik Moskovskogo universiteta. Seriia 8. Filosofiia*, 1972, no. 5, pp. 96–99.

Vysheslavtsev, B. P. *Filosofskaia nishcheta marksizma*. 2d ed. Frankfurt am Main: Possev, 1957.

"Vysokii dolg sovetskikh filosofov." *Pravda*, September 19, 1975, p. 3.

Wetter, Gustav A. *Dialectical Materialism. A Historical and Systematic Survey of Philosophy in the Soviet Union*. Translated by Peter Heath. London: Routledge and Kegan Paul, 1958.

———. *Soviet Ideology Today*. Translated by Peter Heath. New York: Frederick A. Praeger, 1966.

The Works of Aristotle. Vol. 8: *Metaphysics*. Translated by W. D. Ross. Oxford: Clarendon Press, 1954.

"Za tesnuiu sviaz' teorii i praktiki." *Voprosy filosofii*, 1982, no. 1, pp. 3–21.

Zeldovich, Ia. B., and I. D. Novikov. "Contemporary Trends in Cosmology." *Soviet Studies in Philosophy* 14 (Spring 1976), pp. 28–49.

Zel'kina, O.S. *Sistemno-strukturnyi analiz osnovnykh kategorii dialektiki*. Saratov: Izd. Saratovskogo universiteta, 1970.

Zhdanov, Andrei A. *Essays on Literature, Philosophy, and Music*. New York: International Publishers, 1950.

———. *Vystuplenie na diskussii po knige G. F. Aleksandrova "Istoriia zapadnoevropeiskoi filosofii." 24 iiunia 1947 g.* Moscow: Gos. izd. politicheskoi literatury, 1951.

Zhukov, N. I. *Informatsiia (filosofskii analiz tsentral'nogo poniatiia kibernetiki).* 2d ed. Minsk: Nauka i tekhnika, 1971.

Zinoviev, Alexander. *Foundations of the Logical Theory of Scientific Knowledge.* Dordrecht: D. Reidel, 1973.

——. *Logika nauki.* Moscow: Mysl', 1971.

——. *Philosophical Problems of Many-Valued Logic.* Translated by G. Küng and D. D. Comey. Dordrecht: D. Reidel, 1963.

——. *The Yawning Heights.* Translated by Gordon Clough. New York: Random House, 1979.

Zis', Avner. *Foundations of Marxist Aesthetics.* Translated by Katharine Judelson. Moscow: Progress Publishers, 1977.

——. *Iskusstvo i estetika. Traditsionnye kategorii i sovremennye problemy.* 2d rev. ed. Moscow: Iskusstvo, 1975.

——. "Marksistskaia-leninskaia teoriia iskusstva i ee burzhuaznye kritiki." *Voprosy filosofii,* 1980, no. 12, pp. 148–159.

Zoakos, Criton. "The Surfacing of Holy Mother Rus: A Documentary Report." *Executive Intelligence Review,* July 26, 1983, pp. 16–31.

Index

Absolutism, 197–198
Abstract humanism, 284
Academy of Sciences, 27, 154–155
Ackermann, W., 150
Ackoff, Russell L., 157
Activity, 40, 46n, 210–214, 217–219, 247–248, 311, 329
Acton, H. B., 98, 115, 328
Aesthetics, 35, 44, 182, 293–325, 329
Afanasyev, V. G., 13, 207
Agriculture, 228-229, 235
Aksel'rod, L. I., 266–267, 269
Aleksandrov, A. D., 73–74
Alekseev, M. N., 161
Alekseev, P. V., 48n
Alexander the Great, 193
Alienation, 176, 269, 271
All-people's state. See State
All-Union Institute of Scientific and Technical Information, 155
All-Union Research Institute of Technical Aesthetics, 311, 313
All-Union Scientific Research Institute for Systems Investigations, 157
Altruism, 275
Ambartsumian, V. A., 66
Anarchy, 231, 251
Andropov, Iu. V., 234, 238–239, 241, 247, 253, 325
Anisimov, S. F., 280, 283, 285
Anokhin, P. K., 177
Anthropology, philosophical, 40n
Antinomism, 125–133, 165, 329
Aquinas, Thomas, 64
Architecture, 300, 321–323, 325
Aref'eva, G. S., 217–218
Aristotle, 53, 124, 149, 165
Arkhangel'skii, L. M., 268, 273–274, 280

Arsen'ev, A. S., 109
Art, 332; ideological conception of, 294–295, 304–306; philosophy of, 293–325, 327; practical-productive conception of, 309–313, 318; practical-spiritual conception of, 306–309, 311; structural-semiotic conception of, 313–318
Ascent from the abstract to the concrete, 166–167, 170
Ashby, W. Ross, 157
Asiatic mode of production, 187–188, 194–195
Asmus, V. F., 149–150
Astakhov, I. B., 301
Astor, Lady, 286
Atheism, 82n, 97–98
Atom, 62, 88–89
Autonomy, 208, 270
Avenarius, Richard, 58, 68
Avrekh, A. Ia., 198
Ayer, Alfred J., 27

Bach, J. S., 303
Bakhtin, Mikhail, 298
Bakhtomin, N. K., 164
Bakradze, K. S., 109, 128, 151–152, 161
Bakshtanovskii, V. I., 284–286
Bandzeladze, G. D., 269–272, 275, 280, 290
Barabash, Iu. Ia., 316, 324
Barashenkov, V. A., 90
Base. See Foundation and superstructure
Baskin, M. P., 305
Batishchev, G. S., 54–56, 110, 126, 250, 331
Bazhenov, L. B., 83, 85–87
Beauty, 297, 304, 310; laws of, 299, 301, 307, 319

Developed socialism. *See* Socialism
Dialectical logic. *See* Logic
Dialectical materialism. *See* Materialism
Dialectics, 25, 28, 30, 32; categories of,
    101–102, 107–111, 141; laws of, 28–
    29, 31, 102–107, 112–140, 252–255,
    327–328; of nature, 43n; objective 31,
    100–142; principles of, 101; subjective,
    31, 143–181
Dickens, Charles, 14
Dictatorship, 228n; of the proletariat, 11,
    228, 240–243, 245, 253, 259
Dietzgen, Joseph, 89
Differentiation (of philosophical disci-
    plines), 42–45, 190
Divisibility of matter. *See* Matter
Domrachev, G. M., 137
Dostoevskii, F. M., 278, 335
Doublethink, 331–335
Dragalin, A. G., 152–153
Drobnitskii, O. G., 272–273, 287–291
Dubinin, V. V., 205–206, 222
Dubrovskii, D. I., 40, 161n
Duchenko, N. V., 33, 50–51
Dühring, Eugen, 123, 132
Duty, moral, 265

East Germany, 237
Economic determinism, 209, 216–220,
    256, 328–329
Economic materialism, 202–203
Education, 13, 44, 241; moral, 262, 265,
    267, 274–276, 282
Efimov, S. F., 137
Egides, P. M., 176, 269, 271–272, 283,
    290
Ehlen, Peter, 261n
Einstein, Albert, 71–73, 77, 81, 94, 170
Empiricism, 98, 145
Ends and means (in ethics), 279, 283–
    287, 292
Engels, Frederick, 13, 21–22, 34, 37n,
    154, 211n, 248, 330; and art, 294,
    296–297, 304; and the definition of
    philosophy, 23, 39; and dialectics, 25,
    28–30, 100–107, 111, 113–114, 116,
    121–122, 125–126, 128, 133, 136,
    139, 163; and epistemology, 143–144,
    174; and infinity, 83–84, 86; and mate-
    rialism, 24, 58, 60–65, 78, 94, 300;
    and morality, 262–263; and the state,
    226–227, 242–243, 259; and theory of
    history, 33, 184, 191, 196–198, 202–
    203, 219–221
Epistemologism, 32, 36

Epistemology, 143–149, 173–181, 327
Equality, 226, 259
Eremeev, A. F., 294, 296
Essence and appearance, 102, 108, 116,
    320
Ethics, 35, 44, 182, 261–292; profes-
    sional, 277
Evolution, 139, 211n
Existentialism, 21
Expanding universe theory, 81–83
Expressiveness in art, 311, 322

Fatalism, 51
Fedoseev, P. N., 200
Feminism, 275
Feudalism, 134, 188, 194, 197
Fichte, J. G., 134
Fields, material, 59, 62
Finn, V. K., 153
Fischer, Ernst, 306
Fock, V. A., 76–80
Formalism, 150, 295, 314–315
Formation. *See* Socioeconomic formation
Foundation and superstructure, 35, 185–
    187, 197–206, 225–226, 332
Freedom, 208, 270–271, 280–283, 328–
    329; as recognition of necessity, 218–
    220, 220n, 281, 292, 333–335

Gabrielian, G. G., 32
Galanskov, Iu. T., 313
Garaudy, Roger, 306
Gefter, M. Ia., 191
Geography, 200
Gindin, I. F., 191, 193
Ginzburg, A. I., 313
Ginzburg, V. L., 93
Glazunov, I. G., 158–159
God, 24, 64, 82n, 85, 216; existence of,
    58, 60, 62, 97–98, 105, 329
Gol'dentrikht, S. S., 302–303, 306–308
Good, moral, 265
Gor'kii, Maksim, 321
Gor'kii Institute of World Literature, 316
Gorskii, D. P., 151, 153, 173, 177, 180–
    181
Gott (Hott), V. S., 46n, 89
Graham, Loren, 72, 75, 96n, 155
Green Book, 71–72
Gribanov, D. P., 73
Grier, Philip, 261n, 288
Gulyga, A. V., 190
Gurevich, A. Ia., 190, 194, 196–197, 200,
    207–208, 219
Gurgenidze, G. S., 161

INDEX

Happiness, 265, 282
Hegel, G. W. F., 53, 55, 62, 118, 121,
272; and Deborinists, 106, 131, 136,
162, 170; and idealism, 58, 64–65,
108, 131; and objective dialectics, 25,
28–29, 101, 103, 107–110, 113, 127–
128, 134; and subjective dialectics,
147–148, 162, 166–167, 171, 295
Heisenberg, Werner, 75
Heisenberg uncertainty relation, 74–75
Heraclitus, 25
Hevesy, Georg von, 167–168
Hieroglyph, 175
Hilbert, David, 150
Hintikka, Jaako, 154
Historical materialism. See Materialism
Historicism, 263, 271
Historiography, 182–223
History, 50; laws of, 184, 207–208, 329;
philosophy of, 182–223, 327
History of philosophy. See Philosophy
Hobbes, Thomas, 24
Holbach, Baron d', 24
Humanism, 284, 289–292
Human nature, 40, 101, 289–291. See
also New man
Hungary, 237

Ianovskaia, S. A., 149–150, 153
Iatsunskii, V. K., 200
Idealism, 24–25, 31–33, 67, 76, 180, 221,
255, 278, 332
Ideology, 36, 173; and art, 304, 306, 310,
317, 319, 323–325; and Brezhnev re-
gime, 15, 232–252, 268, 274; in Marx,
35, 226; and philosophy, 39, 46, 48–
49, 96, 323; scientific, 38, 48
Iezuitov, N., 297
Il'enkov, E. V., 31–32, 34, 120–121, 126–
127, 141, 162–163, 167
Il'ichev, L. F., 111n, 313
Il'in, A. Ia., 31
Illiushechkin, V. P., 196
Imperialism, 139, 232
Individual and society, 279–283. See also
Freedom
Industry, 228, 235, 310, 313
Inexhaustibility of matter. See Matter
Infinity, 60–62, 81–93, 95–96, 328, 332
Information, 109, 155–156, 174
Institute of Applied Mathematics, 155
Institute of Art History, 310, 313
Institute of Art Studies, 306
Institute of Cybernetics, 155
Institute of History, 191

Institute of Oriental Studies, 196
Institute of Philosophy, 27, 173, 210, 271,
317; work of, 111n, 162, 190, 213,
268, 293, 303
Institute of the History of Science and
Technology, 157
Instruments of labor. See Labor
Interactionism, 220–223, 255
Intermediate links, 129–130, 169
Interpenetration of opposites, law of, 28.
See also Unity and struggle of opposites,
law of
Isotopes, 168–169
Iudin, P. F., 107, 158
Ivanov, G. M., 190
Ivanov, P., 300
Ivanov, V. V., 317

Jakobson, Roman, 318
Jesuitism, 283–284
Jeu, Bernard, 11, 143n
Justification (in ethics), 287–292

Kagan, M. S., 210
Kalinin, M. I., 267
Kant, Immanuel, 53, 61, 269–270, 284
Kantor, K. M., 310, 312
Kapustin, E. I., 249
Karmin, A. S., 86–87
Kasymzhanov, A. M., 161
Kaziutinskii, V. V., 66
Kedrov, B. M., 40n, 75, 88; and the defi-
nition of philosophy, 27–34, 36, 38–39;
and dialectics, 108, 110, 110n, 141,
147, 160–163, 173–176
Keizerov, N. M., 250
Kelle, V. Zh., 34, 49, 211–214, 217–218
Kharin, Yu. A., 41n
Khrapchenko, M. B., 316
Khrushchev, N. S., 13, 230, 237, 239–
240, 244, 259, 267
Khvostov, V. M., 191
Kline, George L., 68n, 82n, 292
Knowability. See Matter
Knowledge, theory of. See Epistemology
Kol'man, Ernst (Kolman, Arnosht), 155;
on contradiction, 124, 128, 131; on
divisibility of matter, 89, 91; on infin-
ity, 84–85, 87
Kondakov, N. I., 151
Konstantinov, F. V., 111n
Kopnin, P. V., 38–39, 173, 175, 177–181
Korostovtsev, M. A., 200
Korsunskii, A. R., 197
Kosichev, A. D., 216

[358]

INDEX

Social consciousness, forms of, 35–36, 38, 184, 262, 273, 294, 304
Social psychology, 200
Socialism: developed, 11, 233–240, 257; transition of, to communism, 115, 119, 151, 227, 230, 238–240, 242–243, 252
Socialist Realism, 293–294, 296, 308–309, 317–318, 320–321, 327, 334
Societalists (obshchestvenniki), 301–305, 310, 313
Socioeconomic formation, 134, 185–188, 193–196, 199–201, 206–209, 213, 228
Sociology, 182
Solzhenitsyn, A., 316, 324–325
Somerville, John, 11
Soul, 24, 58
Soviets (councils), 228
Space, 60–61, 69, 81
Spirkin, A. G., 34–35
Stalin, J. V., 25, 56, 63, 72, 274, 286, 300; and dialectics, 107, 111–112, 136, 151, 160–161; and linguistics, 11, 150, 199, 202, 267, 298; and socialism, 234, 240, 257; and theory of history, 188, 193, 200, 202, 215
State, 15–16, 203–204, 224, 226–228; all-people's, 11, 233, 240–246, 253, 331; withering away of, 15, 230, 241, 259
Stepanov-Skvortsov, I. I., 120
Stolovich, L. N., 301–303, 306–310, 319
Strogovich, M. S., 150
Structuralism, 157–158, 316. See also Systems theory
Subbotin, A. L., 153
Subjectivism, 256, 316
Sublation, 134, 170
Substance, 62–63, 66
Superstructure. See Foundation and superstructure
Surplus value, 166–167, 172, 226
Suslov, M. A., 224
Sviderskii, V. I., 86–87, 109, 118, 120–121, 125, 131, 141
Swiderski, E. M., 300n
Systems theory, 118–121, 156–160, 221–222, 223n, 330

Tarski, Alfred, 150
Tartu State University, 301, 313
Tavenets, P. V., 153
Technology, 186, 204. See also Revolution, scientific-technological
Tectology. See Bogdanov, A. A.
Time, 60–61, 69, 81
Timofeeva, A. V., 137

Titarenko, A. I., 263, 273–276, 281, 284–286, 288
Titles, academic, 43
Tiukhtin, V. S., 87, 118, 173
Tolstoi, L. N., 14, 278, 284, 335
Toporov, V. N., 317
Transformation of quantity into quality, law of, 28, 103–104, 112–121, 253, 327
Truth: absolute and relative, 145–146, 179–180; correspondence theory of, 145, 176; pragmatic conception of, 181
Tsereteli, S. B., 164, 171
Tsotsonova, D. S., 40n
Tsyrkun, A. F., 217
Tugarinov, V. P., 63, 65, 67, 108, 141, 210, 267

Uemov, A. I., 173
Union of Writers, 296
United States, 193
Unity and struggle of opposites, law of, 28, 104–105, 121–133, 253–254
Unity of theory and practice, 106, 274
Ursul, A. D., 46n
Uspenskii, B. A., 313, 316–317

Value theory, 267
Vanslov, V. V., 302, 321
Vasnetsov, A. V., 322–323, 331
Verbin, A. I., 217
Viakkerev, F. F., 128–129, 174
Vinogradov, S. N., 150
Vinogradov, V. V., 150n
Violence, 284–285. See also Revolution
Voishvillo, E. K., 151–153
Volchenko, L. B., 265
Volobuev, P. V., 198
Vulgar sociologism, 266–267, 297–298

War, 232, 283
Weber, Max, 201
Wetter, Gustav, 11, 50, 64, 97–99, 178–179
Wittgenstein, Ludwig, 56
World view, 30, 37–38, 46

Zeno, 126
Zhdanov, A. A., 71, 75, 81–82
Zhiznestroenie (life-building), 312
Zhukov, N. I., 43, 156
Zhuravkov, M. G., 271
Zinoviev, Alexander, 124–125, 127–128, 131, 152–153, 155, 160
Zis', A. Ia., 306, 309, 311–312, 318

Library of Congress Cataloging in Publication Data

Scanlan, James P. (James Patrick), 1927–
  Marxism in the USSR.

  Bibliography: p.
  Includes index.
  1. Philosophy, Marxist—Soviet Union. 2. Philosophy, Russian—20th century. I. Title. II. Title: Marxism in the U.S.S.R.
  B4231.S32 1985   335.43′01   84–45802
  ISBN 0–8014–1649–3 (alk. paper)